Information Security 360

Securing enterprise networks, applications, and cloud native environments against modern cyber threats

Jitendra Tripathi

www.bpbonline.com

First Edition 2026

ISBN: 978-93-78549-373

LIMITS OF LIABILITY AND DISCLAIMER OF WARRANTY

The information contained in this book is true and correct to the best of author's and publisher's knowledge. The author has made every effort to ensure the accuracy of these publications, but the publisher cannot be held responsible for any loss or damage arising from any information in this book.

All trademarks referred to in the book are acknowledged as properties of their respective owners but BPB Publications cannot guarantee the accuracy of this information.

Distributors:

BPB PUBLICATIONS
20, Ansari Road, Darya Ganj
New Delhi-110002
Ph: 23254990/23254991

DECCAN AGENCIES
4-3-329, Bank Street,
Hyderabad-500195
Ph: 24756967/24756400

MICRO MEDIA
Shop No. 5, Mahendra Chambers,
150 DN Rd. Next to Capital Cinema,
V.T. (C.S.T.) Station, MUMBAI-400 001
Ph: 22078296/22078297

Published by Manish Jain for BPB Publications, 20 Ansari Road, Darya Ganj, New Delhi-110002 and Printed by him at Repro India Ltd., Rewari.

www.bpbonline.com

Dedicated to

My parents and my beloved wife, Priti

About the Author

Jitendra Tripathi is an experienced information security professional with over 35 years of expertise in communications and cybersecurity. He has played a key role in securing critical communications networks and information systems and has led security operations for large, mission-critical environments. His experience spans key areas of information security, including security governance, risk management, and security operations. He currently leads cybersecurity operations at Reliance Jio.

Complementing his extensive industry experience with distinguished academic credentials, he holds a master of engineering in telecommunication engineering from the **Indian Institute of Sciences** (**IISc**), Bengaluru, India, and possesses globally recognized certifications, including **Certified Information Systems Security Professional** (**CISSP**), **Certified Information Systems Auditor** (**CISA**), and **Certified Chief Information Security Officer** (**CCISO**). His work reflects a practical, real-world approach to information security, combining strategic insight with operational depth.

About the Reviewers

- **Sandeep Dommari** is a recognized expert in identity-first cybersecurity and enterprise architecture, with over two decades of experience securing critical infrastructure for the public sector and global enterprises. Specializing in modern IAM, **privileged access management** (**PAM**), and AI-driven fraud detection, he has architected solutions protecting billions of digital identities.

  He is a **Fellow of the British Computer Society** (**FBCS**), an IEEE Senior Member, a full member of Sigma Xi, and a Microsoft MVP in Security. He actively contributes to the field as a judge for the **Business Intelligence Group** (**BIG**) Innovation Awards, a session chair for IEEE conferences, and a technical author for major industry publications. He is passionate about advancing Zero Trust architectures and mentoring the next-generation of cybersecurity leaders. Beyond his professional achievements, Sandeep is deeply committed to advancing ethical AI adoption, privacy-first design, and intelligent automation in cybersecurity. He believes that the next frontier of digital trust lies at the intersection of human insight and machine intelligence—a principle that drives his ongoing research and architecture work.

  His overarching mission is to help organizations transition securely into the cloud era, embedding trust, transparency, and intelligence into every layer of their digital ecosystem.

- **Yashasvi Sharma** is a cybersecurity professional with over eight years of experience in **identity and access management** (**IAM**), including SailPoint (certified), cloud, and network engineering. She currently specializes in designing and implementing IAM solutions using tools such as SailPoint, PingFederate, Broadcom SiteMinder, IDM, and Okta. Her expertise lies in creating and managing identity and access frameworks that integrate seamlessly with enterprise applications, IT infrastructure, and operational workflows, with a strong focus on automating access controls, provisioning, and compliance processes to ensure secure and efficient system operations. An avid reader of non-fiction and IT, Yashasvi actively contributes to the professional community by reviewing technical content and providing expert feedback.

Acknowledgement

I wish to express my deepest gratitude to my family and friends for their unwavering support and encouragement throughout the writing of this book, especially my wife, Priti, and my children, Parul and Akash.

I am also grateful to BPB Publications for their guidance and expertise in bringing this book to fruition. It was a long journey of revising this book, with the valuable participation and collaboration of reviewers, technical experts, and editors.

I would also like to acknowledge the valuable contributions of my colleagues and co-workers over many years in the technology domain, whose insights and feedback have greatly enriched my understanding of securing information systems. Your insights and guidance have been truly invaluable.

Preface

In today's hyperconnected digital world, information is one of the most valuable assets, and protecting it is critical to the functioning of nation-states, businesses, and individuals. The rapid adoption of digital technologies, such as cloud computing, **artificial intelligence** (**AI**), and 5G, has transformed the way we live and work. While creating immense opportunities, this transformation has also expanded the attack surface, leading to increasingly sophisticated and frequent cyberattacks.

This book has been written to provide a structured and comprehensive understanding of information security. It is designed to guide readers from core principles to advanced topics, covering both the managerial and technical aspects of the discipline. The aim is to equip readers with the knowledge required to understand security risks, implement protective measures, and respond effectively to evolving cyber threats.

The book covers key domains of modern cybersecurity, including governance, risk and compliance, cryptography, IAM, network and endpoint security, application security, security operations, and cloud security. It also explores the role of AI in information security and examines how emerging technologies are shaping both defensive strategies and AI-powered threat environments.

This book is intended for students, cybersecurity professionals, and IT practitioners who wish to build a strong foundation in information security, as well as for those looking to enhance their understanding of contemporary security challenges. Whether you are beginning your journey in cybersecurity or seeking to strengthen your existing knowledge, this book provides a clear and structured pathway to understanding the complex and evolving landscape of information security.

Chapter 1: Information Security Fundamentals — This chapter introduces the core concepts and essential principles of information security and provides a structured foundation for understanding how to safeguard digital assets. It examines the evolving threat landscape and explores the key frameworks and concepts on which effective security programs are built. This chapter lays the groundwork for the more detailed and technical topics covered in subsequent chapters.

Chapter 2: Threats and Vulnerabilities — This chapter provides a comprehensive understanding of cyber threats and vulnerabilities that impact information systems. It covers different categories of threat actors, their motivations, and levels of sophistication, along with a broad spectrum of cyber threats, such as malware, social engineering, **advanced persistent threats** (**APTs**), supply chain attacks, and AI-driven attacks. The chapter further introduces threat modelling as a structured approach to support the systematic identification, analysis, prioritization, and mitigation of security risks in information systems.

Chapter 3: Security Governance, Risk Management, and Compliance — This chapter focuses on designing and governing an effective information security program aligned with organizational objectives. It covers information security governance, risk management, and the role of compliance in meeting regulatory and business requirements. The chapter outlines the methodology for developing a security strategy and information security policies. It also explains the risk management process and discusses various frameworks that enable a structured and consistent approach to managing information security.

Chapter 4: Information Systems Audit — This chapter covers different types of information systems audits and their objectives, along with the commonly used audit frameworks and standards. The chapter explains how to plan and conduct information systems audits, including the development of audit programs and the key steps involved in the audit process. It also highlights the importance of audit planning and project management in ensuring a structured and effective approach to evaluating the effectiveness of information systems and related controls.

Chapter 5: Cryptography and Data Security — This chapter presents the fundamental principles of cryptography and their application in securing data across its lifecycle. It introduces key concepts and terminology, along with common cryptographic techniques, including symmetric and asymmetric encryption. The chapter also explains the role of **public key infrastructure** (**PKI**) in ensuring data integrity and authenticity. It further covers common cryptographic attacks, data protection techniques such as masking and tokenization, and emerging trends in data security.

Chapter 6: Identity and Access Management — This chapter explores the foundational concepts of identity management and access control in information systems. It covers key areas such as identification, authentication, authorization, and accounting. It also discusses various authentication factors, identity management techniques, federated identity management, and widely used protocols such as SAML, OAuth 2.0, and OpenID Connect. The chapter further examines architectural security and access control models, along with contemporary IAM solutions.

Chapter 7: Network Security — This chapter introduces fundamental networking concepts and their relevance to securing information systems. It covers the OSI and TCP/IP reference models along with the protocols across these models and their inherent security implications. It discusses network devices and core network security components such as firewalls, intrusion detection, and prevention systems. The chapter also addresses secure remote access and wireless security, and provides insights into designing secure network architectures and implementing controls to protect communication networks against evolving threats.

Chapter 8: Endpoint Security — This chapter presents the key concepts and practices required to secure endpoint devices in modern, distributed environments. It addresses the growing challenges posed by diverse endpoints and evolving threats, and covers advanced security solutions such as **endpoint detection and response** (EDR), **extended detection and response** (XDR), and **endpoint protection platforms** (EPPs). The chapter also discusses operating system hardening, secure remote access, virtualization security, and the application of Zero Trust principles to ensure a robust and consistent endpoint security posture.

Chapter 9: Application Security — This chapter outlines the principles and practices essential for developing and maintaining secure applications. It covers the **secure software development lifecycle** (SSDLC) and DevSecOps practices. It also examines common application vulnerabilities, along with security considerations for web, mobile, and API-based applications. The chapter further discusses application security frameworks and emphasizes the integration of security across the development lifecycle to ensure resilient and secure applications.

Chapter 10: Security Operations — This chapter examines the operational aspects of information security, focusing on how organizations monitor, detect, and respond to threats in real-time. It covers the structure and functioning of a **security operations center** (SOC), including its core functions, teams, and processes. The chapter also discusses key technologies such as SIEM, SOAR, and threat intelligence platforms, along with activities like vulnerability management, incident response, and threat hunting. It further provides insights into SOC maturity and the continuous improvement required to maintain an effective and resilient security operations capability.

Chapter 11: Cloud Security — This chapter presents the principles and practices required to secure modern cloud environments. It covers cloud-native architectures, the shared responsibility model, and key security domains such as identity and access management, infrastructure, and network security. The chapter also explores emerging paradigms such as SASE, Zero Trust, **infrastructure as code** (IaC), and automated posture management that redefine security operations in the cloud. It further discusses integrated cloud security platforms that enable continuous monitoring, automation, and risk management in highly distributed and dynamic cloud environments.

Chapter 12: Emerging Technologies and Information Security — This chapter provides a holistic understanding of emerging technologies and trends shaping the future of information security. It examines advances in technologies such as AI, quantum computing, blockchain, and edge computing, and highlights their influence on the threat landscape, security architectures, and defense strategies. The chapter also explores the dual-use nature of these technologies, where innovations enhance security capabilities while simultaneously introducing new risks, and emphasizes the need for adaptive, forward-looking security models to protect modern information systems.

Coloured Images

Please follow the link to download the
Coloured Images of the book:

https://rebrand.ly/7f0b00

We have code bundles from our rich catalogue of books and videos available at https://github.com/bpbpublications. Check them out!

Errata

We take immense pride in our work at BPB Publications and follow best practices to ensure the accuracy of our content to provide an indulging reading experience to our subscribers. Our readers are our mirrors, and we use their inputs to reflect and improve upon human errors, if any, that may have occurred during the publishing processes involved. To let us maintain the quality and help us reach out to any readers who might be having difficulties due to any unforeseen errors, please write to us at:

errata@bpbonline.com

Your support, suggestions and feedback are highly appreciated by the BPB Publications' Family.

Piracy

If you come across any illegal copies of our works in any form on the internet, we would be grateful if you would provide us with the location address or website name. Please contact us at **business@bpbonline.com** with a link to the material.

If you are interested in becoming an author

If there is a topic that you have expertise in, and you are interested in either writing or contributing to a book, please visit **www.bpbonline.com**. We have worked with thousands of developers and tech professionals, just like you, to help them share their insights with the global tech community. You can make a general application, apply for a specific hot topic that we are recruiting an author for, or submit your own idea.

Reviews

Please leave a review. Once you have read and used this book, why not leave a review on the site that you purchased it from? Potential readers can then see and use your unbiased opinion to make purchase decisions. We at BPB can understand what you think about our products, and our authors can see your feedback on their book. Thank you!

For more information about BPB, please visit **www.bpbonline.com**.

Join our Discord space

Join our Discord workspace for latest updates, offers, tech happenings around the world, new releases, and sessions with the authors:

https://discord.bpbonline.com

Table of Contents

1. **Information Security Fundamentals** 1

Introduction 1

Structure 2

Objectives 2

Evolving threat landscape 2

Understanding information security 4

Fundamental concepts of information security 4

CIA triad 5

Confidentiality 5

Types of sensitive data 5

Threat to data confidentiality 6

Measures to protect data confidentiality 6

Integrity 7

Availability 8

Authenticity 9

Non-repudiation 9

IAAA 10

Identification 11

Authentication 11

Authorization 11

Auditing 12

Accountability 12

Least privilege 12

Segregation of duties 13

Defense-in-depth 13

Zero Trust 15

Guiding principles of Zero Trust 15

Tenets of Zero Trust 16

Information security frameworks 17

NIST Cybersecurity Framework 17

ISO 27001 18

CIS Controls framework 18

SOC 2 .... *18*
Other common frameworks *19*
Conclusion 19
Exercises 20
References 20

2. Threats and Vulnerabilities **21**
Introduction 21
Structure 21
Objectives 22
Categories of threat actors 22
Types of cyber threats 23
Malware *23*
Virus *23*
Worm *23*
Ransomware *24*
Cryptojacker *24*
Trojan *24*
Rootkit *24*
Spyware *24*
Adware *25*
Fileless malware *25*
Botnet *25*
Distributed denial of service *25*
Man-in-the-middle *26*
Code injection *26*
SQL injection *27*
Cross-site scripting *27*
Insider threats *27*
Social engineering *27*
Password attacks *29*
Brute-force *29*
Dictionary attack *29*
Credential stuffing *29*
Password spraying *29*

Key logging 30
Spoofing 30
Domain name system attacks 30
Domain name system spoofing 30
Domain name system tunnelling 31
Domain name system hijacking 31
Domain name system amplification 31
Supply chain attacks 31
Internet of Things threats 32
Advanced persistent threats 32
Artificial intelligence threats 33
Common vulnerabilities 34
Threat modelling 35
Threat modelling process 36
Threat modelling approaches 36
Threat modelling methodologies 37
STRIDE 37
PASTA 38
Trike 38
OCTAVE 39
VAST 39
DREAD 39
Conclusion 40
Exercises 40
References 41

3. Security Governance, Risk Management, and Compliance 43
Introduction 43
Structure 44
Objectives 44
Security governance 44
Importance of information security governance 45
Components of information security governance 46
Developing an information security strategy 46
Development techniques 47

Strategic planning ... *49*
Senior management commitment and support ... *49*
Governance structure ... *50*
Roles and responsibilities ... *50*
Creating effective security policies ... *51*
Information security policy ... *52*
Standards, baselines, guidelines, and procedures ... *53*
Monitoring and reporting ... *53*
Security metrics ... *54*
Risk management ... 55
Risk assessment ... *56*
Step 1: System categorization ... *56*
Step 2: Threat identification ... *56*
Step 3: Vulnerability identification ... *57*
Step 4: Control analysis ... *57*
Step 5: Likelihood determination ... *57*
Step 6: Impact analysis ... *58*
Step 7: Risk determination ... *58*
Step 8: Control recommendations ... *59*
Step 9: Results documentation ... *59*
Risk mitigation ... *59*
Mitigation options ... *59*
Control categories ... *60*
Monitoring and evaluation ... *61*
Compliance ... 61
Conclusion ... 63
Exercises ... 63

4. Information Systems Audit ... 65
Introduction ... 65
Structure ... 65
Objectives ... 66
Information systems audit frameworks ... 66
Types of information system audits ... *68*
Financial audits ... *68*

Operational audits ... 68
Compliance audits ... 68
Forensic audits ... 69
Audits vs. assessments ... 71
Aims of information systems audit ... 72
Enhancing security posture ... 73
Regulatory compliance ... 73
Improving efficiency ... 73
Audit project management ... 74
Audit planning ... 75
Developing an audit program ... 76
Aims of the audit program ... 76
Structure of an effective audit program ... 77
Information systems audit process ... 79
Conclusion ... 80
Exercises ... 81

5. Cryptography and Data Security ... 83
Introduction ... 83
Structure ... 84
Objectives ... 84
Fundamentals of cryptography ... 84
Basic terminology of cryptography ... 85
Plaintext ... 85
Ciphertext ... 85
Encryption ... 85
Decryption ... 86
Algorithm ... 86
Key ... 87
Cryptanalysis ... 87
Cryptographic techniques ... 88
Symmetric encryption ... 88
Advanced Encryption Standard ... 89
Data Encryption Standard ... 89
More symmetric algorithms ... 89

Challenges of symmetric encryption 90
Application of symmetric encryption 90
Asymmetric encryption 90
Rivest–Shamir–Adleman 91
Elliptic curve cryptography 92
Diffie-Hellman key exchange 92
Advantages and challenges of asymmetric encryption 93
Application of asymmetric encryption 93
Cryptographic hash functions 93
Properties of secure hash functions 94
Digital signatures 95
Digital certificates 96
Public key infrastructure 97
Data lifecycle 97
Data creation 98
Data in use 98
Data at rest 99
Data in transit 99
Data archival 100
Data disposal 100
Securing data across the lifecycle 101
Encrypting data at creation 101
Safeguarding data in use 101
Protecting data at rest 102
Securing data in transit 102
Encryption for archival 103
Secure disposal 103
Common cryptographic attacks 103
Beyond the cipher data security strategies 105
Data masking and tokenization 105
Access control mechanisms 106
Data loss prevention strategies 107
Auditing and monitoring 107
Emerging trends in data security 108
Post-quantum cryptography 108

Homomorphic encryption 108
AI in data security 109
Conclusion 109
Exercises 110

6. Identity and Access Management 111
Introduction 111
Structure 112
Objectives 112
Access control and information security 112
Access control process 113
Managing identification and authentication 114
Identity registration and proofing 115
Authentication factors 116
Type 1: Something you know 116
Type 2: Something you have 117
Type 3: Something you are 118
Multi-factor and adaptive authentication 118
Multi-factor authentication 119
Adaptive authentication 119
Identity management techniques and protocols 120
Single sign-on 120
Lightweight Directory Access Protocol 120
Kerberos 121
Federated identity management 123
Security assertion markup language 124
Open authorization 125
Open identity 126
Authentication, authorization, and accounting protocols 127
RADIUS 127
TACACS+ 127
Diameter 128
Architectural security models 128
State-machine models 129
Bell-LaPadula model 129

Biba model 129
Clark-Wilson model 130
Information flow model 130
Non-interference model 131
Brewer and Nash model 131
Graham-Denning and Harrison-Ruzzo-Ullman models 131
Access control models 132
Discretionary access control 132
Mandatory access control 133
Role-based access control 133
Attribute-based access control 134
Rule-based access control 135
Contemporary solutions and emerging trends 135
Contemporary IAM solutions 135
Privileged access management 135
Identity governance and administration 136
Identity as a service 137
Identity and access management in cloud environments 138
Emerging trends 138
Password-less authentication 139
Artificial intelligence and machine learning 139
Decentralized identity 140
Identity fabric 140
Conclusion 141
Exercises 141

7. Network Security 143
Introduction 143
Structure 143
Objectives 144
Network models and networking concepts 144
OSI model 144
Application layer 145
Presentation layer 146
Session layer 146

Transport layer 146
Network layer 146
Data link layer 147
Physical layer 147
TCP/IP model 148
Transport layer protocols 149
TCP 149
UDP 149
Internet layer protocols 150
Application layer protocols 151
Routing 152
Static routing 153
Dynamic routing 153
VLAN routing 153
Network address translation 154
Network devices 154
Hubs 154
Bridges 155
Switch 155
Routers 155
Core network security components 155
Firewall 156
Unified threat management 157
Next-generation firewalls 158
Firewall architectures 159
Firewall configuration 160
Web application firewall 160
Detection methodologies 161
Blocking models 161
Proxy 162
Intrusion detection and prevention systems 163
DDoS protection 164
Types of DDoS attacks 164
Attack vectors 165
DDoS mitigation process 166

DDoS mitigation techniques ... 166
Secure remote access ... 167
Virtual private network ... 167
VPN trust model ... 168
Limitations of VPN ... 168
Zero Trust Network Access ... 169
ZTNA architecture ... 169
Advantages of ZTNA ... 170
Wireless security ... 171
Wi-Fi standards ... 171
Wireless security protocols ... 171
Wireless security best practices ... 173
Conclusion ... 174
Exercises ... 175

8. Endpoint Security ... 177
Introduction ... 177
Structure ... 178
Objectives ... 178
Endpoint threats and security challenges ... 178
Endpoint threats ... 178
Endpoint security challenges ... 180
Expanding attack surface ... 180
Evasive malware ... 180
Insider threats ... 180
Software vulnerabilities ... 181
Challenges of virtualized environments ... 181
Endpoint security solutions ... 182
Core components of endpoint security ... 182
Antivirus and antimalware ... 182
Host-based firewalls ... 182
Application control ... 183
Device control and data loss prevention ... 183
Patch management ... 184
Advanced endpoint protection solutions ... 184

EDR ... 184
XDR ... 185
EPP ... 187
Zero Trust for endpoints ... 187
OS hardening ... 188
Windows OS hardening ... 189
Linux OS hardening ... 190
macOS hardening ... 191
Securing remote access ... 192
SSH hardening ... 192
SFTP hardening ... 192
RDP hardening ... 193
Securing virtualized environments ... 194
VM security ... 194
Container security ... 194
Future trends in endpoint security ... 195
Conclusion ... 196
Exercises ... 197

9. Application Security ... 199
Introduction ... 199
Structure ... 199
Objectives ... 200
Secure software development lifecycle ... 200
Phases of SSDLC ... 201
Planning and requirements gathering ... 201
Secure design and architecture ... 202
Secure coding and implementation ... 203
Testing and verification ... 203
Secure application deployment ... 204
Maintenance and monitoring ... 205
DevSecOps ... 205
Principles of DevSecOps ... 206
Security integration in DevSecOps ... 206
Automation and tooling ... 207

Common application vulnerabilities 209
Broken access control 210
Cryptographic failures 210
Injection vulnerabilities 210
Insecure design 211
Security misconfiguration 211
Vulnerable and outdated components 211
Identification and authentication failures 212
Software and data integrity failures 212
Security logging and monitoring failures 212
Server-side request forgery 213
Securing web applications 213
Core principles of web application security 213
Layered defense 214
Authentication and session management 214
Input validation and output encoding 214
Mitigating XSS and CSRF attacks 214
Securing the transport layer 215
Advanced security controls for web applications 215
API and microservices security 216
API authentication and authorization 217
Input validation 217
API abuse prevention 217
Inter-service communication 217
API gateway 218
Continuous protection 218
Mobile application security 219
Mobile Application Security Verification Standard 219
Data storage 219
Secure communication 219
Code protection 220
Runtime protection 220
SDK security 220
Continuous security validation 220
Application security frameworks 221

OWASP ASVS 221
ISO/IEC 27034 222
NIST SP 800-218 222
Emerging trends 222
Supply chain security 223
RASP 223
Zero Trust architecture for applications 223
Application security posture management 224
Security of AI-integrated applications 224
Conclusion 225
Exercises 225

10. Security Operations 227
Introduction 227
Structure 228
Objectives 228
Purpose of security operations 228
Organization of SOC 229
SOC operating models 230
In-house SOC 230
Managed SOC 230
Hybrid SOC 231
Virtual or distributed SOC 231
SOC roles and responsibilities 232
SOC analyst 232
Incident responder 233
Threat intelligence analyst 233
SOC engineer 233
Automation specialist 234
Forensic expert 234
Vulnerability management analyst 234
SOC manager 234
Head of security operations 234
Core functions of SOC 235
Continuous monitoring 235

Incident response 236
Detection 236
Triage 236
Containment 237
Eradication 237
Recovery 237
Post-incident analysis 238
Digital forensic investigation 238
Evidence collection and preservation 239
Evidence examination and analysis 239
Root cause analysis and compromise assessment 239
Threat hunting 240
Threat hunting approaches 240
Threat hunting process 241
Threat intelligence integration 242
Sources of threat intelligence 242
Threat intelligence platforms 243
Vulnerability management 243
Vulnerability assessment 244
Baseline assessment 244
Penetration testing 245
Patch management 245
SOC tools and technologies 246
SIEM 248
Log collection and normalization 248
Correlation and detection logic 248
Advanced analytics 248
Alert enrichment and contextualization 249
Operational visibility 249
SOAR 250
Honeynets and deception technologies 251
Vulnerability scanners 251
Scanning techniques 252
Email security solutions 252
Threat detection techniques 253

Data protection........253
SOC efficacy and maturity........254
Measuring SOC efficacy........254
Detection effectiveness........254
Response efficiency........255
Business impact metrics........255
SOC maturity model........256
Future SOC, unified and autonomous........257
Conclusion........258
Exercises........259

11. Cloud Security........**261**
Introduction........261
Structure........262
Objectives........262
Cloud-native architecture........262
Abstraction and automation........263
Multi-tenancy........263
Characteristics of cloud environments........264
Cloud service models........264
Shared security responsibility........265
IaaS security........265
PaaS security........265
SaaS security........266
Organization management in cloud........267
Organization hierarchy models........267
Organization-level security........268
Organization-level shared services........268
Identity and access management........269
Authentication........269
Authorization........270
Managing permissions in cloud........271
Policy types........271
Privileged user management........272
Conditional access policies and perimeter management........272

Cloud infrastructure security ... 272
Infrastructure security techniques ... 273
Infrastructure as code ... 273
Cloud network security ... 274
Network security controls ... 274
Network security groups ... 274
Cloud firewalls ... 275
Virtual network appliances ... 275
Web application firewalls ... 275
Egress management ... 276
Container networking ... 276
Zero Trust and secure access ... 277
Software-defined perimeter ... 277
Zero Trust Network Access ... 278
Secure access service edge ... 278
Protecting cloud workloads ... 279
Securing virtual machines ... 280
Container security ... 281
Securing PaaS workloads ... 281
Securing serverless workloads ... 282
Data security ... 283
Object storage ... 283
Volume storage ... 283
Database storage ... 283
API security ... 284
Integrated cloud security management platforms ... 284
Conclusion ... 286
Exercises ... 287

12. Emerging Technologies and Information Security ... 289
Introduction ... 289
Structure ... 290
Objectives ... 290
AI in information security ... 290
AI-powered threats ... 291

Defense against AI-driven threats ... 292
AI regulatory frameworks ... 294
Quantum computing and quantum-safe cryptography ... 296
Fundamentals of quantum computing ... 296
Quantum mechanics concepts ... 296
Quantum algorithms ... 297
Applications of quantum computing ... 298
Impact of quantum computing on classical cryptography ... 298
Quantum threat landscape ... 299
Need for cryptographic transition ... 300
Quantum-safe cryptography ... 301
Regulatory standards and frameworks ... 302
Blockchain and information security ... 302
Blockchain principles ... 303
Security applications of blockchain ... 303
Blockchain security challenges ... 303
Edge computing and distributed security ... 304
Edge computing risks ... 304
Securing the edge environment ... 305
Conclusion ... 305
Exercises ... 306

Index ... 307-318

CHAPTER 1
Information Security Fundamentals

Introduction

The rapid digitalization of society has fundamentally transformed how businesses operate and how governments deliver services to their people. In recent decades, the internet has redefined commerce, communication, and administration. Businesses of all kinds and sizes now rely on digital systems and online platforms to reach customers, streamline operations, and expand into global markets. Likewise, governments have embraced digital platforms as the preferred channel to provide essential services, from tax filings and healthcare to social benefits and public records.

The COVID pandemic accelerated this trend, forcing organizations and businesses to rapidly adapt to a new normal of remote operations and digital service delivery. Lockdowns, social distancing, and remote working created an unprecedented reliance on online platforms. Furthermore, remote education, telemedicine, digital payments, and e-governance have become critical lifelines. While this transition enabled continuity, it also increased the attack surface, exposed vulnerabilities in digital infrastructure, and magnified the risks posed by cyberattacks.

In today's interconnected digital world, the protection of data and user trust is more critical than ever. The widespread adoption of digital technology has created vast opportunities but also brought significant risks. Along with increased digitalization and adoption of disruptive technologies like **generative AI (GenAI)**, cloud computing, mobile applications, blockchain, and 5G, cyber threats have grown, not just in sophistication but also in speed and lethality. From widespread precision cyberattacks targeting businesses, governments, and individuals to ransomware attacks disrupting global supply chains, the need for robust information security is at an all time high.

This chapter introduces the fundamental concepts and essential principles of information security, providing a framework for understanding how organizations can safeguard their digital assets. It lays the groundwork for the more detailed and technical topics discussed in subsequent chapters by focusing on the key concepts and methodologies that form the foundation of an effective security posture.

Structure

In this chapter, we will discuss the following topics:

- Evolving threat landscape
- Understanding information security
- Fundamental concepts of information security
- Information security frameworks

Objectives

By the end of this chapter, you will be able to critically examine the emerging information security threat landscape, understand the fundamental concepts and frameworks of information security around which the security programs are designed, and appreciate why information security is a critical business function.

Evolving threat landscape

The digital threat landscape has been evolving rapidly over the last few decades. Attacks on information systems have increased in scale and become more complex and diverse.

From the initial days of the *Morris Worm* in 1988, until the late 90s and early part of 2000, the viruses and malware were mainly focused on exploiting software vulnerabilities and using social engineering attacks to infect systems and spread across networks. These malware variants generally exploited a single attack vector to infect computers. Slowly but gradually, cyberattacks have become more complex and persistent. These attacks now use multiple attack vectors and employ a variety of techniques to exploit vulnerabilities in applications and devices, and carry out supply chain poisoning. They use social engineering techniques to penetrate critical infrastructure and persist in the networks for months and years together as a part of a well-orchestrated plan for data exfiltration and network manipulation, at a time of their choosing. *Operation Aurora,* suspected to be carried out by Chinese hackers around the year 2010, is an apt example of an **advanced persistent threat** (**APT**), wherein the hackers infiltrated the networks of several high-profile companies around the world, including *Google*, by exploiting multiple attack vectors, moving laterally within corporate networks, gaining access to critical systems, and stealing gigabytes of sensitive company data.

Ransomware attacks have also been on the rise during the last decade. In a ransomware attack, cybercriminals gain unauthorized access to networks, encrypt victims' data, and demand a ransom. In 2017, the *WannaCry* ransomware attack infected more than two lac systems across 150 countries and was estimated to have caused damage amounting to over $4 billion worldwide.

Since 2020, the APTs and ransomware attacks have increased in scale and sophistication. These have become more prevalent, persistent, and potent. As per cybersecurity ventures, in 2022, the cybercrime industry was estimated to have cost the global economy over $6 trillion, and it is expected to grow to $11 trillion by 2027[1]. There are two main reasons for this phenomenal rise in cybercrimes:

- The emergence of disruptive technologies like GenAI, 5G, blockchain, and the **Internet of Things** (**IoT**).
- Increased digitalization owing to businesses of all kinds going online, post the COVID pandemic. The increased digitalization and proliferation of applications and devices have increased the attack surface manifold.

Concurrently, the easy availability of GenAI and other niche technologies has lowered the entry barrier for attackers. As a result, we see more sophisticated and targeted attacks by hackers, combining multiple techniques to orchestrate them. GenAI, in particular, has given rise to a whole new strain of attacks of deepfakes where AI-generated fake videos, audio, images, and precision phishing emails are used to target the victims. Another factor contributing to this sophistication is the evolution of the hacker community itself. An entire ecosystem and economy of cybercriminals exists on the darknet. There are hacker groups that specialize in developing zero-day exploits; others have expertise in identifying system vulnerabilities and exploiting them to gain access to networks, yet others conduct the actual attacks by deploying the exploits and carrying out data exfiltration and ransomware attacks. The zero-day exploits, network access, and stolen data are all traded on the darknet for hefty payments. **Ransomware as a service** (**RaaS**) is the new kid on the block!

The rise in geopolitical tensions worldwide has also led to an increase in cyberattacks by the state and state-sponsored actors. In November 2024, the U.S. faced the *worst telecom hack in the nation's history*. A highly sophisticated APT dubbed *Salt Typhoon*[2], attributed to Chinese hackers, that began as far back as 2022, gave the Chinese operatives persistent access to the U.S. telecommunications networks by compromising routers and switches of U.S. telecom companies like *AT&T*, *Verizon*, and *Lumen*, among others.

The primary objective of targeting such **National Critical Information Infrastructure** (**NCII**) is cyber espionage and to carry out disruptive activities during conflicts. All conflicts these days are preceded, accompanied, and followed by cyberattacks on the adversary's networks. We have seen such attacks being played out in the cyber domain during the Russia-Ukraine War and the Gulf Conflict. This is a pointer that future conflicts can be fought entirely in the information domain, using information weapons for control of information and information systems. The cyber-attack by Russian hackers on Estonia in 2007, the most networked country at that time, is a great example of cyber warfare. Outraged by the relocation of a World War II-era statue from Tallinn city center to its outskirts, the Russian hackers had unleashed a series

1 **https://cybersecurityventures.com/wp-content/uploads/2023/11/CybersecurityCost.pdf**

2 **https://www.tenable.com/blog/salt-typhoon-an-analysis-of-vulnerabilities-exploited-by-this-state-sponsored-actor**

of cyberattacks on Estonian networks, completely taking down the country's online services. Banking services, media outlets, and government services all remained impacted for weeks, resulting in widespread disgruntlement against the government.

In the backdrop of the evolving threat landscape where cyberattacks are on the rise, both in scale and lethality, governments and enterprises need to take proactive measures and establish adequate security controls to protect their networks, systems, and data from cyberattacks and leverage information security as a business enabler.

Understanding information security

Information security refers to the processes and measures that protect the **confidentiality, integrity, and availability** (**CIA**) of data. The U.S. **National Institute of Standards and Technology** (**NIST**) defines information security as the *protection of information and information systems from unauthorized access, use, disclosure, disruption, modification, or destruction in order to provide integrity, confidentiality, and availability.* It encompasses the principles, technologies, and practices that protect information assets from theft, corruption, and unauthorized access. It is essential for maintaining trust, ensuring operational continuity, and safeguarding personal and organizational data. At its core, information security is about ensuring that digital information is accessible to authorized users when needed, accurate and trustworthy, and shielded from any unauthorized interference. In the context of organizational operations, this includes not only protecting data from external threats but also managing internal risks such as employee negligence and malicious insider actions. The 2025 data breach of the *Allianz Life Insurance Company,* which affected the majority of its 1.4 million customers, was orchestrated by manipulating unsuspecting employees of the company[1]. Likewise, in May 2025, *Coinbase,* America's largest cryptocurrency exchange, reported a data breach in which its customer support agents had been bribed to access and steal sensitive customer information, including names, account details, and partial **Social Security numbers** (**SSNs**)[2].

Information security is a multidisciplinary field focusing on protecting information and the systems that store, process, and transmit information. The scope of information security extends far beyond just protecting sensitive data; it encompasses a variety of domains, including physical security, network security, application security, data security, and incident response, all working in tandem to protect the overall system.

Fundamental concepts of information security

Information security is based on the three core principles of CIA of information, also known as the **CIA triad**. This CIA triad, along with non-repudiation and authenticity, forms the fundamental pillars of information security. In this section, we will discuss these pillars and some other fundamental concepts of information security, including IAAA, least privilege, **segregation of duties** (**SoD**), defense-in-depth, and Zero Trust.

CIA triad

At the heart of information security, several guiding principles provide a framework for securing information. These principles help organizations design effective security strategies and ensure that their security efforts align with business objectives. The CIA triad is the foundation of information security. CIA guide the protection of information and information systems and are the primary objectives of any security policy and solution deployment. The security controls, to be effective, must address these tenets of information security, as these collectively ensure that the information is protected from unauthorized access, remains unaltered, and is accessible when needed. The following figure illustrates the CIA triad:

***Figure 1.1**: The CIA triad*

Confidentiality

Confidentiality entails the protection and restricted access of sensitive and private information. It ensures that only the authorized users, systems, and processes have access to the information. It prevents unauthorized disclosure or access due to intentional directed attacks or human errors. The primary objective of confidentiality is to preserve the privacy and security of sensitive information and ensure that the information is accessed only by authorized individuals and is processed with proper authorization. The information needs to be protected at rest, while in use, as well as in transit. A variety of security controls, including encryption and access control mechanisms, can be deployed to provide confidentiality during each of these stages, in which the data exists.

Types of sensitive data

The sensitive data that needs to be protected can be of the following types:

- National security information such as classified government documents, military operational plans, or intelligence.
- Intellectual property like trade secrets, application source code of proprietary software, or **research and development** (**R&D**) data.

- Organizational data such as employee records, their personal files, salary and compensation details, or performance appraisal.
- Customer data that includes their profiles or purchase history.
- Citizen's personal information such as **personally identifiable information** (**PII**) like their national SSN, passport information, phone number, birth date, and their address, or medical and healthcare related information such as medical records, treatment plans, health insurance details, or even more sensitive information such as financial data including credit card information, bank account details and financial transactions.

Threat to data confidentiality

Data confidentiality can be compromised in a variety of ways. Some of the threats that can impact the confidentiality of data are as follows:

- Sniffing of traffic over the network.
- Social engineering attacks.
- Password stealing, eavesdropping, shoulder surfing, and impersonation, etc.
- **Man-in-the-middle** (**MitM**) attack, that is, interception of messages and communication between two parties to gain unauthorized access to sensitive information.
- Physical tampering of hardware or storage devices.
- Data interception via unsecured **Wireless Fidelity** (**Wi-Fi**).
- Human error or lack of oversight.
- Inadequate security controls, such as improper encryption and access control mechanisms, can expose sensitive data.

Measures to protect data confidentiality

A number of measures can be employed to safeguard the confidentiality of information. Some of these are as follows:

- The most important proactive measure to ensure data confidentiality is *user awareness and employee training*. This ensures that the users do not fall prey to malicious phishing attacks, thus limiting the attack surface.
- The technical measures that can be employed to ensure data confidentiality include strong encryption, strict access controls, implementing **multi-factor authentication** (**MFA**), deploying **data loss prevention** (**DLP**) techniques, and network segmentation.

- At the policy level, enterprises can apply the **principle of least privilege** (**PoLP**) and grant individuals the minimum level of access required to perform their tasks to prevent unauthorized access to sensitive data.
- Physical security controls, such as access badges, can be implemented to prevent unauthorized physical access to restricted areas housing sensitive assets and information.
- Other measures to safeguard confidentiality include data classification and data labelling, network traffic padding, keeping software and systems updated, using secure communication protocols, and deploying endpoint protection solutions.
- Regular information security audits and assessments help identify vulnerabilities and ensure compliance with the security policies and adequacy of controls to protect data.

Integrity

The principles of integrity and confidentiality are closely intertwined. Without integrity of data, its confidentiality cannot be maintained, as unauthorized alterations could compromise the secrecy of sensitive information. Integrity ensures the reliability and correctness of information. It refers to the assurance that data remains accurate, consistent, and unaltered during its entire lifecycle, from creation to disposal. Accuracy, here, implies that the data is correct, reliable, and free from errors; consistency implies that the data remains logically and structurally consistent, and the unaltered data means that it has not been changed or tampered with. It entails protecting data from unauthorized modifications, whether accidental or malicious, that could compromise the reliability and trustworthiness of the data.

For integrity to be maintained, data must retain its veracity and should be intentionally modified only by authorized persons and processes. Integrity needs to be maintained during the storage, processing, and transit of data. When deploying the security controls, data integrity needs to be examined from three different perspectives: preventing unauthorized users, systems, or processes from making any kind of modifications, preventing authorized subjects from making any unauthorized alterations accidentally, and also by maintaining internal and external consistencies.

Threats to integrity include unauthorized access to systems and data, malicious modification that undermines the integrity of data, intentional replacement, viruses, logic bombs, code injection, data corruption, or unintentional changes and errors that alter the accuracy and reliability of stored data. For data in transit, a MitM attack can allow an attacker to modify data by intercepting and altering communication between two parties. Phishing attacks, code injection, file system manipulation, and backdoors are some of the other threats that can impact integrity. Even physical and environmental threats can undermine data integrity. Events such as fires, floods, and earthquakes can cause damage to hardware and storage devices, thus leading to data corruption or loss. Hardware failures and electromagnetic interference can also affect data consistency and integrity.

A variety of measures can be implemented to safeguard the integrity of information. These include checksum, hash functions, message digest, and **cyclic redundancy code** (**CRC**) to generate unique values and verify and detect any changes to the data. Digitally signing documents is another way to ensure data integrity. Some of the other measures that can be employed to ensure data integrity include strict access control, rigorous authentication, data validation to ensure that data conforms to predefined standards, backup and recovery, **intrusion detection systems** (**IDSs**), and personnel training.

Availability

Availability depends on both confidentiality and integrity. It is essential to ensure the confidentiality and integrity of information systems to maintain availability.

Availability refers to consistent, timely, and uninterrupted access to information systems and resources by authorized users whenever needed. The aim is to prevent disruptions, downtime, or unavailability of assets. It includes efficient, uninterrupted access to resources and implies that the supporting infrastructure, including the network resources, communication channels, and access control systems, is always available to authorized users, whenever required. It implies that the system supports sufficient bandwidth and that timely processing and necessary controls are in place to provide desired access and an acceptable level of performance. The system should be able to handle any interruptions, provide redundancies, and maintain reliable data backups to prevent data loss or destruction. Some of the metrics utilized to describe availability include **mean time to detect** (**MTTD**), **recovery time objective** (**RTO**), **recovery point objective** (**RPO**), **mean time between repairs** (**MTBRs**), and **service level agreement** (**SLA**). These will be dealt with in detail in subsequent chapters.

Threats to the availability of information include **distributed denial of service** (**DDoS**) attacks, which essentially mean overwhelming a system or network with a flood of traffic, rendering a service inaccessible to legitimate users. Network failures due to disruptions or outages in network infrastructure can interrupt communication and, consequently, access to services. Hardware failures, including the malfunctioning or breakdown of hardware components like servers, routers, or storage devices, software errors or bugs, and power outages, can lead to the unavailability of information systems. Malware infections, system configuration errors, and data corruption can compromise the integrity of information systems, leading to disruptions in services. Natural disasters like earthquakes, floods, fires, and hurricanes can physically damage infrastructure and disrupt services. Lack of redundancy in the supply chain can be a major threat to the availability of information systems, as any disruption in the supply chain can lead to the non-availability of critical components when required.

Some of the measures to safeguard availability include deploying DDoS protection solutions, implementing redundant systems and failover mechanisms, load balancing techniques to distribute network traffic evenly across multiple servers, regularly backing up data and establishing robust recovery strategies, and designing networks with in-built resiliency. Additionally, installing an **uninterruptible power supply** (**UPS**) and backup generators to ensure a continuous power supply to the information systems in the event of electrical outages, and providing regular training to employees, following security best practices, and having a strong business continuity plan are measures that ensure availability. The aim is to eliminate a **single point of failure** (**SPOF**) to maintain the availability of critical infrastructure and systems.

Authenticity

Authenticity is a fundamental concept of information security closely associated with the CIA triad, which ensures trustworthiness of users, systems, and data. It is the process of ensuring that data is genuine and has not been tampered with or intercepted during transmission. Authenticity is important for maintaining trust and preventing unauthorized access or fraud. It entails protection against impersonation, spoofing, and other types of identity attacks. The techniques used for ensuring authenticity include authentication, digital certificates, and biometric identification. By employing these techniques, organizations can ensure that unauthorized individuals do not access or misuse confidential data. Authenticity ensures the integrity of data by making sure that the information has not been altered in any manner and that it originated from a legitimate source. It aids availability by verifying the legitimacy of users and processes and preventing any unauthorized interference or DoS attacks.

Non-repudiation

Non-repudiation ensures that someone who caused an event cannot deny that the event occurred, thus implying that the originator of a message, transaction, or action cannot deny having performed it. The concept of non-repudiation provides accountability, making it possible to verify and trust the authenticity and integrity of communications and transactions. It is ensured through identification, authentication, authorization, accountability, and auditing. By leveraging procedural and technical controls, non-repudiation guarantees that parties involved in a digital transaction are held accountable for their actions, whether it is sending an email, signing a contract, or conducting financial transactions. In simple terms, non-repudiation ensures sender accountability, receiver accountability, and transaction integrity.

The following table describes the ingredients of non-repudiation:

Property	Implication
Sender accountability	The sender cannot deny sending the data.
Receiver accountability	The receiver cannot deny receiving the data.
Transaction integrity	The content of the transaction or message has not been altered during transmission.

***Table 1.1**: Implication of non-repudiation*

Non-repudiation fosters trust and can be achieved by implementing strong cryptographic controls, maintaining tamper-proof logging, and adopting emerging technologies like blockchain and AI. Enterprises can enhance non-repudiation mechanisms using specific tools and techniques, often involving a combination of cryptographic methods and procedural safeguards. Digital signatures for signing messages, **public key infrastructure** (**PKI**) for validating them, integrity checks using hashing algorithms for ensuring data integrity, attaching time stamps, and maintaining audit trails are some of the measures to generate this trust.

Despite its robustness, there can be threats to non-repudiation. It can be undermined through compromised keys, and malicious actors can capture and resend valid messages or transactions to disrupt operations using a replay attack. Deprecated or poorly implemented cryptographic algorithms may be susceptible to attacks, or attackers might deceive users into performing certain actions or sharing credentials, complicating non-repudiation claims. Using strong cryptographic algorithms and regularly updating them, proper key management, secure tamper-proof logging, authentication controls like MFA, and awareness training can help counter these threats.

IAAA

IAAA is an access control concept related to information security. It comprises five elements: identification, authentication, authorization, auditing, and accounting.

During the process of accessing a resource, identification implies claiming to be an identity that needs to access a resource; authentication is proving to be that claimed identity; authorization is defining the level of permissions assigned to the authenticated subject for accessing the required resource; auditing is maintaining a log of the activities performed, and accounting or accountability is reviewing the logs to check for compliance or any violations. The following figure illustrates the elements of IAAA:

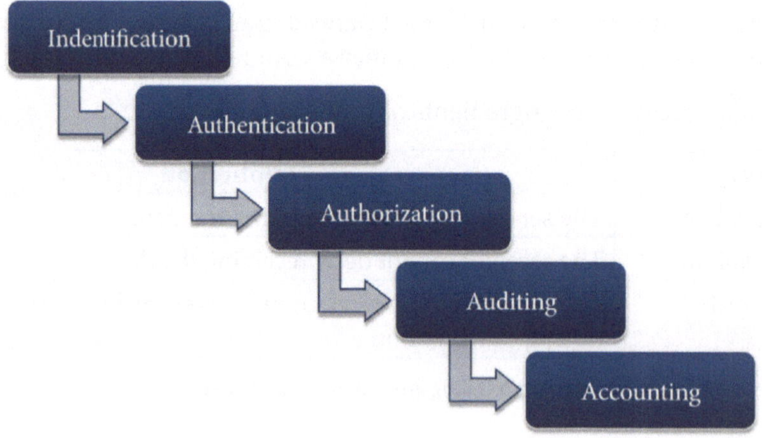

***Figure 1.2**: Elements of IAAA*

Identification

Let us assume that a user wishes to access a resource, for example, a file or a device. Here, the user is the subject, and the file or the device is the object. For the subject to access the object, it has to go through the access control mechanism. First and foremost, the subject needs to establish its identity. So, identification is the process by which a subject professes an identity, after which the authentication process is initiated. The user or subject can be a system, application, individual, or process.

Take the example of an individual trying to login to a web portal. The username, which can be a user ID, email ID, or account number, supplied to the portal, is an identification. In the case of an application or process, it would be the unique process ID or application ID. Most of the time, especially in the case of individuals, the subject's identity is publicly available. For instance, the email address or the name may be known publicly, and hence, a subject cannot be granted access to a resource on the basis of identification alone. The subject needs to prove that he is that identity, and hence the need for authentication. The identity must be authenticated and verified before access to a controlled resource is granted.

Authentication

Authentication is the process of verifying and validating that the identity claimed by the subject is valid. Authentication is achieved by supplying additional information that is supposed to be available to the subject only. Different types of authentication mechanisms can be used to verify the claim. Type 1 authentication, or *something you know,* such as a password, passphrase, or PIN, is the most prevalent type of authentication. The other types are *something you have* (type 2), like smart cards, keys, tokens, and so on; *something you are* (type 3), that is, biometric information such as fingerprint, face recognition, iris recognition, and so on.

When a single type of authentication is used to verify the identity of a subject, it is known as **single factor authentication** (**SFA**). In today's threat environment, it may not be adequate to use a single type of authentication, especially over public networks. Hence, MFA is recommended. MFA is the use of at least two different types of authentication mechanisms. For example, authenticating a web application on the internet using a password (type 1) and SMS or app-based OTP (type 2) is MFA. Similarly, granting an individual access to a restricted area in a complex using a fingerprint (type 3) and an access card (type 2) is an example of MFA. However, using a password and a PIN together is not MFA, since both are of type 1 authentication types.

Authorization

After a subject has been identified and authenticated, it must be authorized to access the given resource(s) as per the assigned rights and privileges. The level of access is generally granted after evaluating an access control matrix that compares the subject, the object, and the intended activity. For example, in the case of a system administrator, once authenticated, he is authorized to perform administrative tasks such as changing the system configuration and so on, whereas a standard user may be authorized to access only certain applications based on the role assigned to him. Authorization is usually provided by using one of the access control models like **mandatory access control** (MAC), **discretionary access control** (DAC), **role-based access control** (RBAC) and **rule-based access control** (RuBAC).

Auditing

Auditing is monitoring and logging the activities performed by the authorized identity. The actions performed by a subject are recorded and tracked programmatically so that they can be held accountable for the activities carried out by them. The purpose of auditing is to establish accountability. It also helps in detecting malicious or unauthorized activities and validating compliance with the laid down security policies.

Accountability

Accountability ensures that the subjects accessing resources can be held accountable for their actions. It is essential for enforcing the information security policies in an organization. Effective accountability can be maintained only if the subjects' identities can be proved, and their activities tracked. In order to establish accountability, the log files collected during the audit are reviewed to check for compliance and violations. During the process, it is verified that the subjects are performing only the activities that they are authorized to, and nothing more. The IAAA elements together ensure accountability and achieve non-repudiation so that a subject cannot deny having performed an activity.

Least privilege

The PoLP implies granting a minimum level of rights to users, processes, and applications that may be required by them to perform their tasks. For instance, a system administrator would need administrative rights on a system, but the other users would require only restricted permissions. Similarly, some groups of users may require read, write, and execute rights on certain files, while others may only need read access. Take also the example of employee payroll in a company. The accounts department would need access to data of all the employees, but the others should be able to view only their own information. The least privilege concept means that the access permissions are so configured that the users and processes can perform their respective tasks, and no more.

One of the main advantages of PoLP is that, in case the credentials of an ID are compromised, the damage is limited to the resources and the level of access granted to that particular user ID. Another concept closely associated with the PoLP is **just-in-time** (JIT) access. This implies that a user or process is given the required level of access to resources for a limited duration, JIT to be able to perform the task, after which the access is revoked. For example, an application administrator performs routine tasks as a part of their daily work and only occasionally performs tasks requiring administrator privileges. In such a scenario, it is a good idea to assign standard permissions to the user and grant them administrative rights, JIT, for the required duration, in order to enable them to perform the administrative tasks. This ensures a secure and efficient environment, catering to the required level of access for the required duration to the required users and processes.

Segregation of duties

SoD, is a foundational concept of information security adopted from finance and accounting. This principle states that no user should have enough access to a critical system or process to misuse it. For instance, a person authorized to grant access to sensitive data or processes should not be the one who requests that access. SoD enhances the overall security posture of an organization and minimizes the risk of unauthorized access or data breach. It prevents accidental errors, as more than one individual is required to complete the task, minimizing the chances of error. It helps in complying with the regulatory requirements and enhances data integrity and availability by applying the four eyes principle, which requires at least two persons to review critical and sensitive processes or actions. SoD also mitigates insider threats and prevents fraud, as no single individual can complete a critical task on their own. It not only prevents internal misuse but also limits damage in case a malicious actor gains unauthorized access to a network or system, as they can perform only those activities that are allowed to the user whose ID was misused to gain unauthorized access.

Defense-in-depth

As the information security landscape continues to evolve, attackers often use multiple attack vectors to target organizations, and no single security control can be adequate to defend against such attacks. Defense-in-depth is a comprehensive strategy of deploying multiple security controls that ensure that if one control fails or is bypassed, other controls are in place to protect the organization's network, systems, and data. NIST defines defense-in-depth as an:

Information security strategy integrating people, technology, and operational capabilities to establish variable barriers across multiple layers and dimensions of the organization. It is the application of multiple countermeasures in a layered or stepwise manner to achieve security objectives. The methodology involves layering heterogeneous security technologies in the common attack vectors to ensure that attacks missed by one technology are caught by another.

The actual implementation of the defense-in-depth may vary from one organization to another, but the objective remains the same: setup a series and variety of controls that an attacker must overcome before they are able to breach the system. The core principles of defense-in-depth are:

- **Layered security**: The security controls are deployed across multiple layers for comprehensive protection. These layers include physical security or perimeter security, network security, endpoint security, and data security.

- **Variety of defenses**: Using different security controls mitigates the risk of a SPOF and makes it harder for the attackers to compromise defenses. For instance, using different types of firewalls ensures that if one type is compromised due to any vulnerability, the other type prevents further lateral movement in the internal network. Likewise, deploying IDSs along with firewalls ensures that if an attack is able to get across the firewall, it gets detected by the IDS.
- **Redundancy**: Controls are deployed in redundant mode so that if one fails, others continue to provide protection.
- **Continuous monitoring and response**: No security is absolute, and attackers will find ways and means to exploit application or device vulnerabilities to infiltrate the network. Continuously monitoring the enterprise network, systems, and devices ensures that any security incident is detected and acted upon promptly.

The following onion-ring figure represents various layers of security controls for defense-in-depth. For each layer, the information security policies and procedures lay down the guidelines and actions required by the stakeholders, and awareness training helps mitigate human errors and educate them against social engineering attacks. As depicted in the following figure, the policies, procedures, and awareness and security monitoring controls are all encompassing and cover all the layers:

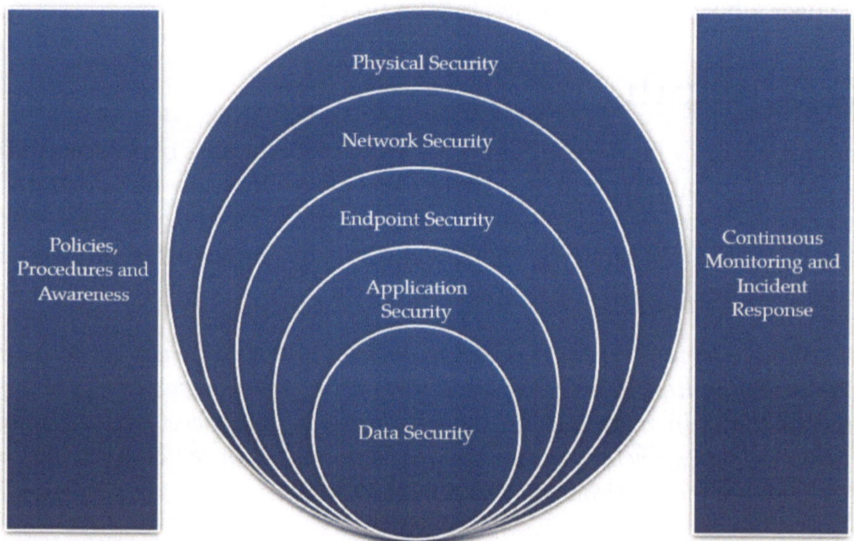

***Figure 1.3**: Layers of defense-in-depth*

Multiple tools, technologies, and solutions are deployed at each layer, in line with the core principles of variety and redundancy. The following figure depicts some of the security controls that can be deployed at various layers:

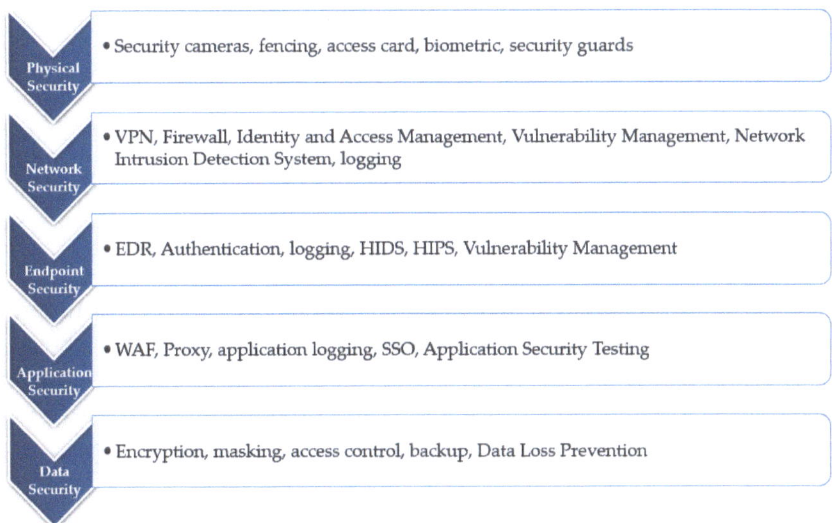

***Figure 1.4**: Security controls at different layers*

Zero Trust

The concept of Zero Trust was introduced by *John Kindervag* of *Forrester Research* in 2010 to develop a framework for protecting enterprise resources through rigorous access control. The Zero Trust concept shifts the focus away from the network perimeter towards individual resources. It presents a shift from a location-centric approach to an identity, context, and data-centric approach with the granular relationship of security controls between users, systems, applications, data, and assets that change over time.

Zero Trust is an information security strategy based on the concept that no subject, user, process, or device, whether inside or outside the enterprise network perimeter, is granted access to a resource unless it is explicitly verified. It is an integrated and proactive approach that explicitly and continuously verifies every connection request and asserts the PoLP. Before allowing any connection, trust is established based on the requesting entity's context and security posture, and access is granted following the PoLP. Thereafter, it is continually reassessed for every new connection, even if the entity was authenticated earlier.

The operative definition of Zero Trust by NIST is that *Zero Trust provides a collection of concepts and ideas designed to minimize uncertainty in enforcing accurate, least-privilege per-request access decisions in information systems and services in the face of a network viewed as compromised.*

Guiding principles of Zero Trust

As the definition above suggests, the guiding principles of Zero Trust are as follows:

- **Verify explicitly**: There is no implicit trust. The principle is never trust, always verify. The security decisions are continually made using all available data points, including identity, location, device health, resource, data classification, and anomalies, before granting access.

- **Use least privilege access**: Implies limiting access to resources by assigning minimum required privileges, JIT, and **just enough access** (**JEA**) based on risk-based adaptive polices.
- **Assume breach**: Assume to be operating in an environment of breach and minimize blast radius with micro-segmentation, end-to-end encryption, continuous monitoring, and automated threat detection and response.

The U.S. **Cybersecurity and Infrastructure Security Agency** (**CISA**) has outlined five distinct pillars for Zero Trust implementation and measuring its maturity level. These are identity, devices, networks, applications, workloads, and data. It also outlines the cross-cutting capabilities of visibility and analytics, automation and orchestration, and governance, which support activities within these pillars and interoperability across the pillars.

Tenets of Zero Trust

The basic tenets of Zero Trust for designing and deploying a Zero Trust architecture are as follows:

- All data sources and computing services in the enterprise are considered resources.
- All communication is secured irrespective of the network location, i.e., a source should not be trusted merely because it is on the enterprise's internal network. It must pass the same tests as a request coming from any outside source. All communication must be explicitly authenticated and should happen in a secure manner to ensure confidentiality and integrity.
- The access to individual resources is granted on a per-session basis, assigning the least privileges required to complete the task. Successful authentication and authorization do not automatically grant access to others. It needs to be authenticated every time, for each resource.
- Access to the resources is determined by a dynamic policy that may include the observable state of the requesting identity, asset, application, or service, and other behavioural and environmental attributes. The policy is a set of access rules assigned to a subject, data asset, or application based on the business process and acceptable level of risk.
- No asset is inherently trusted, and the integrity and security posture of all assets are continually monitored and measured by the enterprise.
- The resource authentication and authorization are dynamic, continually evaluated, and strictly enforced before granting access. The monitoring processes act as a feedback loop for the dynamic policy that strives to strike a balance between security, availability, usability, and cost efficiency.

- In order to improve the security posture and enforce the dynamic policy, as much information as possible about the current state of assets, network infrastructure, and communications is collected and used to refine and update the decision-making.

Information security frameworks

Security requirements of businesses vary depending upon their size, mission, goals, location, industry sector, etc. The information security frameworks are a set of standards, guidelines, and best practices that provide organizations with a structured approach for implementing a security program. The frameworks can be applied to businesses of all types and sizes and provide a comprehensive roadmap for identifying and mitigating risks. Aligning information security controls to a framework helps organizations follow a consistent approach to security, measure the maturity level, and meet regulatory requirements. It demonstrates management commitment to security and instills confidence in the stakeholders.

In this section, we will introduce some of the most commonly adopted information security frameworks.

NIST Cybersecurity Framework

The NIST **Cybersecurity Framework (CSF)** was first released in 2014, with the current version, CSF 2.0, released in 2024. Along with ISO 27001, it is one of the most commonly used frameworks that can be adopted by industry, government agencies, and other organizations to manage cybersecurity risks effectively. Refer to the following figure:

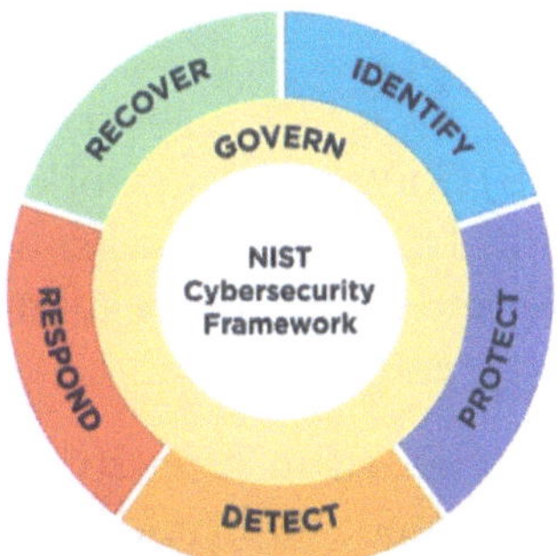

***Figure 1.5:** CSF functions*
*(**Source:** NIST)*

The NIST CSF comprises three components: core, profile, and tiers. The core describes a set of outcomes that an organization can aspire to achieve. It is organized into six core functions of govern, identify, protect, detect, respond, and recover, which are further divided into 22 categories and 106 sub-categories. The profile describes the current and the desired or target maturity state of the organization in terms of the core outcomes. A gap analysis between the desired and current state is carried out to arrive at an action plan to close the gap. The tiers characterize the maturity level of an organization's information security governance and management practices and provide a progressive model for transitioning from informal to a continuously improving maturity level. These tiers in the order of maturity are partial, risk-informed, repeatable, and adaptive.

ISO 27001

Published by the **International Organization for Standardization** (**ISO**) in partnership with the **International Electrotechnical Commission** (**IEC**), ISO 27001 is an internationally accepted standard for information security. It is widely adopted across the world by organizations and businesses of all types and sizes to implement and demonstrate commitment to security. The framework lays down requirements for defining, implementing, operating, and improving an **information security management system** (**ISMS**). It requires the management to systematically examine the organization's security risks, design and implement a coherent and comprehensive set of security controls, and adopt a management process to ensure that the controls continually fulfill the organization's information security needs. Organizations can implement the framework and get certified by an accredited agency.

The latest version of the standard, published in 2022, is organized into 11 clauses. The ISO 27001 requirements are given in clauses 4 to 10. Implementation of the requirements laid down in these clauses is mandatory for any organization that wishes to be compliant with the standard. The seven clauses encompass the context of the organization, leadership, planning, support, operation, performance evaluation, and improvement. In addition, there is an annexure of 93 discretionary security controls which may be scoped for managing and mitigating risks and to meet any additional regulatory requirements.

CIS Controls framework

The **Center for Internet Security** (**CIS**) Controls framework provides a set of best practices for safeguarding and protecting networks from cyberattacks. It attempts to align with the latest industry regulations and frameworks and is updated regularly by professionals from different fields, including government, industry, and academia.

The latest CIS Controls version 8.1, released in June 2024, includes 18 controls focused on inventory control, configuration management, audit and logging, data protection, vulnerability management, penetration testing, email and web security, network security, access control, application security, incident response, awareness training, and service provider management.

SOC 2

System and Organization Controls 2 (**SOC 2**) is a non-financial, information security-focused framework by the **American Institute of Certified Public Accountants** (**AICPA**). It specifies how service organizations should protect customer data and is developed around the five **Trust Services Criteria** (**TSC**) that include security, availability, processing integrity, confidentiality, and privacy. Service organizations can voluntarily choose to be SOC 2 attested by AICPA-approved auditors to demonstrate compliance with the framework. The SOC 2 report is tailored to an organization's unique business needs and reports on the adherence to the TSC criteria in scope for the business. Security is the only mandatory criterion; others need to be included only if they are relevant to the services being provided by the organization. There are two types of SOC 2 reports:

- **SOC 2 Type 1**: It is a point-in-time report and evaluates whether the security controls have been designed properly to comply with the relevant trust criteria.
- **SOC 2 Type 2**: This is a more technical and detailed report on how the controls function over time and reports on the operational effectiveness of these controls.

Other common frameworks

We previously discussed some commonly adopted security frameworks for implementing overall security in an organization. There are other industry-focused and function-specific frameworks. Some of these are as follows:

- The EU **General Data Protection Regulation** (**GDPR**) is a regulation focused on data protection and privacy rights. Compliance with GDPR is mandatory for businesses to operate in the EU.
- ISO 27701 **Privacy Information Management System** (**PIMS**) is an extension of ISO 27001 for privacy management. It is designed for use by any organization or entity handling **personally identifiable information** (**PII**).
- ISO 42001 **Artificial Intelligence Management System** (**AIMS**) is a framework that specifies requirements for establishing, implementing, maintaining, and continually improving an AIMS. It provides a structured way to manage AI risks and opportunities, balancing innovation with governance.
- **Payment Card Industry Data Security Standard** (**PCI DSS**) is a standard by the PCI **Security Standards Council** (**SSC**) for safe payments worldwide and applies to businesses handling credit card information and payments.
- The **Health Insurance Portability and Accountability Act** (**HIPAA**) is a U.S. legislation to protect patient healthcare data and medical records. It prohibits any entity from sharing such information unless authorized by the patient or their representative.

Conclusion

The information security landscape has been evolving rapidly over the years. From simple viruses and worms exploiting single software vulnerabilities to infect computers and networks, the threats have evolved to sophisticated APTs exploiting multiple attack vectors. AI-assisted deep fake attacks have also been on the rise due to the easy availability of GenAI. The famous deepfake scam that impacted *Arup Engineering*, a UK-based engineering firm, is only a pointer of things to come. In early 2024, Arup Engineering fell victim to a sophisticated deepfake scam in which fraudsters used AI-generated video to impersonate a senior executive during a video conference and convinced one of their finance professionals in Hong Kong to transfer approximately £20 million to fraudulent accounts[3].

The objective of information security is to protect the CIA triad of data and ensure authenticity and non-repudiation. There are other fundamental concepts, including IAAA, least privilege, SoD, defense-in-depth, and Zero Trust, which are essential for implementing and maintaining the security of information systems. Adopting an information security framework helps in providing a structured way for designing, implementing, and maintaining an information security program. A security framework not only helps in following a consistent approach and measuring progress, but also demonstrates management commitment and instills confidence among stakeholders.

In the next chapter, we will discuss various types of information security threats and vulnerabilities and explore various threat modelling methodologies that can be employed to identify and mitigate information security risks.

Exercises

1. Critically examine the current threat landscape with reference to your business or organization. Research a recently discovered APT and analyze the **tactics, techniques, and procedures** (**TTP**) used by the threat actors.
2. Explain the CIA triad.
3. What are the concepts involved in IAAA? Differentiate between authentication and authorization.
4. Discuss the strategies of defense-in-depth and Zero Trust in the context of your organization.
5. Review the information security framework adopted by your organization and verify the current maturity state of the security controls to ascertain whether and how these fulfill the organization's security requirements.

References

1. **Allianz Life July 2025 data breach: https://www.forbes.com/sites/steveweisman/2025/08/10/allianz-data-breach-exposes-vulnerabilities-affecting-everyone/**
2. **Coinbase cryptocurrency exchange May 2025 data breach: https://www.coinbase.com/en-in/blog/protecting-our-customers-standing-up-to-extortionists**
3. **Arup Engineering deepfake scam: https://www.theguardian.com/technology/article/2024/may/17/uk-engineering-arup-deepfake-scam-hong-kong-ai-video**

Chapter 2
Threats and Vulnerabilities

Introduction

Cyber threat, vulnerability, and risk are some of the terms often discussed in the context of information security. Cyber threat is an act intended to compromise the integrity of information systems with the objective of stealing, corrupting, destroying, or exposing data or disrupting information systems and networks. Threats can originate from a variety of sources and target different elements of information systems, i.e., people, processes, and technology, including applications, software, servers, endpoints, network devices, etc. Vulnerabilities are weaknesses or flaws in information systems that threat actors exploit to compromise information systems. They can employ a variety of techniques to compromise systems and networks, ranging from directly exploiting vulnerabilities in systems and services to spreading or amplifying false and malicious content. The tactics and techniques used by the threat actors depend upon the objective of the attack, the opportunity presented by the prospective target, and the skill level of the threat actors. The attackers can be cyber criminals, hacktivists, malicious insiders, or state actors, each of whom presents unique challenges and risks.

A comprehensive understanding of cyber threats and vulnerabilities in information systems and the motivation, objectives, and methodologies used by various threat actors is essential for developing effective information security strategies. A structured and proactive threat modelling approach can be adopted for identifying, analyzing, and prioritizing security risks in information systems and focusing efforts on implementing suitable controls to mitigate them.

Structure

In this chapter, we will discuss the following topics:

- Categories of threat actors
- Types of cyber threats
- Common vulnerabilities
- Threat modelling

Objectives

By the end of this chapter, you will be able to understand different categories of threat actors, their motivations, and sophistication levels. You will be able to understand different types of threats and vulnerabilities and appreciate how threat actors exploit vulnerabilities in information systems to target organizations and businesses. You will also be able to comprehend various threat modelling methodologies and be able to apply these techniques to identify and mitigate information security risks in various scenarios and situations.

Categories of threat actors

The threats to information systems can come from a variety of actors with varying motivations and skill levels. They can be individuals, groups of hackers, cyber criminals, or state actors, and can be operating from anywhere across the world. Also, not all threat actors have a similar skill level and capabilities. Some may be highly trained and organized with unlimited resources to plan and execute their mission, while others could be individual hackers or *script kiddies* with limited understanding and resources. The objectives and motivation for the attacks could also range from cybercrime, hacktivism, espionage, data stealing, to corrupting and disrupting information systems. Thus, the attacks vary in complexity, scale, and sophistication depending on the type of threat actors. The threat actors can be broadly categorized into the following categories:

- **State actors**: State actors or state-sponsored actors operate in support of advancing geopolitical objectives. By far, they are the most sophisticated threat actors who have the backing of nation-states and have dedicated resources and expertise to plan, coordinate, and execute the attacks. The motivation could be espionage or seeking control of networks for carrying out disruptive activities at a time of their choosing. Most of the **advanced persistent threats** (**APTs**) that use complex and protracted campaigns are perpetrated by state-sponsored actors.
- **Cybercriminals**: The primary motive of cybercriminals is financial gain. The attacks carried out by this category of threat actors can vary in complexity and sophistication. An organized group of cybercriminals with requisite planning, technical expertise, and easy availability of niche technology can run a well-orchestrated campaign to target individuals and businesses.
- **Hacktivists**: These are the threat actors who carry out hacking activities to prove a point in support of their ideologies. They generally utilize readily available cyber tools to launch attacks and compromise applications and networks. The complexity and level of sophistication of the attacks are much lower, and their effect on the target may be for a limited duration only.
- **Script kiddies**: They use readily available techniques to exploit the well-known vulnerabilities in applications and devices. The motives could be to prove a point, try out new things, or just for the thrill. AI-assisted exploit code generation has led to a rise in script kiddies.

- **Malicious insiders**: They are disgruntled or rogue employees who harbour a grudge against an organization. The insider threat actors are particularly dangerous as they have complete knowledge of the internal environment and have legitimate access to the organization's network and systems, making it that much easier to perform the malicious activities.

Types of cyber threats

Cyber threats are actions carried out by threat actors to compromise the confidentiality, integrity, or availability of information by exploiting vulnerabilities in information systems. These can manifest in a variety of ways; the most common of these are discussed in the following sections.

Malware

Any type of malicious software that is designed to exploit vulnerabilities and perform malicious actions to harm or compromise applications, systems, networks, or end user devices can be categorized as malware. Malware is created with the intention of gaining unauthorized access, stealing information, or disrupting normal operations. They can exploit various attack vectors like email, malicious websites, removable drives, or infected software downloads. Viruses, worms, Trojans, rootkits, keyloggers, spyware, adware, and ransomware are all examples of malware. Some of these are discussed in the following sections.

Virus

A virus is an executable code that attaches itself to legitimate applications. It executes and replicates when the infected application is run. The primary goal is to replicate and spread across the infected systems, deleting files, corrupting storage, and operating systems, thereby disrupting operations. The *ILOVEYOU*[1] virus, which spread in the year 2000 through emails disguised as love letters, is one of the most infamous viruses. It is estimated to have caused damages worth $10 billion worldwide by infecting files and corrupting databases.

Worm

A type of malware that can replicate and spread across networks without any user interaction. They can self-replicate by exploiting software or device vulnerabilities. Similar to viruses, the worms can cause damage to information systems by deleting files, corrupting data, and draining network resources. The *Stuxnet* worm[2], which targeted multiple Windows vulnerabilities, exploited flaws in *Siemens Industrial Control Systems* in 2010, and disrupted Iran's nuclear program by sabotaging the centrifuges, is a well-known example. Others include *Mydoom, Sasser, Conficker, Blaster worm*, etc.

Ransomware

In a ransomware attack, threat actors gain unauthorized access to systems and encrypt the files and data on the system, rendering it unusable. The system is held hostage until the owners agree to pay the demanded ransom. The primary objective of a ransomware attack is financial extortion. Ransomware attacks have been on the rise in recent years. *WannaCry*[3], which exploited the Windows **Server Message Block** (**SMB**) protocol (*EternalBlue*), is a well-known ransomware. In 2017, it affected more than 0.2 million systems across 150 countries, significantly disrupting services, resulting in estimated damages of $4 billion. Another example is the *NotPetya*[4] ransomware, which initially targeted Ukrainian infrastructure, spread globally, and caused an estimated damage of $10 billion to businesses and enterprises across the world. *NotPetya* also exploited the SMB vulnerability and combined other techniques to spread rapidly.

Cryptojacker

Threat actors deploy malicious software to leverage the computing resources of the victim system for crypto mining. As the crypto mining software hogs the system resources, it may become slow and unstable.

Trojan

These are malicious programs disguised and embedded in legitimate software. Trojans provide unauthorized access to networks and systems, create backdoors, and help in stealing sensitive information.

Rootkit

Malicious software that provides administrative privileges to applications, firmware, operating system kernels, or hypervisors. They provide full control over the system, permitting any kind of modifications, including modifying the antimalware software itself. They help in maintaining persistence while evading detection and enabling attackers to carry out various malicious activities, including information stealing, launching attacks, and maintaining control over the compromised systems.

Spyware

Spyware is used to secretly monitor user and system activities, without the knowledge or consent of the owner. Spyware remains covert and is used for activities like keystroke logging, monitoring surfing habits, and capturing user credentials. These can also be used for accessing and turning on the device's camera and microphone for remote surveillance.

Adware

Adware or advertising software displays targeted advertisements on the affected system. It may not be inherently malicious, as the main objective is to generate revenue by delivering tailored online advertisements. However, it can be a nuisance due to frequent pop-ups and distractions. Adware often spreads through software bundling, where it is included with legitimate free software downloads.

Fileless malware

Fileless malware operates entirely in the system memory, without leaving any traces on the storage disk. This type of malware exploits legitimate system tools, processes, and memory to execute without residing on the disk. Hence, it is also known as **Living of the Land** (**LOTL**) malware. These are extremely difficult to detect, as no additional software is installed, and native files, like PowerShell and **Windows Management Instrumentation** (**WMI**), are leveraged to enable the malicious functions.

Botnet

A botnet is a network of hijacked computers and devices, also called bots or zombies, that are infected with malware and in the control of threat actors, who can leverage them to launch coordinated attacks without the knowledge of the owners. Botnets regularly scan the internet to identify vulnerable devices. Once a vulnerable device is found, it is infected with the malware and made part of the botnet to utilize its computing and network resources. Botnets can be used to launch a variety of attacks, such as **distributed denial of service** (**DDoS**) attacks, sending spam emails, spreading malware, crypto mining, and carrying out password attacks like credential stuffing and password spray attacks.

Modern antivirus and **endpoint detection and response** (**EDR**) solutions employ a variety of techniques such as signature-based detection, heuristic and behavioural analysis, **machine learning** (**ML**), and **artificial intelligence** (**AI**) to handle not only known malware but also unknown and zero-day threats as well. The antivirus and EDR solutions are combined with cloud threat intelligence and real-time monitoring and response solutions, such as **security information and event management** (**SIEM**) systems and **security orchestration and automated response** (**SOAR**) solutions for automatic containment and remediation.

Distributed denial of service

A DoS attack is a type of attack that is aimed at overwhelming network and system resources of the target, to the extent that normal operation is disrupted and the system is unable to service legitimate requests, resulting in a denial of service to the genuine users. A DDoS attack is initiated from multiple devices that are part of a botnet. The difference lies in the magnitude and coordination of the attack. In a DDoS attack, the impact is much more severe, as the coordinated attack quickly exhausts the target's resources, including bandwidth, memory, and processing power, causing the system to become slow, unresponsive, or completely unavailable. A multitude of techniques, including flooding, resource exhaustion, and protocol exploitation, can be used for DDoS attacks. In flooding attacks, the target is flooded with a high volume of requests, such that it is not able to service additional requests, leading to a denial of service. The techniques used can be TCP SYN flooding, **User Datagram Protocol** (**UDP**) flooding, ARP flooding, etc. In resource exhaustion attacks, the target's resources, such as bandwidth, compute, and memory, are consumed by exploiting system vulnerabilities. In protocol exploitation, vulnerabilities in network and application layer protocols are exploited to disrupt the services.

Man-in-the-middle

A **man-in-the-middle** (**MitM**) attack occurs when a threat actor secretly intercepts communication between two parties without their knowledge. This could be between the victim and a website, like, say, a banking website or any other application. The victims remain under the illusion that they are communicating directly and securely with the legitimate website. The attackers position themselves between the victim and the target website to intercept the data being transmitted. Once in the middle, the threat actors can monitor communications, reroute traffic, deliver malware, and harvest personally identifiable or other sensitive information, like personal messages, login credentials, credit card information, etc. The attackers might also alter the information in the communication, for instance, modify payment instructions to divert funds to another account or alter the contents of a message to manipulate the conversation. A typical MitM attack in action is illustrated in the following figure:

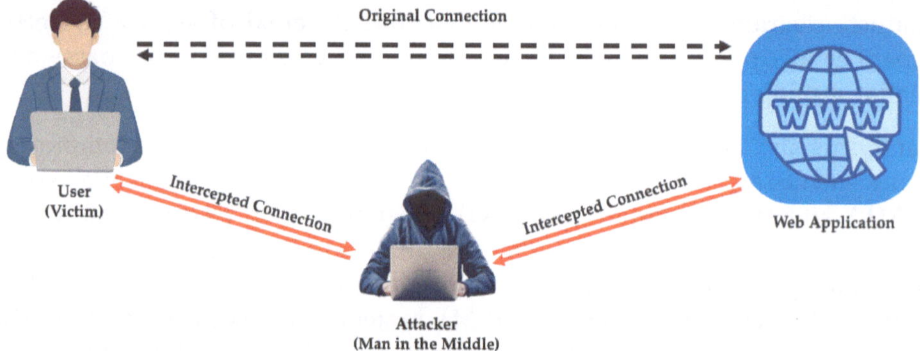

Figure 2.1: *MitM attack*

Code injection

In this type of attack, the threat actors introduce malicious code in a program or a website, taking advantage of programming flaws or how data is interpreted. The attack occurs when the input is not validated and sufficiently sanitized. SQL injection and **cross-site scripting** (**XSS**) are the most prevalent injection attacks.

SQL injection

This type of attack is targeted against websites that use databases in the backend to service user requests. Malicious code is injected into an SQL query through a user request, which is run against the application's backend database server. A successful SQL injection attack can allow the attacker to read, modify, and perform privileged operations, leading to data exfiltration, data deletion, or database corruption.

Cross-site scripting

XSS allows threat actors to inject malicious scripts by manipulating user input into websites without proper input validation and sufficient data sanitization. The attackers use clickable content in the vulnerable website to transmit the scripts that get delivered to the victims when they visit the website. When clicked, the scripts are executed in the context of the victim's browser. This can provide the attacker access to sensitive information, like session cookies and tokens, and can lead to data theft or even facilitate the attackers in carrying out further exploitation and malicious activities.

Insider threats

Insider threats are threats from individuals who are part of an organization and have authorized access to its information systems and resources. Disgruntled employees, partners, or other trusted entities can intentionally or unintentionally misuse their legitimate access rights to the systems, leading to the compromise of confidentiality, integrity, and availability of data or information systems. For instance, a disgruntled system administrator or an application admin can intentionally steal sensitive information, collude with other threat actors, and create a backdoor for them to enter the network or disrupt operations for personal gains or with malicious intent. Likewise, a negligent employee may fall victim to a social engineering attack and inadvertently expose sensitive company data.

Social engineering

Social engineering is manipulating unsuspecting users and tricking them into revealing sensitive information or taking actions that provide attackers with unauthorized access to their or the company's systems, to perform further malicious activities or exploitation. Social engineering attacks exploit human psychology to trick users and then exploit technical vulnerabilities to further their attack. The attackers can lure or coerce the victims into taking actions by invoking fear, empathy, or urgency. Threat actors use a variety of social engineering techniques, like phishing, baiting, smishing, pretexting, and tailgating. Some of these are as follows:

- **Phishing**: Threat actors impersonate as trusted and legitimate entities, and send emails or messages with malicious links or attachments to a large number of recipients and trick them into clicking malicious links or opening the attachments, which may lead to revealing sensitive information or installing malicious software on the victim's system. This can be used to exfiltrate data or gain unauthorized access to the organization's network. Phishing attacks can be categorized as follows:

- o **Spear phishing**: It is a targeted phishing attack. In a spear phishing attack, the threat actors send precise and tailored messages to a selected set of recipients. The threat actors thoroughly research the targets before crafting and sending an email that has context and appears genuine. The targets are more likely to perform the intended actions as the mail appears relevant and seems to be originating from a trusted source. A spear phishing attack is called so because of the targeted nature of the attack.
- o **Whaling**: Whaling or whale-phishing attack is targeted at the senior executives or individuals with higher levels of privilege and authority, i.e., the *big fish* or the whales in the organization. For obvious reasons, if such attacks succeed, the impact is much higher, as these victims are likely to have more valuable and sensitive information.
- o **Smishing**: Smishing or SMS phishing is conducted through text messages. Attackers send SMS with malicious links and lure the victims into clicking them. When users click the link, they are directed to a website from which malicious software gets downloaded on the victims' devices. This can allow the attacker to control the device functionalities or gain access to sensitive information.
- o **Vishing**: It is voice phishing used by cybercriminals. The threat actors make fraudulent voice calls and trick individuals into revealing sensitive information, which can be used to defraud them.

- **Baiting**: In this type of social engineering attack, the threat actors throw a bait to the users by making false promises to lure them into revealing sensitive information or taking such actions that permit installing malicious software on their device. The bait can be in the form of offering free software, movie or music downloads, free gaming, prizes, or money, etc., to lure victims into clicking on malicious links or downloading malware-infected files.
- **Pretexting**: In pretexting, the threat actors shape the target before orchestrating the attack. In this type of attack, the attackers pretext the prospective targets posing as a person of authority, such as a bank employee, tax official, government employee, member of a law enforcement agency, or a person from any private entity in which the victims may have an interest, such as an insurance agency, talent hunting agency, etc. After pretexting and explaining the context, the attackers would seek personal and sensitive information or ask them to access a link to install malicious software, which could then be used to advance the attack further.

Password attacks

These are attempts by hackers or unauthorized individuals to gain access to user accounts, systems, or networks by guessing, stealing, or brute forcing passwords. These attacks can be carried out in a variety of ways to exploit weaknesses in information systems to compromise user credentials and gain unauthorized access to sensitive information or resources. The password attacks can be conducted from a single source or through botnets to speed up the process. Some common types of password attacks are discussed in the following sections.

Brute-force

In a password brute-force attack, the attackers use automated tools to systematically try out all possible combinations of alphabets, digits, and special characters to brute-force the passwords. Brute-force attacks can be time-consuming, as all possible combinations need to be tried out until the correct password is discovered. The time taken depends on the complexity of the password, and hence, these attacks are effective against weak or easily guessable passwords.

Dictionary attack

This can also be considered a type of brute-force attack. The difference lies in the fact that, instead of attempting to brute-force the passwords character by character, a compiled list of commonly used passwords and their variations is used to discover the passwords. Dictionary attacks are faster and are successful against users who tend to use simple or commonly used passwords.

Credential stuffing

People tend to use the same passwords across multiple platforms and systems, as they find it difficult to remember too many passwords. In a credential stuffing attack, the threat actors rely on the tendency to reuse passwords and use stolen username-password combinations obtained from previous data breaches. The stolen set of user credentials is tried out for a large number of users on the target application, with the objective and hope that some users may have reused the credentials, and the attack would succeed for those accounts. Credential stuffing attacks can be conducted from a single source or by employing a botnet to do simultaneous credential stuffing for a large number of accounts.

Password spraying

In password spraying attacks, rather than brute forcing an individual account's password, the attackers try out a few commonly used passwords for multiple accounts simultaneously, maybe thousands or even millions. The idea is that some users in the organization would be using those passwords. While increasing the possibility of finding the right combination, it also prevents the chances of account lockout, reducing the risk of detection.

Key logging

Keyloggers spy on the victims by recording the keystrokes. These are malicious software programs installed on previously compromised systems that capture all keystrokes, including passwords. Keyloggers are especially dangerous as they operate with stealth, without the knowledge of the users, and are capable of capturing the most difficult passwords, which otherwise cannot be guessed easily.

Spoofing

Spoofing is when a sender forges or disguises themselves as a trusted or authorized source. Spoofing attacks take advantage of the trust relationship between a legitimate source and the recipients. The spoofing can happen at any layer, from the application to the **Media Access Control** (**MAC**) layer. Some of the techniques used by the attackers are call spoofing, in which the caller's phone number is spoofed, email spoofing, where the sender's email ID is spoofed, **domain name system** (**DNS**) spoofing, IP spoofing, and ARP spoofing. Though conducted at different layers of the **Open Systems Interconnection** (**OSI**) model, the modus operandi to achieve the goal remains the same, i.e., impersonate as a trusted source and exploit the trust relationship to execute the attack to gain unauthorized access, steal data, access sensitive information, and spread malware.

Domain name system attacks

DNS is a service that resolves the human-readable internet addresses into IP addresses, which are used by computers and network devices to communicate with other devices. All organizations generally allow DNS traffic to flow in and out of their networks without any restrictions. Also, due to the sheer volume of DNS traffic, it requires enormous resources and niche technology to monitor the traffic and derive any actionable insights from it. As a result, in most organizations, it remains unmonitored. In DNS attacks, the threat actors attempt to disturb the normal functioning of the DNS servers, redirecting the users to malicious websites, exfiltrating data through DNS tunnelling, or even disrupting the DNS operations altogether. DNS spoofing, tunnelling, hijacking, amplification/reflection are some of the DNS attacks.

Domain name system spoofing

DNS spoofing is the manipulation of the DNS servers by poisoning their cache to direct traffic from legitimate websites to a spoofed and malicious site. The attackers send fake DNS responses to the DNS server and trick it into storing the IP address of the malicious site for an authentic domain. When the users try to visit the actual website, they are directed to the malicious site that mirrors the original. Once the users are directed to the attacker's website, the attacker can perform all kinds of malicious activities, including harvesting login credentials, stealing personal or sensitive information like credit card numbers, bank account details, etc.

Domain name system tunnelling

As the name suggests, DNS tunnelling is used to bypass firewalls and exfiltrate data using the DNS protocol and the DNS ports. Data is sent to a remote server, disguised as DNS queries, and then directed to the attacker in the form of DNS responses. Such attacks are extremely difficult to detect due to the high volume of DNS traffic flowing through the networks.

Domain name system hijacking

DNS hijacking is a type of attack in which the DNS queries are resolved incorrectly and unexpectedly, redirecting users to malicious sites. DNS hijacking, also called **DNS redirection**, can be achieved in several ways. The attackers can modify the local DNS settings and host file entries on the end user device to redirect the requests to a malicious site. The DNS settings of a router can be overwritten, affecting all users connected to the router. MitM attacks can capture DNS resolution requests and divert users to a malicious site. The DNS records of a compromised DNS server can be changed such that the domain name is resolved to the attacker's fake site.

Domain name system amplification

Unlike the above attacks, where the objective is to redirect the users to a malicious website, DNS amplification is a type of DDoS attack. It involves exploiting open DNS resolvers to flood the target with DNS responses. The technique used is to send DNS requests to the open resolvers with a spoofed IP address, which then respond with a response much larger than the initial query. When multiple open resolvers and spoofed IP addresses are used together, the target can be overwhelmed with traffic, rendering it unavailable for the legitimate users.

Supply chain attacks

The information systems deployed by various organizations comprise hardware and software from different vendors. There is a need for organizations to collaborate with vendors and other service providers, and hence, provide these partners access to their organization's information systems to manage operations. The threat actors exploit this trust relationship to launch supply chain attacks. They target the weakest link in the supply chain and infiltrate the systems or tools of a third-party vendor with weak security by exploiting vulnerabilities in their products and processes. Once the initial foothold has been gained, the trust relationship with the third-party vendor is exploited to launch attacks against the target organizations. Typically, the hardware supplied by the vendor may be compromised, or an application or software component may be injected with malicious code. When the compromised hardware or software is in the target's network, it can be exploited to launch further attacks. Whatever the method, supply chain attacks can have a devastating effect on businesses, even to the extent of impacting their continuity.

The *SolarWinds* attack of 2020 and the *Kaseya Virtual System Administrator (VSA)* attack of 2021 are two of the most infamous supply chain attacks reported in recent years. In the *SolarWinds*[5] attack, attackers infiltrated the company's software build system and planted a backdoor, known as *Sunburst*, in its Orion IT infrastructure monitoring and management platform. When the backdoored software was deployed in the customers' network, it gave the attackers access to their internal network and sensitive systems. More than 18,000 customers, including government organizations and Fortune 500 companies, were estimated to have been impacted by the attack. In the *Kaseya*[6,7] attack, vulnerabilities in its VSA software were exploited in a ransomware attack, giving attackers access to the company's systems and spreading the ransomware further to its customers. The attack affected nearly 1,500 businesses worldwide, disrupting operations globally.

Internet of Things threats

There has been a proliferation of **Internet of Things** (**IoT**) and **industrial IoT** (**IIoT**) devices in recent years. Along with an increase in the number of IoT devices, the threat surface has expanded, and new security risks and challenges have emerged. Most of the IoT devices are not sufficiently secure and do not have basic security features implemented. Due to device performance issues and the costs associated with implementing security, the IoT vendors tend to implement only the required operational functionalities, overlooking the security aspects. In certain cases, the devices are deployed outside the secure network perimeter of the organization, making it challenging to secure them. The risks associated with successful IoT attacks are also higher, as these are physical devices or devices controlling critical real-world systems, and any successful attack on these could have devastating and lethal effects.

The threat actors can exploit vulnerabilities in the hardware, software, or communication channels connecting the IoT devices. Insecure hardware components, outdated firmware, and insecure default device settings can pose a threat. Vulnerabilities in the IoT application software can also be exploited to launch an attack. The attackers can intercept, manipulate, or disrupt communications by taking advantage of vulnerabilities in the communication channels connecting the IoT devices, leading to large-scale disruptions and damage.

The 2010 *Stuxnet* virus attack, which targeted industrial control systems and exploited flaws in Siemens software to cause physical damage and sabotage the Iranian centrifuges, is a good example of an IoT attack. Another example is the Mirai malware, which infects IoT devices and leverages them to initiate DDoS attacks. Multiple security controls can be implemented to protect IoT devices from DDoS and malware attacks. Some of these include strong authentication mechanisms, strong encryption, encrypting the communication channel, regular firmware updates and software patching, and proactively monitoring the IoT networks to detect and mitigate potential threats before they can cause any harm.

Advanced persistent threats

APTs are sophisticated cyberattacks, meticulously planned and executed by highly skilled threat actors. These attacks are not random. APT attacks are well-researched, meticulously planned, and adequate resources are allocated to conduct the attacks clandestinely over a prolonged time. The threat actors exploit multiple attack vectors to infiltrate the targets with stealth and persist in the network for long durations, to exfiltrate data or carry out other malicious activities at a time of their choosing. These threat actors are organized groups, generally state-sponsored. The targets of the APTs are high-value targets, like sensitive government organizations and networks, national critical infrastructures, and large businesses and enterprises. Once inside the target network, the APTs aim to retain long-term control of the target for espionage, i.e., steal national secrets, trade secrets, patents, proprietary information, and carry out large-scale disruptions by sabotaging critical infrastructure to further their geo-political goals.

The APTs differ from traditional attacks in several ways and can be identified by their characteristics. Unlike the opportunistic attacks, the APTs are deliberate, targeted towards specific targets, and tailored for specific organizations with clear objectives. These attacks are resource-intensive, requiring a strong financial backing. They are highly sophisticated and use cutting-edge technologies and zero-day exploits. They follow a targeted approach, and instead of adopting hit-and-run tactics, they carry out multi-stage attacks and persist in the network for long durations to execute their activities with stealth to achieve their objectives. *APT28 (Fancy Bear),* attributed to the Russian military, *APT29 (Cozy Bear),* attributed to Russia/Eastern European nations, *APT14 (Anchor Panda),* attributed to the Chinese Navy, and *APT35 (Phosphorus and Newscaster Team),* believed to be Iran-sponsored, are some of the APTs suspected to be involved in well-known attacks.

Each APT attack follows unique tactics and techniques to progress the attack. Generally, the anatomy of an APT attack can be grouped into three stages as follows:

- **Infiltration**: During this stage, the threat actors carry out reconnaissance to gather information about the target by employing a variety of techniques, like social engineering, **Open-Source Intelligence** (**OSINT**), and network scanning. Thereafter, the target is infiltrated using techniques such as spear phishing or by exploiting the identified vulnerabilities. Once an initial foothold is gained, the attackers deploy malware and backdoors to maintain control.
- **Expansion**: In this stage, they carry out reconnaissance of the internal network to map the network, identify critical resources, and harvest credentials for privilege escalation. Thereafter, they move laterally in the network by exploiting vulnerabilities in the internal systems and databases using the compromised credentials. During the process, they also collect vital data and sensitive information.
- **Exfiltration**: During this stage, the collected data is exfiltrated out of the target network, evading detection throughout. Finally, the cleanup is done, and all the traces are erased to avoid attribution.

Artificial intelligence threats

As the AI technology matures and its usage becomes more prevalent, it presents associated social, ethical, environmental, and information security-related threats and challenges that need to be addressed. Some of the potential AI threats in the context of information security are discussed as follows:

- **Lack of transparency**: AI and deep learning models are difficult to understand. Additionally, the AI companies do not reveal much about their products. It is not known how and why AI concludes, and what algorithms are used. This leads to a lack of transparency.
- **Lack of accountability**: Closely associated with transparency is the lack of accountability, i.e., who is to be held accountable and liable if AI systems go wrong and make a damaging decision. This needs to be incorporated into the AI governance strategy.
- **AI bias**: The AI models are developed by humans, who have their own biases that can creep into the AI systems. Also, if the data used for training the AI systems is biased and unrepresentative, it can lead to unexpected and unwarranted outcomes.
- **Privacy and security issues**: AI systems collect and process a large amount of personal and sensitive data to customize user experience or train the AI models. Such large amounts of data concentrated in the AI tools raise data privacy and security concerns.
- **Misinformation and manipulation**: Malicious actors and vested interest groups can misuse AI-generated content, like fake videos, images, and voices, to spread misinformation and disinformation to manipulate public discourse, influence public opinion, and damage reputations.
- **Increase in cybercrime**: Cybercriminals can misuse the AI technology to carry out more sophisticated and effective cyberattacks. AI tools can be used to analyze large amounts of data to gather precise and actionable intelligence about potential targets, which permits them to customize the attack. Using AI, they can automate complex tasks, allowing them to conduct attacks at scale. It can be used to code and create polymorphic malware to avoid detection and interception. Highly convincing phishing emails can be generated, tailored for specific individuals and targets, giving the right context and mimicking their writing style.

Common vulnerabilities

Information systems comprise multiple hardware and software components. These include servers, end user devices, network components, and security devices. People and the processes managing these components all form part of the information systems. There can be different types of information systems, such as server-based systems, client-based systems, distributed systems, industrial control systems, IoT systems, web-based systems, or mobile systems. Each of these may have weaknesses and vulnerabilities that can be exploited by threat actors. The vulnerabilities discovered in different components can be broadly categorized as outlined in the following list:

- **Hardware vulnerabilities**: These are weaknesses or flaws in the physical components that can be exploited by attackers. The vulnerabilities could emerge due to inadequate security considerations, design flaws, or supply chain poisoning. End-of-life and unsupported devices can introduce additional vulnerabilities, as the vendors do not provide any support or upgrades.
- **Software vulnerabilities**: These are weaknesses in the software, such as the operating systems, web servers, email servers, DNS servers, and custom application software, among others. The vulnerabilities in the software can arise from programming errors, design flaws, unpatched software bugs, or supply chain vulnerabilities. The **Open Web Application Security Project** (**OWASP**) Top 10 and OWASP Mobile Top 10 represent the most critical web and mobile application vulnerabilities. Some of these include SQL injection, XSS, lack of input validation, improper authentication and authorization, and weak or missing encryption.
- **Network vulnerabilities**: These are weaknesses in the network components, like routers, switches, network security devices, etc. These can range from poorly configured or missing **access control lists** (**ACLs**) in the routers, misconfigured firewalls and proxies, unprotected wireless access points, and insecure network management planes. Vulnerabilities in the network segment can provide attackers with an ingress route in the organization's network for further exploitation and lateral movement in the internal network.
- **Configuration vulnerabilities**: System misconfigurations are the most common and easily exploitable vulnerabilities. Attackers regularly scan networks to identify misconfigured systems and applications, and those with default settings. It provides them with easy and quick access to the enterprise network and resources.
- **Process vulnerabilities**: Security governance is an important facet of information security. Even the most effective technical security controls will fail if the procedures for operating and exercising oversight are not adequate or missing altogether.
- **Human vulnerabilities**: This refers to the vulnerabilities arising out of human actions, behaviour, and psychology. Falling prey to social engineering attacks, poor password management, and failing to take timely actions to patch software, or not following the security instructions, all introduce vulnerabilities in information systems, which can be exploited by malicious actors.

Threat modelling

Having discussed various types of threats and vulnerabilities, let us understand what threat modelling is and its importance in securing information systems. We saw that information systems comprise multiple hardware and software components, and over a period of time, several vulnerabilities of varying severity may be discovered in these systems. These need to be fixed promptly to limit the possibility of exploitation by threat actors. However, it is not feasible for organizations to fix all the vulnerabilities due to budgetary and resource constraints. It is also not required to fix them all, as not all threats may be relevant to an organization's information system. They need to prioritize mitigation based on the severity, likelihood of exploitation, and the consequent impact.

Threat modelling is the process of identifying potential threats to an organization's information systems, the vulnerabilities that could be exploited by these threats, and implementing measures that proactively mitigate the associated risks. It is a structured and proactive approach to identify, analyze, prioritize, and mitigate risks in the information systems.

Threat modelling process

The threat modelling process involves several steps, which are as follows:

1. **Scope definition**: This involves defining the scope for threat modelling, i.e., the infrastructure, systems, and applications to be included and the objective of the threat modelling exercise.
2. **Asset identification**: All assets within the scope of the applications, systems, and infrastructure are identified. This helps in identifying the assets that are important for the business and those that are likely to be the target of attackers. It helps in identifying their criticality and the potential impact of threats.
3. **Threat identification**: This step involves identifying all the vulnerabilities in the assets in scope and potential threats that could exploit these vulnerabilities.
4. **Risk analysis and prioritization**: In this step, the potential impact and the likelihood of occurrence of each of the identified threats and vulnerabilities are assessed. The risks are prioritized based on the criticality, potential impact, and the organization's risk tolerance.
5. **Mitigation**: Devise and develop appropriate mitigation strategies for mitigating the identified risks. It would involve implementing technical, operational, and administrative security controls.
6. **Monitoring and review**: The information system, the attack surface, and the threat environment all continue to evolve with time. Threat modelling, therefore, needs to follow an iterative approach to identify and address the emerging threats.

Threat modelling approaches

Depending upon the applicability, suitability, and preference, organizations may use different approaches for threat modelling. These may be categorized as:

- **Asset-centric approach**: This approach focuses on identifying and safeguarding valuable assets of the organization. A catalog of all the assets is created, their interconnections and dependencies are worked out through visual representations, and the potential risks to the assets are identified. This helps in focusing on the risks to valuable assets. For this reason, it is also known as a **risk-based approach**.

- **Attacker-centric approach**: Here, the aim is to identify the attackers and the potential threats based on their assessed goals and objectives. This helps in identifying the assets that need to be protected. A downside of this approach is that new threat actors may emerge with time, representing threats that may not have been considered.
- **Application-centric approach**: This approach focuses on the application. The process egins by gaining a thorough understanding of the application's components, processes, data flows, and users. This helps in comprehending the application's functionality and identifying any possible vulnerabilities. Thereafter, the potential risks to the application are identified and categorized to recognize and classify the prospective threats based on their likelihood and impact. This helps in designing and implementing suitable security controls, leading to a more secure and resilient application.

Threat modelling methodologies

There are several threat modelling methodologies; each has its advantages and limitations. Some could be more suitable for a particular scenario than others. These need to be carefully evaluated to select a model that suits the needs for a specific scenario and environment. Some of the threat modelling methodologies are discussed in the following sections.

STRIDE

The STRIDE threat modelling methodology was initially created by *Microsoft*. It has evolved and is widely used in application-centric threat modelling as well as other scenarios to classify and quantify risks. The acronym STRIDE stands for Spoofing, Tampering, Repudiation, Information Disclosure, DoS, and Elevation of Privilege, representing the type of major threat classes that an information system may face. The different categories of threat classes are as follows:

- **Spoofing**: It is impersonating a legitimate identity to gain unauthorized access. Spoofing typically compromises the authentication process. Attackers can spoof MAC addresses, IP addresses, usernames, process names, system names, email IDs, and many other logical identities.
- **Tampering**: It is the unauthorized modification of data or communication. Tampering compromises both integrity and availability.
- **Repudiation**: Malicious actors can deny performing an activity, and the challenging party is unable to prove it. Attackers resort to repudiation attacks to maintain deniability, so as not to be held accountable.

- **Information Disclosure**: Unauthorized disclosure of confidential and restricted data to individuals who are not authorized to view it. This could be due to design flaws or misconfigurations.
- **DoS**: Rendering a service or system unavailable or degrading it to an extent that normal activity by legitimate users is hampered.
- **Elevation of Privilege**: A subject can acquire privileges higher than what is assigned to them. This can be achieved by exploiting system vulnerabilities or by merely misusing the credentials of a higher privileged account.

PASTA

Process for Attack Simulation and Threat Analysis (**PASTA**) is a risk-based technique that helps in selecting and implementing controls based on the criticality and value of the assets. It provides a thorough understanding of the threat actors' attack methodology, which helps in deciding the points at which the security controls need to be implemented. It is a dynamic methodology that continuously assesses evolving threats to evaluate risks and efficiently develop countermeasures. The PASTA threat modelling process involves seven stages. Each stage has specific objectives and deliverables that are used for the next stage:

1. **Define the objectives**: This is aligned with the business goals and objectives.
2. **Establish technical scope**: This helps in identifying the critical components within the scope.
3. **Application decomposition and analysis**: Detailed data flow diagrams are prepared to decompose the complex application to clearly identify any weaknesses.
4. **Evaluate threats**: The threats are evaluated based on the historical data and current trends.
5. **Weakness and vulnerability assessment**: The vulnerabilities are evaluated to identify and address the most severe ones.
6. **Attack modelling**: It helps in identifying and categorizing attacks associated with various vulnerabilities and those that impact the most valuable assets.
7. **Risk analysis and mitigation**: This is the stage in which risks are evaluated and mitigation measures are implemented to manage the risks.

Trike

Trike is an open-source, risk-based threat modelling methodology. It follows a structured approach for recognizing threats and reducing risks. Trike provides insights into how various security controls are integrated and function together to protect information systems. It provides reliable and repeatable procedures for audits and a consistent framework for communication and collaboration among various stakeholders. The methodology adopted in the Trike threat modelling helps in arriving at an acceptable level of risk for each class of assets and in determining an appropriate response for mitigation actions.

OCTAVE

Operationally Critical Threat, Asset, and Vulnerability Evaluation (OCTAVE) is a structured, risk-focused threat modelling methodology that provides a comprehensive framework for mitigating risks across organizations of all sizes. It is focused on mitigating organizational risks rather than technological risks. This asset-centric and risk-centric approach has three phases: building asset-based threat profiles, identifying infrastructure vulnerabilities, and developing a security strategy by identifying critical assets. This allows for a more comprehensive understanding of organizational risks, facilitating informed decision-making to improve information systems security.

VAST

Visual, Agile, and Simple Threat (VAST) is a threat modelling concept based on agile programming and project management principles. VAST is very well-suited for fast-paced development environments that need rapid adjustments to the security policies. This technique employs two independent threat modelling methodologies—architectural and operational, which provide unique actionable outputs for various stakeholders like architects, developers, and information security personnel. VAST is easily scalable and can be seamlessly adapted to extensive and concurrent development environments to facilitate the administration of intricate development situations.

DREAD

The DREAD threat model was initially introduced by *Microsoft* for ranking or rating threats. Though Microsoft discounted its use due to probable inconsistencies in the ratings, it is still used by many organizations in conjunction with other threat modelling techniques. The model provides flexible ratings based on the responses to five questions for each of the identified threats, as follows:

- **Damage potential**: The extent of damage a threat is likely to cause, if exploited.
- **Reproducibility**: How easy or difficult it is for an attacker to reproduce the attack.
- **Exploitability**: What is the effort required to launch an actual attack?
- **Affected users**: Number of users likely to be impacted if the exploit is widely available.
- **Discoverability**: How hard it is for the attackers to discover the threat.

Conclusion

Information systems face a multitude of cyber threats from different threat actors, including cyber criminals, hacktivists, malicious insiders, and state actors, each of whom presents unique challenges and risks. A comprehensive understanding of the threats and system vulnerabilities is essential for developing a holistic strategy to protect information systems. Threat modelling, a structured and proactive methodology for identifying and mitigating risks, can be employed to identify threats and vulnerabilities and prioritize mitigation of the resulting risks.

Some of the common cyber threats that organizations face are malware infections, bot attacks, DDoS, social engineering attacks, spoofing, password attacks, DNS attacks, and MitM attacks. More sophisticated and complex threats include APTs, IoT threats, supply chain attacks, and AI-based threats. Each of these threats poses different challenges to information systems, depending on the skill and motivation level of the threat actors and the complexity of the attack. However, not all threats apply to all situations and environments. A threat presents a risk only if an information system has weaknesses or vulnerabilities that can be exploited. These could pertain to hardware, software, processes, or people managing the information systems. It is therefore essential to carry out threat modelling to identify and prioritize risks and develop effective mitigation strategies. By adopting suitable threat modelling methodologies, organizations can develop a thorough understanding of the threat landscape and develop security strategies tailored to their specific needs.

In the next chapter, we will discuss information security governance, risk, and compliance. These functions ensure that the information security goals of an organization are aligned with business goals, the information security risks are identified and addressed suitably, and the business remains compliant with the applicable information security regulations.

Exercises

1. Distinguish between threat, vulnerability, and risk in the context of information systems.
2. Discuss different types of malware along with examples.
3. Supply chain attacks can have a devastating effect on information systems. However, such attacks are very complex to execute and require thorough planning and careful execution. Discuss in the context of the Solar Winds supply chain attack.
4. While AI can aid in securing information systems efficiently and effectively, it can also be misused by malicious actors to target individuals and information systems. Discuss some of the emerging AI-based and AI-powered threats.
5. What is the importance of threat modelling? Discuss the methodology employed in your organization and critically examine how it helped in identifying, prioritizing, and mitigating the risks.

References

1. **ILOVEYOU: The virus that loved everyone: https://www.kaspersky.co.in/blog/cybersecurity-history-iloveyou/24432/**
2. **Stuxnet worm attack on Iranian nuclear facilities: http://large.stanford.edu/courses/2015/ph241/holloway1/**
3. **WannaCry: https://www.malwarebytes.com/wannacry**
4. **NotPetya: A Columbia University case study: https://www.sipa.columbia.edu/sites/default/files/2022-11/NotPetya%20Final.pdf**
5. **SolarWinds hack explained: Everything you need to know: https://www.techtarget.com/whatis/feature/SolarWinds-hack-explained-Everything-you-need-to-know**
6. **Safeguarding our future: https://www.dni.gov/files/NCSC/documents/SafeguardingOurFuture/Kaseya%20VSA%20Supply%20Chain%20Ransomware%20Attack.pdf**
7. **Kaseya press release: https://www.kaseya.com/press-release/kaseya-responds-swiftly-to-sophisticated-cyberattack-mitigating-global-disruption-to-customers/**

Join our Discord space

Join our Discord workspace for latest updates, offers, tech happenings around the world, new releases, and sessions with the authors:

https://discord.bpbonline.com

Chapter 3
Security Governance, Risk Management, and Compliance

Introduction

Governance, risk, and compliance (**GRC**) is a structured way to align information security goals and objectives with the business goals while managing information risks and meeting the regulatory compliance requirements. GRC is one of the most important functions of information security management that directly concerns the leadership and the senior management. The three related functions of information security governance, risk management, and compliance ensure that the information security efforts in an enterprise are aligned with the business goals, risks are identified and addressed most appropriately and efficiently, and the business meets all the information security regulatory compliance requirements. It helps organizations know that they are doing their security correctly and doing so on an ongoing basis.

Information security governance is the collection of defining, supporting, and directing the information security efforts of an organization. It integrates the security program into corporate governance to ensure that organizational goals and objectives are supported by the information security program. It entails developing an information security strategy in accordance with a governance framework and establishing and implementing information security policies to communicate management's directives and guide the development of standards, procedures, and guidelines. Information security governance defines the roles and responsibilities of various stakeholders and empowers them to undertake their responsibilities to support the security mission.

Risk management is the process that allows an organization to balance the operational and economic costs of security controls and enhance the mission capability by protecting the information systems and data that support the organization's mission. It includes risk identification, assessment, mitigation, and continuous evaluation of the implemented controls to ascertain their effectiveness.

The compliance function ensures that the controls are effective on an ongoing basis and are effectively reducing the risk to acceptable levels and achieving the objectives intended by the organization. Compliance with the laid down laws, regulations, standards, and frameworks is also a necessary control mandated by governments. The primary aim is to ensure that appropriate processes are in place, people in the enterprise are aware of their responsibilities, and the technical controls are appropriately implemented and managed. Regulatory compliance ensures that organizations exercise due diligence and commit necessary resources to meet the requirements laid down by the laws and government regulations.

Structure

In this chapter, we will discuss the following topics:

- Security governance
- Risk management
- Compliance

Objectives

By the end of this chapter, you will be able to understand the mechanics of developing and governing an information security program to support and achieve business goals and objectives. You will be able to appreciate the importance of information security governance in achieving organizational goals, develop an information security strategy, create effective security policies and guidelines, and understand the structure required for a successful security program. The processes involved in risk management, including risk assessment, risk mitigation, and monitoring and evaluation, will emerge clearly. You will also be able to understand the need for security control frameworks and standards, and how these contribute towards meeting the regulatory compliance requirements.

Security governance

The **National Institute of Standards and Technology** (**NIST**) defines information security governance as:

The process of establishing and maintaining a framework and supporting management structure and processes to provide assurance that information security strategies are aligned with and support business objectives, are consistent with applicable laws and regulations through adherence to policies and internal controls, and provide assignment of responsibility, all in an effort to manage risk.

It emerges that information security is a business-driven activity and security governance is not a technical issue alone, but a business support function, and the senior management and the board of directors are accountable for it. Information security governance is all about aligning the information security program with the business goals and objectives. It is part of enterprise governance and entails developing an information security strategy and a suitable governance structure to support and enhance the business. It involves adopting a security framework tailored and scoped to business needs, depending upon the industry and region in which the enterprise operates, creating and implementing policies and guidelines to enforce information security in the organization, setting appropriate security controls to manage risks appropriately, and establishing necessary measurement metrics and reporting mechanisms. Being a critical aspect for the success and continuity of the business, it is essential that the senior management in the organization lends complete support to the security program and has a clear understanding of the information security activities and how this supports and enhances the business.

Importance of information security governance

Information security governance transcends information systems and acts as a business enabler, and the lack of it can have serious consequences for businesses. The 2017 data breach of Equifax, in which personal data of more than 143 million people was exposed, is an example of how a lack of governance can adversely impact a business. The breach occurred due to the failure to patch a known vulnerability in the company's web application. Investigations pointed towards multiple lapses in the firm's security governance process that led to the incident. Absence of a clear patch management policy, lack of accountability for security controls, and inadequate audit and risk management practices together resulted in the massive data breach. Consequently, Equifax faced class action lawsuits, regulatory fines amounting to about $700M towards settlements, and massive reputational damage. Drawing lessons from historical events and learning from their own experiences, businesses have been adopting better security governance practices over the years. For instance, *Microsoft Corporation* has developed a proactive security governance model to embed security into its software development process. This has helped Microsoft build a strong security culture and enforce accountability across teams, which has resulted in dramatically reducing vulnerabilities in its products.

The benefits that accrue from successful information security governance are as follows:

- **Alignment of information security program with business goals**: Ensures that the information security efforts support and enhance business objectives.
- **Helps manage risks efficiently**: Provides a structured approach and firm foundation for efficient and effective risk management, reducing the potential impact of security incidents.
- **Ensures compliance**: Assures regulatory and policy compliance and helps in meeting legal and regulatory requirements related to security, avoiding penalties.
- **Resource optimization**: Ensures effective management of information security resources by providing a structure and framework for efficient use of limited resources, aligning security investments with the organization's priorities.
- **Enhances brand reputation**: By protecting the brand against any damage to the business reputation due to security incidents.

- **Builds trust:** Improves trust level among partners, customers, and other stakeholders by showcasing management's commitment to information security.
- **Operational predictability**: Reduces uncertainty in business operations by reducing the residual risk to acceptable levels.
- **Improves decision-making**: Facilitates informed decision-making by providing a level of assurance that critical decisions are based on accurate data and information.

Components of information security governance

The information security governance should be integrated with the enterprise governance by ensuring top management commitment and involvement of enterprise-wide leadership and teams. The activities that comprise information security governance and facilitate this integration include:

- Strategic planning
- Organizational design and development
- Establishment of roles and responsibilities
- Integration with enterprise architecture
- Documentation of security objectives in policies and guidance

Developing an information security strategy

The goal of an information security strategy is to protect the business assets and value. Information security strategy is a living document with a long-term proposition of the manner in which the enterprise proposes to secure its business. Like any other strategy, it has a mission, goals, and objectives which follow from the business vision, goals, and objectives. There are factors like the organization's culture, asset value, risk tolerance, legal obligations, and the market conditions that need to be considered while evolving a security strategy.

Factors to be considered:

- **External environment**: Businesses do not operate in isolation; they function in the context of a larger environment and are subject to several external factors. They need to be conversant with the regulatory environment of the industry and the territory they operate in. They should be aware of the emerging threat landscape and the security strategies being adopted by their competitors and the industry. The research work done in the field by independent organizations can also be leveraged to benefit from the emerging trends and strategies for securing information systems.
- **Organizational culture**: The culture of the organization will have an impact on how well the security program is received and implemented. The organizational culture

plays an important role as each business and its management views security differently; some consider it to be an enabler, while others may think it to be a necessary evil that must be taken care of to meet the regulatory requirements. Some may have a larger risk appetite, while others could be averse to taking risky decisions. The size of the organization, speed of adoption of new technologies, the trust level in the stakeholders, and the outsourcing posture will have an impact on the plans and strategy.

- **Audit reports and prior security incidents**: The audit reports, both internal and external, can provide great insight into the security posture of the organization and add value to the information security strategy. Likewise, evaluation of prior security incidents can help focus and orient the security efforts in the right direction.
- **Asset value**: Carefully looking at the assets that need to be protected and their value to the business will help in identifying the associated risks and implementing suitable controls to reduce the risks to an acceptable level.

Development techniques

Every strategy has a desired end state in sight that it proposes to achieve in the long run, say three to five years. The current state of security in the organization is ascertained, and a gap analysis is carried out to identify the gaps and develop a road map to achieve the desired state. The following list outlines some of the techniques that can be employed to develop the information security strategy:

- **SWOT analysis**: This is a proven technique to assess the **strengths, weaknesses, opportunities, and threats** (**SWOT**) of a business and can be used in the development of a security strategy to identify areas where security could make a positive and visible impact. The strengths and weaknesses can be identified by analyzing the past performance of the organization and its systems and processes. Brainstorming and discussions are required to identify the opportunities that can be seized, and threats can be understood as events or actions that adversely impact the existing environment and future plans.
- **Capability Maturity Model Integration (CMMI)**: It is a capability improvement framework that provides guidance for organizations to elevate their performance. It helps organizations benchmark their capabilities against industry best practices and build maturity by identifying the gaps. The CMMI model classifies the maturity states into initial, managed, defined, quantitatively managed, and optimizing.
- **Balanced scorecard (BSC)**: It takes the customer, quality, and learning perspectives into consideration besides the financial profitability measures. The idea is that the financial profitability of the organization can be improved by focusing on other measures. BSC provides metrics to measure the progress made by an organization in achieving its goals. The BSC technique can be used to develop security strategies and build measures to track how the customer, quality, learning, and financial perspectives are being enhanced by the security strategy.

The following table provides a comparison among the three techniques:

Aspect	SWOT analysis	CMMI	BSC
Purpose	Strategic planning involves identifying internal and external factors.	Process improvement and capability maturity of an organization.	Performance measurement and strategic management.
Focus	High-level assessment of SWOT.	Process maturity across people, process, and technology.	Balanced view of financial and non-financial metrics across multiple perspectives.
Advantages	Simple and quick to perform, it encourages strategic thinking and broad applicability.	Provides a detailed process improvement roadmap. Standardized framework. Helps in benchmarking and continuous improvement.	Aligns business activities with strategy. Balanced focus on financial and operational **key performance indicators** (**KPIs**). Clear visualization of strategy execution.
Disadvantages	Lacks quantifiable measures, is subjective, prone to biases, and does not offer specific solutions.	Complex to implement, time-consuming, and resource-intensive, it requires cultural change	Implementation can be complex. May overemphasize measurement over action. Requires consistent data gathering.
When to use	At the early strategic planning stages. For high-level situational analysis, when time or resources are limited.	When process optimization and capability maturity are needed. For software development, manufacturing, and services. To improve process consistency and quality.	To track strategy execution over time. When aligning departmental goals with corporate vision. To measure performance and take corrective actions.
Suitable for	High-level strategy and brainstorming.	Process-heavy industries need structured improvement.	Performance-driven organizations focus on strategy execution.

***Table 3.1**: Comparison of SWOT analysis, CMMI, and BSC techniques*

Strategic planning

Planning ensures that organizations manage security proactively rather than reacting to security incidents. Effective security plans focus on goals and objectives to be achieved and help in decision-making. However, the best of the security plans may turn out to be ineffective in the absence of senior management approval and commitment. Organizations need to develop strategic, tactical, and operational plans to focus and prioritize their efforts and help the enterprise progress towards achieving the desired state.

Based on the time horizon, information security plans can be classified as follows:

- **Strategic plan**: A strategic plan is a long-term plan that defines the security purpose and is aligned with the business goals and objectives. It has a long-term horizon, generally has a three to five years perspective to guide the long-term security activities. It is reviewed and updated annually to ensure that it remains contemporary and relevant. The high-level goals and vision are included in strategic planning to provide direction for security projects to achieve business objectives.
- **Tactical plan**: Tactical plans are medium-term plans that provide the broad initiatives to support and achieve the goals specified in the strategic plan. These plans are more specific and are typically useful for a year. Tactical plans may include multiple projects and lay down the tasks required to be performed to achieve the organizational goals.
- **Operational plan**: These are detailed short-term plans based on the objectives laid down in the strategic and tactical plans. These plans state the detailed methodology for achieving the laid down goals and objectives. Budgeting requirements, resource allocation, detailed scheduling, and implementation procedures are laid down in the operational plans. These need to be updated frequently, quarterly, or maybe even monthly, to ensure that the objectives are met in the given time frame.

Senior management commitment and support

The **chief information security officer** (**CISO**) or similar role in the organization is responsible for the security function. The CISO needs to build a business case for the security program to showcase to the management how information security supports the business goals and objectives, and why it is a critical business issue for regulatory compliance and creating a positive business environment. Putting things across in simple business terms is essential for obtaining the management's approval and backing. The senior management can demonstrate its commitment and support in a variety of ways. They can champion the cause by getting directly involved in the approval and implementation process, which drives home the message that security is taken very seriously at the top. They can also demonstrate their support by prioritizing security in the budget allocation and allocating sufficient resources for the security program.

Governance structure

The board and senior management are accountable for the security of the organization. Clearly defined roles and responsibilities help the board exercise effective governance and oversight. The security strategy that is issued with the approval of the upper management provides directions to all the stakeholders. Based on the directions provided in the strategy document, the middle-level management formulates the policies, procedures, guidelines, and baselines to be implemented by the operational managers and adhered to by the end users. Once the program gets into the implementation stage, continuous monitoring and regular reporting are essential to ascertain the progress of the security program and its effectiveness and to carry out any mid-course correction, if necessary. Organizations need to establish a suitable governance structure and feedback mechanism to exercise proper oversight to ensure the effectiveness of the security program. In larger organizations, the board may assign the role to a subcommittee to exercise closer oversight.

Roles and responsibilities

The information security roles and responsibilities in an organization may be dispersed across different business verticals and teams. As such, information security turns out to be an enterprise-wide responsibility. Shared and overlapping responsibility can, at times, lead to ambiguity and a lack of ownership, leaving a hole in the security structure. Training workshops and awareness campaigns can help employees understand their security roles better and understand their responsibilities in the larger scheme of things. The importance of the security role should be emphasized in the job descriptions, and compliance with the security policies, guidelines, and regulations by the employees should be evaluated regularly and during the appraisal process.

Defining security roles helps in establishing communications and support structure in the organization, which facilitates the implementation and enforcement of the security policies. The typical security roles that are found in an organization are as follows:

- **Senior management**: The senior management is accountable to the board for the security of the business. An **Information Security Steering Committee** (**ISSC**) or **Information Security Council** (**ISC**), which has senior managers as members drawn from various areas of the organization, is responsible for the governance and success of the security program. The ISSC forms the backbone of sustaining the organizational support for the security program. The purpose of the steering committee should be clearly defined, and its vision should be well understood by all the members. The mission and goals of the committee are stated objectively and communicated unambiguously. The ISSC champions the organization's security effort, and its mission, among other things, includes project initiatives, prioritizing the information security effort, reviewing and recommending security policies, and establishing program oversight.

- **CISO**: The CISO is responsible for driving the security program. He is responsible for the planning, budgeting, and performance of the information security component. He prepares a business case for the program and seeks approval and commitment for the security program from the senior management. The CISO needs to have leadership as well as technical competencies to successfully build and drive the security program. He needs to understand the organizational culture, communicate the risks objectively and clearly, set realistic goals, engage with the business owners and other internal stakeholders, and collaborate and network with stakeholders outside the organization.
- **Business owners**: The business owners are responsible for the information and data pertaining to their business. They are the decision makers who decide who has access to the applications, systems, and data, and what level of access is assigned to them. They are responsible for classifying and authorizing access to the information, as it is ultimately their responsibility to protect it. The CISO needs to network and engage with the business owners for the effective implementation of security solutions to secure the IT systems and processes supporting critical business processes.
- **System administrators**: The device and system administrators are responsible for implementing the prescribed protection measures laid down in the security policies and processes. They are the custodians of the information processed and stored on their systems and are responsible for implementing the security controls. The activities performed by them may include deploying security solutions, managing data storage as per the classification, checking data integrity, and taking backups.
- **Users**: Any individual who has access to a system or application is a user. Access to secured systems must be authenticated, and the level of access provided to the users should be commensurate with their role and the tasks they need to perform. The principle of least privilege needs to be applied to ensure only necessary permissions are assigned. The users are also responsible for ensuring that they are aware of the information security policies and fully understand and follow the prescribed procedures correctly. This is essential so that security is not compromised intentionally or unintentionally.
- **Auditors**: They are responsible for reviewing and verifying that the security policies are properly implemented, and the security controls deployed are adequate and effective, i.e. they are reducing the identified risks to acceptable levels. The audits are conducted internally and by external auditors, and the audit reports are reviewed by the senior management. The deficiencies identified are addressed by issuing new directives to be acted upon by the stakeholders concerned.

Creating effective security policies

Policies, standards, procedures, and guidelines formalize the process of implementing security in an organization and form the basis for ensuring compliance with the security program.

This somewhat hierarchical documentation helps produce a robust and reliable security infrastructure. These documents form the cornerstone of a security program and represent the organization's intention to secure the business and the actions and behaviour expected from the users and employees. While those in charge of security in an organization are responsible for developing the policies, procedures, and guidelines, it is a collaborative effort to ensure that the business aspects are addressed. The directives endorsed and approved by the business leaders are accepted and received well, as against those issued by the information security function.

Information security policy

NIST defines information security policy as an aggregate of directives, regulations, rules, and practices that prescribe how an organization manages, protects, and distributes information. It is a high-level document that provides the foundation for an effective security program. It defines the scope and main security objectives and outlines the security framework of the organization. It identifies the major functional areas of data processing and brings out the criticality of assets and the importance of securing them. It defines roles, assigns responsibilities, specifies compliance requirements, and defines the acceptable risk levels. It is used to demonstrate that the senior leadership has exercised due care to protect the business and information. Best practices followed for creating an information security policy are as follows:

- It should clearly define the process followed for creating the policy. The process followed for initiating, creating, reviewing, and approving the policy is well defined and communicated so that all are aware of their responsibilities.
- It should be a broad-level document that is relevant for at least two to three years. However, an annual review must be carried out for any updates.
- The length of the document should be kept to a minimum, technical implementation details should be avoided, and the tone should be directive.
- The policy should be reviewed by the management and given a sign-off before publishing.
- Periodic review of the policy should be carried out, at least annually.
- Consequences for non-adherence and non-compliance should be included for effective implementation.

Organizations may have several security policies to cover the overall security strategy. These include organizational or program policy, issue-specific policies, and system-specific policies. The program policy addresses the overall issues relevant to the organization, and, as the names suggest, the other two types of policies focus on specific issues and systems or applications.

Standards, baselines, guidelines, and procedures

An information security policy is a broad-level document that defines what needs to be done to secure the organization. It forms the basis for crafting standards, guidelines, and procedures that provide the managers, admins, and end users with a specific approach and directions for implementing the policy to meet the organizational objectives. The details included in each of these documents and their intended purpose are as follows:

- **Standards**: The mandatory requirements for homogeneous use of technology, controls, hardware, and software are defined in the standards. They provide the methodology by which technology and procedures are uniformly implemented in the organization. Standards facilitate integration, improve efficiency, and simplify the operation of security controls.

- **Baselines**: The baselines establish the minimum level of security that the systems in the organization must adhere to. This is the common basic secure state for systems and devices upon which further stringent controls can be built, depending upon the environment and the envisaged risk. Baselines are system, platform, or application-specific and provide the description of settings and configurations to be implemented for secure deployment.

- **Guidelines**: Imposition of standards may not always be feasible, appropriate, or cost-effective. Guidelines recognize that systems and environments may vary considerably and offer recommendations on how the standards and baselines are to be implemented. These are discretionary controls that can be customized for unique systems and environments based on the user's judgment and prevalent conditions. They describe the methodologies to be adopted and are descriptive rather than prescriptive.

- **Procedures**: The procedures are the final document in the hierarchy of structured policy formulation. These are detailed documents with a technical orientation that provide a step-by-step description of the actions to be taken to implement specific security solutions and controls. A procedure can cover an entire system deployment, or it can be product, system, or software specific, like deployment of firewalls, proxies, WAF, antivirus solution, etc. Procedures are also created for accomplishing specific tasks like creating user accounts and assigning the required level of privileges. Procedures ensure the integrity of business processes and help ensure the standardization of security across all systems.

Monitoring and reporting

Effective security governance requires continuous monitoring, regular feedback, and reporting. This is required to evaluate the implementation and maintenance of the security program and to ascertain that the security controls are effective and meet the desired objective. It also helps in ensuring that the policies and procedures are current and align with the evolving technologies and emerging threat scenarios. If not monitored properly and updated regularly, the program may become deficient and ineffective due to a variety of reasons, like changes in the operational requirements, threat environment, compliance requirements, and the organization's goals and business processes. Periodic review and reporting demonstrate management's commitment to the security program and help in meeting regulatory compliance requirements. Regular assessments and reports also provide valuable feedback to the management, administrators, and users for evaluating systems and operational performance and initiating course correction measures, where required. The performance of the security program is assessed in terms of metrics that provide realistic feedback to the management. Not all stakeholders need similar metrics; different levels in the organizational hierarchy require different types of metrics. Whatever the metrics are, they should be accurate, cost-effective, repeatable, predictive, and actionable.

Security metrics

A good security metric should be **specific, measurable, attainable, relevant, and timely** (**SMART**). *NIST SP 800-55 Rev1: Performance Measurement Guide for Information Security* and *ISO 27004:2009* on *Information Security Measurement Techniques* are useful references for developing security metrics. Security metrics that can be used for the measurement and improvement of a security program are as follows:

- **Strategic alignment metrics**: Information security needs to be aligned with the business objectives. Some indicators of strategic alignment would be the extent to which the security program enables specific business activities, the business activities impacted due to inadequate management of risks, the percentage of security activities mapped to organizational objectives, and the security objectives that are understood by the stakeholders, measured by awareness testing.
- **Value delivery metrics**: The value delivery KPIs include the measure of security activities designed to achieve objectives in a cost-effective manner, i.e., the cost of security is proportional to the asset value, effectiveness, and utilization level of the security controls deployed to achieve the desired objectives, and the adequacy and appropriateness of the controls in reducing the risks to acceptable levels.
- **Resource management metrics**: Indicators of effective resource management would include effective knowledge dissemination, extent of standardization of security-related processes, clarity in definition of roles and responsibilities, incorporation of information security in business plans, the percentage of information assets and related threats adequately addressed, resource utilization levels, staff productivity, and establishment of organizational structure of the information security function.
- **Performance management metrics**: Measuring and reporting on information security processes is necessary to ensure that the program remains on track and the organizational goals are effectively met. Some indicators of effective performance management include **mean time to detect** (**MTTD**) and **mean time to remediate** (**MTTR**) security incidents, number of frequently occurring and unreported incidents, cost-effectiveness, ability to determine effectiveness of security controls, effective

means of detecting vulnerabilities, knowledge of emerging threats, tracking of evolving risks, extent of monitoring of critical controls and results of business continuity and disaster recovery tests and exercises.

Risk management

Risk management is the process of identifying the risks to the business and taking such measures as to reduce the risks to acceptable levels. It encompasses risk assessment, risk mitigation, and continuous monitoring and evaluation to minimize risks to organizational assets, operations, and individuals. It is a business process that supports the management in decision-making. The CISO acts as the facilitator for the risk decisions by objectively bringing out the risk involved and the likely impact if not mitigated appropriately. The decision on addressing the risk is to be taken by the management since they own the risk. To be effective, risk management should be done in a timely and efficient manner.

The typical steps involved in the risk management process are depicted in the following figure:

***Figure 3.1**: Risk management process*

The success of the risk management program would depend upon:

- Senior management's commitment and backing.
- Complete support and participation of the technical operations teams.
- Expertise and competence of the risk assessment team and their ability to apply the methodology and provide cost-effective safeguards.
- Awareness and cooperation of the end users who must follow the laid down procedures to comply with the controls.
- Continuous assessment and evaluation of the risks and effectiveness of the controls.

Risk assessment

Risk is a function of the likelihood of threats exploiting potential vulnerabilities in systems and processes and the resulting adverse impact on the business. Risk assessment is carried out to determine the potential threats and associated risks to the IT processes supporting the business processes. It is an important process to understand the state of security in the organization, and it helps uncover the effectiveness of existing controls in protecting the organization's information assets. It provides visibility into the risks that an organization is exposed to and helps to prioritize the information security expenditure and allocate funds for appropriate security controls. The likelihood of future adverse events is determined by analyzing the threats, potential vulnerabilities, and the controls in place. Impact is the harm that is caused to the business in the event of the vulnerability being exploited by the threat actor. The level of envisaged impact helps determine the value of the asset and the associated resources. The risk assessment can be carried out in a step-by-step manner by following the methodology developed by NIST.

Step 1: System categorization

The first step of risk assessment is to define the scope, establish the boundaries of the information system, and identify the resources and the information that are within the system. The business specifics of the system should be described first. This helps establish the scope and boundaries of the exercise. Once the business processes have been identified, the technical infrastructure is identified, and the technical components and processes supporting the business processes are reviewed. The controls to be implemented will depend upon the criticality and sensitivity of the system, categorized based on the impact on confidentiality, integrity, and availability of the system and the information. The system categorization is an important first step, as all other steps and controls flow from the categorization.

Step 2: Threat identification

Threat is an adverse event or the potential for a threat actor to exploit a vulnerability in the information system, i.e., those dangers that have the potential to cause harm to the business and the supporting systems. A threat source presents a risk only if a vulnerability exists in a system or process. The goal of threat identification is to identify the threats that apply to the systems and processes in scope. While identifying the threats, it is important to consider all types of threats, which may include human, environmental, and technical threats. Specific threats pertaining to the business, i.e., the industry and the regions in which it operates, should be considered. The motivation and expertise of the threat sources should also be considered when identifying the threats.

The threats to an organization or information system can be broadly classified as follows:

- **Human threats**: While human resources in an organization are the most valuable asset, they can also be the weakest link in organizational security. Adverse events caused by malicious intent or unintentional acts are considered to be the biggest threats. Human errors and omissions are reported to have caused maximum loss to businesses.

- **Environmental threats**: These include natural threats like floods, earthquakes, tornadoes, etc., and threats focused on environmental systems protecting the computing environment in data centers and server rooms.
- **Technical threats**: Misconfigured systems, unauthorized access, and successful exploitation of application and system vulnerabilities can lead to compromise and unauthorized access to information.

Step 3: Vulnerability identification

After the threat identification step is complete, the next step is to identify the vulnerabilities that could be exploited. Vulnerabilities may exist in information systems if a consistent baseline has not been applied or the software and firmware patches are not current. Even if the systems are fully patched, previously unknown zero-day vulnerabilities may emerge. The goal of vulnerability identification is to generate a list of system and application vulnerabilities that could be exploited by potential threat actors. This can be achieved using vulnerability resources, vulnerability assessment, penetration testing, and developing a security requirements checklist. Previous risk assessments, audit reports, security advisories, vendor advisories, and vulnerability databases are some of the vulnerability sources that can be used to identify vulnerabilities. Proactive vulnerability scanning and penetration testing can be used to complement the process. When developing a security requirements checklist, it is ascertained whether existing and planned controls meet the desired objectives or not. This process is used to identify asset vulnerabilities in all the security areas, including management, operational, and technical areas.

Step 4: Control analysis

Unless the business is starting afresh, certain security controls would already be in place. During this step, the existing and planned controls are analyzed. Both technical and non-technical controls should be considered. The technical controls are the safeguards incorporated in the systems and software, and the non-technical controls are the managerial and operational controls. These control types are further categorized into preventive and detective controls based on the actions they perform. The controls can be analyzed in a systematic manner by developing a security requirements checklist or using an existing one.

Step 5: Likelihood determination

In this step, the likelihood of a vulnerability being exploited, given the existing security controls, is determined. Motivation and expertise of the threat source, nature of vulnerability, and the effectiveness of existing controls are all considered to determine the likelihood of exploitation of a potential vulnerability. A qualitative description of low, medium, and high is generally assigned. This assessment is done by the business owners, facilitated by the information security professionals.

Step 6: Impact analysis

During the impact analysis, the severity of the impact resulting from the successful exploitation of the vulnerability is determined. Mission criticality and sensitivity of the system and data are considered to arrive at the impact. This is available from the **business impact analysis** (**BIA**) report, which prioritizes the impact levels due to the compromise of assets based on qualitative and quantitative assessments of the criticality and sensitivity of assets involved. The adverse impact can be described in terms of loss or degradation of confidentiality, integrity, and availability. Some tangible impacts may be measured in terms of loss of revenue, while the intangible impacts, like damage to the company's reputation and loss of public trust, can be classified qualitatively. The benefits and downsides of quantitative and qualitative assessment are as follows:

- **Quantitative assessment**: It assigns a dollar value to the impact, which can be utilized in the cost-benefit analysis for recommending controls. The disadvantage is that it is time-consuming and requires expertise to carry out a quantitative assessment.
- **Qualitative assessment**: Instead of calculating and expressing in terms of cost, the impact is classified qualitatively, such as high, medium, or low. The advantage is that it prioritizes the risks and identifies the areas for immediate improvement.

Step 7: Risk determination

Until now, the discussion has centered around the likelihood of the threat and its impact. This is the step in which the risk level is determined, which is a function of the likelihood of a given threat source attempting to exploit a vulnerability, the magnitude of impact should the vulnerability be successfully exploited, and the adequacy of the existing or planned controls in reducing the risk to an acceptable level. The risk level can be determined by creating a risk level matrix with inputs from threat likelihood and impact. A sample matrix in *Table 3.2* shows a 3x3 matrix for risk level determination. A more granular matrix may be used depending upon the granularity desired and the organization's requirements:

Threat likelihood	Impact		
	Low	Medium	High
Low	Low	Low	Low
Medium	Low	Medium	Medium
High	Low	Medium	High

Table 3.2: Risk level matrix

Step 8: Control recommendations

Once the risk level is determined, necessary control measures need to be identified to mitigate the risk and reduce the residual risk below the acceptable levels. Typically, the focus is on prioritizing the mitigation of high-level risks. For a high-risk level, there would be a strong need for immediate corrective measures; for medium risk, the plan should be developed to address the risk in a reasonable timeframe. In case of low risks, the decision-making authorities may choose to mitigate or accept the risk. Effectiveness of the controls, organizational policy, legislation and regulations, operational impact, and safety and reliability are some of the factors that are considered while recommending the controls and alternative solutions.

The control recommendations are the final output of the risk assessment process and form an input for the risk mitigation process. Depending upon the risks identified, multiple security controls such as network security solutions, **data leak prevention** (**DLP**), email filtering, endpoint protection, data encryption, **multi-factor authentication** (**MFA**), and strong password policies may have to be implemented. When recommending the security controls, a cost-benefit analysis should be carried out to demonstrate that the control is efficiently reducing or alleviating the risk, i.e., the cost of the control can be justified by the reduction in risk level. The operational impact of introducing the control should also be carefully evaluated during the risk mitigation process.

Step 9: Results documentation

The recording of the results of the risk assessment is done by creating a risk assessment report. This report helps the senior management and the business owners in making policy and procedural decisions, budget allocation, and any operational and management changes. The risk assessment report describes the threats and vulnerabilities, the resultant risk levels, and provides recommendations for the implementation of controls. The report should follow a systematic and analytical approach to facilitate the senior management to understand the risk and take necessary measures to address it.

Risk mitigation

The next process after risk assessment is risk mitigation. It entails evaluating, prioritizing, and implementing appropriate security measures to reduce or eliminate the risks. The goal is to reduce the risks effectively in the most efficient manner. The senior management and business managers would select the most cost-effective and appropriate controls to reduce the risk to acceptable levels to safeguard the organization's mission.

Mitigation options

The risks can be mitigated by employing a variety of controls. The appropriate option would depend upon the organization's mission, goals, and culture. It may also not be feasible to address all risks simultaneously. The organization needs to prioritize the mitigation depending upon the potential of the risk to cause harm and adversely impact the organization's mission. The risk mitigation options available to organizations include:

- **Risk acceptance**: Based on the risk appetite of the organization, it may choose to accept the risk and continue to operate the information systems without addressing it. The decision to accept the risk is that of the business, and the senior-most manager in the hierarchy should accept the risk. The process of risk acceptance should be formalized and recorded. Even if the business chooses to accept the risk, it may decide to act and mitigate it in the future.
- **Risk avoidance**: Risk can be avoided by eliminating the cause of the risk or its consequence. For instance, if a risk is identified in a system, the business may decide to shut down the system and not use the functionalities provided by it. Similarly, if an application vulnerability is identified that can be exploited over the internet, the business may decide to limit the exposure and not expose the application on the internet.
- **Risk reduction**: This is where the controls are deployed to reduce the risk to an acceptable level or eliminate it altogether. The most cost-effective and appropriate controls are employed. The selected control could be technical, physical, or administrative, or a combination of these. Each of these could be further categorized into preventive, detective, and corrective controls.
- **Risk transference**: The organization decides to transfer the risk to a third-party, like purchasing insurance to compensate for any loss, instead of addressing the risk by deploying security controls.

Control categories

Control types can be categorized as technical, physical, and administrative. Different types of controls are as follows:

- **Technical controls**: These are also known as logical controls and are technical solutions implemented to protect systems and applications. These are hardware and software controls and require system design and security engineering to implement. Access control, encryption, **intrusion detection system** (**IDS**), **intrusion protection system** (**IPS**), firewall, proxy, **web application firewall** (**WAF**), **distributed denial of service** (**DDoS**) protection tools, endpoint protection solutions, **security information and event management** (**SIEM**) system, and honeynet are some examples of technical controls.
- **Physical controls**: These are the controls that are implemented to control access to sensitive areas like data centers and server rooms to prevent unauthorized access to sensitive information, systems, and materials. Fences, **closed-circuit television** (**CCTV**) cameras, security guards, steel doors, biometrics, access control cards, and environmental control systems are some of the examples of physical controls.

- **Administrative controls**: These are the management and operational controls. The management controls include the security policies, procedures, and guidelines issued by the management to control access and usage of information systems. The operational controls are the implementation and execution of procedures and mechanisms by people to ensure security. Incident response, change management, configuration management, business continuity planning, and disaster recovery are some of the operational controls.

The preceding security controls can be broadly categorized as protective, detective, and corrective controls depending upon the purpose they achieve:

- **Protective controls**: These are the controls that prevent exploitation or unauthorized access. IPS, firewall, access control mechanisms, endpoint protection, segregation of duties, awareness training, fences, and security guards are some examples of protective controls.
- **Detective controls**: Even after the security controls are implemented to reduce the risk below an acceptable level, there remains some residual risk. New risks may also emerge due to changes in the operational environment or newly discovered vulnerabilities in systems and software, which may be exploited. Detective controls are put in place to detect such exploitation attempts. Examples include IDS, SIEM, honeynet, CCTV cameras, internal and external audits, etc.
- **Corrective controls**: These are the controls that are implemented to remediate and mitigate the effects of a security incident. They complement the preventive and detective security controls. Patching and software updates, implementation of business continuity and disaster recovery, and incident response are some of the corrective measures that organizations take.

Monitoring and evaluation

Continuous monitoring and regular evaluation are necessary to ensure that the security controls are effective and maintain the risk below an acceptable level. The organization's business environment continues to evolve with time. New systems, applications, and software may be incorporated into the information system, leading to an increase in the attack surface. Additionally, previously unknown vulnerabilities may be discovered, due to which the existing controls may not be fully effective or degrade. Therefore, it is important that the risk management in an organization remains an ongoing and evolving process.

Compliance

Governments and their agencies enact and issue a variety of laws and regulations to ensure that businesses operate securely, and the information entrusted to them by the principals always remains secure. A variety of security control frameworks and standards have evolved with time to help meet the regulatory requirements. While the laws and regulations lay down what needs to be done, the standards and frameworks act as tools to plan, organize, implement, test, and monitor security. The landscape of acts, regulations, frameworks, and standards provides the structure for what must be complied with to protect the organization's information systems and data.

Compliance is ensuring that the controls are being adhered to on an ongoing basis. It ensures that due diligence has been exercised by the organization to meet the regulatory requirements. The primary objective of the regulatory environment is to ensure that the organizations have appropriate processes and technical controls in place and people are aware of their responsibilities for managing security effectively, which requires following the laid down processes and managing systems appropriately. Depending upon the region and the industry, an organization may have to simultaneously comply with multiple laws and regulations. However, it is important to understand that compliance with regulations does not necessarily imply that the risks have been mitigated to acceptable levels. It only provides an assurance that the requirements as laid down by the laws and regulations are being met, and there is no regulatory non-compliance. It is important to carry out proper risk assessment as discussed above to identify the real risks to the organization and take necessary mitigation actions to address the risks.

While compliance with standards alone may not be enough to mitigate the risk to an acceptable level, adopting control frameworks helps in creating a roadmap for a successful security program and provides an opportunity to create a baseline for ongoing security. There are a variety of frameworks that can be adopted. A preferred approach would be to use the NIST Cybersecurity Framework in conjunction with ISO 27001 and 27701 controls, the COBIT controls, and any other security requirements specified by industry. This helps in addressing the security requirements holistically. COBIT can be used for the high-level IT environment and for establishing an audit structure. IS27001 and 27701 can provide the notion of a formalized **information security management system** (**ISMS**) and **Privacy Information Management System** (**PIMS**), and a description of the processes for ISMS and PIMS. Greater granularity can be provided by the NIST controls. The industry-specific controls, such as the **Health Insurance Portability and Accountability Act** (**HIPAA**), Federal security rules, **Payment Card Industry Data Security Standard** (**PCI DSS**), and region-specific controls for the EU's **General Data Protection Regulation** (**GDPR**), can provide the requirements necessary to comply with the applicable acts and regulations. These controls exist at different levels and complement one another. By implementing the common sum of requirements, an organization can implement an effective security program.

Once the control frameworks are selected, scoped, and implemented, it is important to review them regularly. Internal and external audits should be conducted to review and assess the controls and identify any gaps. The identified gaps should be mitigated promptly to ensure the effectiveness of the security program over time.

Conclusion

Information security governance, risk management, and compliance are the basis of information security management. It is the senior management that is accountable for security in the organization, and unstinted support and commitment from the senior management are essential for the security program to succeed, as it prioritizes security and ushers in a security-aware culture in the organization.

Security governance is a business-driven activity and should be closely dovetailed into the overall enterprise governance to ensure that the security effort fully supports the organization's mission. Risk management is carried out to identify risks to the organization and take such actions to reduce them to an acceptable level. The process involves a systematic approach of risk assessment, risk mitigation, and continuous monitoring and evaluation. The risk assessment process helps in identifying and classifying the risk level based on its likelihood and impact. Once the risk levels are identified, risk mitigation actions are taken to bring the residual risk to an acceptable level. Since the security environment continues to evolve, continuous monitoring and evaluation of the controls is necessary to ensure that the residual risk remains below the acceptable level. The compliance function ensures that the information security policies, standards, and guidelines are followed on an ongoing basis and the organization remains compliant with the applicable laws and regulations. The effectiveness of the security controls and compliance with the laid down policies and regulations can be assessed by conducting security audits. In the next chapter, we will discuss information security audit and its significance in maintaining a successful security program.

Exercises

1. Discuss the importance of information security governance in designing, implementing, and maintaining a successful information security program.
2. Information security governance should be dovetailed into the enterprise governance. Discuss.
3. What are the factors to be considered while developing an information security strategy? Discuss the techniques that can be followed for evolving an effective information security strategy.
4. What is an information security policy? Discuss the other documents an organization needs to create for the successful enforcement of the information security policy.
5. Review and critically examine the information security governance structure in your organization.
6. What is risk assessment? Discuss the various steps involved in risk assessment.
7. Discuss the risk mitigation options and types of security controls.

8. Regulatory non-compliance is a huge business risk. Review various information security and privacy-related acts and regulations applicable in your region to understand the compliance requirements.

Chapter 4
Information Systems Audit

Introduction

Information systems audit is an independent evaluation of an organization's information systems. It involves the collection of evidence of the implemented security controls and the examination of the collected evidence to assess the effectiveness of the systems, processes, and controls. On completion of the audit, a report is prepared by the information systems auditor to objectively present the findings on the effectiveness and efficiency of controls and provide recommendations for remediation. Information systems audit can be undertaken for a variety of reasons, such as evaluating existing security controls to ascertain the level of protection of the information assets, identifying potential risks, or demonstrating compliance with regulatory requirements. If any gaps are identified, these can be fixed in a timely manner to ensure continued compliance. Information systems audit also serves as an assurance function and provides confidence to the customers, management, and other stakeholders that the business is well-protected.

Information systems audit is a logical corollary of the security governance function that provides an objective and holistic view of an organization's information system. Its overarching goals are data security, compliance with regulations, and supporting business objectives. Such audits help in ascertaining whether the confidentiality, integrity, and availability of information systems and data are being achieved, whether security controls are effective and functioning efficiently, and whether information systems comply with the applicable regulations, acts, and industry guidelines. An audit is not merely about checking boxes. It plays a proactive role in safeguarding sensitive data and maintaining business trust. The *Equifax* data breach that we discussed in *Chapter 3, Security Governance, Risk Management and Compliance,* could probably have been prevented or timely mitigated if routine information systems audits were performed, ensuring proper vulnerability management and adherence to compliance standards.

Structure

In this chapter, we will discuss the following topics:

- Information systems audit frameworks
- Audit vs. assessments
- Audit project management

- Audit planning
- Developing an audit program
- Information system audit process

Objectives

In this chapter, you will learn how to conduct audits, assessments, and **control self-assessment** (**CSA**). By the end of this chapter, you will become familiar with common audit frameworks used for information systems audits and understand how to conduct information systems audits in accordance with various standards, guidelines, and industry best practices. You will be able to distinguish between various types of audits and assessments and understand the purpose of each. You will also learn about the need and importance of audit project management and get a detailed insight into developing an audit program and the various steps involved in the audit process.

Information systems audit frameworks

Several widely recognized frameworks and standards provide guidance and structure for conducting effective information systems audits. These frameworks are live documents that have evolved over time to help businesses protect their information systems against evolving threats. **Control Objectives for Information and related Technology** (**COBIT**) by the **Information Systems Audit and Control Association** (**ISACA**) is one of the prominent frameworks for governance and management of enterprise information technology systems. The latest version of COBIT was released in 2024. It offers a comprehensive set of best practices and control objectives that auditors utilize to assess and strengthen an organization's technical controls. It provides a flexible and modern approach to **information technology** (**IT**) governance and ensures that the information systems are aligned with business goals and the associated processes achieve their objectives effectively and efficiently.

Information Technology Infrastructure Library (**ITIL**) is another widely recognized framework. The latest version is ITIL4, which was released in 2019. It focuses on IT service management best practices and provides guidance on the delivery and support of IT services. It is particularly relevant to the operational aspects of information systems auditing and can help auditors in assessing the efficiency and effectiveness of IT service management processes in supporting the business needs.

ISO 27001, ISO 27701 and *ISO 42001* by the International Organization for Standardization provide frameworks for establishing, implementing, maintaining, and continually improving an **information security management system** (**ISMS**), **Privacy Information Management System** (**PIMS**) and **Artificial Intelligence Management System** (**AIMS**). Information system audits often assess an organization's security controls against these standards to ensure that sensitive and personal data is adequately protected. Compliance with these standards demonstrates an organization's commitment to information security and ensuring customer data privacy. An updated version of ISO 27001 was released in October 2022. The ISO/IEC 27001:2022 introduced a revised structure and updated controls, emphasizing areas like cloud security and data protection. Likewise, ISO/IEC 27701:2025 expands upon its predecessor and provides more comprehensive privacy information management guidelines.

Besides these key frameworks, other relevant standards and frameworks provide necessary guidance for auditing information systems. The **Information Technology Audit Framework (ITAF)** by ISACA is a comprehensive audit framework that establishes standards that address the roles and responsibilities, ethics, expected professional behaviour, and the required knowledge and skills of auditors of information systems. It defines various terms and concepts specific to information system audits and provides guidance and techniques for planning, performing, and reporting of information system audits and assurance engagements. Depending on the industry and the regulatory requirements, auditors may also refer to other standards like the NIST Cybersecurity Framework, which provides a comprehensive framework for managing cybersecurity risk, or the **Payment Card Industry Data Security Standard** (**PCI DSS**), which is specific to organizations that handle credit card information. SOC 1 and SOC 2 audits are also popular audits related to SOC. The SOC 1 audits focus on a service organization's internal controls over financial reporting, and the SOC 2 audits assess controls related to security, availability, processing integrity, confidentiality, and privacy. While these are some of the most common frameworks, auditors need to refer to and take guidance from regulations relevant to the specific industry and region in which a business operates. The selection of the most appropriate framework or standard would depend upon the specific objectives and scope of the audit and the industry and regulatory environment in which the organization functions. Whichever framework one decides to go by, information systems auditors must take care to adopt and follow the latest version, as the frameworks continue to evolve.

The following table summarizes the major frameworks/standards and their purpose:

Framework/Standard	Purpose
COBIT	Governance and management of enterprise IT, providing best practices and control objectives.
ITIL	IT service management best practices for the delivery and support of IT services.
ISO 27001	International standard for ISMS.
ISO 27701	International standard for PIMS.
ISO 42001	International standard for AIMS.
ITAF	Professional practices framework for IT audit.
SOC 1 and SOC 2	Compliance audits assessing controls at service organizations relevant to financial reporting (SOC 1) and security, availability, integrity, confidentiality, privacy, etc. (SOC 2).

Framework/Standard	Purpose
NIST Cybersecurity Framework	Comprehensive framework for managing cybersecurity risk.
PCI DSS	A data security standard for organizations that handle credit card information.

Table 4.1: *Common frameworks and standards and their purpose*

Types of information system audits

Security requirements of businesses vary depending on their size, mission, goals, and location. Therefore, information systems audits are not monolithic; they encompass different types, each with a specific focus and objectives. Let us discuss some of the scenarios for information systems audits.

Financial audits

In the context of information systems, financial audits are concerned with the reliability and integrity of financial data processed by these systems. These audits ensure that adequate controls are in place to prevent fraud and errors that could materially affect financial reporting. Such information systems are designed to create an audit trail, allowing every financial transaction to be traced back to its origin and through the processing steps. Information systems auditors in this context collaborate with financial auditors and work to ensure that the information system supports business objectives and complies with relevant financial regulations.

Operational audits

Operational audits evaluate the effectiveness, operational efficiency, and economy of an organization's information system. These audits focus on assessing the overall control of the information system's operational environment and examining the policies and procedures for adequacy and compliance with the relevant laws, regulations, and standards. The goal is to identify gaps and inefficiencies and recommend measures for improvement to streamline operations and ensure that the information systems effectively support business goals. This type of audit involves reviewing the implemented policies and procedures to ascertain that necessary resources are available to perform the assigned tasks and that the employees consistently adhere to the laid down policies and procedures.

Compliance audits

Compliance audits specifically examine whether an organization's IT systems and processes comply with the applicable laws, regulations, industry best practices, and internal policies. Compliance audit is particularly critical in industries with strict regulatory requirements, such as the healthcare industry under the **Health Insurance Portability and Accountability Act (HIPAA)**, or the finance sector under the **General Data Protection Regulation** (GDPR). The objective of a compliance audit is to ensure that IT practices and information systems align with these standards, thereby minimizing the risk of non-compliance and consequent legal penalties or reputational damage.

Forensic audits

Forensic audits represent another type of information system audit. These are typically conducted in response to a suspected security incident, data breach, or fraudulent activity. Forensic audits involve a detailed investigation of the information system to uncover evidence, determine the scope and impact of the incident, and identify the perpetrators. Forensic audits would invariably require specialized tools and techniques for data recovery and analysis. The information system auditor should either be conversant with the use of these tools or seek support from forensic experts to complete the engagement.

The following table summarizes the primary focus and objectives of the above audits:

Type of audit	Primary focus	Typical objectives	Example areas covered
Financial audit	Reliability and integrity of financial data processed by information systems.	Ensure adequate controls prevent fraud and errors affecting financial reporting, and verify information systems support financial objectives and regulatory compliance.	Audit trails, transaction processing controls, and segregation of duties within financial systems.
Operational audit	Effectiveness, efficiency, and economy of IT operations.	Identify inefficiencies and recommend improvements, ensure information systems support business goals effectively, and assess compliance with operational policies and procedures.	IT resource utilization, service level agreements, incident management processes, and business continuity planning.
Compliance audit	Adherence to laws, regulations, industry standards, and internal policies.	Verify that information systems and processes meet the requirements of relevant regulations, industry standards, and internal policies, and minimize the risk of non-compliance.	Data privacy controls, security policies and procedures, adherence to regulatory requirements, and record retention policies.
Forensic audit	Investigation of suspected security incidents or fraudulent activities.	Uncover evidence of security breaches or fraud, determine the scope and impact of incidents, identify perpetrators, and recommend measures to prevent recurrence.	Data recovery and analysis, log analysis, digital forensics, and investigation of system vulnerabilities.

***Table 4.2**: Information systems audit focus areas and objectives*

In addition to these primary types of audits, there are several other specialized information systems audits. Development audits, for instance, involve system designers and auditors working together during the development lifecycle to ensure that the application being developed has adequate controls and security built in. An application review is a process where auditors review existing applications to ensure that necessary controls are in place to provide reasonable assurance that transactions are valid, recorded accurately, and completed in a timely manner. A management audit concentrates on the management practices of an information system organization to assess how well the controls are designed, implemented, and monitored. A technology audit is designed to review a specific technology used in processing business data to assess how well information systems controls are implemented for that technology. In addition, audits can focus on specific areas such as systems and applications, network security, data integrity, disaster recovery, and internal controls. The variety of audit types reflects the complexity of modern information systems and the diverse needs of organizations for managing their information systems. The following table highlights the focus and objectives of various specialized audits and the typical areas covered:

Specialized audits	Primary focus	Typical objectives	Example areas covered
Development audit	Security and controls during the system development lifecycle.	Ensure that applications under development have adequate security and controls built in from the design stage itself.	Security requirements definition, secure coding practices, and testing of security controls during development.
Application review	Controls within specific applications.	Ensure that adequate controls exist within applications to provide reasonable assurance that transactions are complete, valid, accurate, and timely.	Input validation, processing controls, output controls, and user access management within applications.
Management audit	Management practices of the information systems organization.	Assess how well controls of the information systems environment are designed, implemented, and monitored by the management team.	IT organizational structure, roles and responsibilities, IT governance frameworks, monitoring, and oversight of IT operations.
Technology audit	Implementation of controls for specific technologies.	Assess how well information systems controls are implemented for specific technologies used in processing business data (e.g., file servers, security tools, network equipment).	Configuration reviews, vulnerability assessments specific to the technology, and adherence to best practices.

Specialized audits	Primary focus	Typical objectives	Example areas covered
Network security audit	Protection of sensitive data from cyber threats.	Evaluate firewalls, intrusion detection systems, and security protocols to ensure the network is robust and secure.	Firewall rule sets, intrusion detection system configurations, network segmentation, and wireless security protocols.
Data integrity audit	Accuracy, consistency, and reliability of business data.	Ensure that systems store and process data without errors, safeguarding decision-making and customer trust.	Data validation processes, data backup and recovery procedures, data access controls, and data reconciliation processes.
Disaster recovery audit	Effectiveness of data backups and disaster recovery plans.	Ensure that data backups and disaster recovery plans are effective and ready to deploy in an emergency in order to minimize downtime in case of a breach or failure.	Testing of backup and recovery procedures, review of disaster recovery plans, assessment of recovery time objectives, and recovery point objectives.
Internal control audit	Procedures to protect against fraud, errors, and unauthorized access.	Review an organization's procedures to protect against fraud, errors, and unauthorized access, strengthening the foundation of information systems audit and control.	Segregation of duties, authorization processes, physical security controls, and change management procedures.

***Table 4.3**: Specialized audits*

Audits vs. assessments

It is important for information systems auditors to understand the difference between audits, assessments, and CSA, and the associated procedures. In general, the auditees can leverage assessments and self-assessments to improve the effectiveness and efficiency of information systems and the audit score between audits.

Information systems audits involve a formal examination and verification of the controls to verify whether the applicable standards and guidelines are being followed, the controls are effectively and efficiently mitigating the risks to an acceptable level, and accurate records and audit trails are being maintained. Formal audits provide higher levels of assurance than assessments, and the audit results can be used for external reporting and demonstrating regulatory compliance.

Assessments, on the other hand, are less formal, where the goal is to determine the value of the existing controls. These may be conducted by internal teams or by professional auditors and are perceived to be more cooperative activities focused on assessing the efficiency and effectiveness to reduce costs and improve efficiency. These can also be used for training and awareness, creating a sense of ownership, and working towards improving the audit score. The results of assessments are internal to an organization and do not qualify for external reporting or regulatory licensing.

CSA is an assessment carried out by the auditee. The auditors in this case act as facilitators and help guide the auditee towards improvement. CSA assures the management and other stakeholders that the internal controls of the organization are reliable and effectively protect the business. It can help uncover high-risk or previously unknown risks, which can then be investigated in detail. CSA also helps in developing a sense of ownership among the process and asset owners and helps in reducing resistance to changes for control improvement. Like any other assessment, CSA is also an internal activity of the organization and cannot be used for regulatory compliance reporting. The following table provides a comparison between audit, assessment, and CSA:

	Audit	Assessment	CSA
Purpose	Independent verification of compliance and controls.	Evaluate the effectiveness of controls, processes, and risks.	Self-evaluation of controls by the process owners.
Conducted by	External or internal auditors	Internal teams or consultants.	Process owners and the management team.
Formality	Structured, follows audit standards.	Flexible approach	Participative approach
Focus area	Compliance with laws, regulations, and frameworks.	Control effectiveness, risk identification.	Ownership and accountability of controls by staff.
Output	Audit report with findings, non-conformities, and recommendations.	Assessment report with gaps and improvement suggestions.	CSA report identifying control gaps and action plans.
Frequency	Periodic	Periodic or as-needed	Continuous or periodic
Key benefit	Independent assurance to stakeholders.	Identifies improvement areas.	Increases process owner accountability and awareness.

Table 4.4: *Audit vs. assessment vs. CSA*

Aims of information systems audit

The information systems audits serve a multitude of purposes and can be undertaken for a variety of reasons in different settings and situations. The objective of information systems audit is to enhance the organization's security posture, ensure regulatory compliance, and improve operational efficiency.

Enhancing security posture

One of the primary objectives of information systems audits is to enhance the security posture of the organization. It involves a thorough assessment of information security risks and the implemented controls to assess their effectiveness in protecting the confidentiality, integrity, and availability of information assets. Auditors evaluate existing systems and processes designed to secure data, identify potential risks to information assets, and recommend ways to minimize those risks. This would include reviewing policies, procedures, and processes, technical, administrative, and operational controls, access, incident detection and response procedures, and preparedness for security incidents and data recovery. The goal is to identify vulnerabilities and weaknesses that could be exploited by attackers, thereby helping to strengthen the organization's defences against external and internal threats.

Regulatory compliance

Another key objective of information systems audit is to ensure regulatory compliance. These audits are conducted to verify whether the information systems comply with applicable laws, regulations, and contractual agreements to ensure protection against legal penalties and reputational damage. This includes adherence to industry and region-specific regulations like HIPAA for healthcare information security or GDPR for data protection. The auditors review the IT practices to ensure alignment with relevant standards, minimizing non-compliance risk and potential legal issues. With governments worldwide shifting focus to data privacy and confidentiality, this is a crucial objective for regulatory compliance as it demonstrates due diligence and a commitment to best practices.

Improving efficiency

Improving operational efficiency and effectiveness of the information systems is also one of the main objectives of the information systems audit. The auditors examine whether information systems are being used effectively and efficiently to support business processes and help identify ways to improve operations, reduce costs, and enhance productivity. This involves evaluating the existence and effectiveness of the laid down policies and procedures and ensuring their alignment with business objectives and strategies. By identifying the gaps and inefficiencies in the information systems and associated processes, audits help streamline operations and optimize resource allocation, resulting in overall improvement in business performance. Furthermore, auditors assess whether IT investments yield the expected returns and contribute to the organization's overall success.

The objectives of information systems audit can be summarized as follows:

- Ascertain that the existing controls are adequate and are effectively and efficiently mitigating the intended risk.

- Ascertain that the resource allocation within the information system is done efficiently.
- Provide assurance that risks are properly mitigated and the assets are safeguarded.
- Ensure that the accuracy, availability, and reliability of information are maintained.
- Provide assurance that necessary controls and processes are in place to prevent, detect, correct, and report any omissions and irregularities.
- Review of information systems to ascertain compliance with policies, standards, procedures, and regulatory requirements.
- Review of applications and systems to verify application functionalities, documentation, and audit trails to ensure that compliance is achieved and data integrity, security, and privacy are maintained.
- Identify and uncover any potential vulnerabilities and threats that can impact the confidentiality, integrity, and availability of information assets.
- Ensure that management adequately prioritizes security and takes appropriate measures to align the information security objectives with the business goals, and ensures reasonable preventive, detective, and corrective actions for the effectiveness of the information security program.

Audit project management

When an audit is planned, there are several steps that must be performed to conduct an audit. Thorough planning is an essential first step for the successful conduct of an audit engagement. There is also a need to carry out an overall risk assessment to ensure efficient utilization of audit resources. The next step would be to develop an audit program that consists of the objectives, scope, and audit procedures to be followed to achieve the audit objectives. The actual engagement involves an audit process where the auditors gather evidence, evaluate the security controls, and prepare an audit report to present the findings and observations to the management in an objective manner.

Project management techniques with which information security auditors need to be familiar with include:

- **Planning the audit engagement**: This entails planning the audit, considering the project-specific risks.
- **Creating the audit plan**: Developing an audit plan requires charting the necessary audit tasks, optimizing resource allocation, and making realistic time estimates.
- **Executing the plan**: Once the audit plan has been made, it needs to be put into action. This requires pre-audit planning, developing an audit program, and conducting the audit.

- **Monitoring**: This is necessary to ensure that the audit activities are on track and any challenges are managed proactively to ensure the audit is completed within budget in a timely manner.

Auditing modern information systems is a complex activity, and organizations are increasingly adopting integrated audit tools to plan, execute, and monitor audits to ensure compliance, improve efficiency, and increase transparency. A variety of audit-specific platforms are available that can be utilized by auditors to automate audit workflows, evidence collection, and reporting. Information systems auditors can also leverage project management and planning tools like *Gantt charts* and *Scrum boards* to structure audit activities, assign tasks, and monitor progress.

Audit planning

Effective audit planning is paramount to the success of an information systems audit. This initial phase involves several crucial steps that define the scope and direction of the entire audit process. A fundamental aspect of audit planning is defining the scope and objectives. This involves clearly identifying what aspects of the information systems will be audited and what the audit aims to achieve. Audit planning considers the six W's for an engagement. It considers data and assets involved (*What?*), the rationale for the audit (*Why?*), the processes to be examined (*How?*), the individuals or organizations involved (*Who?*), the network infrastructure (*Where?*), and the relevant timelines (*When?*). Understanding the organization's current technological maturity level is essential to determine the appropriate time, cost, and overall scope of the audit. Establishing clear objectives and a well-defined scope ensures that the audit remains focused and addresses the organization's specific needs, regulatory requirements, and the prevailing risk landscape.

Another vital component of audit planning is risk assessment. As we discussed in *Chapter 3, Security Governance, Risk Management, and Compliance,* risk assessment involves a comprehensive evaluation of potential vulnerabilities and threats to the organization's information assets. By identifying and evaluating the levels of vulnerability and threat associated with different information assets, auditors can determine the impact of the potential risk. Taking a risk-based approach allows for the prioritization of audit efforts and the allocation of resources to the areas where the potential impact of a failure is the greatest. This includes identifying security vulnerabilities, assigning risk rankings (e.g., high, medium, low), and evaluating methods for assigning risk ratings to systems.

Resource allocation is also a key consideration during audit planning. This involves determining the necessary resources, including the audit team's manpower and their skillset, the allocated budget, and the tools and technologies required to conduct the audit effectively within the defined timeline. Proper allocation of resources ensures that the audit can be conducted thoroughly and efficiently.

Another crucial element that is often overlooked is the need for the auditor to gain a thorough understanding of the business and IT environment of the organization being audited. This includes understanding the company's critical business activities and the role that information systems play in supporting these activities. This contextual understanding is essential for identifying relevant risks and controls and ensuring that the audit is aligned with the organization's overall business objectives.

Finally, effective audit planning also involves establishing clear communication and expectations with the auditee. This includes communicating the audit's scope, objectives, timeline, and the resources that will be required from the auditee. Careful planning and agreeing on the audit requirements and activities help in minimizing disruptions to normal business operations and avoiding subsequent misunderstandings.

Common pitfalls in audit planning are as follows:

- **Ambiguous objectives**: Audit scope and goals are not defined precisely.
- **Ambitious timelines**: Unrealistic schedules that ignore resource constraints.
- **Ignoring risk prioritization**: Not focusing on high-risk processes.
- **Poor stakeholder engagement**: Limited communication with auditees or management.
- **Inadequate resource allocation**: Lack of skilled staff, tools, or budget.
- **Failure to integrate past lessons**: Not considering findings from previous audits.
- **Weak documentation**: Incomplete planning records that reduce transparency.

Developing an audit program

The audit program serves as a detailed roadmap for conducting the information systems audit. It outlines the specific procedures, timelines, and resources necessary to achieve the audit objectives. At the core of an audit program are the audit procedures, which are the step-by-step instructions that auditors follow to gather evidence and assess the effectiveness of controls. These procedures can include a variety of techniques such as interviews with personnel, observation of processes, review of documentation (e.g., policies, procedures, system configurations), and testing of systems and data. The audit program may also specify the use of **Computer Assisted Audit Techniques** (**CAATs**) to analyze large volumes of data or automate certain audit tasks. Depending upon the audit requirement, it can also include evaluation and recommendation of automated assessment tools, administrative safeguards, and penetration testing to identify system vulnerabilities.

Aims of the audit program

The audit program is a critical product of the audit process. It serves as a guide for performing and documenting the audit and ensures that the audit goals are met. The main objectives of developing an audit program are:

- Formally document the audit objectives and scope, audit methodology, and the sequential steps to be followed during the audit.
- Develop standard procedures that are repeatable and easy to use by the auditors who need to perform similar audits. This calibrates the audit and alleviates personal biases.
- Document the type of testing to be carried out, i.e., compliance testing or substantive testing for various systems and sub-systems to achieve the audit objectives.
- Meet the generally accepted audit standards that pertain to the planning phase of the audit process.

Structure of an effective audit program

The audit program should clearly reiterate the audit objectives and scope that were defined and agreed to during the planning phase. This ensures that the boundaries of the audit engagement are clearly defined and the audit team remains focused on what needs to be achieved. A detailed timeline and schedule are also critical components of the audit program. It outlines the various phases of the audit, key milestones to be achieved, and the expected duration for each audit activity. A well-defined timeline helps in managing expectations and ensuring that the audit is completed within the planned timeframe and budget.

The audit program also details resource allocation, specifying the roles and responsibilities of each member of the audit team, the required expertise for different audit tasks, and how resources will be assigned to various activities. This ensures that the audit is adequately staffed with resources, having the necessary skills and expertise.

Reporting requirements are another essential element of the audit program. This section outlines the format, content, and frequency of audit reports that will be provided to management and other relevant stakeholders. It may specify the types of findings to be included, the level of detail required, and the process to be followed for communicating the recommendations.

To ensure thoroughness and consistency during the conduct of the audit, the program may include checklists and questionnaires that auditors can use to guide their work and ensure that all relevant areas are covered. These tools provide a structured approach to gathering information and documenting observations.

In cases where it is not feasible to examine all data or transactions, the sampling methodologies that will be used to select the representative subset for testing should be clearly specified. This is essential to ensure that the audit conclusions are based on a statistically valid sample.

Finally, the audit program should define the requirements for working paper documentation. Working papers serve as the record of the audit work performed, the evidence gathered, and the conclusions reached. The program will specify the format, content, and retention requirements for these documents, ensuring that there is a proper audit trail to support the findings and conclusions.

The following table provides a concise and practical sample template for an ISMS audit program aligned with ISO/IEC 27001:2022 requirements:

Control area	Audit step (what to check)	Evidence to collect	Status (Yes/ No/NA)
ISMS scope	*Has the organization clearly defined and documented its ISMS scope?*	Scope statement, approvals	
Management commitment	*Is there a signed and communicated Information Security Policy?*	Policy, communication records	
Risk assessment	*Are risks identified, assessed, and actions planned to treat them?*	Risk register, assessment report	
Statement of Applicability (SoA)	*Does the SoA list the chosen controls and match the risk treatment plan?*	SoA version history	
Policies and procedures	*Are information security policies and processes documented and circulated?*	Policy repository, awareness evidence.	
Training and awareness	*Do employees understand their ISMS responsibilities?*	Training records, survey results.	
Access control	*Are user accounts and access rights properly managed and reviewed?*	Access matrix, logs	
Incident handling	*Are incidents logged, investigated, and resolved systematically?*	Incident log, **root cause analysis** (**RCA**) report.	
Business continuity	*Are backup and recovery plans in place and tested?*	Test reports, recovery results.	
Internal audit	*Is an internal ISMS audit performed regularly?*	Audit reports, findings, corrective and improvement actions.	
Management review	*Does management review ISMS performance and risks periodically?*	Review minutes, action items.	
Improvements	*Are gaps fixed and improvements tracked continuously?*	Record of corrective and improvement actions, improvement register.	

***Table 4.5**: Sample template for ISMS audit*

Information systems audit process

During the information systems audit process, auditors need to gather evidence, evaluate the strengths and weaknesses of the implemented controls based on the evidence gathered through various tests, and prepare a report that objectively presents the weaknesses in the information system and recommendations for remediation. The audit process typically follows a structured approach comprising several key phases. Broadly, it consists of three key phases: planning, field work, and reporting. Depending upon the requirement and extent of the audit, organizations may decide to break down these main phases into several other phases. *Figure 4.1* depicts typical phases of the audit process:

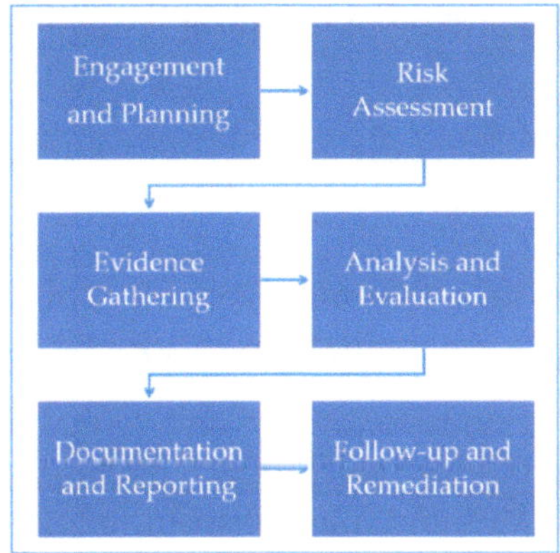

***Figure 4.1**: Typical audit process phases*

The audit process usually begins with the initial engagement and planning phase. This involves formally agreeing to conduct the audit, understanding the auditee's business and IT environment, and clearly defining the scope and objectives of the audit. During this stage, the area to be audited, the purpose of the audit, and the specific systems, functions, and units of the organization to be audited are identified. This is a crucial stage of the audit process as the auditor needs to understand the information system and its components and assess the maturity level of the information system to determine the necessary resources, time, and budget for the audit. During this phase, a preliminary audit plan is developed, outlining the overall approach and timelines.

The next phase is the risk assessment phase, which involves a detailed analysis of potential risks and vulnerabilities within the information system. This may include conducting vulnerability scans and penetration testing to identify weaknesses in the organization's information infrastructure, such as firewalls, proxies, intrusion detection systems, and encryption protocols, etc. Conducting a risk assessment is important for setting the final scope of a risk-based audit. For other types of audits, such as the compliance audit, carrying out risk assessment is a good practice as it helps the auditors to justify the engagement and refine the audit scope. The findings of the risk assessment also aid the auditors in focusing the subsequent audit efforts on the areas presenting the highest risk.

After the risk assessment is complete, the evidence gathering and testing phase starts. During this phase, the auditors employ a variety of techniques to gather evidence about the design and effectiveness of the security controls. This can include conducting interviews with relevant personnel, observing processes, reviewing documentation such as policies and procedures, examining system logs and configurations, and performing tests on transactions and outputs. The use of CAATs may be employed to analyze data and perform automated testing.

The evidence gathering and testing phase is closely intertwined and followed by the analysis and evaluation phase. It is in this phase that auditors analyze and evaluate the collected evidence to identify any findings, assess the severity of identified weaknesses or vulnerabilities, and determine the overall effectiveness of the controls in place. This step requires professional judgment and a thorough understanding of the audit criteria and the organization's business context.

The findings and conclusions of the audit are then documented and communicated in the reporting phase. The audit report typically includes an executive summary, the audit scope and objectives, a description of the audit procedures performed, detailed findings and observations, and recommendations for improvement. The audit report should be clear, concise, and provide actionable recommendations to address the identified weaknesses.

The final phase of the audit process is follow-up and remediation. After the audit report is issued, management is responsible for developing and implementing corrective actions to address the identified findings. Auditors may perform follow-up reviews to assess whether the recommended actions have been implemented effectively and have achieved the desired outcomes. This phase ensures that the audit process leads to tangible improvements in the organization's information systems and controls.

Conclusion

Information systems audits ensure that security controls are aligned with business goals, improve decision-making, and reduce the risk of financial or reputational loss. They help build customer trust by demonstrating data protection, service reliability, and security of personal information. From the shareholders' and investors' perspective, they enhance confidence in the organization’s governance and long-term resilience.

Information systems audits serve as a cornerstone for ensuring the **confidentiality, integrity, and availability** (CIA) of information and information systems. These audits help in improving the efficiency and effectiveness of information systems, as well as in meeting the regulatory compliance requirements. Increased digitalization and an ever-evolving threat landscape make it paramount for organizations to conduct regular and proactive audits of their information systems. The dynamic nature of technology necessitates continuous evaluation of security controls and processes to identify emerging threats and ensure ongoing protection of organizational information assets. The increasing number and complexity of regulatory requirements across various industries also mandate that organizations prioritize compliance.

The information systems audits provide a vital mechanism for verifying adherence to the applicable laws, regulations, and standards.

The value of information systems audits extends beyond mere technical assessments. By aligning information systems with the overall business strategy and risk management efforts, the audits contribute significantly towards achieving organizational goals and building resilience against potential disruptions. The commitment to regular and thorough information systems audits also demonstrates an organization's proactive approach to safeguarding data, maintaining operational integrity, and fostering confidence amongst the stakeholders.

In the next chapter, we will focus on the core principles of cryptography and its practical applications for data security.

Exercises

1. What are the common frameworks for information systems audit? Briefly discuss the general performance and reporting standards of the ITAF by ISACA.
2. Information systems audits can be conducted standalone or as part of an overall audit. Discuss various types of information systems audits and assessments.
3. What are the benefits of CSA?
4. Information systems audits can be conducted to achieve a multitude of objectives. Discuss the objectives of an information systems audit.
5. What are the ingredients of an audit program?
6. Discuss various steps involved in the audit process.
7. You are part of your organization's internal audit team reviewing a procurement tracking system that is integrated with payment and financial reporting systems. During the audit, you notice that access logs are not regularly reviewed, the same individual can both approve procurement and process payments, and the backup procedures have not been tested in the last 12 months. As an information systems auditor, identify the two key risks and recommend suitable controls to address them.
8. A cloud-based **software as a service (SaaS)** provider recently experienced a service outage due to a malware infection. The incident revealed gaps in their information systems governance wherein regular vulnerability assessments were not performed, incident response procedures were not formalized, and previous audit findings were not acted upon. While conducting a follow-up information systems audit, what areas would you prioritize, and how would you link the findings to management accountability and regulatory compliance?

Join our Discord space

Join our Discord workspace for latest updates, offers, tech happenings around the world, new releases, and sessions with the authors:

https://discord.bpbonline.com

CHAPTER 5
Cryptography and Data Security

Introduction

Data is the most valuable asset of an organization. It drives performance, innovation, customer service, and business growth. The primary goal of threat actors targeting businesses or organizations is to seek sensitive data for financial gain or cyber espionage. The other objectives are service disruption and denial of service attacks. It is, therefore, essential for organizations to protect sensitive data under their control and ensure its confidentiality and integrity at all times. While organizations implement a range of security controls for comprehensive data protection and defense-in-depth, encryption remains a critical control for securing data throughout its lifecycle.

Although cryptography is a vast field, this chapter focuses on the basic concepts of cryptography as relevant to data security in the digital world. Broadly speaking, cryptography is the practice of securing communications and information through the use of codes. The concept dates back centuries, evolving from simple ciphers used in ancient times to the sophisticated computer-based encryption methods employed today. This evolution of cryptography from rudimentary techniques to complex algorithms reflects a constant adaptation to the changing technological advancements and the enduring need for secure information exchange in the ever-evolving threat landscape. From the early days of the Spartan scytale and the Caesar Cipher, which employed basic substitution and transposition of characters, cryptography as a field has seen tremendous evolution with the development of sophisticated and complex cryptographic techniques to secure data and communication channels. The historical example of the *Enigma machine* during World War II and the efforts to break its code underscore the perpetual interplay between the development of cryptographic systems and the cryptanalysis techniques to break these systems. Today, cryptography is deeply embedded in the information systems that support businesses, and it forms the bedrock for protecting critical applications and services that organizations rely upon. It also plays a vital role in meeting regulatory and compliance requirements by ensuring the confidentiality and integrity of sensitive data as required by various standards and regulations such as PCI DSS, HIPAA, and GDPR.

Structure

In this chapter, we will discuss the following topics:

- Fundamentals of cryptography
- Advantages and challenges of symmetric and asymmetric encryption
- Data lifecycle
- Securing data across the data lifecycle
- Common cryptographic attacks
- Beyond the cipher data security strategies
- Emerging trends in data security

Objectives

This chapter will focus on the core principles of cryptography and its practical applications for data security. By the end of this chapter, you will have an understanding of the fundamental concepts and the basic terminology of cryptography and different types of cryptographic techniques. Specifically, you will be able to explain the differences between symmetric and asymmetric encryption and understand how **Transport Layer Security** (**TLS**) uses both. You will also be able to comprehend the working and implementation of **public key infrastructure** (**PKI**). The chapter also explores the interconnectedness of encryption and data security with the other domains of information security, demonstrating how they collectively contribute to a resilient and secure information ecosystem. By establishing a strong understanding of these foundational elements, you will be better equipped to appreciate the complexities and nuances of the wider information security landscape.

Fundamentals of cryptography

The English word *Cryptography* is adapted from the Greek words *kryptos,* meaning *hidden,* and *graphien,* meaning *to-write.* It is a branch of mathematics dedicated to the principles, techniques, and methods of transforming plaintext data into a secure form such that it is accessible only to those who are authorized to access it. It involves protecting the confidentiality, integrity, and authenticity of data. NIST defines cryptography as a branch of mathematics concerned with the transformation of data to protect information, which is a critical tool for computer security. *NIST SP 800-175B (Rev.1)* further elaborates that cryptography embodies the principles and methods for transforming data to conceal its meaning, prevent unauthorized usage, and prevent undetected modification.

Modern cryptography extends beyond the traditional focus on secrecy. While ensuring confidentiality remains one of the primary objectives, contemporary cryptography also provides mechanisms for authentication, data integrity, and non-repudiation. In the realm of information security, modern cryptography serves as a fundamental control for defence against cyberattacks, thus safeguarding communications and protecting data from unauthorized access.

Basic terminology of cryptography

We begin by introducing the basic terminology used in cryptography, and then build upon it to examine different types of cryptographic techniques and their application in securing data across different stages of its lifecycle.

Plaintext

Plaintext refers to the original, unencrypted data or message in a format that is readable by humans or computers. It is the input that is fed into an encryption system, and the desired output obtained after decryption. Examples of plaintext can include text documents, email messages before encryption, images, audio files, and any other type of digital data in its original and unconcealed state, are all examples of plaintext in the context of cryptography. Plaintext is inherently vulnerable to unauthorized access and disclosure. It can easily be read and potentially misused by anyone who can access the storage location or the transmission channel. This inherent risk underscores the need for encryption when dealing with confidential data, whether at rest, in use, or in transit across networks. While the terms plaintext and cleartext are often used interchangeably, there is a subtle distinction between the two. Plaintext specifically refers to the input and output of cryptographic processes. Cleartext is a broader term that includes any data that is not encrypted. It also includes data such as binary files, which may not be human-readable but still exist in an unconcealed form.

Ciphertext

When plaintext is encrypted using a cryptosystem, it is transformed into ciphertext. It is the encrypted form of the original message or data that is rendered unreadable and incomprehensible to anyone who does not possess the key to decrypt it. Ciphertext appears as a random sequence of characters, numbers, and symbols, making it difficult to decipher in the absence of an appropriate key.

Ciphertext helps safeguard the confidentiality of information. Even if someone manages to intercept or gain unauthorized access to the ciphertext, they will not be able to comprehend it easily to utilize the information. The transformation from plaintext to ciphertext is done using an encryption algorithm and a specific key. The plaintext can be derived from the ciphertext only by using the corresponding decryption key or cryptanalysis techniques.

Encryption

Encryption is the fundamental process that converts plaintext into ciphertext using a cryptographic algorithm and a key. The core objective of encryption is to ensure data confidentiality, security, and privacy by rendering the information unintelligible to unauthorized parties.

There are two primary categories of encryption techniques: symmetric-key encryption and asymmetric-key encryption. Symmetric-key encryption is also known as secret key encryption, and it utilizes a single secret key for both the encryption and decryption processes. This method is faster and more efficient, which makes it suitable for encrypting large volumes of data. The **Advanced Encryption Standard** (**AES**) and the **Data Encryption Standard** (**DES**) are examples of symmetric-key algorithms. The other category is asymmetric-key encryption, also known as public key encryption. It employs a pair of mathematically related keys: a public key and a private key. The public key can be freely distributed and used by anyone to encrypt messages intended for the owner of the corresponding private key, who is the only one capable of decrypting them. The private key can also be used by the owner to digitally sign messages to ensure message integrity and demonstrate non-repudiation. Asymmetric encryption is particularly valuable for secure key exchange over insecure channels and for implementing digital signatures. Commonly used asymmetric algorithms include **Rivest–Shamir–Adleman** (**RSA**) and **elliptic curve cryptography** (**ECC**). Regardless of the type of encryption, the strength of the encryption relies on the robustness of the algorithm and the security of the keys used. Practical real-world implementations of cryptosystems combine the advantages of both symmetric and asymmetric encryption, often using asymmetric methods for key exchange and symmetric methods for encrypting the actual data.

Decryption

Decryption is the reverse process of encryption for transforming ciphertext back into its original plaintext form. This permits authorized recipients of encrypted data to access and understand the original information. Successful decryption hinges on having the correct decryption key and using the corresponding algorithm that was employed during encryption. Depending upon the encryption technique, the decryption method is also symmetric or asymmetric. In symmetric decryption, the secret key that is used for encryption is also used for decryption. In asymmetric decryption, the private key of the key pair is used to decrypt data that was encrypted using the corresponding public key. The ability to decrypt data is essential for legitimate users to access any protected information, highlighting the symbiotic relationship between encryption and decryption.

Algorithm

A cryptographic algorithm is a well-defined computational procedure that specifies how encryption and decryption are to be performed. During encryption, the algorithm takes the plaintext and a key as input to produce the ciphertext. Conversely, for decryption, it takes the ciphertext and the corresponding key as input to output the original plaintext.

Cryptographic algorithms are broadly of two types, substitution ciphers and transposition ciphers. In substitution ciphers, characters, or groups of characters in the plaintext are replaced with other characters or symbols. Caesar Cipher, in which each letter is shifted a certain number of positions down the alphabet, is a classic example of a substitution cipher. The transposition ciphers rearrange the order of the characters in the plaintext to create the ciphertext, instead of changing the characters themselves. The rail fence cipher is an example of a transposition cipher. The modern cryptographic algorithms, like AES and RSA, employ far more complex cryptographic techniques. These algorithms combine elements of both substitution and transposition ciphers along with intricate mathematical functions to achieve a high-level of security. The strength of an algorithm is paramount as it determines the resistance of the encrypted data to cryptanalytic attacks. They achieve this through multiple rounds of encryption involving **substitution boxes (S-boxes)**, permutations, and a mix of linear and nonlinear transformations to ensure diffusion across the data.

Key

A cryptographic key is a piece of secret information, typically a string of bits, numbers, or characters, that controls the operation of a cryptographic algorithm. The key determines the specific transformation of the plaintext into ciphertext during encryption and vice versa during decryption. The security of the encrypted data is critically dependent on the secrecy and strength of the key.

There are two main types of cryptographic keys, secret keys and public/private key pairs. In symmetric cryptography, a single secret key is shared between the sender and the receiver, which is used for both encryption and decryption. In asymmetric cryptography, two mathematically related keys are used: a public key and a private key. The public key can be freely distributed and is used for encryption, while the private key is kept secret by its owner and is used for decryption. The length and randomness of a cryptographic key are crucial factors in its strength. Longer and more random keys are significantly harder to guess or break. Current best practices recommend minimum key sizes such as AES-128 or AES-256 for symmetric encryption, RSA-2048 or RSA-3072+ for asymmetric encryption, and ECC keys of at least P-256 or P-384 for equivalent strength. Keys should also be rotated periodically to minimize exposure from potential compromise.

For secure key generation, high-entropy sources must be used to ensure unpredictability. Cryptographically secure random numbers should be generated using **deterministic random bit generators (DRBGs)** or hardware-based **true random number generators (TRNGs)**. For the overall security of a cryptosystem, it is essential to have robust key management practices, including secure generation, storage, distribution, and destruction of keys in accordance with standards such as NIST SP 800-57.

Cryptanalysis

Cryptanalysis is a complementary field to cryptography. It focuses on the study of methods to defeat cryptographic techniques and plays a vital role in the security landscape by identifying weaknesses and vulnerabilities in cryptographic algorithms and their implementations. It entails analyzing and decrypting ciphers, codes, and encrypted text without prior knowledge of the key. In essence, while cryptography is about creating secure codes, cryptanalysis is about breaking them.

The primary objective of cryptanalysis is to discover the secret key used to encrypt a message. However, through cryptanalysis, it is also feasible to discover a functionally equivalent algorithm for decryption and deduce information about the original plaintext even without finding the secret key. Cryptanalytic attacks are often categorized based on the amount of information available to the attacker. Ciphertext only attacks occur when the attacker only has access to the encrypted message. Known-plaintext attacks involve the attacker having access to both the plaintext and its corresponding ciphertext. Chosen-plaintext or **chosen-ciphertext attacks** (**CCAs**) represent scenarios where the attacker can choose plaintexts to be encrypted or ciphertexts to be decrypted to gain more insight into the cryptographic process. Modern cryptographic protocols such as TLS and encryption schemes using **Authenticated Encryption with Associated Data** (**AEAD**) are explicitly designed to be resistant to CCAs, ensuring robustness against such exploit scenarios.

Cryptographic techniques

Cryptographic techniques can be broadly categorized into symmetric and asymmetric encryption. There are several other related techniques and practical implementations, like cryptographic hash functions, digital signatures, digital certificates, and PKI, that play crucial roles in securing information systems.

In modern applications, encryption is often implemented using AEAD modes such as **Galois/Counter Mode** (**GCM**), **Counter with CBC-MAC** (**CCM**), and **Offset Codebook Mode** (**OCB**). These modes provide both confidentiality and integrity in a single, efficient operation and have become the default standard for protecting data in transit and at rest.

We will delve into each of these to gain a comprehensive understanding of cryptographic techniques employed to secure digital systems.

Symmetric encryption

Symmetric encryption is a fundamental cryptographic technique that employs a single secret key to both encrypt and decrypt data. This necessitates that both the sender and the recipient of the encrypted information must possess the same key, and it should be kept confidential from anyone who is not authorized to have it. The symmetric encryption process involves transforming plaintext into ciphertext using the secret key and an encryption algorithm. To retrieve the original information, the recipient needs to use the same secret key and a corresponding decryption algorithm to convert the ciphertext back into plaintext. The simplicity and efficiency of symmetric encryption enable it to be widely used for securing data, particularly for large volumes. *Figure 5.1* represents the symmetric encryption and decryption process:

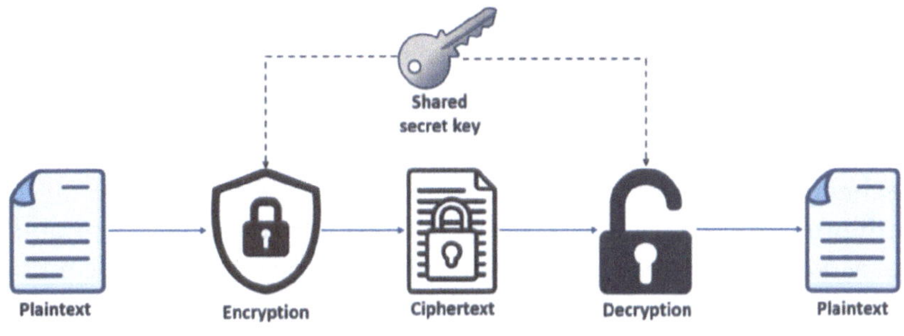

Figure 5.1: Symmetric encryption

There are several symmetric algorithms that have been developed over the years, each one with its own characteristics and security strengths. Let us discuss some of these.

Advanced Encryption Standard

The AES, which is widely considered the gold standard for symmetric encryption, is among the most prominent ones. AES is a block cipher that operates on fixed-size blocks of data (128 bits) and supports key lengths of 128, 192, and 256 bits. The number of repetitions performed in the encryption process varies depending on the key length: 10 rounds for 128 bit keys, 12 rounds for 192 bit keys, and 14 rounds for 256 bit keys. Each round involves several sub-processes, which enhance the complexity of the relationship between the plaintext, the key, and the ciphertext, thus enhancing the security of the system.

Data Encryption Standard

The DES, which uses a 56 bit key and operates on 64 bit blocks, is another historically significant symmetric algorithm. Given the modern-day computing power and the relatively short key length of DES, it is now considered vulnerable to brute-force attacks. To address this weakness, **triple DES (3DES)** was developed. 3DES applies the DES algorithm three times to each data block using either two or three different keys, effectively increasing the key length to 112 or 168 bits. While 3DES is more secure than DES, it is slower and has largely been superseded by AES. NIST has not allowed the use of 3DES for new applications since 2023. The existing systems using 3DES should migrate to AES, preferably to authenticated encryption modes like AES-GCM, which provide both confidentiality and integrity.

More symmetric algorithms

Several other notable symmetric algorithms are used for securing digital data and communications. Blowfish is a fast and flexible cipher with a variable key length ranging from 32 to 448 bits. Twofish, the successor of Blowfish, offers enhanced speed and security with key lengths up to 256 bits. **Rivest Cipher 4 (RC4)** is a stream cipher known for its speed and simplicity, but it has been found to have a number of vulnerabilities and is therefore not used in modern cryptosystems. Other symmetric algorithms include *Salsa20, ChaCha20, CAST, IDEA, Serpent, RC5, RC6, Camellia, ARIA,* and *SM4,* each designed with specific performance and security characteristics.

In traditional schemes, while encryption ensures confidentiality, separate mechanisms such as **message authentication codes** (**MACs**) are used to verify the integrity and authenticity of the message. Modern cryptosystems employ AEAD, which integrates confidentiality and integrity within a single unified operation. Besides encrypting the plaintext, AEAD schemes simultaneously generate an authentication tag to ensure that the ciphertext is not altered. Common AEAD modes include GCM, CCM, and OCB. These techniques are widely used in modern protocols such as TLS, **Internet Protocol security** (**IPsec**), and **Secure Shell** (**SSH**).

Challenges of symmetric encryption

The primary challenge of symmetric encryption lies in key management. Since the same key is used for both encryption and decryption, it is extremely important to securely generate, distribute, store, rotate, and revoke the keys. As the number of users and systems that need to communicate securely increases, the complexity of managing and sharing these secret keys grows exponentially. There are several solutions to address these challenges, including centralized **key management systems** (**KMS**) that streamline the key generation, storage, and distribution processes. A **hardware security module** (**HSM**) is a common implementation that provides a secure and tamper-proof environment for storing and managing cryptographic keys. Many enterprise KMS solutions integrate with HSMs to meet stringent security and regulatory requirements. Advanced deployment models such as **bring your own key** (**BYOK**) and **hold your own key** (**HYOK**) give organizations greater control over key ownership and residency in cloud environments. Another best practice is the use of envelope encryption, where a master key encrypts **data-encryption keys** (**DEKs**), which in turn encrypt the actual data.

Application of symmetric encryption

Due to its speed and efficiency, symmetric encryption finds widespread usage in many real-world applications. It is the preferred encryption technique for encrypting large volumes of data, especially file and disk encryption, where performance is a critical factor. For secure browsing using **Hypertext Transfer Protocol Secure** (**HTTPS**) over the internet, while symmetric encryption is used to encrypt the actual data transferred between the browser and the web server, the session keys are exchanged using asymmetric encryption during the TLS/SSL handshake. The latest version, TLS 1.3, uses AEAD to provide both confidentiality and integrity. TLS 1.3 also supports session resumption through session tickets or pre-shared keys, which allows faster re-establishment of secure sessions without the need for a full handshake. **Virtual private networks** (**VPNs**) also utilize symmetric encryption to secure the data transmitted through the VPN tunnels, often employing AES in GCM or CBC mode depending on the protocol. Similarly, databases often employ symmetric encryption to protect sensitive information. Even for internal communications, where key sharing can be managed effectively, symmetric encryption is considered most suitable. The wireless protocols like **Wi-Fi Protected Access 2** (**WPA2**) and **Wi-Fi Protected Access 3** (**WPA3**) used for securing communications over wireless networks also employ symmetric encryption algorithms like AES. WPA3 provides enhanced security through the **Simultaneous Authentication of Equals** (**SAE**) handshake. It mandates the use of AES-GCMP-128 to provide both encryption and authentication for the wireless data frames.

Asymmetric encryption

Asymmetric encryption employs a pair of keys: a public key for encryption (or digitally signing messages) and a private key for decryption. This encryption method leverages the fact that the public key can be freely shared with anyone and used to encrypt data, but only the owner of the corresponding private key can decrypt that data. This fundamental property of asymmetric encryption resolves the key distribution problem associated with symmetric encryption, since there is no need for a secure channel to exchange the secret key. The asymmetric encryption and decryption processes are shown in *Figure 5.2*:

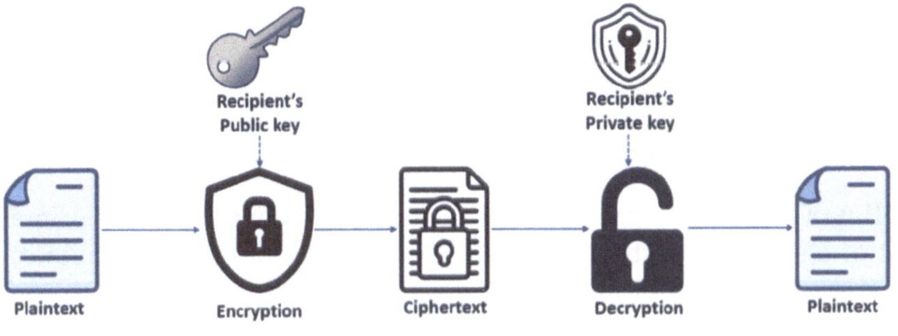

Figure 5.2: Asymmetric encryption

There are several prominent asymmetric algorithms that are widely used for secure messaging. The following section outlines some of these.

Rivest–Shamir–Adleman

RSA is one of the oldest and most prevalent asymmetric encryption algorithms that relies on the mathematical difficulty of factoring large integers into their prime factors. The key generation process in RSA involves selecting two large prime numbers, calculating their product (the modulus), and then determining the public and private exponents. Encryption is performed by raising the plaintext to the power of the public exponent modulo the modulus, while decryption involves raising the ciphertext to the power of the private exponent modulo the same modulus. The length of the RSA key typically ranges from 2048 to 4096 bits. **Optimal**

Asymmetric Encryption Padding (**OAEP**) for RSA encryption and **Probabilistic Signature Scheme** (**PSS**) for RSA-based digital signatures are recommended in modern implementations. These techniques introduce randomness and structural integrity checks, making them more resistant to chosen-ciphertext and adaptive attacks as compared to the earlier schemes. The older RSA PKCS#1 v1.5 padding scheme should be avoided in new implementations due to known vulnerabilities and lack of semantic security.

Elliptic curve cryptography

ECC is a more recent asymmetric algorithm based on the algebraic structure of elliptic curves over finite fields. It offers comparable security to RSA with significantly smaller key sizes, thus improving the efficiency and strength of encryption. For instance, a 256 bit ECC key is often considered equivalent in strength to a 3072 bit RSA key. ECC is used in various cryptographic operations, including digital signatures through the **Elliptic Curve Digital Signature Algorithm** (**ECDSA**) and key exchange via the **Elliptic Curve Diffie-Hellman** (**ECDH**) protocol. Standardized curves such as NIST P-256 and P-384 are commonly used in practical implementations for compatibility and interoperability across systems. However, newer curves such as Curve25519 and Curve448, which offer enhanced security properties, improved performance, and better resistance to implementation attacks, are being increasingly adopted. These curves are widely used in TLS 1.3, Signal, and other contemporary secure communication protocols.

Diffie-Hellman key exchange

The **Diffie-Hellman** (**DH**) key exchange is an asymmetric technique that is primarily used for the agreement of a secret key rather than direct encryption of data. It facilitates two parties with no prior shared secret to jointly establish a secret key over an insecure communication channel. Essentially, the process involves the exchange of public parameters and the use of private keys to compute a shared secret based on the difficulty of the discrete logarithm problem. The classical DH scheme operates over modular arithmetic, while ECDH achieves equivalent security with a smaller key size and improved efficiency by using elliptic curve mathematics. To enhance security further, most practical implementations employ **Ephemeral Diffie-Hellman** (**DHE**) or **Ephemeral ECDH** (**ECDHE**), where new temporary key pairs are generated for each session. This provides forward secrecy and ensures that even if long-term keys are later compromised, past communications remain protected.

The basic DH exchange is considered vulnerable to **man-in-the-middle (MitM)** attacks and is combined with suitable authentication mechanisms to overcome the problem during the key exchange process, as seen in the TLS protocol.

Advantages and challenges of asymmetric encryption

The primary advantage of asymmetric encryption lies in its simplified key distribution. The public key can be openly shared, which permits anyone to encrypt messages for the intended recipient, who alone possesses the private key for decryption. However, the security of asymmetric encryption hinges on the computational difficulty of the underlying mathematical problems. The advent of quantum computing poses a significant threat to asymmetric algorithms like RSA and ECC, particularly due to Shor's algorithm, which can very efficiently solve the integer factorization and discrete logarithm problems that these algorithms rely upon. Compared to symmetric encryption, asymmetric algorithms typically require longer key lengths to achieve equivalent security due to their mathematical structures.

Application of asymmetric encryption

Asymmetric encryption finds usage in several real-world applications. It is fundamental to digital signatures for providing authentication, integrity, and non-repudiation for the exchange of electronic documents and messages. It is also used for secure key exchange, enabling the establishment of shared secrets for symmetric encryption. Email encryption technologies like **Pretty Good Privacy** (**PGP**) and **Secure/Multipurpose Internet Mail Extension** (**S/MIME**) also employ asymmetric encryption to protect the confidentiality and integrity of messages. Websites using HTTPS also use asymmetric encryption through TLS/SSL certificates to authenticate the server and establish secure connections. Asymmetric encryption also plays a crucial role in blockchain technology for ensuring the security and integrity of transactions.

Cryptographic hash functions

Cryptographic hash functions are mathematical algorithms that take an input of arbitrary length and produce a fixed-size output that is commonly referred to as a hash value or digest. These functions act like digital fingerprints for ensuring data integrity by producing a unique hash for each unique input. Any alteration to the input data results in a significantly different hash output, making it easy to detect any tampering. Hash functions are fundamental for ensuring data integrity and are used in file integrity checks to verify that a file has not been altered during transmission or storage. In message transmission, these are used to confirm the sender's identity and the integrity of the message. They also play a critical role in password storage, where the hashed version of a password is stored instead of the plaintext.

Historically, **Message Digest Algorithm 5** (**MD5**) and **Secure Hash Algorithm** (**SHA**) families are the most widely used cryptographic hash algorithms. MD5 is an older algorithm that generates a 128 bit hash value. While MD5 was widely used in the past, it is now considered insecure due to collision vulnerabilities, meaning it is relatively easy to find two different inputs that produce the same hash. The SHA family has SHA-1, SHA-2, and SHA-3 types of algorithms. SHA-1, which produces a 160 bit hash, is also considered insecure and is generally deprecated. The SHA-2 and the more recent SHA-3, with variants that produce 224, 256, 384, or 512 bit hashes, are considered secure algorithms and are extensively used in blockchain technologies, digital signatures, and many other security applications.

For message transmission, the **Hash-based Message Authentication Code** (**HMAC**) is the most common keyed construction. It combines a secret key with a hash function such as HMAC-SHA-256 to ensure that the message is not altered and that it originates from an authenticated source. HMAC is the standard approach used in secure communication protocols such as TLS, IPsec, and SSH. For password storage, the general-purpose hash functions like SHA-256 or SHA-3 are not adequate, as they are designed for speed and can be exploited by brute-force attacks. Instead, dedicated password hashing functions such as Argon2id, scrypt, and bcrypt that are deliberately slow should be used. These functions should always be implemented to incorporate a unique salt per password and appropriate work-factor or memory cost parameters to withstand large-scale cracking attempts.

Properties of secure hash functions

For a hash function to be considered cryptographically secure, it must possess the following essential properties:

- **Pre-image resistance**: It is a one-way property, which means that it should not be computationally feasible to find the original input given only the hash value. This is crucial for applications like password security, where the hash of the password is stored instead of the password itself.
- **Collision resistance**: It should not be computationally feasible to find two different inputs that produce the same hash output. This is vital for the integrity of digital signatures, as collisions could allow an attacker to create a fraudulent document with the same signature as a legitimate one.
- **Deterministic**: The function must be deterministic, i.e., the same input should always yield the same output.
- **Uniformity:** The function should produce uniform hashes evenly distributed across the output space.

Several real-world applications, such as digital signatures and digital certificates, employ encryption and hashing techniques to ensure message confidentiality, integrity, and non-repudiation. Typical encryption and hashing processes for communication of data over an insecure channel are depicted in *Figure 5.3*, where asymmetric encryption and hashing are used for data confidentiality, integrity, and non-repudiation:

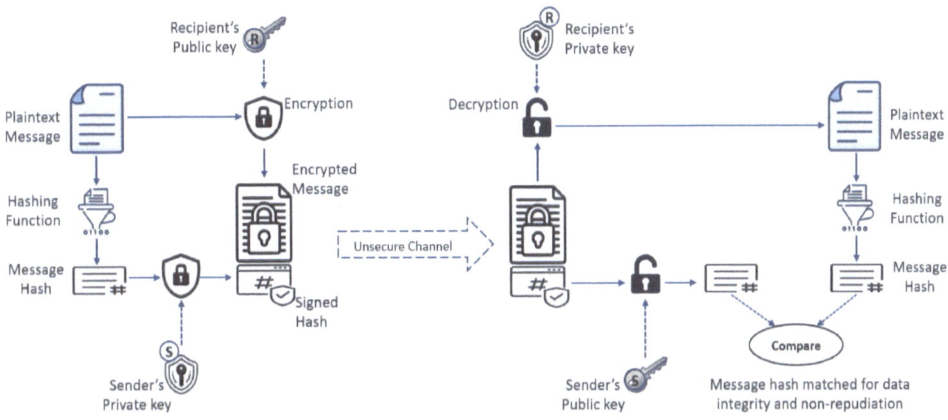

Figure 5.3: Sign and encrypt

Digital signatures

Digital signatures provide a mechanism to ensure the authenticity and integrity of digital messages and documents. They serve several crucial purposes, which include authentication of the sender to ensure that the message indeed originated from the claimed sender, data integrity to verify that the message has not been altered during transmission, and non-repudiation, which ensures that the sender cannot deny having sent the message.

The creation of a digital signature involves a step-by-step process. First, the message or document to be signed is processed through a cryptographic hash function to create a unique message digest or hash. This hash value is then encrypted using the sender's private key to form the digital signature. Signing a hash instead of the entire document ensures efficiency, as signing a shorter hash value is computationally less intensive. Encrypting the hash with the private key provides authentication and non-repudiation since it is only the sender who possesses the private key.

The verification of a digital signature is a reverse process. The recipient of the digitally signed message uses the sender's public key to decrypt the digital signature to obtain the original hash of the message. The recipient then hashes the received message independently using the same hash function that the sender used and compares the two hash values. If the two hashes match, it confirms that the message was indeed sent by the claimed sender and that it has not been altered during transmission. Several cryptographic algorithms support digital signatures. Modern systems adopt RSA-PSS and ECDSA as they provide improved resistance to adaptive chosen-message attacks. Due to their high performance, resistance to side-channel attacks, and simpler implementation, the **Edwards-curve Digital Signature Algorithm (EdDSA)**, particularly Ed25519 and Ed448, is increasingly used.

Digital signatures have become indispensable in various modern applications. These are widely used for securing email communications through protocols like S/MIME and PGP.

These are also used extensively for digitally signing software packages. Verifying the integrity of software through code signing involves using digital signatures to confirm the authenticity and origin of software packages. Further, digital signatures play a crucial role in e-commerce transactions for authenticating the parties and ensuring the integrity of financial transactions.

Digital certificates

Digital certificates are electronic documents used to verify the ownership of a public key by a specific entity, like an individual, organization, or server. These certificates act as a form of digital identification, assuring that the public key belongs to the claimed entity. A digital certificate typically contains several details including the certificate holder's identity e.g. name, email address, organization etc., the public key itself, the details of the **Certificate Authority** (**CA**) that issued the certificate, the digital signature of the CA which verifies the certificate's authenticity, an expiration date indicating the period of validity and a unique serial number for identification. These components collectively provide a verifiable identity and the means to establish secure communication.

Digital certificates are of different types, each serving specific security needs. SSL/TLS certificates are commonly used to secure websites, enabling HTTPS and establishing trusted connections between browsers and web servers. Software developers use code signing certificates to digitally sign their applications to ensure their authenticity and integrity. For email security, email certificates are often used with S/MIME to secure and authenticate email communications. For remote access, client certificates are used to authenticate users accessing secure systems and networks.

TLS certificates vary in the level of identity validation performed by the issuing CA. **Domain validation** (**DV**) certificates verify that the applicant controls the domain. These are the most commonly used certificates for general website encryption. **Organization validation** (**OV**) certificates provide additional verification steps to confirm the legitimacy of the organization owning the domain. **Extended validation** (**EV**) certificates represent the most rigorous verification process and display enhanced identity details in browsers to provide users with higher assurance of trust.

The most crucial entity in the issuance and management of digital certificates is the CA. They provide a secure online environment by offering a reliable mechanism to verify digital identities. CAs are trusted third-party organizations responsible for verifying the identity of various entities before issuing the digital certificates. The certificates are digitally signed by the CAs using their private keys to ensure the authenticity and integrity of the certificates issued by them. Anyone can verify this signature by using the CA's public key, thus establishing a chain of trust. This process establishes the chain of trust that is the basis of the PKI. The hierarchy typically includes a root CA, one or more intermediate CAs, and the end-entity certificate. These collectively form the foundation of secure communication and authentication over the internet.

The status of the certificates can be checked from the **Certificate Revocation Lists** (**CRLs**) that are periodically published by CAs or by using the **Online Certificate Status Protocol** (**OCSP**), which allows clients to query the revocation status of a specific certificate in real-time. Modern TLS implementations often use OCSP stapling, where the server provides a signed OCSP response during the handshake. This eliminates the need for the client to contact the CA directly, improving performance and privacy.

Public key infrastructure

PKI is a comprehensive framework comprising a set of roles, policies, hardware, software, and procedures needed to manage digital certificates and public key encryption. It provides a structured approach to managing digital certificates and cryptographic keys throughout their lifecycle. Its primary purpose is to facilitate the secure transfer of information for a wide range of online applications. PKI establishes and manages digital trust, ensuring that the communicating parties can exchange information securely and verify each other's identity.

PKI relies on several key components working together. CAs are the trusted entities that issue, store, and sign digital certificates of applicants. **Registration Authorities** (**RAs**) are used to verify the identity of the entities requesting digital certificates. Digital certificates are indexed and stored in secure certificate repositories from which they can be accessed when needed. The entire lifecycle of certificates, including their issuance, renewal, revocation, and access control, is managed with the help of a certificate management system. The requirements, procedures, and practices of PKI are outlined in an overarching certificate policy that provides a framework for its operation and trustworthiness.

Automation plays a critical role in maintaining PKI efficiency and scalability in practical deployments. Protocols such as the **Automated Certificate Management Environment** (**ACME**) enable automated certificate issuance, renewal, and deployment. In enterprise environments, PKI management is often integrated with device management platforms to automate certificate distribution and renewal across a large number of managed endpoints. This ensures continuous compliance, operational consistency, and improved security posture.

For organizations maintaining private or internal PKI, it is important to follow robust security practices. The root CA should be kept offline to prevent compromise, while intermediate CAs can operate online to issue and manage the certificates. The CA's private keys should be stored in an HSM. This is essential to protect the CA's private keys and ensure that the cryptographic operations occur in a secure, tamper-resistant environment. The trust is further enhanced by regular audits, implementing strong access controls, and the use of short-lived certificates wherever feasible.

Data lifecycle

Before we understand securing data using various cryptographic techniques, it is important to understand the data lifecycle. The journey of data from creation to destruction involves several distinct stages, each presenting its own unique set of security risks. Refer to the following figure, which depicts various stages of the data lifecycle:

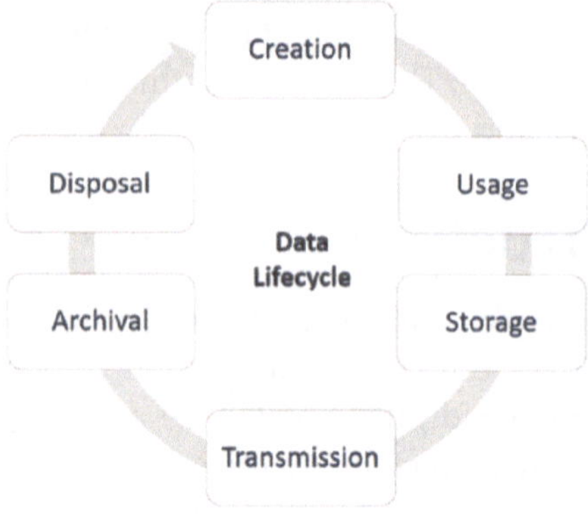

Figure 5.4: *Data lifecycle*

Data creation

The initial stage of the data lifecycle involves the generation of new data or the gathering of existing data from different sources. This can range from user input in applications to sensor readings and the acquisition of data from external databases. Vulnerabilities can arise from this stage itself, and the importance of securing data at its genesis cannot be overstated since weaknesses introduced early in the lifecycle can have cascading effects on subsequent stages. Lack of proper system configurations and insecure processes involved in data creation and collection can introduce significant weaknesses. Unauthorized access to systems or environments where data is being created or collected poses a major risk. Data infected with malware can also get into a system during the collection process, especially when acquiring data from external or untrusted sources.

To strengthen data protection from the outset, data classification and tagging should be implemented at the point of creation itself. This enables policy-driven encryption and access control measures to be applied consistently throughout the data's lifecycle. Additionally, during data ingestion from external sources, integrity checking mechanisms such as cryptographic hashes and digital signatures should be employed to ensure that the data is not tampered with or corrupted even before entering the organizational systems.

Data in use

Once data has been created or collected, it undergoes processing and is actively used for a variety of purposes. This may include data transformation, analysis, reporting, and powering application functionalities. Data in use remains vulnerable to a range of security threats, particularly because traditional encryption methods require data to be decrypted before processing, which can expose the data to a variety of threats. Unauthorized access by malicious software operating on the systems processing the data is a significant concern. Inadequate access controls on the systems and applications used to process the data can lead to breaches of confidentiality by unauthorized users or even legitimate users misusing data beyond their authorized scope. Any vulnerabilities in the applications running on the systems processing data may also be exploited by attackers to gain unauthorized access to the data. To mitigate these risks, **Trusted Execution Environments** (**TEEs**) such as *Intel SGX*, *AMD SEV*, and *Arm CCA* are used, which provide hardware-based isolation to safeguard sensitive data and code during execution. For enhanced data protection during use, extensive research is being carried out in advanced techniques such as homomorphic encryption to permit computations to be performed on encrypted data without requiring decryption, thereby preserving confidentiality even during processing.

Data at rest

After collection, creation, and processing, data needs to be securely stored. It can reside on a variety of media such as hard drives, databases, cloud storage platforms, and archival systems. Data at rest is a prime target for attackers seeking to exfiltrate sensitive information, and the risks associated with it are diverse. Physical theft of storage media like laptops and external drives can directly compromise the data stored on them. Unauthorized access using compromised credentials or by exploiting system and application vulnerabilities poses a significant threat to data at rest. Similarly, insider threats resulting from malicious or careless employees can also lead to unwarranted exposure and misuse of stored data. To ensure robust protection, it is essential to employ strong encryption techniques with authenticated encryption modes that provide confidentiality as well as data integrity. For instance, AES-XTS is generally used for full disk encryption, and AES-GCM is used for encrypting files and objects in storage systems and databases.

In the context of cloud storage, misconfigurations of cloud security settings can inadvertently result in the public exposure of sensitive data. Therefore, implementing strong encryption and robust access control mechanisms is essential to effectively secure data at rest. For sensitive data, the default encryption typically enabled by the **cloud service providers** (**CSPs**) should be further enhanced by leveraging **customer-managed keys** (**CMKs**) through cloud KMS. Envelope encryption patterns that entail encrypting data keys with a master key stored in the KMS can be used to balance scalability with security and simplify key rotation.

Data in transit

Data frequently needs to be transmitted over various types of networks. This movement of data, known as **data in transit**, introduces its own set of security risks. The data being transmitted over networks is susceptible to interception, eavesdropping, and manipulation by unauthorized parties. Interception of communications between two parties by attackers employing MitM attacks is a major threat to data in transit. Sniffing packets on insecure networks can also allow attackers to gain access to sensitive information. The use of unencrypted file transfer protocols and weak security protocols during transmission further increases these risks.

To counter these threats, TLS 1.3 is used as the baseline standard for encrypting communications. The earlier versions of TLS are now formally deprecated due to known weaknesses. TLS 1.3 mandates strong authenticated encryption modes like *AES-GCM* and *ChaCha20-Poly1305*, which provide both confidentiality and integrity. For email communications, different encryption mechanisms are employed depending on the desired security level. PGP/GPG and S/MIME provide end-to-end encryption and digital signing. STARTTLS, on the other hand, encrypts the connection between **mail transfer agents** (**MTAs**) and offers only hop-to-hop encryption. This implies that mail content can be accessed at the intermediate mail servers.

Data archival

Data that is no longer in active use but is still required to be retained for compliance, historical analysis, or any other reasons is often moved to archival storage for long-term retention. While the archival data is not accessed as frequently, it may still contain sensitive information and therefore, remains a lucrative target for attackers. There is a greater risk of unauthorized access to archival data, particularly if it is stored on older systems that may have weaker security controls than the infrastructure used for active data.

When encrypting archival data, it is essential to consider key longevity and crypto-agility. This is required to ensure that encryption mechanisms remain secure over time as algorithms and key strengths evolve. Organizations must have a crypto-agility plan that enables a smooth transition to stronger algorithms or longer keys when existing ones are deprecated or no longer meet regulatory standards. Periodic re-encryption of archived data using contemporary algorithms and new keys should be part of routine maintenance to ensure long-term confidentiality of data.

The practice of retaining backups beyond their intended lifespan can also introduce security risks, as these backups may have outdated controls that are not adequate to protect sensitive information. It is therefore necessary to implement strong and effective security controls, including encryption and stringent access control measures, to ensure the continued protection of information archived for long-term retention.

Data disposal

The final stage in the data lifecycle is the secure destruction and disposal of data that is no longer needed. This process is critical for preventing unauthorized access to sensitive information that may reside on retired storage media. Improper data disposal practices can lead to significant data breaches if storage media such as hard drives and tapes are not properly sanitized before being discarded or reused.

Incomplete data destruction, where remnants of the original data remain on the storage media, can permit determined attackers to recover sensitive information even after disposal.

Therefore, secure data destruction is crucial in preventing data leaks from systems and storage that have reached the end of their useful life. Established sanitization standards, such as NIST SP 800-88 (Rev.1), should be followed for comprehensive guidance on secure data destruction methods. The appropriate sanitization technique often depends on the type of storage media. While traditional **hard disk drives** (**HDDs**) can typically be sanitized using overwriting or degaussing methods, **solid-state drives** (**SSDs**) require specialized techniques due to their internal wear-levelling mechanisms that may retain residual data. Many modern **self-encrypting drives** (**SEDs**) support crypto-erase, where deleting the encryption key renders all stored data permanently inaccessible.

Securing data across the lifecycle

To address the diverse security risks present at various stages of the data lifecycle, a variety of encryption techniques can be employed. The choice of technique depends on the specific requirements of the stage, the state of the data, and the performance considerations.

Encrypting data at creation

One of the most effective ways to secure data is to encrypt it as early as possible in its lifecycle, ideally at the point of creation or collection. At the application-level, this is achieved by integrating encryption functionalities directly into the applications that generate or modify data. This ensures that the data is encrypted even before it is written to storage media. For data collected from untrusted sources, encryption can be applied immediately upon ingestion. This minimizes the time window during which data exists in an unencrypted state, thus reducing the potential for exposure. There are a variety of techniques that can be employed to facilitate encryption at the creation or collection stage. This includes leveraging APIs that enforce encryption during data transfer and storage or implementing secure data ingestion methods that encrypt data as it is being input.

Safeguarding data in use

A significant challenge faced by security professionals is protecting data while it is being actively processed or used. Traditional encryption methods typically require data to be decrypted before any operations can be performed on it, which opens a window of vulnerability. Homomorphic encryption, which is an emerging cryptographic technique, presents a promising solution to this problem. This encryption technique allows computations to be performed directly on encrypted data without the need for prior decryption. The results of these computations remain in encrypted form, and only the authorized key holders can decrypt them to reveal the outcome. While homomorphic encryption does hold immense potential for secure data processing, it is not yet widely adopted due to current limitations in performance and complexity. Continued advancements in this field could significantly enhance data security across the lifecycle by facilitating secure data processing in previously challenging scenarios.

Protecting data at rest

Securing data at rest is a critical aspect of the data lifecycle, and several encryption algorithms and techniques are available for this purpose. Symmetric encryption algorithms utilize a single secret key for both encryption and decryption of data. AES, which is a highly robust symmetric block cipher, is the most used method for encrypting data at rest. It supports various key sizes, including 128, 192, and 256 bits. The different key sizes offer varying levels of security and performance, with the longer keys providing greater protection, though at the cost of increased computational overhead. Older symmetric algorithms like DES, which uses a 56 bit key, are now considered weak. An improved version of it is the 3DES algorithm, which offers improved security by applying the DES algorithm three times, but is slower than AES. Other symmetric block ciphers, such as Twofish and Blowfish, known for their speed and effectiveness, also find usage in protecting data at rest.

Beyond algorithm-specific encryption, several other techniques can also be applied to protect data at rest. Disk encryption encrypts the entire storage volume, safeguarding all data contained within it. Tools like *BitLocker* for *Windows* and *FileVault* for *macOS* utilize full disk encryption to protect data on devices. Database encryption techniques focus on securing data stored within databases. This can involve encrypting the entire database or specific tables or columns within the database. **Transparent data encryption** (**TDE**) is a technique used to encrypt entire database files. File-level encryption provides a more granular approach by encrypting individual files or folders, permitting tailored protection based on the sensitivity of the data.

Securing data in transit

Protecting data as it travels across networks is crucial, and several protocols have been developed to facilitate secure transmission. TLS/SSL is a ubiquitous protocol that encrypts data transmitted over networks. TLS employs a combination of asymmetric encryption for the initial handshake process, in which the client and server authenticate each other and agree on a shared secret key, and symmetric encryption for the subsequent bulk data transfer using the negotiated key. IPsec is a suite of protocols that secures IP communications by providing authentication and encryption for each IP packet in a communication session. IPsec is commonly used to establish secure VPN connections. **Secure File Transfer Protocol** (**SFTP**) offers a secure method for transferring files over an SSH connection, ensuring both encryption of the data and secure authentication of the parties involved. SFTP provides a significant security upgrade over the standard FTP protocol, which transmits data in clear. Likewise, HTTPS represents the secure version of HTTP, which leverages TLS/SSL to encrypt all web traffic exchanged between a browser and a web server. For email security, protocols, and methods like PGP/GPG and S/MIME are used. PGP and GPG often utilize a hybrid approach, employing symmetric encryption for encrypting the email message body and asymmetric encryption for securely exchanging the symmetric-key. On the other hand, S/MIME depends upon public key cryptography and digital certificates to provide email security. The selection of an appropriate protocol for data in transit depends on the specific application requirements and the network environment over which the data is being transmitted.

Encryption for archival

Long-term retention of data is necessary for regulatory purposes and forensic investigations. Government regulations and standards mandate the duration for which different categories of data must be retained to meet legal, regulatory, or business obligations. Securing the archival data is essential to prevent its misuse. Implementing encryption for data at rest in archives provides a critical layer of defense against unauthorized access over extended periods. Given the potentially large volumes of data stored in archives, symmetric encryption algorithms like AES are frequently used due to their performance characteristics. When selecting an encryption algorithm for archival data, organizations need to consider the longevity of the algorithm and the strength of the encryption key to ensure that the data remains protected against future advances in cryptanalysis techniques. Another important aspect is the security of the archival key since it needs to be retained for as long as the archived data itself. HSMs can provide a secure and robust solution for storing the encryption keys associated with archival data.

Secure disposal

While encryption is not always directly involved in the destruction process, it can play a crucial role in ensuring data is rendered unrecoverable after disposal. Cryptographic erasure involves encrypting data with a strong encryption key and then securely destroying or deleting that key. Without the decryption key, the data becomes practically inaccessible. This method is especially effective for contemporary storage technologies like SSDs and SEDs. The secure overwriting or physical destruction of the encryption key is essential for this technique to be effective. Even though it is not an encryption technique, physical destruction of storage media through shredding or degaussing is also an effective way to ensure that data is permanently destroyed.

Common cryptographic attacks

Despite the strength of modern cryptographic algorithms, various types of attacks can target weaknesses in their implementation or the way they are used. Understanding these common cryptographic attacks and the strategies to mitigate them is crucial for ensuring data security. Some of these attacks are as follows:

- **Brute-force attacks**: These are the most common type of attacks, which involve systematically trying every possible combination until the correct one is found. The protection strategies against brute-force attacks include using strong keys and implementing account lockout policies after multiple failed attempts. In the context of password brute-force, dictionary attacks use a list of common words and passwords to try to guess the correct one. Using complex, unpredictable passwords that are not based on dictionary words can help prevent such attacks.

- **Frequency analysis**: This cryptanalysis technique is effective against simple substitution ciphers, which involve analyzing the frequency of characters in the ciphertext to deduce the plaintext. Modern ciphers, such as polyalphabetic and block ciphers, are designed to be resistant to this type of attack.
- **Known-plaintext**: These attacks occur when the attacker has access to both the plaintext and the corresponding ciphertext, which together can be used to deduce the key or the algorithm.
- **Chosen-plaintext**: Such attacks are even more potent. In these types of attacks, the attacker can choose arbitrary plaintexts to be encrypted and obtain the corresponding ciphertexts, which helps reveal information about the encryption key. Using strong encryption algorithms and frequently rotating the keys can mitigate the risk associated with these attacks.
- **Side-channel attacks**: These attacks exploit unintended information leakage, such as timing of operations or power consumption during the execution of cryptographic algorithms, to gain insights into the cryptographic processes or keys. Implementing countermeasures like constant-time algorithms and power analysis resistance techniques can help prevent side-channel attacks.

In addition to the above, implementation vulnerabilities in cryptographic systems can also be exploited by attackers. Padding oracle attacks, for instance, exploit error messages or timing differences in systems using unauthenticated CBC mode, and replay attacks target protocols that fail to validate message freshness. Similarly, protocol downgrade attacks can be used to trick systems into using weaker protocol versions or cipher suites. The RNG and entropy failures can also compromise cryptographic keys at the source itself.

The following table lists some of the common cryptographic attacks and mitigation measures:

Cryptographic attack	Mitigation measure
Side-channel/timing attacks	Employ constant-time operations and side-channel hardening.
Padding oracle attacks	Use AEAD modes such as AES-GCM, ChaCha20-Poly1305, and avoid unauthenticated CBC.
Replay attacks	Implement nonces or sequence numbers, and validate message freshness.
RNG/entropy failures	Use FIPS-validated DRBGs, ensure adequate system entropy.
Protocol downgrade attacks	Enforce TLS 1.3 or higher, disable deprecated versions, and weak cipher suites.

Table 5.1: Cryptographic attack types and mitigation measures

Vulnerabilities in the key management process, such as employing weak keys, improper storage, lack of timely rotation, or insecure distribution, can also lead to compromise of the cryptographic system. Implementing robust key management practices is essential for ensuring the security of cryptosystems.

The following table summarizes governance and operational controls for effective key management:

Governance	Operational controls
Rotate keys periodically to minimize exposure.	Store and use keys within a certified HSM to ensure tamper-resistant protection.
Ensure separation of duties by dividing key management roles so that no single individual controls generation, storage, and usage.	Securely back up key encryption keys in protected locations to ensure recoverability.
Regularly audit and continuously monitor all key access and usage events to detect unauthorized activity.	Define escrow and break-glass procedures for emergency or lawful access, under stringent audit.
Ensure complete and verifiable key destruction at the end of life to prevent future decryption.	Align crypto policy with organizational cryptographic standards and compliance requirements to maintain consistency.

***Table 5.2**: Considerations of effective key management*

Beyond the cipher data security strategies

While encryption is vital for protecting data confidentiality, a comprehensive data security strategy should involve a layered approach that incorporates other complementary strategies. When implemented alongside strong encryption practices, these strategies would create a more robust and effective data security posture for providing layered defense against a wide range of threats.

Data masking and tokenization

Both data masking and tokenization aim to protect sensitive data, but they differ in their approach and reversibility. Data masking typically reduces or eliminates the presence of sensitive data in datasets in a way that might not be easily reversible. Tokenization replaces sensitive data with non-sensitive tokens, and the original data is usually stored securely and can be retrieved by reversing the tokenization process, if required.

Data masking involves creating a fake but realistic version of the original data to protect sensitive information. This is particularly effective when used in non-production environments for testing, training, and software development purposes. The objective is to alter the data values while preserving their format and structure, thus rendering the data unusable by unauthorized individuals while still allowing realistic testing and analysis. Data masking can be achieved through a variety of techniques, which include the following:

- **Randomization**: Replacing sensitive data with randomly generated values.
- **Substitution**: Data is replaced with similar but fictitious data.
- **Shuffling**: Data values within a column are reordered.
- **Encryption**: Transforming data into an unreadable format. This is generally combined with other techniques.
- **Hashing**: Data is converted into a fixed-length string.
- **Nulling or redaction**: Original data is replaced with null values or asterisks.
- **Date shifting or aging**: Dates associated with the data are altered by a fixed amount.
- **Variance or averaging**: Individual values in the data are replaced by statistical measures.

Data tokenization, on the other hand, replaces sensitive data with non-sensitive equivalents known as tokens. These tokens have no intrinsic value and are used as placeholders for the actual sensitive data, which is stored securely in a separate environment. Tokenization is used to protect data both at rest and in transit and offers several benefits, such as minimizing the impact of data breaches, enhancing data security by rendering stolen tokens unusable without access to the vault, simplifying data management by isolating sensitive data, and enabling flexible data usage for analytics purposes without exposing the original sensitive information. Tokenization is commonly employed in high-security contexts such as protecting payment card data under PCI DSS, where sensitive values like PANs are replaced with tokens that have no mathematical relationship to the original data.

It is important to understand that tokenization is not encryption. Unlike encryption, tokenization does not depend on cryptographic keys for reversible transformation. Instead, it relies on a secure token vault that maintains the mapping between tokens and original data. In certain cases, **format-preserving encryption** (**FPE**) may be used as an alternative, which allows ciphertexts to retain the structure of the original data. However, tokenization offers stronger isolation since the sensitive values can be completely removed from operational systems.

Access control mechanisms

Access control is a fundamental security practice that governs who can access specific resources within a computing environment and with what privileges. It is vital for ensuring the confidentiality, integrity, and availability of data by preventing unauthorized access. Access control depends upon the fundamental components of identification, authentication, and authorization.

Depending upon the need, different types of access control models can be employed in an information environment. **Discretionary access control** (**DAC**) provides the resource owners with the authority to decide who can access their resources. MAC uses a centralized authority to assign access levels to users and security labels to resources, granting access only when the level matches or exceeds the label. **Role-based access control** (**RBAC**) assigns access rights based on a user's role within the organization. **Rule-based access control** (**RuBAC**) grants or denies access to resources based on predefined rules and conditions. **Attribute-based access control** (**ABAC**) uses a combination of attributes associated with the user, the resource, and the environment to make access decisions. The fundamental principles guiding access control are the principle of least privilege, which dictates that users should be granted only the minimum level of access that is necessary to perform their job, and just-in-time access, which grants the authorized access only for the required duration. We will further discuss the access control models in greater detail in the next chapter on **identity and access management** (**IAM**).

Data loss prevention strategies

Data loss prevention (**DLP**) encompasses a set of tools, processes, and strategies designed to detect, prevent, and manage unauthorized access, transmission, or leakage of sensitive data. The primary objectives of DLP are to maintain the integrity and security of sensitive information and prevent data breaches. DLP strategies are particularly effective in mitigating risks associated with insider threats and human error that significantly contribute to data loss incidents. There are different types of DLP solutions that can be implemented by organizations. These include network DLP, which is used to monitor data in transit, endpoint DLP to protect data on end user devices, cloud DLP to secure data in cloud environments, and email DLP to control the sharing of sensitive information via email.

The DLP solutions typically offer key capabilities like data identification and classification to identify what sensitive data exists and where it is located, continuous monitoring of data to detect any policy violations or suspicious activities, and action enforcement to block, encrypt, quarantine, or alert on unauthorized data handling.

Implementing a successful DLP strategy requires following several best practices. Organizations need to begin by identifying and classifying their sensitive data and defining clear objectives and policies that outline acceptable data handling practices. Encryption should be used to protect sensitive files, and access controls should be enabled to limit who can view or modify sensitive data. Monitoring data movement and access is essential for detecting potential breaches or policy violations. Educating employees about data security policies and best practices to be followed plays a crucial role in minimizing data loss incidents. Finally, it is important to conduct regular security audits and reviews to assess the effectiveness of the DLP strategy and identify any weaknesses for improvement.

Auditing and monitoring

Auditing and monitoring are indispensable components of a robust data security framework and play a critical role in ensuring the effectiveness of security controls. When it comes to the effectiveness of encryption, there are specific aspects that need to be monitored. It is important to ensure proper implementation of encryption algorithms and protocols by verifying that strong and up-to-date methods are being used. Handling of cryptographic keys is another aspect that must be regularly monitored to prevent any compromise. Adherence to encryption policies across the entire data lifecycle also needs to be monitored to ensure that data is protected consistently while in transit, at rest, or in use. Finally, security monitoring should also include detection of any attempts to bypass or tamper with encryption, which could indicate malicious activity or misconfigurations.

Auditing and monitoring must also encompass crypto-agility monitoring, which is the ability to detect and respond to the use of weak algorithms, deprecated protocol versions, and misconfigured cipher suites. Certificate expiration alerts should be set up to prevent service outages due to expired digital certificates. All certificates and cryptographic identities used across servers, applications, containers, and IoT devices should be tracked and governed to ensure that cryptographic trust is continuously validated.

Emerging trends in data security

The field of data security and encryption is constantly evolving, driven by advancements in technology and the emergence of new threats. Two significant developments poised to reshape this landscape are **post-quantum cryptography** (**PQC**) and **artificial intelligence** (**AI**).

Post-quantum cryptography

The advent of quantum computing presents a potential threat to many of the current encryption methods, including the widely used asymmetric algorithms like RSA and ECC. The speed at which quantum technology is progressing means that quantum computers could soon be able to break these algorithms by leveraging techniques such as Shor's algorithm. To counter this threat, researchers are actively working towards developing PQC, which involves creating new cryptographic algorithms designed to be secure against attacks from quantum computers. These algorithms are considered to be secure even against the computational power of quantum machines. Lattice-based cryptography is a promising area of research that uses mathematical structures called lattices for developing quantum-resistant cryptographic algorithms. These structures are believed to be resistant to quantum attacks and may offer potential alternatives to RSA and ECC. Another area of research is hash-based signatures, which rely on the security of cryptographic hash functions and are not vulnerable to quantum algorithms like Shor's algorithm.

Homomorphic encryption

As we discussed earlier in the chapter, homomorphic encryption allows computations to be performed on encrypted data without decrypting it. This capability could revolutionize the fields of cloud computing and data privacy. Homomorphic encryption allows operations to be performed on ciphertexts and generates an encrypted result. The result can be decrypted using the authorized keys to reveal the correct outcome without ever exposing the original plaintext data. This would be particularly beneficial when data is required to be shared with third-parties for processing. For instance, a user could upload encrypted data to a cloud for processing, and the CSP can perform computations on the encrypted data without ever seeing the actual content, thus ensuring data privacy. Homomorphic encryption is still in very early stages of development. One of the biggest challenges being faced is the high computational cost associated with performing operations on encrypted data, which, as of now, makes it impractical for real-world applications. However, homomorphic encryption holds great promise, and as improved and more efficient techniques are developed, it could find usage in privacy-preserving data analytics and secure outsourcing.

AI in data security

AI has already started playing a significant role in enhancing data security. AI technologies are being used for a variety of security applications, including threat and anomaly detection by analyzing patterns and identifying suspicious activities. AI is also being leveraged for **security orchestration and automated response** (**SOAR**), enabling faster and more efficient handling of security incidents. In the realm of data protection, AI can enhance data classification and governance by automatically categorizing information based on its sensitivity. Furthermore, AI is contributing towards the advancement of encryption techniques like adaptive encryption, which adjusts security levels based on detected threats, and homomorphic encryption by facilitating efficient computation on encrypted data. AI-powered behavioural analytics is also being used to improve access control by monitoring user activity and detecting anomalous behaviour. Neural cryptography is another emerging field where AI is being actively used to develop security solutions. Neural cryptography explores the use of artificial neural networks for encryption and cryptanalysis, offering new approaches to secure communications.

Conclusion

In this chapter, we explored the foundational concepts and diverse applications of encryption and data security within the broader context of information security. We examined the terminology and core principles of encryption, the fundamental differences between symmetric and asymmetric encryption algorithms, and the critical role of hashing in ensuring data integrity. We also discussed digital signatures and certificates for establishing trust and authenticity, and various encryption techniques for securing data across its lifecycle. Further, we delved into the complementary techniques of data masking and tokenization for protecting sensitive information and discussed the necessity of robust access control mechanisms and the strategies for preventing unauthorized data exfiltration through DLP techniques. Finally, we touched upon common cryptographic attacks and vulnerabilities in encryption implementations, as well as the evolving landscape of post-quantum cryptography and the role of AI in enhancing data security.

Encryption and data security are not merely technical implementations but foundational pillars upon which a resilient and secure information ecosystem is built. A comprehensive approach to data security requires a multi-layered strategy that integrates technical controls with robust security policies and fosters a culture of security awareness. As the threat landscape continues to evolve with the emergence of new technologies like quantum computing and AI, organizations must take proactive measures to safeguard their data. By embracing robust and contemporary data security strategies, organizations can ensure a more secure and trustworthy information system. In the next chapter, we will discuss and understand the foundational concepts of IAM and their practical implementations.

Exercises

1. Explain symmetric and asymmetric encryption techniques. Discuss their use in real-world applications for data security and how the two techniques complement each other to provide practical cryptographic solutions.
2. Distinguish between digital signatures and digital certificates.
3. Explain how asymmetric cryptography helps ensure data integrity and non-repudiation.
4. Discuss various stages of the data lifecycle and the cryptographic techniques employed to protect data at each of these stages.
5. Write a note on different types of cryptographic attacks and their mitigation measures.
6. What is post-quantum cryptography? Discuss the evolving trends in the field of cryptography.
7. Consider a secure web application handling financial transactions, such as a secure online payment platform. Choose and justify appropriate cryptographic algorithms (e.g., AES-GCM, ECDSA, Curve25519, etc.), suitable key sizes, modes of operation, and key management approach, including generation, rotation, and protection mechanisms. Consider both performance and security trade-offs.
8. Using OpenSSL or an equivalent cryptography tool, perform the following steps:
   a. Generate an asymmetric-key pair.
   b. Create a self-signed digital certificate.
   c. Use the certificate to establish a TLS connection between a local client and server.
   d. Inspect and record the cipher suites, key exchange mechanisms, and encryption algorithms negotiated during the connection.
   e. Verify the cryptographic standards used by the setup, such as TLS 1.3, AES-GCM, or ChaCha20-Poly1305.

Chapter 6
Identity and Access Management

Introduction

Identity and access management (**IAM**) is one of the fundamental pillars of information security. At its core, IAM is a framework designed to govern access to an organization's systems, applications, and networks. It entails assigning a unique digital identity to each entity, i.e., user or device, authenticating that identity, authorizing appropriate access to resources, and continuously monitoring and managing these identities in accordance with the organizational policies.

Over the years, the IAM landscape has transformed significantly. Increased adoption of cloud technology has reshaped the information environment, with identity emerging as the new security perimeter. The traditional network perimeter that was once protected by firewalls has dissolved with the advent of cloud adoption, distributed computing, and widespread remote working. Data and applications are no longer confined inside central data centers but are distributed across multiple cloud environments and are accessed from diverse locations and devices. The traditional security models that relied heavily on network perimeters and assumed trust within organizational boundaries have proved to be inadequate in addressing the security concerns of modern business operations. In Zero Trust networks, organizations operate in an environment of assumed breach where every access request must be explicitly verified and continuously monitored, regardless of the network location. In such an environment, the identity of an entity remains the only consistent element across all access points, emerging as a crucial control plane that redefines the concept of security perimeter. This paradigm shift has led to the development of sophisticated IAM solutions that can adapt to dynamic business needs while maintaining stringent security controls for Zero Trust.

Contemporary IAM solutions address many complex security challenges, including privileged access management, federated identity services, enforcing dynamic access control policies, and adhering to regulatory compliance requirements while maintaining usability and operational efficiency. With the integration of advanced authentication mechanisms, automated provisioning lifecycle management, and sophisticated access control models, IAM has evolved from a basic security function into a strategic business enabler that balances security requirements with operational demands. NIST SP 800-63 on digital identity management provides a comprehensive framework for using and managing digital identities securely, ensuring both usability and trustworthiness. Several other frameworks and standards, such as the **Identification, Authentication, and Access Control** (**IA/AC**) controls in NIST SP 800-53, ISO/IEC 27001, and the CIS Controls, also provide authoritative guidance for implementing IAM programs aligned with established industry best practices.

Structure

In this chapter, we will discuss the following topics:

- Access control and information security
- Managing identification and authentication
- Multi-factor authentication
- Adaptive authentication
- Identity management techniques and protocols
- Federated identity management
- Authentication, authorization, and accounting protocols
- Architectural security models
- Access control models
- Role-based access control
- Contemporary solutions and emerging trends

Objectives

The objective of this chapter is to explore various foundational concepts of IAM and their practical implementations. By the end of this chapter, you will be able to critically analyze the interplay between access control and the core principles of information security. You will gain a clear understanding of the access control process, identity registration and proofing, various identification techniques, and authentication protocols. You will be able to appreciate the importance of **single sign-on** (**SSO**) and **federated identity management** (**FIM**) in reducing IAM vulnerabilities and enhancing user experience. You will be able to distinguish between **security assertion markup language** (**SAML**), **open authorization 2.0** (**OAuth 2.0**), and **OpenID Connect** (**OIDC**) protocols and the scenarios in which to use each of these. You will also be able to understand various architectural security and access control models and their application in the design and development of IAM solutions.

Access control and information security

The foundation of effective access control rests upon the core principles of information security, i.e., confidentiality, integrity, and availability, also known as the **CIA triad**. These principles provide the conceptual framework for understanding how access control mechanisms should be designed and implemented for safeguarding sensitive information and maintaining operational integrity.

To ensure confidentiality, information must be protected from unauthorized access, use, or disclosure. This is ensured by implementing access controls that enforce restrictions on who can view or retrieve sensitive information. Users are granted access only to the information explicitly required for their tasks, and merely for the duration it is needed. Integrity is ensured by implementing access controls that limit who can modify, create, or delete data, and under what circumstances, thus preventing unauthorized alteration. While access controls primarily focus on confidentiality and integrity, indirectly, they support availability as they are designed in such a way that legitimate access to authorized users is not hindered, and they have timely, reliable, and uninterrupted access to information and information systems whenever needed. However, a persistent challenge is encountered in striking the right balance between robust security controls and practical usability. Overly restrictive access controls can hamper business operations and impede productivity, while inadequate controls can expose organizations to unwarranted security risks. By following the **principle of least privilege (PoLP)** and carefully controlling access to resources, organizations can maintain the confidentiality and integrity of sensitive information while ensuring that legitimate users retain the access necessary to perform their job functions effectively.

The evolving threat landscape, additionally, demands a dynamic approach to information security. The traditional static and rigid access control mechanisms may not be adequate to protect against sophisticated threats like polymorphic malware and **advanced persistent threats** (**APTs**). This calls for the development of adaptive and context-aware access control mechanisms, which dynamically adjust permissions based on real-time risk assessment and changing user context. Such dynamic access controls are essential for maintaining security without unduly impeding user activity.

Access control process

The access control process involves the following foundational steps that are critical for establishing an effective access control system:

1. **Identification and classification of data**: This is the initial and most crucial step that entails gaining a comprehensive understanding of the organization's digital assets. It requires identifying different data types, ascertaining their storage locations, and assessing their sensitivity levels. Data owners and data custodians are identified, and classification levels are mapped to policies and labels that help define access controls, **data loss prevention** (**DLP**) rules, and encryption requirements. Data classification is a prerequisite to effective access control, as it helps in choosing the right access control model and defining appropriate policies.

2. **Selecting an access control model**: Once data has been classified, the next step is to select an appropriate access control model. Common models include **role-based**

access control (RBAC), **attribute-based access control** (ABAC), **discretionary access control** (DAC), and **mandatory access control** (MAC). We will discuss these models in the following sections of this chapter. The selection of a model depends on a variety of factors, including the nature of the data being protected, the granularity desired, and the operational flexibility required.

3. **Defining policies and roles**: This step involves developing unambiguous and explicit rules that dictate who can access specific resources, under what conditions, and with what permissions. It includes listing all organizational functions and their associated responsibilities to identify necessary roles.
4. **Setting up access control mechanism**: This step involves the technical implementation of the chosen access control model. Once the policies and roles are defined, the access control system is configured to manage and enforce the rules based on the chosen model.
5. **Implementing authentication and authorization**: The final step in the access control process involves integrating robust authentication and authorization processes. While authentication verifies a user's claimed identity, authorization ensures that the authenticated user possesses the necessary rights to access specific resources.
6. **Monitoring and logging**: Once the access has been implemented, the access attempts, approvals, and denials must be continuously logged. This is essential to detect anomalous activities and policy violations.
7. **Access review and revocation**: Regular audits are conducted to ensure compliance and ascertain the effectiveness of the access controls. Access rights are reviewed periodically to ensure alignment with current roles and responsibilities, and adjusted or revoked as per business needs.

The access control process is inherently iterative, and these steps need not be followed in any sequential manner. The dynamic nature of organizations, evolving roles, new data, and emerging threats require these steps to be iterative and not a one-time activity. This iterative approach is essential for maintaining an adaptive and resilient security posture in the face of constant change.

Managing identification and authentication

The foundational elements of IAM revolve around a clear understanding and meticulous management of identification, authentication, authorization, and accountability. These are discrete, sequential processes within the IAM framework and act in concert to regulate access to systems and resources.

Identification is the process by which a subject requiring access to resources asserts its identity by providing a unique identifier. This typically involves furnishing unique credentials within the context of the organization. This is required during the initial account setup as well as every time an entity attempts to access any resource. Followed by identification is the authentication process, where the asserted identity is verified. This entails matching the user-supplied input with the previously stored information. Authentication helps validate that the user is indeed who they claim to be. During the authorization process, a successfully identified and authenticated subject is granted the appropriate level of access to resources based on predefined permissions and contextual factors. After access has been granted, session management and token lifetime/refresh techniques are used for monitoring and ongoing accountability. This ensures that the subjects use the access privileges appropriately, and any misuse or anomaly is detected and addressed promptly.

The **authentication, authorization and accounting** (**AAA**) processes are often referred to together as the AAA framework, with identification serving as a precursor to authentication. This is a comprehensive security framework where each component is interdependent, and weakness in any single link of this chain, be it flawed identification, weak authentication, or improperly configured authorization, can compromise the entire security posture of an organization.

Identity registration and proofing

The identity registration and proofing process prepares the foundation for all subsequent identity and access management activities. Identity registration is the initial act of creating a digital identity within an information system, and identity proofing is the process of verifying the claimed identity against real-world evidence. The rigor of identity proofing procedures must be commensurate with the level of trust and access privileges associated with the identity. For high-privilege accounts or access to sensitive resources, identity proofing may require enhanced verification procedures to establish trust in the digital interactions. The need for advanced proofing techniques is also necessitated due to the increased sophistication of identity fraud. With the exponential rise in identity theft and fraud, traditional document checks alone are not sufficient against modern threats like deepfakes. The identity proofing mechanisms must evolve from static verification to dynamic, real-time assessments to counter the increased sophistication of such advanced identity threats.

Further, regulatory compliance requirements also serve as a driving force for developing a robust identity proofing process. Regulations such as **know your customer** (**KYC**) and **Anti-Money Laundering** (**AML**) explicitly require businesses to verify customer identities to prevent illicit activities like money laundering or terror financing. Adherence to these guidelines requires customer due diligence and the use of trusted and reputable data stores, such as government databases or financial institutions, for verifying identities. Organizations also need to have a well-established identity lifecycle management process to regularly review and update the registered identities to ensure that they remain accurate and appropriate at all times. Periodic re-proofing of identities, especially for privileged users and those in high-risk roles, is essential to ensure that the identities remain valid over time. Additionally, strong governance over the **Joiner–Mover–Leaver** (**JML**) lifecycle should be ensured, i.e., proper identity proofing and onboarding of new users should be done, changes in roles or responsibilities of existing users must trigger timely access reviews and adjustments, and credentials of departing users must be promptly revoked.

The NIST SP 800-63 on *Digital Identity Guidelines* provides identity, authentication, and federation assurance levels to address different dimensions of trust in digital identity systems. Section 63A of the framework defines **Identity Assurance Levels (IALs)** that reflect the degree of confidence in the binding between a subject and their digital identity. IAL1 implies no identity proofing with minimal assurance, IAL2 is remote identity proofing with validated information, and IAL3 means in-person identity proofing with physical presence and strong verification of identity evidence. Organizations can select the appropriate IAL based on the risk associated with the data or system to be accessed.

Authentication factors

The NIST SP 800-63B provides comprehensive guidance on authentication and lifecycle management. It defines three **authentication assurance levels (AALs)** to measure the strength of the authentication process: AAL1, **single factor authentication (SFA)**; AAL2, **multi-factor authentication (MFA)** using secure authenticators; and AAL3, MFA with hardware-based authenticators and strong cryptographic protocols. The authentication factors are categorized primarily into three types based on the nature of the evidence they provide, i.e., something you know, something you have, and something you are. Modern authentication systems have expanded this categorization to include additional factors such as something you do and somewhere you are. Let us explore these authentication factors.

Type 1: Something you know

Knowledge-based authentication factors (something you know) are the most common and widely used form of authentication. This factor relies on information that should be known only to the legitimate user. Passwords are the most common example of this factor type. Use of passwords for authentication is popular due to their simplicity, low cost of implementation, and universal compatibility with existing systems and applications. However, it has significant inherent weaknesses that have become increasingly problematic, as threat actors have developed sophisticated techniques to attack password-based authentication. **Personal identification numbers (PINs)**, security questions, and passphrases are some of the other examples of knowledge-based authentication.

The main challenge with knowledge-based factors lies in the difficulty of creating and maintaining secrets that are both sufficiently complex and easy to recall. Users often choose passwords that are easy to remember, but these are also easy to guess and crack through automated attacks. *How often do we see people using dictionary words, personal information, and simple patterns as passwords and reuse them across multiple systems and applications?* These weaknesses are further exacerbated due to the proliferation of systems and applications that depend upon passwords for authentication, which results in password fatigue and poor password hygiene. As standard practice, for memorized secrets, one should use long passphrases (at least 12–14 characters in length), as longer phrases provide greater resistance to brute-force attacks. NIST SP 800-63B suggests that length and resistance to known-breach reuse are more effective security measures than traditional composition rules, such as forced combinations of symbols, numbers, and uppercase alphabets. These tend to reduce usability without significantly improving protection.

Type 2: Something you have

This is a possession-based factor that validates a user's identity by requiring them to possess a specific physical item or device that is known to belong to them. Possession factors add a physical layer of security, making it difficult for malicious actors to gain unauthorized access without the physical device. When combined with knowledge-based factors in MFA, they substantially reduce the likelihood of credential compromise. Common examples of possession-based factors include hardware tokens that generate **one-time passwords** (**OTPs**), hardware security keys, and smart cards containing user information. Mobile devices are frequently used as possession factors, receiving OTPs via SMS messages, push notifications or generating codes through authenticator applications like *Google Authenticator*, *Authy*, or *Microsoft Authenticator*.

Hardware security tokens provide cryptographically strong authentication mechanisms that are highly resistant to remote attacks. These devices typically generate time-synchronized OTPs or respond to cryptographic challenges from authentication servers, providing proof of possession without transmitting long-term secrets over insecure communication channels. Smart cards are devices that can securely store cryptographic keys and digital certificates while providing standardized interfaces for authentication protocols such as **public key infrastructure** (**PKI**) and **Fast Identity Online** (**FIDO**). The security of smart card-based systems depends on the tamper-resistant properties of the card hardware and the secure implementation of cryptographic operations within the card's secure element.

Mobile devices are used as possession-based authentication factors through the use of SMS-based OTPs and mobile authenticator applications. While SMS-based authentication is a convenient way for delivering time-sensitive authentication codes, it suffers from various security weaknesses related to SIM swapping attacks, SMS interception, and vulnerabilities in mobile communication networks. To overcome these weaknesses, mobile authenticator applications that implement cryptographically secure time-based or challenge-response authentication mechanisms locally on the device should be preferred. The software-based authenticator applications implement standard protocols such as **time-based OTP** (**TOTP**) or **Hash-based message authentication code** (**HMAC**) **based OTP** (**HOTP**) algorithms. The HOTP algorithm generates OTP by applying an HMAC function to a shared secret and a counter. The TOTPs are a variant of the HOTP algorithm in which the moving factor is derived from the current time rather than a counter, ensuring codes expire within a short interval. While the software-based authenticators provide a stronger authentication mechanism as compared to the SMS-based solutions, it is important to understand that the security of the software-based authenticators depends on the security of the underlying mobile device platform and the secure implementation of cryptographic operations within the application.

Type 3: Something you are

Also known as biometrics, this type of authentication factor provides identity verification based on unique physiological or behavioural characteristics of the users. Physiological biometrics include fingerprint scan, facial recognition, iris scan, retina scan, handprints, and speech patterns. Behavioural biometrics leverage patterns in user behaviour such as typing rhythm, mouse movement patterns, or gait analysis. Biometric factors offer a significant advantage over knowledge and possession-based factors since they are inherently tied to individuals and cannot be easily transferred, shared, or stolen. However, biometric authentication can present challenges related to privacy, permanence, and accuracy due to the statistical nature of biometric matching algorithms.

Physiological biometrics rely on measurable physical characteristics that are unique to each individual and relatively stable over time. Fingerprint recognition is the most widely used form of biometric authentication since it offers a good balance of accuracy, convenience, and cost-effectiveness. With the advancements in image recognition technology, facial recognition is also commonly used for biometric authentication. However, both fingerprint scan and facial recognition systems can be vulnerable to spoofing attacks that use artificial fingers, photographs, or videos and, therefore, may require liveness detection mechanisms for high-security applications. Among the biometric systems, iris recognition is one of the most accurate forms of authentication. Iris recognition systems take advantage of the complex and unique patterns present in the human iris to achieve low false acceptance and false rejection rates and are relatively resistant to spoofing attacks.

Other, not-so-common biometrics systems include voice recognition systems that analyze speech patterns and vocal characteristics to verify a speaker's identity and behavioural biometrics systems that analyze patterns in user behaviour, such as typing rhythm, mouse movement patterns, or gait analysis for authentication. The behavioural biometric systems typically have lower accuracy than physiological biometric systems and are more susceptible to environmental factors and changes in user behaviour over time.

While biometric authenticators provide convenience and resistance to credential sharing, they introduce unique challenges. If biometric traits are compromised, they cannot be rotated and hence require strong template protection mechanisms to prevent theft or misuse of the biometric data. Revocation of biometrics is also inherently difficult, as an individual cannot change their fingerprint or iris pattern. To mitigate these risks, biometric authentication should be paired with device-bound secure hardware systems such as **Trusted Platform Module (TPM)** that store and process biometric templates locally, ensuring that raw biometric data never leaves the user's device.

Multi-factor and adaptive authentication

Each of the preceding types of authentication mechanisms has its own strengths and weaknesses. The increased sophistication of authentication attacks in the ever-evolving threat environment implies that organizations can no longer depend on a single authentication mechanism to protect their applications, especially those facing the internet. To counter these advanced threats, MFA and adaptive authentication techniques are employed.

Multi-factor authentication

MFA requires users to provide two or more different types of authentication factors to gain access to a system or account. For instance, combining password authentication (something you know) with mobile authenticator-based OTP (something you have) significantly increases security by making it much more difficult for an attacker to compromise an account. This layered approach makes it substantially harder for an intruder to overcome multiple authentication mechanisms as compared to a single factor. However, to have the desired effect, it must be ensured that the authentication factors are from different types, i.e., knowledge-based, possession-based, and biometric authentication. For instance, using a combination password and PIN for authentication is not considered MFA as both are knowledge-based factors.

It is important to adopt a risk-based approach and implement suitable MFA methods based on the assessed risks. For high-risk and sensitive environments, organizations should prioritize phishing-resistant MFA over the traditional OTP or push-based methods. Phishing-resistant MFA technologies such as FIDO2/WebAuthn authenticators or smart card–based credentials like **Personal Identity Verification** (**PIV**) and **Common Access Card** (**CAC**) use cryptographic challenge–response mechanisms bound to specific devices and relying parties, making them resistant to credential replay and **man-in-the-middle (MitM)** attacks.

Adaptive authentication

A persistent challenge in authentication is the inherent trade-off between security strength and user friction. Increasing the number of authentication factors or the complexity of the login process can make access more cumbersome, which increases the risk of *MFA fatigue* and may lead to increased attempts to bypass security. Adaptive authentication based on anomaly detection, rate limits, and number matching seeks to mitigate this by dynamically adjusting authentication requirements based on a real-time assessment of user behaviour and contextual factors. It leverages **machine learning** (**ML**) algorithms and **artificial intelligence** (**AI**) to analyze numerous data points, such as user behaviour, location, time of day, device type, and other contextual information, to assign a risk level to the login request. If the login appears risky, the system steps up authentication, and the user is prompted for an additional authentication factor. For the logins that are considered less risky, the system minimizes unnecessary authentication friction. This enhances the user experience by minimizing unnecessary MFA prompts, thus reducing *MFA fatigue* and improving security without compromising the user experience.

Identity management techniques and protocols

Effective identity management relies on a suite of interconnected systems and protocols that streamline access and enable secure interactions across diverse environments. The identity management models can be broadly categorized into two categories; centralized and decentralized or federated. These systems have their own advantages and challenges. While centralized systems offer simplicity in management, they can become a source of a single point of failure. On the other hand, the decentralized or federated systems offer greater resilience and flexibility, but there can be challenges to trust management and data privacy.

Single sign-on

SSO is an authentication method that enables users to securely access multiple systems, applications, and websites using a single set of login credentials. This is accomplished by establishing trust relationships between **identity providers (IdPs)** and service providers, which enables secure sharing of authentication assertions across organizational boundaries and eliminates the need for repetitive logins without compromising security. Contemporary SSO implementations typically rely on standard protocols such as SAML, OIDC, or OAuth 2.0 for secure communication between IdPs and relying parties. SAML is the most widely adopted web SSO protocol in enterprise environments, enabling organizations to federate identities across on-premises and cloud-based applications. For modern applications and **application programming interface (API)**, OIDC and OAuth 2.0 are the preferred standards as they provide lightweight authentication and authorization mechanisms that integrate well with mobile and web services.

The SSO systems provide streamlined authentication, enhanced security, improved user experience, and compliance monitoring. They help in implementing consistent security policies across the connected applications and facilitate visibility into user access patterns and behaviours. They also facilitate the implementation of advanced security controls such as risk-based authentication, adaptive access controls, and automated threat detection and response. While streamlining security, the centralized nature of SSO systems creates risks for security management, as a compromise of the central authentication system could potentially provide attackers with access to all the dependent applications and systems. This necessitates robust protection of the SSO infrastructure using strong protective and detective security controls. To enhance security, the systems should be hardened by using signed and encrypted assertions, enforcing strict audience and recipient restrictions, setting short token lifetimes, enabling replay protection, and continuously monitoring IdP activity for anomalies.

Lightweight Directory Access Protocol

The **Lightweight Directory Access Protocol (LDAP)** is a standardized protocol used for querying and modifying directory services. LDAP directories store information about users, groups, devices, and network resources that are used in access management. Its primary function is to access and maintain distributed directory information services to facilitate user authentication, authorization, and resource management.

The LDAP architecture functions around three main components: the LDAP server, the LDAP client, and the **directory information tree** (**DIT**). The server stores and manages the directory data and processes requests received from the clients. The LDAP client initiates a connection to the server to query or modify directory information. The DIT represents the hierarchical structure of the directory that organizes entries in a tree-like format. Each entry within the DIT represents a single object, such as a user, a group, or a device, and contains a set of attributes that describe that object. Once connected, an LDAP client can perform a variety of operations on the directory, including search, compare, add, delete, or modify.

LDAP facilitates seamless interoperability among different systems and applications, allowing them to work together in a coherent manner. It is extensively used in authentication and authorization systems for verifying user credentials and managing access control. Organizations also leverage LDAP to maintain a single, centralized directory of users, groups, and resources. The centralized directory services help simplify administration and enhance security by providing a single source of truth for identity management. LDAP is also commonly used to manage email and contact directories and store information about network resources, facilitating efficient resource management and access control.

LDAP transmits credentials and directory data in clear text and is therefore insecure on untrusted networks. It is therefore essential to use secure communication channels such as LDAP over SSL/TLS (LDAPS) or LDAP with STARTTLS/TLS when using directory services over untrusted networks. Many enterprises use **Active Directory** (**AD**) or other LDAP-compatible directories as the central repository for managing user identities, groups, and access permissions. Effective governance of these directories is essential and entails careful schema management and thoughtful group design. Schema management ensures that the objects and their attributes remain consistent and secure. This prevents unauthorized or accidental modifications. Group design helps structure access rights, enforces the PoLP, and enables consistent access control across the organization.

Kerberos

Kerberos is an authentication protocol that employs symmetric-key cryptography to provide strong mutual authentication between a client and a server in distributed network environments. It is the primary authentication protocol used within the domain context in modern AD environments. The protocol relies on **service principal names** (**SPNs**) to identify services and requires strict clock synchronization across systems. It provides secure authentication over insecure networks by eliminating the need to transmit passwords during the authentication process. Instead of using long-term secrets, Kerberos uses a trusted **Key Distribution Center** (**KDC**) to issue time-limited tickets that establish the identity of users and services throughout the network.

The Kerberos authentication process is depicted in *Figure 6.1*. It involves the following steps:

1. The user requiring access to a service initiates a request to the authentication server, which is part of the KDC.
2. The authentication server authenticates the user, and upon successful authentication, issues a **ticket granting ticket** (**TGT**) encrypted with a key derived from the user's password.
3. The user decrypts the TGT and presents it to the **ticket granting server** (**TGS**), also part of the KDC, to obtain service-specific tickets for accessing network resources.
4. The TGS verifies the TGT and issues a service ticket for accessing the required service.
5. The user then presents the service ticket to the server, providing the service, which validates the service ticket and grants access.

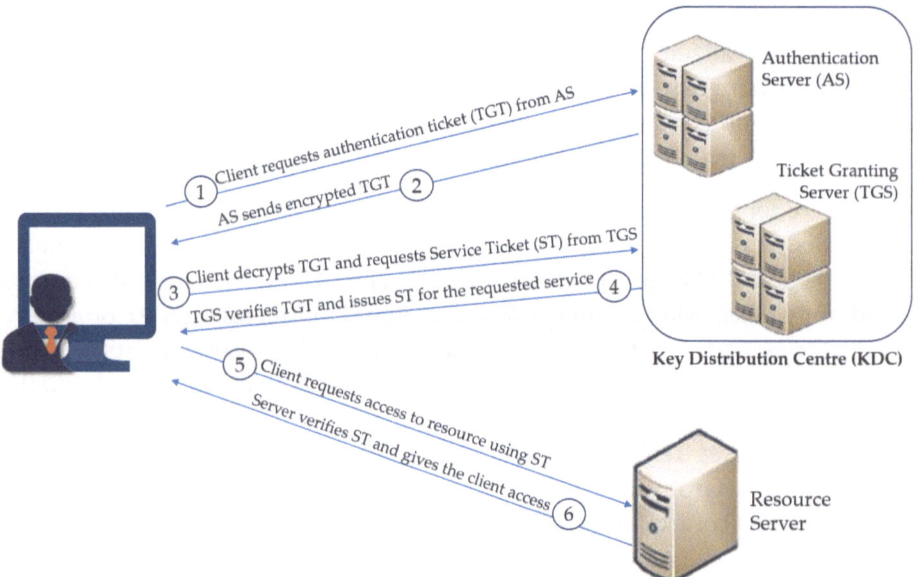

***Figure 6.1**: Kerberos authentication*

Kerberos authentication relies on symmetric encryption algorithms and shared secrets managed by the KDC. All network entities, including the KDC, share symmetric-keys that are used to encrypt and decrypt authentication messages and tickets. This ensures efficient cryptographic operations along with strong security. While the time-sensitive nature of Kerberos tickets provides inherent protection against replay attacks, it is vulnerable to forged tickets and kerberoasting attacks. The kerberoasting attack involves offline cracking of Kerberos service tickets of service accounts with weak passwords. Enforcing strong service account credentials, using **group managed service accounts** (**gMSAs**), and configuring services to use AES-only encryption can help mitigate the weakness to a large extent.

Federated identity management

With the proliferation of online services and applications, there is a need for organizations to grant access to resources across disparate systems and applications beyond organizational boundaries. Identity federation provides solutions to enable this seamless access, facilitating collaboration while maintaining security. FIM establishes a trusted relationship between different organizations and third-party entities, enabling users to access resources and services provided by external organizations using mutually trusted credentials. This trusted relationship enables the sharing of identities and the authentication of users across different domains. The primary benefit of FIM is that a user can authenticate to one domain and then access resources in other domains without the need to perform a separate login process. This effectively facilitates cross-domain SSO, and for this reason, FIM is often referred to as federated SSO. Reliable operation of federated systems requires robust management of the underlying dependencies, such as metadata exchange to synchronize trust configurations, regular rotation of certificates and signing of keys to maintain cryptographic assurance, and careful handling of clock skew to handle time-sensitive token validation. In addition, federated tokens must be validated rigorously to prevent any misuse or acceptance of forged assertions.

The key components of FIM include an IdP, the entity responsible for authenticating users and issuing authentication tokens, and a service provider or relying party that controls access to the requested resources and relies on the IdP to verify the user's identity. The IdP and service provider have formal agreements that define the trust relationship and information exchange protocols between them. When a user initiates a login into a service provider, instead of directly authenticating the user, it redirects the request to the IdP. The IdP authenticates the user and, upon successful authentication, issues a secure token using open identity federation standards like SAML, OAuth, or OIDC back to the service provider. Since the IdP and service provider have a trust relationship, the service provider trusts this token and grants the user access to the requested resource. The following figure shows the identity federation process:

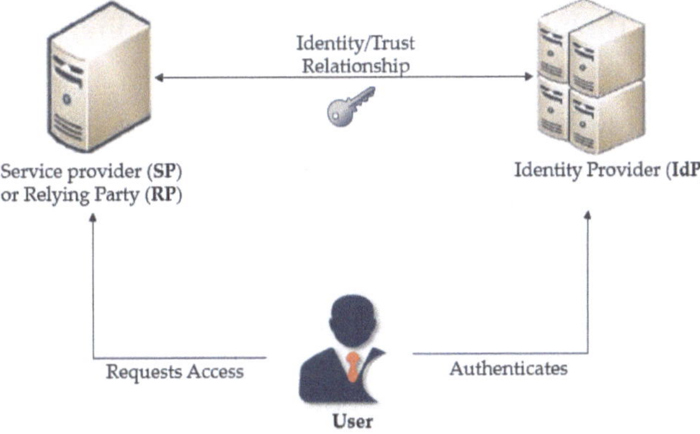

Figure 6.2: *Identity federation*

Security assertion markup language

SAML is an open standard for identity federation designed for exchanging authentication and authorization data between the IdP and service provider. It is mostly used in web-based authentication as it relies on using the browser agent to broker the authentication flow.

The fundamental components of SAML include the following:

- **SAML assertions**: These are XML-based statements that provide information about a user's identity, authentication status, and authorization attributes. These are issued by IdPs and are used to securely share authentication and authorization data with service providers. There are three primary categories of assertions: authentication assertions, attribute assertions, and authorization decision assertions.
- **SAML bindings**: These are mechanisms that define how SAML messages are exchanged between different entities, detailing how authentication requests and responses are delivered using standard communication protocols. Some of the common SAML bindings are **Hypertext Transfer Protocol** (**HTTP**) redirect binding, HTTP post binding, HTTP artifact binding, and **Simple Object Access Protocol** (**SOAP**) binding. Each binding serves a specific purpose and is selected based on factors such as security, transport protocol, and the capabilities of the systems involved.
- **SAML profiles**: These are predefined combinations of protocols, assertions, and bindings tailored for real-world use cases. Common SAML profiles include web browser SSO, single logout, attribute sharing, attribute query, and IdP discovery profiles.
- **SAML flows**: These are the steps required to complete the authorization and authentication process. SAML flows can be service provider-initiated or IdP-initiated. The service provider-initiated flow is typically triggered when an end user tries to access a resource or sign in directly on the service provider. In case of an IdP-initiated sign-in flow, the IdP initiates a SAML response that is redirected to the service provider to assert the user's identity.

SAML is extensively used in enterprise SSO systems due to its robust security features and compliance capabilities. It supports digital signatures, encryption, and strong access control policies, making it highly secure and compliant with industry regulations. It provides identity verification, secure authentication, and protection against interception through TLS and HTTP bindings. However, the security of a SAML deployment depends not only on the protocol itself but also on its implementation. Assertions should always be signed, and unsigned responses must be avoided. Where feasible, the post binding method, which offers stronger protection as compared to redirect or artifact methods, should be enforced. Replay protections, such as enforcing expiration times and one-time-use identifiers, are also essential to prevent token reuse. In addition, since SAML is an **Extensible Markup Language** (**XML**)-based protocol, it is inherently sensitive to issues like canonicalization errors and signature wrapping attacks. To mitigate these risks, organizations should use only vetted SAML libraries.

Open authorization

OAuth is an open-standard authorization protocol that allows unrelated servers and applications to securely permit authenticated access to their assets without requiring the user to share their actual login credentials. The primary focus here is on authorization rather than on authentication. OAuth 2.0 is an evolved version of OAuth that provides a simpler, more flexible, and more secure authorization as compared to OAuth and is particularly well-suited for mobile applications.

The architectural components of OAuth include the following:

- **Resource owner (user)**: The end user who owns the protected data and is authorized to grant access permissions.
- **Client**: This is the application or service that requests access to the data.
- **Authorization server**: The authorization server authenticates the user and issues the access tokens, ensuring that only authorized clients receive tokens.
- **Resource server**: The server or application that holds the user's protected data. It grants access to the data only when presented with a valid access token.

OAuth is widely used for identity and access management in a variety of scenarios, particularly in third-party integrations for delegated access, microservices communication, mobile and desktop applications, third-party login integration, and API authorization. It is primarily an authorization framework that decouples authentication from authorization, implying that OAuth does not authenticate the user's identity itself but delegates the permission for a client to access specific resources on the user's behalf. It provides secure delegated access and is preferred in scenarios where applications need limited, secure access to user data without handling sensitive login credentials.

OAuth defines multiple authorization grant types, and organizations need to select the most appropriate type to balance security and usability. Use of the Authorization Code grant with **proof key for code exchange** (**PKCE**) is recommended for public and native applications, and the Client Credentials grant is considered suitable for service-to-service or **machine-to-machine** (**M2M**) communication. Legacy flows such as Implicit Flow and **Resource Owner Password Credentials** (**ROPC**) are now deprecated due to inherent security weaknesses, and their use is discouraged. Central to OAuth security is its token management. The access tokens should have short lifetimes to limit exposure, and refresh tokens that enable longer-term sessions must be rotated securely. Mechanisms like token binding or **Demonstration of Proof-of-Possession** (**DPoP**) are used to provide additional protection by ensuring that intercepted tokens cannot be reused. OAuth also supports fine-grained access control through scopes that define the resources or actions a client may request. Combined with user consent, scopes help enforce the PoLP to ensure that applications receive only the permissions explicitly granted.

It is important to note that OAuth itself does not provide authentication. For scenarios where asserting user identity is required, OIDC extends OAuth 2.0 by issuing ID tokens that authenticate users, thus bridging the gap between authorization and identity verification.

Open identity

OpenID is a protocol that simplifies user authentication by facilitating login to multiple applications using a single set of credentials provided by an OpenID provider. OIDC builds upon this concept and is used as an authentication layer directly above the OAuth 2.0 authorization protocol. OIDC standardizes user authentication by leveraging the existing OAuth 2.0 framework for authorization and adding functionalities for identity verification. It utilizes the standard message flows of OAuth 2.0 for providing identity services.

The OIDC framework includes an OpenID provider or IdP and a relying party or client. An OpenID provider is the entity that implements the OIDC and OAuth 2.0 protocols and is responsible for authenticating users. The relying party is an application that delegates its user authentication function to the OpenID provider or IdP.

The typical OIDC access flow is as follows:

1. The initial step is client registration. For any authentication to occur, the clients, i.e., web applications and services, must be registered with the OpenID provider.
2. When a user attempts to login to a resource through a client, it initiates an authentication request to the OpenID provider, specifying the requested scopes and the redirection endpoint.
3. The OpenID provider authenticates the user and seeks approval for sharing of specific data access scopes requested by the client.
4. Upon successful authentication and user consent, the OpenID provider issues an **Identity** (**ID**) token or access token. The ID token is a **JSON Web Token** (**JWT**) and contains verifiable assertions about the user's identity. The access token acts as a digital key permitting the client to retrieve resources on behalf of the user.
5. When the client receives the ID token, it validates the token to ensure its authenticity and integrity. If an access token is also issued, the client can use it to request further claims about the end user from the OpenID provider.
6. On successful validation, the client authenticates the user and grants access to the requested application or resource.

OIDC is explicitly designed to support native and mobile applications. It offers significant benefits by simplifying authentication and offloading the burden of user authentication from individual services. It provides enhanced security and improved user experience and, owing to its adaptability, is used in a wide range of applications, including mobile, TV console, and web applications. Secure implementation of OIDC requires careful handling of authentication artifacts. ID tokens must be rigorously validated, which entails checks for the issuer, audience, signature, and nonce to prevent token replay or forgery. Additionally, proper token management, including token generation, expiration, and its secure transmission, should be ensured to maintain the integrity and confidentiality of user identity information.

Authentication, authorization, and accounting protocols

AAA protocols provide standardized frameworks for managing network access control and resource usage monitoring in distributed environments. **Remote Authentication Dial-In User Service** (**RADIUS**), **Terminal Access Controller Access-Control System Plus** (**TACACS+**), and Diameter are three prominent AAA protocols, each with distinct characteristics and suitability for different network environments.

RADIUS

RADIUS is a standard networking protocol that provides centralized AAA management for users and devices connecting to a network service. It operates as a client-server protocol within the application layer, where network access servers such as routers and firewalls function as RADIUS clients that forward user-supplied credentials to a central RADIUS server for processing and response.

RADIUS provides an authentication function via access requests by verifying the identity of users or devices against a centralized database. Once authentication is successful, it determines the specific resources the user is permitted to access based on predefined policies and grants access according to user roles and permissions. The accounting function provides comprehensive logging by meticulously tracking and logging user activity, such as the number of logins, session duration, data usage, and resources accessed.

For secure deployment, RADIUS should be configured to use RadSec (RADIUS over TLS) to ensure that credentials and accounting information are protected in transit. In environments where RadSec is not feasible, other mechanisms must be implemented to secure the communication channels between clients and servers. RADIUS also supports attribute-based authorization through **vendor-specific attributes** (**VSAs**), which allow fine-grained access control based on user or device characteristics. Security can be further strengthened by chaining the RADIUS server to an IdP or MFA system to enforce additional verification before granting network access.

TACACS+

TACACS+ is an AAA protocol that offers enhanced security and more granular access control capabilities. It is an advanced proprietary protocol developed by *Cisco* that addresses limitations in earlier TACACS implementations and RADIUS capabilities. It provides more flexible authorization mechanisms and full encryption of communication between clients and servers. TACACS+ is now widely used in enterprise network environments for controlling administrative access to network devices such as routers, switches, and firewalls. It is typically used to enforce fine-grained command-level authorization, facilitating organizations to restrict the commands that individual administrators can execute on the network devices.

TACACS+ separates AAA functions, facilitating more flexible implementation and granular control over access decisions. Authentication and authorization can be configured independently or combined into a single step, providing greater flexibility. The accounting capability of TACACS+ provides detailed per-command logging of administrative activities on network devices, enabling organizations to maintain comprehensive audit trails to support security monitoring, compliance reporting, and forensic investigation.

Diameter

Diameter is a next-generation AAA protocol designed to address limitations and scalability issues in RADIUS while providing enhanced security and functionality for next-generation network services. It is specifically designed to support the demands of modern telecommunications networks such as **long-term evolution** (**LTE**) and **IP Multimedia System** (**IMS**) networks. Unlike RADIUS and TACACS+, this protocol is based on a **peer-to-peer** (**P2P**) architecture that allows either party in a communication session to initiate messages and relies on **Transmission Control Protocol** (**TCP**) and **Stream Control Transmission Protocol** (**SCTP**) for reliable message transmission.

Diameter protocol offers greater flexibility and enables more complex communication flows as compared to the client-server model. It provides enhanced scalability and reliability by employing server redundancy, load balancing, and automated failover techniques. For robust encryption and integrity protection, it uses **Transport Layer Security** (**TLS**) and **IP Security** (**IPSec**). Diameter protocol also supports enhanced policy control, dynamic rules, **quality of service** (**QoS**), and bandwidth allocation. The accounting and billing capabilities of Diameter include support for real-time charging, prepaid services, and complex billing models required in commercial service provider environments.

Architectural security models

Architectural security models are theoretical models that provide conceptual frameworks for designing robust and secure IAM systems. These models establish formal methods for implementing controls to enforce confidentiality and integrity. Security professionals need to have an understanding of these models as they provide the foundation for designing and evaluating access controls.

State-machine models

The state-machine models assume that if a system begins in a secure state and the security properties are preserved during all state transitions, then the system will remain secure regardless of the operations performed. These models are especially relevant when analyzing MAC systems where security policies are system-enforced rather than left to the discretion of users. The secure state concept is fundamental to other security models, including the *Bell-LaPadula* and *Biba models*.

Bell-LaPadula model

The Bell-LaPadula model is a foundational MAC model that addresses data confidentiality in multilevel security systems. It assigns security levels to both subjects and objects and prevents unauthorized disclosure of information by implementing strict rules about how subjects at different security levels can access objects with different classification levels. This model is particularly useful when developing security systems for government and military applications where protecting classified information from unauthorized disclosure is a primary concern.

The two core properties of the Bell-LaPadula model that ensure confidentiality are the Simple Security Property (no read up) and the Star Property (no write down). The Simple Security Property dictates that users cannot read information classified at a higher security level than their own clearance level. This prevents users from accessing information for which they are not authorized. The Star Property prevents subjects from writing information to objects at lower classification levels. This prevents higher security classification information from being inadvertently or maliciously leaked through lower classification channels. The model also supports DAC through the Discretionary Security Property, where access control is enforced through an access matrix that allows some level of DAC.

Biba model

The Biba model is a complementary model to Bell-LaPadula and addresses data integrity issues. It is designed to protect the accuracy and reliability of information by preventing data corruption due to errors or malicious intent. The Biba model finds application in financial systems, safety-critical controls, and data processing systems where information integrity is paramount.

The Biba model defines two primary integrity properties that complement the confidentiality properties of the Bell-LaPadula model. These are the Simple Integrity Property (no write-up) and the Integrity Star Property (no read-down). The Simple Integrity Property prevents subjects from modifying objects at higher-integrity levels than their own. This ensures that higher-integrity information cannot be corrupted by a less trustworthy subject. The Integrity Star Property dictates that a subject at a specific integrity level cannot read an object of lower integrity. This property prevents higher-integrity subjects from being contaminated by low-integrity data, thus protecting subjects from being influenced by potentially unreliable or corrupted information. There is a third property called the Invocation Property, which ensures that a process from a lower integrity level cannot request higher access and can interact only with subjects at an equal or lower integrity level.

Figure 6.3 represents the complementary relationship between the Bell-LaPadula and Biba security models:

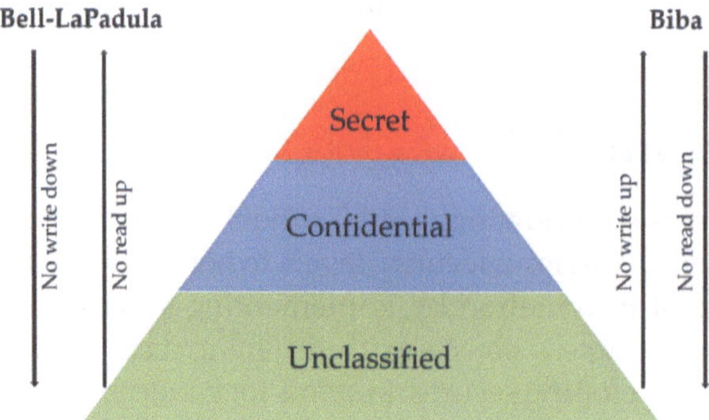

Figure 6.3*: Bell-LaPadula and Biba models*

Clark-Wilson model

The Clark-Wilson model is an integrity model that builds upon the Biba model and protects the integrity of information by preventing authorized users from making unauthorized changes to data, thereby preventing errors and fraud. The model restricts direct data manipulation and requires data to be accessed and modified only through a set of authorized programs. This ensures that the transactions are well-formed and adhere to specified rules and constraints. The model also enforces strict separation of duties, assigning different critical tasks to different individuals. It prevents any single individual from completing entire business transactions independently. This reduces the risk of fraud and malicious activities, as no single individual has complete control over a sensitive operation.

Information flow model

While the basic state-machine models function on the premise that a system is secure if all the states in which it operates are secure, the information flow model is based on the principle of data flows and consists of objects, state transitions, and lattice states. It tracks data movement within an information system with the objective of preventing any unauthorized data propagation. Unlike the traditional models like Bell-LaPadula and Biba, which focus on applying controls at the point of access, the information flow model examines the environment from the perspective of data being exchanged between various entities. The primary objective is to prevent unauthorized and insecure flow of information in any direction.

The security controls, in this model, are so designed that information transfer cannot take place without sufficient risk mitigation, especially when the information propagates from a higher security level object to lower security level objects. This is achieved by defining lattice-like structures to represent security relationships between different information categories and ensuring that data propagates only upwards, i.e., from a lower security context to a higher security context.

Non-interference model

As the name suggests, the non-interference model is a security model designed to enforce confidentiality by ensuring that the actions at a higher security level of an information system do not interfere with lower security levels. This model focuses on what a subject knows about the states of the system rather than on the flow of information. The non-interference property ensures that the behaviour of a higher security level visible to the subjects at a lower security level remains identical regardless of what actions are performed at the higher level. This ensures that users of the lower security context are not able to deduce any information from the activities at the higher levels, effectively ensuring that secret inputs do not implicitly leak any information to publicly observable outputs.

Brewer and Nash model

The Brewer and Nash model, also known as the **Chinese Wall model**, is a dynamic access control model developed to address conflict of interest issues. In this model, a system is structured into three levels of abstraction: objects (individual data items), datasets (collections of objects), and conflict classes. A subject is allowed to make the initial decision of accessing a dataset, but once that decision is made, access to other conflicting resources is blocked to prevent any conflict of interest. This is achieved by defining dynamic read and write access rules. The read rule ensures that a subject can read an object only if they have never read any object from a conflicting dataset. This rule ensures that a single user does not breach the proverbial Chinese Wall by accessing information from conflicting classes. The write rule defines that a subject can write to an object only if they have permissions to read that object, and they have not read an object from a dataset other than the one for which write access is requested. This prevents collaborative breaches by multiple subjects.

Graham-Denning and Harrison-Ruzzo-Ullman models

While the preceding security models define the rules of engagement, they do not delve into the specifics of implementation. The Graham-Denning model specifies how subjects and objects should be securely created and deleted and how specific access rights should be assigned. The Harrison-Ruzzo-Ullman model is an extension of the Graham-Denning model that focuses on the safety and security of information systems, particularly concerning the integrity of access rights. It outlines how access rights can be changed and how subjects and objects should be created and deleted.

The following table lists the primary focus areas of various security models and maps their typical use cases:

Security model	Primary focus	Typical use cases
Bell-LaPadula	Confidentiality	Classified government systems, defence networks.
Biba	Data integrity	Financial systems, transaction processing, integrity-critical applications.
Clark-Wilson	Data integrity / well-formed transactions	Banking, ERP systems, and accounting systems.
Brewer and Nash model	Conflict of interest	Consulting firms, financial, audit, and advisory services.
Graham-Denning	Secure creation, deletion, and access control of subjects and objects	System design and OS-level security, foundational access control policies.
Harrison-Ruzzo-Ullman	Formal access control policy enforcement, safety analysis	Security analysis, verification of access control policies.

Table 6.1: Primary focus areas of security models and typical use cases

Access control models

Access control models are practical implementations of the architectural security models. These models define frameworks that dictate how permissions are granted or denied to subjects interacting with objects. There are different types of access control models, including mandatory, discretionary, role-based, rule-based, and attribute-based models.

Discretionary access control

The DAC model is the least restrictive access control model. It gives the resource owners complete control over the resources they own. This implies that resource owners have the complete authority to grant or revoke permissions. They can specify who can access which resources and under what conditions. DAC is generally implemented by establishing a resource hierarchy and defining **access control lists** (**ACLs**) to specify the access permissions.

The main advantage of DAC is its flexibility and ease of use. It empowers resource owners to manage access to their data without the need for central administration. This is particularly useful in collaborative and fast-paced environments where users need to enable and disable access frequently and quickly. This model is also fairly simple and straightforward to implement. Since users are familiar with their needs, they can directly control the access, doing away with the requirement of laying down elaborate policies.

However, flexibility also makes DAC significantly vulnerable. The decentralized nature and lack of adequate oversight may lead to the granting of excessive privileges, thereby increasing the probability of data leaks and unauthorized access. A major concern is that the permissions granted by an end user can be inherited by programs they execute. This effectively means that if a user inadvertently executes a malicious program, it could exploit the user's privileges to compromise the system and access sensitive information. A malware executing under a user's account inherits the same privileges as that user. To mitigate this risk, DAC is combined with application control and a whitelisting mechanism to restrict unauthorized code execution. Due to its discretionary nature, the DAC model requires active oversight, continuous monitoring, and regular audits to manage permissions effectively and identify any anomalies.

Mandatory access control

In the MAC model, policies are system-enforced based on preconfigured rules rather than by the users. The administrators or owners do not have the discretion to determine the access rights. The access decisions are based on security labels. Users are assigned clearance levels, and data is classified based on sensitivity. Access decisions are made on the basis of the clearance level of the user and classification of the data, as per the configured rules. This requires that each subject and object must have security labels associated with it for the system to make decisions.

The MAC model provides strict controls and is particularly useful in environments dealing with sensitive information, such as military, government agencies, and advanced research organizations, where security and confidentiality are of utmost importance. In enterprise and server contexts, MAC principles are implemented in technologies such as *SELinux* and *AppArmor*, which enforce fine-grained policies at the operating system level. However, these implementations are complex to author and maintain, and their deployment at scale requires careful planning and expertise. While MAC ensures consistency and minimizes human error, the biggest downside of this model is a lack of flexibility, which can pose challenges to collaborative tasks and the rapid response required during security incidents or emergencies. Therefore, to balance security with usability, organizations generally adopt RBAC, which provides a more adaptable access management model.

Role-based access control

The RBAC model assigns permissions to users based on predefined roles within an organization rather than directly to individual users. This approach simplifies administration and enhances security by aligning access privileges with job functions. The RBAC model defines permissions that are grouped into roles. Each role is granted a specific set of permissions that are necessary to perform the tasks associated with that role. Thereafter, individual users are assigned to the roles. A single user may be assigned to one or more roles depending on their job requirements.

The primary advantage of the RBAC model is its simplicity and scalability. As the users are grouped into roles based on access needs, provisioning and deprovisioning can be easily automated, reducing the administrative load. If a user needs access to organizational resources, he is added to one or more of the required roles. If there is a job change, he is simply added to or removed from a role group, which automatically adjusts his access permissions across all associated applications. The RBAC model also helps in implementing the PoLP by ensuring that users are given access to only what they need to perform their job functions. To achieve greater granularity in role assignment, the RBAC model can be augmented or used in conjunction with rule-based or ABAC models.

While RBAC has its benefits, it introduces other unique challenges. For instance, poorly designed role hierarchies can result in role explosion, where an excessive number of roles makes management unwieldy. Another challenge organizations encounter is role mining, the complex task of deriving appropriate roles from existing access patterns. To address these issues, structured role engineering should be ensured during the implementation of RBAC, and it should be followed by periodic role reviews to ensure that role definitions remain current, efficient, and aligned with the business needs.

Attribute-based access control

ABAC is a highly granular and flexible access control model that makes context-aware and risk-adaptable access decisions based on the attributes associated with the subject, object, environment, or the actions requested. Access decisions are made in real-time by analyzing these attributes. Any information that can be expressed as an attribute can be used for developing the access control policies, which can be adapted to an organization's specific needs and conditions. This flexibility makes ABAC particularly suitable for environments with diverse access control needs.

The attributes in the ABAC model are organized into different categories, such as subject attributes, object attributes, action attributes, and environmental attributes. The subject attributes include information like user identity, user role, clearance level, and departmental affiliations. The object attributes include classification, owner, and sensitivity of the object. Action attributes are the actions that a subject can perform on the object, such as read, write, or execute. Finally, the environmental attributes can be parameters like time, geo-location, or threat level, etc. When a user attempts to access a resource or application, the system evaluates the request based on a combination of these attributes and determines whether access should be granted or denied. Multiple attributes can be considered simultaneously to define fine-grained access control policies.

While ABAC provides for flexibility and granularity, it is a complex model to implement. It requires elaborate policies to define the multitude of attributes and rules, and a robust governance and management structure to govern and manage the access provisioning lifecycle. In practice, ABAC is often implemented through frameworks such as the **Extensible Access Control Markup Language** (**XACML**) or modern policy engines like **Open Policy Agent** (**OPA**) using the Rego language. While these enable expressive and fine-grained controls, they also introduce governance overhead to avoid policy sprawl and reduce the risk of misconfigurations. However, the advancements in cloud-native and access-control technologies have accelerated the adoption of ABAC-based IAM systems, as they offer enhanced security without adversely impacting the user experience.

Rule-based access control

Rule-based access control (**RuBAC**) model builds upon the attribute-based foundation of ABAC and introduces dynamic, context and risk-aware decision-making to adjust access permissions in real-time. It operates on if-then logic to make automated access decisions about who can access what resources, at what times, and under what circumstances.

The RuBAC model offers granular control and efficient administration. It facilitates defining a precise set of rules based on different attributes such as location, time of day, device type, and user actions to help achieve granularity. Once the rules are configured, the system automatically grants or denies access based on the predefined rules, doing away with the need for manual intervention, thus improving efficiency. The model provides adaptability and flexibility in implementing time-specific access permissions and vastly simplifies the user onboarding process. However, effective implementation of the RuBAC model requires meticulous planning, thorough testing, and careful implementation.

Contemporary solutions and emerging trends

Thus far in the chapter, we discussed the foundational concepts of IAM. Let us now explore some practical implementations and cutting-edge developments in the field.

Contemporary IAM solutions

The IAM technology has been constantly evolving to cater to the specialized needs and complex security challenges of modern organizations. In recent years, it has transformed rapidly to provide secure, scalable, and flexible access solutions. Specialized and sophisticated IAM solutions have been developed to counter the risks posed by increasingly potent cyber threats, while meeting the growing demand for a seamless user experience.

Privileged access management

Privileged accounts are prime targets of threat actors due to their elevated permissions to critical systems and sensitive data. A compromise of such an account can be catastrophic, resulting in widespread system compromise. **Privileged access management** (**PAM**) is an IAM solution that focuses on controlling and monitoring access to resources by privileged users and accounts.

A PAM system works on the PoLP and **just-in-time** (**JIT**) access. All privileged users are required to access critical systems and resources through the PAM system, which grants the bare minimum access permissions necessary for performing the required tasks. The access is granted for a limited duration, and all activity is monitored and recorded for audit purposes. This reduces the attack surface to a large extent.

The key components and functionalities of a PAM solution include the following:

- **Password vault**: This is a secure storage to store and manage secrets such as passwords, keys, and tokens. It also enforces the password policies and automates password rotation.
- **Session monitoring and recording**: It provides real-time insights into privileged user activities. This involves recording and analyzing user activities to detect any potential privilege abuse.
- **Least privilege enforcement**: It ensures that the elevated privilege is granted only when needed and for a strictly limited duration.
- **Credential rotation**: The password and key rotation process is automated to reduce the risk of compromise.
- **MFA**: Enforcing MFA for privileged user accounts further enhances security by making it difficult for threat actors to gain access to systems, even if the credentials are compromised.

Contemporary PAM solutions incorporate additional patterns and technologies to enhance security and usability. Credential brokers and ephemeral access models are often implemented to provide short-lived credentials or JIT privilege elevation to reduce the exposure window of sensitive accounts. PAM solutions are also integrated with secrets management platforms, such as cloud **key management services** (**KMS**) or Secret Manager, to centrally store and rotate credentials securely.

Identity governance and administration

Identity governance and administration (**IGA**) is a larger concept that goes beyond the scope of traditional IAM and encompasses governance and compliance requirements as well. While traditional solutions focus on the operational aspects of provisioning and controlling access, IGA stresses continuous monitoring, compliance, audit, and risk reduction. It provides a comprehensive view of all user identities and their access privileges across the organization. The primary objective of IGA is to ensure that all assets are protected from unauthorized access and that the organization consistently adheres to the regulatory compliance requirements.

The IGA solutions offer the following capabilities:

- **Centralized visibility**: IGA creates a single, authoritative view of access permissions and actions performed by users. This helps in promptly detecting any unauthorized access, policy violations, or ineffective controls that could pose a risk to the organization.

- **Automated workflows**: They streamline the process for users to request access to resources and simplify the approval process, reducing errors and manual overhead.
- **Automated provisioning and de-provisioning**: IGA automates the entire user provisioning and de-provisioning lifecycle, including onboarding, offboarding, and role changes, etc.
- **Permission management**: Administrators can precisely specify and verify what permissions users have for accessing various resources.
- **Access review**: It periodically carries out an automated review of access permissions to ascertain the appropriateness of access levels.
- **Segregation of duties (SoD)**: IGA solutions can detect risk-based access outliers and identify toxic combinations of permissions that could lead to policy violations or potential fraud by ensuring no single user has conflicting permissions.
- **Advanced analytics**: It provides insights into access privileges and actions performed to detect suspicious activities.

Identity as a service

The evolution towards cloud-based computing and proliferation of **software as a service** (**SaaS**) applications have led to widespread adoption of integrated identity services that provide comprehensive IAM capabilities through third-party providers, **identity as a service** (**IDaaS**) provides a cloud-based, centralized IAM solution for managing and authenticating user access to organizational resources. It allows an organization to outsource the operational tasks of its IAM solution to a specialized third-party provider, leveraging their expert capabilities and reducing administrative overhead.

IDaaS solutions provide comprehensive identity lifecycle management capabilities, authentication services, and authorization policy enforcement. They can integrate with diverse applications in varied environments, including on-premises, multi-cloud, and hybrid environments. This enables organizations to implement consistent identity and access management policies across their entire technology stack. The centralized nature of IDaaS facilitates the implementation of advanced security features such as risk-based authentication, behavioural analysis, and automated threat detection and response.

IDaaS solutions typically support standards such as **System for Cross-domain Identity Management** (**SCIM**) for automated user provisioning, JIT provisioning via SAML, or OIDC. While adopting IDaaS, organizations need to be aware of dependency risks and must cater to contingencies in case of non-availability of the IDaaS platform to ensure operational continuity. Planning for failover strategies and offline contingencies, such as cached credentials, is essential to ensure uninterrupted access to resources during service disruptions.

Identity and access management in cloud environments

Advancements in cloud technology and its widespread adoption have reshaped the IAM landscape. While the cloud environments offer unmatched flexibility and scalability, they also introduce unique challenges that require specialized strategies for effective IAM.

Implementing IAM across hybrid and multi-cloud environments is inherently complex. Each cloud has its own distinct IAM solution, which, if not managed cohesively, can lead to identity fragmentation and inconsistent policies, resulting in significant risks. The dynamic and distributed nature of cloud environments makes it difficult to maintain a unified view of identities and associated permissions. As a result, organizations may choose to grant excessive permissions to users to avoid hindering their activity. This may lead to access creep, increasing the risk of security breaches. Managing access permissions for machine and service identities across different clouds adds yet another layer of complexity. These identities require continuous monitoring and a dynamic approach to access management.

The cloud service providers offer robust cloud-native IAM solutions designed and optimized for their native environments. However, they still need to be meticulously implemented and managed to ensure comprehensive security.

The following best practices can be adopted for cloud-based IAM solutions:

- **Centralized identity management**: Consolidating identities, groups, and access permissions across diverse cloud ecosystems simplifies control, management, and governance.
- **Automated provisioning and deprovisioning**: Automating the user account lifecycle across cloud and on-premises environments for SaaS as well as legacy applications reduces manual overhead and enhances security by ensuring timely access revocation.
- **SSO**: Implementing SSO enables users to access multiple cloud applications with one set of credentials, improving user experience and reducing password fatigue.
- **MFA**: MFA enforces an additional layer of security. Adaptive MFA that dynamically adjusts authentication requirements based on risk scores can be used to further enhance the security of applications.
- **Use of temporary credentials**: Instead of using long-term access keys, temporary credentials obtained from an IdP should be used to access cloud resources. This would significantly reduce the risks associated with compromised static credentials.

Emerging trends

The emergence of new paradigms like AI, ML, blockchain, and **Internet of Things (IoT)** is redefining the IAM landscape. Sophisticated IAM solutions are being developed, as the traditional solutions have proved insufficient to address the unique challenges and complexities introduced by these modern technologies. Let us discuss some of the advancements in the IAM technology.

Password-less authentication

Password-less authentication is a verification method that eliminates the need for the good old password by leveraging more secure and user-friendly alternatives. These methods include biometrics, web authentication-based FIDO2, synced passkeys, mobile authentication apps, certificate-based smart cards, and pattern-based authentication, etc. The motivation for adopting password-less authentication is two-fold: enhancing security by mitigating password-related vulnerabilities and improving user experience by eliminating the burden of remembering and managing multiple complex passwords. This convergence of security and user convenience is accelerating the adoption of password-less authentication methods, so much so that we may see passwords being eliminated altogether in the near future.

FIDO2 and WebAuthn with device-bound passkeys have emerged as the most secure and phishing-resistant password-less authentication approaches. Synced passkeys maintain strong cryptographic protections while allowing users to authenticate seamlessly across devices. When adopting password-less authentication, it is also important to have robust fallback and recovery strategies to ensure continuity of access in case of device loss or failure.

Artificial intelligence and machine learning

AI and ML present both unique security challenges as well as enormous new capabilities for IAM. While the existing IAM systems find it challenging to define and manage identities of AI entities and control their access permissions, the use of AI/ML technology can significantly enhance the effectiveness and capabilities of IAM systems.

The ways in which AI/ML can help enhance the effectiveness and efficiency of IAM systems are as follows:

- **AI-driven threat detection and anomaly detection**: ML algorithms can learn normal patterns of user behaviour and quickly detect any anomalies pointing towards potential security risks.
- **User and entity behaviour analytics (UEBA)**: AI-powered UEBA baselines can be established for users and entities such as applications, service accounts, and APIs to detect anomalies efficiently.
- **Risk-based and adaptive authentication**: AI-enabled IAM systems can make decisions based on contextual factors by dynamically adjusting authentication requirements and prompting additional authentication factors only when necessary.
- **Enhanced monitoring of privileged sessions**: AI-driven systems can efficiently analyze privileged user activities, detect unusual actions, and provide real-time alerts for policy violations and privilege abuse.

- **Predictive identity security**: Predictive AI systems can identify patterns that typically precede attacks and predict security incidents even before they occur.
- **Autonomous response capabilities**: AI systems can provide autonomous response capabilities such as automatically adjusting authentication requirements, isolating compromised accounts, and temporarily restricting access of suspicious entities. However, AI/ML models are susceptible to model drift and bias, which can lead to inconsistencies over time. For high-impact actions, frequent human review should be ensured to validate or override automated decisions, and all model decisions should be logged for auditability, compliance, and forensic investigation.

Decentralized identity

Decentralized identity (**DID**) is a framework that leverages cryptography and blockchain technology for identity management. The DIDs of users are stored in distributed ledgers and secured cryptographically. The individuals retain control over their identity, shifting control away from centralized authorities to individuals and providing them with greater sovereignty over their data and digital identities. The DID framework comprises cryptographically secured **verifiable credentials** (**VCs**) that are issued by an issuing authority and contain claims about the user. Anyone who wishes to verify the credentials of the user can do so by using the issuer's public key. This allows individuals to prove their identity selectively without sharing the underlying data.

DID is still an emerging trend that signifies a move from identity management by organizations to identity sovereignty by individuals. The standards for DID are being developed under the **World Wide Web Consortium** (**W3C**), the international body responsible for defining core web standards. While the consortium has published the DID and VC specifications to promote interoperability across platforms and issuers, these are still maturing, and challenges remain around interoperability, scalability, and governance. However, the technology has the potential to significantly impact the way identities will be managed, shared, and verified in the future.

Identity fabric

Identity fabric or identity mesh architecture is an emerging architectural framework that provides a unified, decentralized approach to managing identities across complex, distributed IT environments, encompassing on-premises, hybrid, and multi-cloud setups. An identity fabric acts as a scalable, independent identity architecture forming an 'identity mesh' around an entire organization. It provides all entities in an organization with a single, streamlined point of access across all cloud and on-premises environments. Fundamentally, the framework allows identity to define the security perimeter, aligning with Zero Trust principles.

An effective identity fabric ensures consistent policy enforcement across heterogeneous environments, enables unified lifecycle orchestration for users and machines, and supports standardized protocols such as OIDC, SAML, and SCIM for interoperability. It extends governance to non-human identities and ensures that machine and workload identities are subject to the same rigorous controls as human users.

Conclusion

We began this chapter by discussing the interplay between access control and the core principles of information security. Thereafter, we delve into the foundational concepts of IAM, including the access control process, management of identities, and various authentication factors and protocols. We also discussed SSO, identity federation, and different access control models. Having understood the fundamentals, we went on to explore contemporary IAM solutions and future trends in the context of cloud and other emerging technologies such as AI/ML and blockchain.

Identity and access management systems have evolved significantly over the years. From simple password-based authentication mechanisms, the IAM systems have evolved into sophisticated frameworks that integrate identification, authentication, authorization, and accountability across diverse environments. With Zero Trust rapidly transforming security from a network perimeter-based approach to an identity-centric approach, the future holds great promise for the IAM technology. It would be characterized by increased automation, intelligent decision-making, and user empowerment. The evolving threat landscape and emerging technologies would require IAM systems to have enhanced predictive and automated response capabilities. Organizations would need to adopt solutions that can seamlessly manage identities across hybrid and multi-cloud environments and leverage AI/ML capabilities to detect anomalies and enforce dynamic context-aware access policies. The ultimate objective is to have sovereign, decentralized identities where the owner has full control over their personal data.

We saw how IAM has emerged as the center of gravity for digital security and how identity has become the de facto network perimeter. We now shift our focus towards network security. In the next chapter, we will cover various aspects of computer networking and network security, including wireless networks.

Exercises

1. Discuss how confidentiality, integrity, and availability, the core principles of information security, impact the design and development of IAM systems.
2. Explain the access control process and discuss the significance of identity registration and the proofing process in identity and access management.
3. What is identity federation? Explain SAML, OAuth 2.0, and OIDC open standards used for FIM.
4. What are the types of architectural security models? Discuss the Bell-LaPadula and Biba models and explain how they complement each other.

5. It is essential to have a clear understanding of the access control models to be able to design effective IAM systems. Discuss various access control models, their strengths and weaknesses, and their suitability for different scenarios and organizations.
6. Discuss how AI/ML can be leveraged to enhance the effectiveness and efficiency of IAM systems.
7. Design an IAM architecture for an enterprise whose workloads span across on-premises and multiple cloud environments. In your design, specify which SSO protocols you would use, the MFA method, how ABAC policies would be structured, and explain your PAM strategy. Provide justification for each choice based on security, scalability, and usability considerations.

Chapter 7
Network Security

Introduction

The digital world comprises a heterogeneous network of computers, servers, and routing devices that are networked for resource sharing and data exchange. These networks form the backbone of digital operations. Online services are hosted on systems connected to the internet and are accessed by users remotely. The ability to share information online, collaborate across geographical boundaries, and access distributed resources remotely forms the basis of modern commerce and governance.

While networks form the backbone of digital operations, their very ubiquity and pervasiveness make them a prime target of cyberattacks. The evolving threat landscape and the increased frequency of such attacks have made it imperative for organizations to adopt a strong network security posture. Any vulnerability in an organization's network can undermine even the most advanced endpoint security measures and expose critical systems to exploitation by attackers remotely. Therefore, it is important that information security professionals develop an in-depth understanding of computer networks and network security concepts to effectively secure interconnected systems and navigate the complexities of modern information systems.

This chapter introduces essential networking concepts relevant to security, including the **Open Systems Interconnection** (**OSI**) and **Transmission Control Protocol/Internet Protocol** (**TCP/IP**) reference models, which provide a structured framework for understanding data flow and control points across networks. Thereafter, key protocols at various layers are examined from a security perspective, followed by an overview of core network security components, including firewalls, proxy servers, **web application firewalls** (**WAFs**), **intrusion detection systems** (**IDS**), and **intrusion prevention systems** (**IPS**). These fundamentals form the basis for understanding secure network architecture design and the effective implementation of network security controls.

Structure

In this chapter, we will discuss the following topics:

- Network models and networking concepts
- TCP/IP models
- Transport layer protocol

- Network devices
- Core network security components
- Secure remote access
- Wireless security

Objectives

The objective of this chapter is to provide a comprehensive understanding of computer networking and network security concepts, equipping information security professionals with the theoretical knowledge and practical understanding necessary to design, implement, and maintain secure networks. By the end of this chapter, you will have a clear understanding of the OSI and TCP/IP network models. You will learn about various layers and protocols in each of these network models and their inherent security implications. You will also learn about the core network security components, such as firewalls, proxies, intrusion detection and prevention systems, and other devices that form the bedrock of network defense. You will also learn how to design secure networks and explore protocols and methodologies essential for safeguarding communication channels. Having gone through the chapter, you will be able to apply the theoretical knowledge to design, implement, and maintain secure and resilient communication networks, which is crucial for information security in the evolving threat landscape.

Network models and networking concepts

Before we go on to discuss network security, let us understand how computers and digital systems exchange data. In this section, we will first delve into the OSI and TCP/IP network models and then go on to discuss some important networking concepts that are essential for a thorough understanding of network security.

OSI model

The OSI model is a conceptual framework for network communications. It provides an open network architecture for vendors to develop networking products that can seamlessly integrate with the devices from other vendors. While the actual data exchange between computers or network devices happens over the physical medium, wired or wireless, the OSI model provides seven logical layers to facilitate network communication. The devices at each end of the communication channel communicate with each other at the corresponding layers using the protocols laid down in the model. These layers are numbered 1 to 7 from bottom to top and also given identifiable names based on their functionality. At each end, a layer communicates with the layers immediately above and below it. At the sender end, the data flows down the protocol stack, and a protocol header (maybe a footer as well) is added before it is passed on to the layer below. At the receiver end, the reverse happens. The data flows up the stack, and at each layer, the header is stripped before sending the data up the stack. In networking terminology, the process of adding the header information is called **encapsulation,** and removing it is called **decapsulation**.

The following figure represents the seven layers of the OSI model and the logical communication channels:

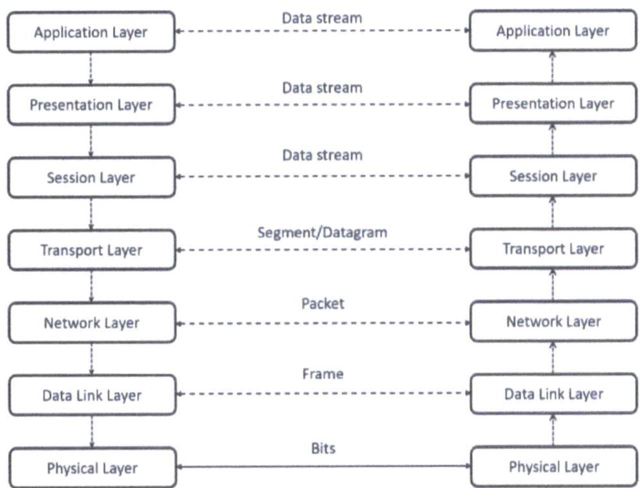

Figure 7.1: *Seven layers of the OSI model and logical channels*

The message to be sent across the network is created at the application layer and is passed down the stack through the presentation layer down to the physical layer. At the physical layer, the message is transmitted to the distant end, where it is recreated and sent up the protocol stack, stripping the header information at each layer.

Let us briefly discuss the functionalities of each of these layers and the role they play in network communication.

Application layer

The application layer, not to be confused with the actual application, is the top-most layer of the protocol stack. It interfaces the user applications, network services, and operating systems with the protocol stack and facilitates end user applications to communicate with the stack. It includes, among others, services and protocols required for web browsing, file transfer, message exchange, and remote terminal sessions. Common protocols at this layer include **File Transfer Protocol** (FTP), **Hypertext Transfer Protocol** (HTTP), **Simple Message Transfer Protocol** (SMTP), Telnet, **Post Office Protocol version 3** (POP3), **Internet Message Access Protocol** (IMAP), **Simple Network Management Protocol** (SNMP), etc. When an application needs to transmit data over the network, it passes the data along with suitable instructions to the protocols at the Application layer, which processes and formats the data in the required format before sending it to the next layer, i.e., the presentation layer.

Presentation layer

The presentation layer acts as a translator. It transforms data received from the application layer into a format suitable for network transmission. It translates the data into a common format that can be understood and processed by any receiving system that follows the OSI model. The presentation layer is primarily concerned with the syntax and format of the data rather than the meaning of the data itself. This ensures that an application at the receiving end can use the data as long as it understands the format. Most formats for audio, video, images, web pages, emails, and documents operate within this layer. Some of the common file and data formats that are handled in the presentation layer include **American Standard Code for Information Exchange** (ASCII), **Extended Binary Coded Decimal Interchange Code** (EBCDIC), **Graphic Interchange Format** (GIF), **Tagged Image File Format** (TIFF), **Joint Photographic Experts Group** (JPEG), **Moving Picture Experts Group** (MPEG), **Musical Instruments Digital Interface** (MIDI), **Portable Document Format** (PDF). The presentation layer is also responsible for data encoding, encryption, and compression.

Session layer

The session layer sets up communication between two applications that need to communicate or exchange data. It manages and controls communication sessions between the applications and is responsible for the establishment, maintenance, and termination of sessions to ensure organized and synchronized data exchange. The communication between the applications can happen in three different modes: simplex or unidirectional, half duplex, where the communication takes place in both directions but in one direction at a time, and full duplex, i.e., simultaneous two-way communication. **Remote Procedure Call** (RPC), **Network Basic Input Output System** (NetBIOS), **Network File System** (NFS), and **Structured Query Language** (SQL) are protocols that operate in the session layer. It is important to appreciate that session layer protocols manage application-to-application communication as opposed to transport layer protocols that handle computer-to-computer communication.

Transport layer

The transport layer provides the exchange of data between the sender and the receiver by ensuring end-to-end communication between them. This is achieved through data segmentation, data flow controls, and error-checking mechanisms. **Transmission Control Protocol** (TCP) and **User Datagram Protocol** (UDP) are the key protocols at the transport layer. While TCP is a reliable connection-oriented protocol, UDP is a connectionless protocol used for faster communication. Other protocols at this layer include **Secure Socket Layer** (SSL), **Transport Layer Security** (TLS), and **Sequenced Packet Exchange** (SPX).

Network layer

The primary function of the network layer is to add routing information to the data and route it to the correct destination. It handles logical addressing through IP addresses and is responsible for routing the data packets across different networks. The network layer accepts data segments from the transport layer, breaks them into smaller packets for efficient movement, routes them through the best available routes to the destination, and reassembles them at the destination. The packets from the same source may take different paths to reach a destination. The routing protocols at this layer maintain their routing tables, and when packets are received, they are routed through the most efficient path. While IP is the most common protocol at the network layer, some others include **Internet Control Message Protocol** (**ICMP**), **Internet Group Management Protocol** (**IGMP**), **Open Shortest Path First** (**OSPF**), **Border Gateway Protocol** (**BGP**), and **Routing Information Protocol** (**RIP**).

Data link layer

The data link layer is responsible for the transmission of data across the physical network. It packages raw bits into frames, manages error detection and correction, and handles data transfer between directly connected nodes. The data format at this layer is determined by the hardware and technology used in the network. The data link layer is divided into two functional sublayers. One that includes **Media Access Control** (**MAC**) for encapsulating data frames and **Address Resolution Protocol** (**ARP**) for translating IP addresses to MAC addresses, and the other, **Logical Link Control** (**LLC**), which communicates with the network layer and takes care of flow control and error checking. The data link layer adds the hardware address or the MAC address of the device to the data frame. The MAC address is a 6 byte address written in hexadecimal notation, the first 3 bytes of which denote the **Organization Unique Identifier** (**OUI**) of the hardware manufacturer, and the last 3 bytes represent the unique number assigned to the interface. The MAC sublayer is aware of the underlying physical layer and formats the data accordingly for transmission over the physical network. Some of the protocols at the data link layer include Ethernet, token ring, **Asynchronous Transfer Mode** (**ATM**), **Point-to-Point Protocol** (**PPP**), **Layer 2 Tunneling Protocol** (**L2TP**), and **fiber distributed data interface** (**FDDI**).

Physical layer

The physical layer is the lowest layer in the stack and is responsible for the physical connection of the network nodes through wired or wireless medium. At the sender end, it receives the data frames from the data link layer and converts them into bits for transmission over the physical medium. At the receiver end, it receives the bits and converts them into a frame before passing them to the data link layer. The physical layer includes protocols, electrical specifications, optical specifications, and interface standards such as X.21, V.24, V.35, **High Speed Serial Interface** (**HSSI**), **Synchronous Optical Networking** (**SONET**), **Wireless Fidelity** (**Wi-Fi**), Bluetooth, and various other standards by the **Telecommunications Industry Association** (**TIA**) and **Electronic Industry Alliance** (**EIA**). The physical layer employs the hardware through these standards and the device drivers to control the transmission and reception of bits over the physical medium. **Network interface card** (**NIC**), hubs, and repeaters are some of the devices that function at the physical layer.

TCP/IP model

The TCP/IP model was developed by the **Defense Advanced Research Projects Agency (DARPA)** of the U.S. **Department of Defense (DoD)** for its network, which later evolved into the internet. The TCP/IP model consists of four layers, as opposed to seven in the OSI model, and precedes it.

The four layers of the TCP/IP model are as follows:

- **Application layer**: This is the topmost layer that interacts directly with user applications and programs. It handles data representation for user applications and forwards it to the transport layer to offer services like email and remote system access, etc.
- **Transport layer**: This layer, also called the **host-to-host layer**, is responsible for establishing connections between the sending and receiving devices. It splits the data received from the application layer into chunks of packets and puts them into sequence for transmission. It ensures error-free transfer of data and controls the data flow rate for smooth transmission.
- **Internet layer**: This layer, also called the **network layer**, controls data transmission over the network and manages protocols related to packet transmission. It specifies the path data packets will use for transmission and provides IP addresses for system identification over the network.
- **Link layer**: This layer is also called the **network access layer**. It combines the functionalities of the data link and physical layers of the OSI model and is responsible for sending and receiving data in binary format over a physical communication medium, and uses the physical address of the device for mapping the transmission path.

The following figure shows various layers of the TCP/IP model and depicts how they correspond to those of the OSI model:

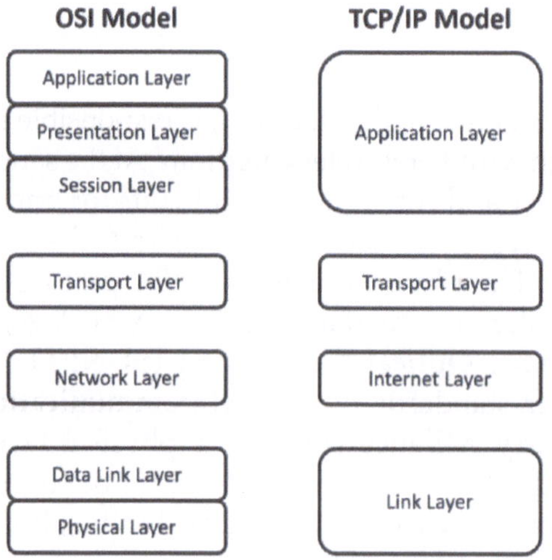

***Figure 7.2**: TCP/IP model layers and correspondence with the OSI layers*

TCP/IP is a widely adopted and platform-independent protocol suite. It comprises numerous individual protocols at different layers. Some of the important protocols that will aid our understanding of network security are discussed in the following sections.

Transport layer protocols

The transport layer is responsible for end-to-end communication between systems and primarily utilizes two core protocols: TCP and UDP. Communication between two systems takes place using sockets, which are a combination of IP address and port number. The port numbers range from 0 to 65,536 (2^{16}), out of which the first 1024 are the well-known ports reserved for standard services, port numbers from 1024 to 49151 are used for registered software, and beyond that are ephemeral ports used randomly as source ports. The TCP and UDP protocols have their unique features and are useful for different scenarios.

TCP

TCP is a connection-oriented protocol, which essentially means the communicating devices first establish a connection through a three-way handshake process involving **synchronization** (**SYN**) and **acknowledgment** (**ACK**), and then proceed with the exchange of data. The initiating device sends a SYN packet, the recipient responds with a SYN-ACK packet, and thereafter the initiator sends a final ACK to confirm the connection. The protocol provides reliable, sequenced, and error-checked delivery of data over an IP network. It ensures reliability through positive acknowledgment with re-transmission, packet sequencing for ordered delivery, and checksums for error detection. From a security perspective, these mechanisms enhance data integrity and resilience against packet loss, corruption, and unintended modification during transmission, making TCP well-suited for applications that require reliable and consistent data delivery. The TCP protocol also implements flow control and congestion control to prevent the sender from overwhelming the receiver and prevent network congestion. It is ideally suited for applications where data integrity is important, such as web browsing, email, file transfer, and online banking transactions. However, the connection-oriented nature of TCP exposes it to **denial of service** (**DoS**) attacks such as SYN floods, in which attackers exploit half-open connections to exhaust server resources. Since TCP is optimized for accurate delivery rather than timely delivery, it is less suitable for real-time applications like **Voice over IP** (**VoIP**) due to potential delays from retransmissions.

UDP

UDP is a connectionless, lightweight protocol that prioritizes speed over reliability. It does not establish a session before sending data, nor does it guarantee delivery. Each UDP packet, referred to as a **datagram**, is treated independently. The packets can take different routes to the destination and arrive in any order. The protocol supports multicasting and permits a single packet to be sent to multiple recipients simultaneously. This helps with bandwidth optimization. The lower overhead and reduced latency make the UDP protocol ideal for real-time applications where timely delivery is critical, and some packet loss may be acceptable, such as video streaming, online gaming, VoIP, and **domain name system** (**DNS**) lookups.

Internet layer protocols

At the internet layer, also known as the **network layer**, IP is the most important and commonly encountered protocol. It is responsible for providing routing and addressing information for transmitting data packets across diverse networks. Like UDP, it is also a connectionless protocol that does not guarantee packet delivery, which must be handled at the transport layer, if required. There are two types of IP addressing schemes used in IP-based networks: **IP version 4** (**IPv4**) and **IP version 6** (**IPv6**). The IPv4 addressing scheme uses 32 bits and is more commonly used than IPv6, which uses 128 bits and thus has a larger address space. The IPv6 addressing scheme also provides many additional features that are not present in IPv4 networks.

The IPv4 addresses are grouped into classes and subnets, with each address having a host part and a network part. They are categorized into four classes (A, B, C, D, and E). This scheme hierarchically organizes the IP addresses to support networks of different sizes and complexity. The details of IP addresses in various classes are as follows:

- Class A IP addresses are allocated for very large networks. The first octet is used for the network portion, and the other three for hosts. The range includes addresses from 1.0.0.0 to 126.255.255.255, out of which 10.0.0.0 to 10.255.255.255 is used in private networks. The default subnet mask is 255.0.0.0.
- Class B IP addresses serve moderate-sized networks. Here, the first two octets are for the network and the remaining two for hosts. Their IP range is from 128.0.0.0 to 191.255.255.255, with 172.16.0.0 to 172.31.255.255 reserved for the private address range. The default subnet mask is 255.255.0.0.
- Class C IP addresses are earmarked for small networks. The first three octets are used for the network, and the last for hosts. Their address space ranges from 192.0.0.0 to 223.255.255.255, and 192.168.0.0 to 192.168.255.255 is reserved for private networks. The default subnet mask here is 255.255.255.0.
- Class D IP addresses ranging from 224.0.0.0 to 239.255.255.255 are used for multicasting.
- Class E IP addresses are for experimental purposes and are reserved for research. The range includes IP addresses from 240.0.0.0 to 255.255.255.255.

Classless Inter-Domain Routing (**CIDR**) notation can be used instead of the classical dotted decimal notation subnet masks to combine multiple non-contiguous sets of addresses. For instance, for 255.255.0.0 dotted decimal notation, the CIDR notation /16 can be used. The CIDR notation also simplifies the process of splitting large networks into smaller subnets and managing IP addresses more effectively and efficiently. This helps in micro-segmentation and implementing **virtual local area networks** (**VLANs**), which are crucial for controlling network traffic.

Theoretically, the IPv4 addressing scheme can provide approximately 4.3 billion IP addresses. However, this address space is not adequate due to the large-scale proliferation of IP devices. This constraint is addressed by IPv6. It addresses the limitations of IPv4 by using a 128 bit alphanumeric address format (e.g., 2405:0bd6:0000:0000:0000:29ff:0033:8bc8), which vastly expands the address space to 2^{128}, i.e., approximately 3.4 × 10^38 unique IP addresses. IPv6 also provides several advanced features compared to IPv4. It includes native support for **IP security** (**IPsec**), built-in **quality of service** (**QoS**) support, and eliminates the need for **network address translation** (**NAT**). It has a simplified header format that improves routing efficiency. In certain situations, IPv6 can be faster due to the elimination of NAT. However, despite the technical superiority of IPv6, IPv4 is still the preferred and more widely used protocol, though the adoption of IPv6 is gradually increasing.

Besides IP, the internet layer has many other protocols in use, such as IGMP, ICMP, and ARP. IGMP facilitates systems to support multicasting. ICMP is used primarily for determining the health of networks. Utilities such as ping and traceroute utilize the ICMP protocol. The versatility of the ICMP protocol makes it a lucrative target for malicious actors to launch DoS attacks. As a result, many features and the throughput of ICMP are by default restricted in most networks. As discussed earlier, the ARP protocol helps in the interoperability of logical and physical addresses. The traffic on the network segment travels from the source to the destination using physical addresses, i.e., the MAC addresses. The ARP protocol resolves IP addresses into MAC addresses and vice versa to facilitate this communication. This is achieved by maintaining the ARP cache at the routing devices. The ARP caches are at times abused by attackers and filled with false information, resulting in ARP poisoning.

Application layer protocols

The application layer of the TCP/IP model broadly corresponds to the session, presentation, and application layers of the OSI model. There are numerous protocols at this layer that support user applications to provide access to the underlying network. Some protocols that support common user functions such as web browsing, email exchange, file transfer, and network administration are as follows:

- For web browsing, HTTP and **HTTP secure** (**HTTPS**) are used to serve web pages to the browser at the user's end. While HTTP uses TCP port 80, HTTPS works on TCP port 443. HTTP is a plaintext protocol and is inherently vulnerable to interception, modification, and ingestion of malicious data. The vulnerabilities of HTTP are overcome by HTTPS by encrypting the communication between client and server using SSL/TLS certificates.
- For a remote terminal emulation application, two of the most common protocols used are Telnet and SSH. In the Windows environment, **Remote Desktop Protocol** (**RDP**) is used. Telnet uses TCP port 23, SSH uses TCP port 22, and RDP uses TCP port 3389. Since Telnet is a plaintext protocol, it is generally not used these days, and SSH, which provides encrypted communication and a stronger authentication mechanism, is preferred.

- For file transfer, FTP and **SSH FTP** (**SFTP**) are used. FTP uses TCP ports 20 and 21, and SFTP works on TCP port 22. SFTP is a secure protocol where encryption is provided through SSL/TLS. Though SSL was originally designed to support HTTPS, it can be used to secure the communication of any application layer protocol. Another lightweight protocol used for file transfer is **Trivial FTP** (**TFTP**). This protocol works on UDP port 69 and does not require any authentication.
- Multiple protocols support email communication. SMTP is used to send messages from a client to an email server and between email servers. To pull email messages from a mailbox, POP3 and IMAP are used. IMAP is more secure than POP3 and provides additional features of downloading email headers and deleting the messages directly on the server without the need for downloading. SMTP works on TCP port 25, POP3 on TCP port 110, and IMAP on TCP port 143. Each of these protocols also supports secure communication using TLS encryption. The TCP ports used for the secure versions are SMTP - 465/587, POP3 - 995, and IMAP - 993.
- SNMP is used to collect network health and status information. It functions over UDP ports 161 and 162. The initial versions of SNMP relied upon community strings and plaintext communication, making them vulnerable to interception and attacks. The current version, SNMPv3, allows for encrypted communication and a robust authentication mechanism.
- DNS transforms human-readable domain names into machine-readable IP addresses. It operates on port 53. DNS was never designed with security in mind. The main objective was ease of use. The inherent weaknesses in the protocol expose it to DNS poisoning and DNS hijacking attacks. This can be overcome by enabling **DNS security extensions** (**DNSSEC**) to provide an authentication mechanism and ensure data integrity.
- **Dynamic Host Control Protocol** (**DHCP**) automates IP address allocation and configuration of network parameters such as subnet mask, default gateway, and DNS server. This significantly simplifies the administrative burden for the network administrators. The inherent simplicity and absence of robust security features make it vulnerable to attacks such as DHCP starvation and replay attacks. As a mitigation measure, DHCP snooping and ARP binding should be implemented on the network switches to counter such attacks.

Routing

Routing and switching facilitate network segmentation and data transmission across networks. They are the fundamental building blocks for network security. Proper design and configuration of VLANs, inter-VLAN routing, and routing protocols are essential for implementing robust network segmentation and enforcing access controls. Routing can be dynamic or static. Practical network implementations typically employ a combination of static and dynamic routing to manage traffic flow.

Static routing

Static routing is simple and predictable. The routes are configured manually by the network administrators. It is ideal for small networks where specific and fixed paths need to be defined due to security reasons. However, to provide even basic failover capabilities, static routing needs to be combined with technologies such as **Virtual Router Redundancy Protocol** (**VRRP**) or **Hot Standby Router Protocol** (**HSRP**). In large and complex networks, it can be cumbersome for administrators, as any changes in the network condition need to be updated manually. Since the routing does not adapt to changes dynamically, it can lead to inefficiencies and outages.

Dynamic routing

Dynamic routing employs protocols that enable routers to automatically adapt to changing network conditions by frequently updating and exchanging the route information. It provides a higher level of failover capability and is highly effective for large and continuously evolving networks. Dynamic routing protocols maintain the current routing information and automatically update new optimal paths if the current ones become inaccessible. They offer scalability, fault tolerance, higher availability, and rapid convergence. OSPF and BGP are two of the commonly encountered dynamic routing protocols. OSPF is a link-state routing protocol that implements Dijkstra's SPF algorithm. It is an **Interior Gateway Protocol** (**IGP**) that operates within a specific routing domain or **autonomous system** (**AS**). It supports multipath routing and uses various network metrics such as reliability, bandwidth, and latency to determine optimal paths. BGP is an **Exterior Gateway Protocol** (**EGP**) primarily used to exchange routing information between **Internet Service Providers** (**ISPs**) and different AS. It is a path-vector protocol that employs an optimal path selection technique for the transfer of data packets. The routing decisions are based on parameters such as adjacent IP addresses, router designation, path distance, and origin type, with the routing algorithm typically selecting routes with the shortest path to the destination. Both OSPF and BGP employ authentication mechanisms to ensure data security during network modifications. BGP offers greater flexibility and control than OSPF, though it is comparatively more complex to implement and maintain.

VLAN routing

VLANs provide logical network segmentation within physical network infrastructure. They operate by applying tags to network packets and associating them with each VLAN. While routing packets, the network switches read these tags and forward the packet exclusively to the intended VLAN. For routing a packet to another VLAN, inter-VLAN routing is used. When a device in one VLAN needs to communicate with a device in another VLAN, it sends the request to the routing device, typically a router or a layer 3 switch. The router (or the layer 3 switch) examines the VLAN tags, determines the destination, and routes the packet to the appropriate VLAN. In the case of router implementation, a single physical Ethernet interface on the router is logically divided into sub-interfaces, each associated with a specific VLAN.

This allows the single physical interface to route traffic between multiple VLANs. Layer 3 switches utilize **Switched Virtual Interfaces** (**SVIs**) to perform the routing function. SVIs are virtual interfaces created on the switch for various VLANs. Layer 3 switches are preferred in modern enterprise networks as they provide higher packet processing rates compared to traditional routers due to their hardware-based switching capabilities.

Network address translation

NAT enables multiple devices within a private network to share a single public IP address for external communication. It converts the private IP addresses used by devices within a private network into a single public IP address when those devices communicate with external networks and translates the public IP back to the corresponding private IP for incoming responses. This alleviates the need for multiple public IPs, streamlines network management, and enhances security by masking details of the internal network.

NAT can be achieved in the following ways:

- **Static NAT (SNAT)**: This involves a one-to-one mapping between a single private IP address and a single public IP address. SNAT is typically used when a particular internal device, such as a web server, needs to be made accessible from an external network.
- **Dynamic NAT (DNAT)**: This dynamically maps private IP addresses to public IP addresses from a pool of available addresses. The mapping changes with each session, and a device may be assigned different public IP addresses for different connections.
- **Port Address Translation (PAT)/NAT overload**: This is the most widely used and efficient type of NAT. It allows multiple devices on an internal network to share a single public IP address by assigning a different port number to each outbound connection. The router distinguishes between sessions by using these unique port numbers, enabling thousands of devices to share one public IP address.

Network devices

Network devices are part of the physical and logical infrastructure of a computer network. These devices facilitate secure data transmission by routing packets, managing data flow, and contributing towards the overall functionality and security of the network. Understanding the capabilities and functionalities of various network components is essential for designing and maintaining a secure and resilient network infrastructure.

Hubs

Hubs are the most basic networking devices that operate at the physical layer. They are physical interconnects that function as multiport repeaters. Hubs simply broadcast the data received on a port to all other connected ports. The security implication is that any device connected to the hub can see and potentially intercept all traffic on the network segment. It can also lead to data collisions that can adversely impact network efficiency in congested network environments.

Bridges

Bridges operate at the data link layer and connect two separate physical network segments. A bridge discovers and maintains the MAC addresses of devices on each network segment. If the destination address of the incoming traffic is on the same side of the bridge as the source, the bridge filters out the data frame and keeps it local. If the destination is on the other segment, the frame is forwarded across the bridge. While bridges handle the network traffic more efficiently as compared to hubs by segmenting the collision domains, they still forward all broadcast and multicast traffic across both segments.

Switch

A network switch connects multiple devices within a single network segment. Switches primarily operate at layer 2, i.e., the data link layer, though there are models that can perform limited routing functions on the network layer, i.e., layer 3 as well. Switches maintain MAC address tables and have intelligence built-in to filter the incoming traffic and send data only to the intended destinations rather than broadcasting it to all the connected devices. This significantly reduces unnecessary traffic and improves network performance. It also reduces unnecessary exposure of sensitive data. In addition, switches, especially of the managed types, can incorporate additional security features such as VLAN and **access control list** (**ACL**), which facilitate logical segmentation of the network and granular filtering of traffic, thereby further restricting exposure.

Routers

Routers operate at the network layer and typically connect **local area networks** (**LANs**) and **wide area networks** (**WANs**). They route packets over different networks based on their IP addresses. The routing decisions are made based on the route entries in the routing tables maintained by the routers. These entries can be static or updated dynamically to determine the most efficient paths for data transfer to different networks. The state of the connected networks and the routing information is discovered by the routers through routing protocols such as OSPF, BGP, and RIP.

Core network security components

The main function of the network devices that we discussed in the preceding section is the transmission of data from the source to the destination. We also saw that the networking protocols were primarily designed to achieve data transfer across networks, not necessarily with security in mind. As the networks grew and the need was felt to secure data exchange across varied networks and geographical locations, new protocols such as SSL and TLS were developed to ensure communication security. Some of the existing protocols were upgraded, and security features were built into them. However, this alone is not adequate for a secure network architecture. Networks need to be secured by deploying core network security components whose main purpose is to protect the network infrastructure from any cyberattacks. Together, these devices must provide protection against attacks at any layer of the protocol suite. This is essential for defense-in-depth. Firewall, WAF, IDS, and IPS are some of the devices deployed in a network to protect against external and internal threats. In addition, **distributed DoS** (**DDoS**) protection tools are used on the internet-facing segment to protect against DDoS attacks and ensure that only legitimate traffic reaches the internal network. These components come in different form factors: specialized appliances, software-based, or can be provided as a service. Some of the core network security components are discussed in the following section.

Firewall

When we think of network protection, the first thing that comes to mind is a firewall. Firewalls are network devices that are deployed to segment networks and regulate traffic across different segments. They act as a barrier between trusted internal networks and untrusted external networks and scrutinize the traffic to determine whether it should be permitted, denied, or dropped. For instance, a firewall placed at the perimeter of an organization's network filters the incoming and outgoing packets based on predefined rules to control the flow of traffic in and out of the network. Similarly, a network connected to the internet is generally segmented into a **demilitarized zone** (**DMZ**) and a trust zone. The internet-facing servers, such as web servers and email servers, are placed in the DMZ protected by the perimeter firewall. Other servers, such as application servers and database servers, are deployed in the trust zone and are accessible from the organization's internal network only. The internal network may be further divided into a user segment and a server segment, and an identity-aware firewall may be used to control access to the servers.

The firewall rules are generally defined in ACLs, and the decision to allow, block, or drop packets is taken based on parameters such as IP address, port, protocol, application, and content. Based on the filtering parameter and functionality, firewalls can be categorized as packet filtering firewalls, circuit-level gateway firewalls, application-level gateway firewalls, and stateful inspection firewalls. A firewall solution may offer more than one of these functionalities and incorporate additional advanced features such as behavioural analytics and **artificial intelligence** (**AI**) to provide comprehensive network protection. The common firewall types are categorized as follows:

- **Packet filtering firewalls**: These are first-generation firewalls that operate at the network layer. The decision to allow or block traffic is taken based on a predefined set of rules, which include parameters such as source IP address, destination IP address, port number, and protocol available in the packet header. These firewalls provide basic security but can be easily spoofed as they do not scrutinize the payload.

- **Circuit-level gateway firewalls**: These firewalls, also known as circuit proxies, operate at the session layer and examine session-level connections such as TCP/UDP to verify their legitimacy. These are second-generation firewalls that monitor the network protocol session initiation messages to determine whether the session being initiated is legitimate or otherwise, implying whether the remote system initiating the connection is trusted or not. The decision to allow or deny is based on the validity of the communication session, and not on the content of the traffic, as the circuit proxies do not carry out deep packet inspection. While these firewalls provide a higher level of security as compared to the packet filtering firewalls, they need to be used alongside other types, such as the application gateway firewalls, for comprehensive network security.
- **Application-level gateway firewalls**: These firewalls, also called **proxy firewalls**, make protocol connections on behalf of other devices and applications. A proxy firewall accepts incoming and outgoing messages from the source, inspects them for any malicious content, and if found clean, sends them to the destination. Unlike the packet filtering or circuit-level firewall, a proxy firewall breaks the communication channel between the source and the destination. It terminates the session and restarts it on behalf of the sender. This protects the internal network and identities. An application gateway operates at the application layer, and each application has its own proxy server. Thus, a proxy firewall would have numerous proxy servers, a unique one for each application. Proxy firewalls may increase latency and adversely impact network performance since each packet must be examined and processed as it passes through the firewall.
- **Stateful inspection firewalls**: These are third-generation firewalls that operate at the network and transport layers. Also referred to as dynamic packet filtering firewalls, they evaluate the state and content of the network traffic. They keep track of the state of active network connections, and by understanding the context of the traffic, they can detect and block malicious packets that do not conform to established connection states. For instance, in the case of TCP, various steps and states of the protocol are well defined and follow a laid down sequence. A stateful firewall would keep track of these states for each of the packets passing through it and their acknowledgments and sequence numbers. If they are not found in order, it points towards malicious activity, and the firewall blocks the connection to protect internal systems. Likewise, in the case of UDP, since it is a connectionless protocol, the source and destination address and ACL rules are stored in the firewall state table. Since the protocol does not have a specific tear-down stage, if a prolonged period of inactivity is observed, the firewall simply times out the connection and removes the entry from the state table.

Unified threat management

Unified threat management (**UTM**) devices combine various firewall functionalities with other security functions such as website filtering, content filtering, antivirus, IPS/IDS, **virtual**

private network (**VPN**), and **data loss prevention** (**DLP**) capabilities. They are primarily designed for small networks and businesses with simplicity and ease of use in mind. They provide protection against a wide range of threats with a centralized interface for configuration and monitoring. They offer a cost-effective solution and simplify network protection and management by consolidating multiple security features in a single device. UTMs come with a user-friendly central management console that greatly simplifies deployment, configuration, administration, and monitoring tasks, thus reducing the administrative overhead of security teams. While UTMs simply secure operations to a large extent, they have capability limitations and can become a single point of failure. A misconfigured UTM appliance or its failure can expose the entire network to threats, leading to a complete security breakdown.

Next-generation firewalls

As the cyber threat landscape has evolved, network protection technologies have advanced beyond the capabilities of traditional firewalls. NGFWs are an evolution of conventional firewall technologies, which integrate multiple security functions into a single, cohesive platform. Unlike traditional firewalls that primarily operate at the network and transport layers, NGFWs provide deeper visibility and control over network traffic for more effective protection against sophisticated threats. They are typically built on specialized hardware and optimized software architectures, which allow them to inspect traffic at scale in high-throughput environments.

NGFWs are capable of performing deep packet inspection, which involves analyzing not only packet headers but also the payload of network traffic. This capability facilitates the detection of malware, malicious command-and-control communication, and other advanced threats that may evade conventional firewalls. NGFWs are also application-aware, enabling them to identify, monitor, and control traffic based on specific applications rather than relying solely on ports or protocols. This, combined with user and device awareness, enables these firewalls to enforce highly granular security policies aligned with business requirements.

Key capabilities of NGFWs are as follows:

- **Deep packet inspection**: Enables detailed analysis of traffic payloads to detect malware and sophisticated attack patterns.
- **Application awareness and control**: Allows policies to be defined based on applications and their specific functionalities.
- **Integrated IPS**: Detects and blocks known threats using signatures and identifies anomalous behaviour indicative of attacks.
- **Content filtering**: Restricts access to malicious or inappropriate websites to reduce exposure to web-based threats.
- **Web application protection**: Provides protection against common web application attacks such as SQL injection and **cross-site scripting** (**XSS**).

- **Encrypted traffic inspection:** Allows inspection of encrypted traffic (SSL/TLS) to identify hidden threats, though this feature must be enabled with care due to potential performance and privacy considerations.

Modern NGFWs increasingly incorporate AI and **machine learning** (**ML**) techniques to enhance real-time threat detection and improve protection against previously unseen attacks. By combining advanced inspection capabilities with automation and intelligence, NGFWs provide a more proactive defense against evolving cyber threats.

Firewall architectures

Firewalls can be deployed in a number of ways to meet the network protection requirements of an organization. There are mainly three types of firewall deployment architectures: single-tier, two-tier, and three-tier. In a single-tier architecture, a single firewall is placed between the organization's internal network and the external network. All traffic moving in and out of the internal network must pass through this firewall. In a two-tier firewall architecture, two firewalls are used in tandem. This segments the internal network into segments: the DMZ, which is accessible from the external environment, and the trusted zone that is accessible only internally. The three-tier architecture further segments the internal network. Besides the DMZ and trusted private network, a transaction subnet is created, and all data exchange between the DMZ and trusted zone takes place through this transaction subnet. This provides added security to the assets in the trusted zone.

The following figures depict various firewall deployment architectures:

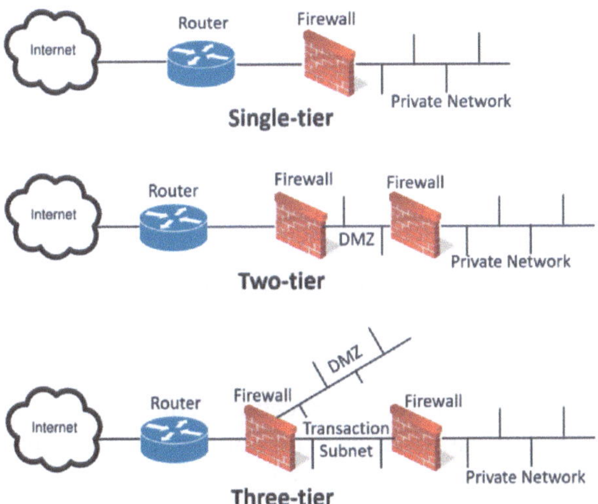

Figure 7.3: Firewall deployment architectures

Firewall configuration

The most advanced firewalls will be rendered ineffective unless configured properly. Therefore, effective firewall configuration is paramount for network security. Some of the best practices for firewall configuration are as follows:

- **Implicit deny**: The default action for any firewall should be implicit deny, i.e., block by default any packet that has not been explicitly allowed. This approach of blocking all traffic by default and explicitly allowing only specific, known, and necessary traffic is the most secure approach. This strategy provides for strong control and significantly reduces the risk of a breach due to any misconfiguration.
- **Principle of least privilege**: The firewall access control rules should be as specific as possible, and only specified traffic should be allowed. This implies specifying parameters such as source IP address(s), destination IP address(s), destination port(s), and the protocol associated with the traffic. Unless necessary, the use of any in these fields should be avoided.
- **Specify destination IP and port**: The exact IP address of the destination servers and the precise ports to be allowed should always be specified. Opening all ports may create holes in the security and expose the server to attacks from the external network.
- **Secure management ports**: Management and database ports should, preferably, be accessed internally over the private network and not exposed to the external environment. If unavoidable, access should be restricted to specific source IP addresses and ideally provided through a VPN for added security.

Web application firewall

WAF operates at the application layer and is designed to protect web applications and **application programming interface** (**APIs**). Unlike a firewall, a WAF is not used for network segmentation. Its primary function is to protect internet-facing web applications from application layer attacks such as SQL injection, command injection, XSS, and cookie manipulation. A WAF inspects the header and payload in the HTTP and HTTPS requests and analyzes them for any anomalies against a set of WAF rules. This deep-packet inspection allows the WAF to distinguish between legitimate traffic and malicious requests.

WAF is typically placed in front of the web application, which enables it to analyze every packet and enforce policies before the traffic reaches the application and web servers. Depending on an organization's needs and infrastructure, WAFs can be deployed as network-based, host-based, or cloud-based. Each of these deployments has its advantages. Network-based WAFs are generally hardware appliances that offer low latency and high performance, which is critical for real-time applications. Host-based WAFs are software solutions that offer greater customization and integration with the application environment, but are slower. Cloud-based WAFs are offered as a service and require minimal on-site setup and maintenance. They are highly scalable and can easily absorb massive traffic volumes.

Detection methodologies

WAFs have evolved along with the emerging threat landscape. There has been a paradigm shift from static signature-based detection to dynamic anomaly-based detection. The WAF methodologies are as follows:

- **Signature-based detection**: In this method, the incoming traffic is compared against a database of known attack patterns. It is effective for known threats but is totally blind to new attacks. Experienced attackers can easily bypass the static rules by using various obfuscation techniques, such as payload padding, encoding, or modifying the attack slightly so that the pattern no longer matches a known signature. As a result, a large number of actual threats may pass through the WAF undetected.
- **Anomaly-based detection**: Anomaly-based detection addresses the limitations of signature-based detection methodology. It leverages AI and ML. This method first establishes a dynamic, behavioural baseline of normal application traffic and then flags any traffic that deviates from the baseline as anomalous and potentially malicious. This enables the WAF to detect and block novel, unknown, and polymorphic attacks that would easily bypass a static rule set.

Blocking models

WAFs operate on models that are based on the manner in which decisions are made to allow or block traffic. They can operate on a negative security model or a positive security model, which are commonly referred to as blacklisting and whitelisting, respectively. A combination of the two can also be used for better results. The three models are as follows:

- **Negative security model (blacklisting)**: This model explicitly blocks malicious traffic. The database of attack signatures is regularly updated, and traffic not matching any of the signatures is allowed to pass through. This approach is very effective against known attacks and high traffic volume. However, it is inherently reactive and does not protect against previously unknown threats and zero-day attacks.
- **Positive security model (whitelisting)**: This approach blocks all traffic by default and only allows requests that are explicitly defined as legitimate. To be effective, it requires a learning period to establish a baseline of the normal application behaviour. This is a proactive approach and is highly effective against new attacks, since anything outside the established baseline is automatically detected. However, this model is highly resource-intensive and, if not tuned properly, may result in unintentional blocking of legitimate traffic.
- **Hybrid approach**: Contemporary WAFs generally combine the strengths of both models for a more comprehensive defense. They use the blacklist approach to efficiently stop known threats and simultaneously employ the whitelisting approach to provide robust protection against unknown and sophisticated attacks. This approach offers an effective balance of security, performance, and management efficiency.

Proxy

A proxy is a server that acts as an intermediary between two devices, typically a user and a website. The connection request from the source does not go to the destination server directly. Instead, the request from the source or client is sent to the proxy, which further initiates a request to the destination, keeping track of the incoming request. When a response is received from the server, the proxy forwards it to the client. Effectively, the intermediary server acts as a proxy for the client. The proxy manages the traffic based on predefined and pre-configured rules and provides a range of benefits, such as improved performance and enhanced security by enforcing organizational policies.

Depending on the direction of the traffic they manage, proxies can be categorized as a forward proxy or a reverse proxy. The key distinction between the two types is as follows:

- **Forward proxy**: A forward proxy, or simply a proxy, acts on behalf of a client. It accepts outbound requests from the clients and forwards them to external servers on the internet. If we look from the server's perspective, the request appears to originate from the proxy server. This effectively masks the client's identity and location. Forward proxies help enforce content filtering policies and provide anonymity.
- **Reverse proxy**: A reverse proxy acts the other way round, i.e., on behalf of a server. It is deployed in front of one or more web servers. It intercepts the incoming requests from external clients and routes them to the appropriate server in the backend. Effectively, the external clients interact only with the reverse proxy. This conceals the IP addresses and details of the actual servers. This is the basic architecture that is used for WAFs, load balancers, and **content delivery networks** (**CDNs**).

In addition to performing their primary intermediary role, proxies provide several other critical network security functions:

- **Security**: Proxies can filter malicious traffic and block access from unauthorized sources. They also enhance security by masking the client or server IP addresses, limiting their exposure to the external environment, and protecting their identity.
- **Performance enhancement**: Proxies can vastly improve network performance. This is achieved through caching frequently accessed websites, which reduces response times and bandwidth usage for subsequent requests. Reverse proxies can provide load balancing by distributing incoming traffic across multiple servers, ensuring efficiency and high availability.
- **Policy enforcement**: Both forward and reverse proxies can be configured to enforce organizational security and access policies, such as content filtering to restrict access to unwarranted websites and rate limiting to prevent request floods.

Intrusion detection and prevention systems

IDS and IPS are both critical components of network security that provide complete visibility into network activity. The core distinction between the two lies in their response mechanism. An IDS passively monitors the network traffic for suspicious activity. When it detects an intrusion attempt, it generates an alert, which then must be investigated and mitigated manually. In contrast, IPS is an active system that takes immediate actions to block any malicious traffic in real-time. When a threat is detected, an IPS automatically takes action to neutralize it and minimize any potential damage.

IDS and IPS employ similar detection techniques; only the response consequent to detection differs. They leverage a blend of predefined rules and behavioural analysis for detection. The predefined rules employ signature-based detection methodology to identify threats by comparing the network traffic against a database of known attack signatures. While this method is fast, it is fundamentally reactive and does not detect threats for which a signature does not exist. The other methodology is anomaly-based detection. This method follows a proactive approach by establishing a baseline and leveraging ML to continuously monitor real-time traffic and flag any significant outliers as a potential intrusion. This approach is highly effective at detecting previously unknown attacks that signature-based systems would miss. However, the baseline needs to be properly calibrated to reduce false positives. Practical implementations follow a hybrid approach that combines both detection methods. Signature-based detection is used for quick and accurate blocking of known threats, while anomaly-based detection is employed to proactively detect new and sophisticated attacks.

The deployment of IDS and IPS in a network differs owing to the functionalities that they provide and the impact they have on the network throughput. The deployment architecture and its impact are as follows:

- **IDS deployment**: An IDS is deployed out-of-band and not placed directly in the network traffic path. The network traffic is mirrored to the IDS via a span port or network tap, where it is monitored. Since it is deployed out-of-band and operating in detect mode, it does not impact the network performance or introduce latency. This makes IDS ideal for networks with high volumes of traffic where even minor delays are unacceptable.
- **IPS deployment**: An IPS is deployed in-line and placed directly in the network traffic flow. It is typically positioned between a firewall and a switch. All network traffic in the segment passes through the IPS, where it is inspected and filtered. While the in-line positioning enables real-time blocking, it may introduce network latency and become a traffic bottleneck if the system is misconfigured or the traffic is excessive.

The following table provides a comparison between the features of IDS and IPS:

Feature	IDS	IPS
Functionality	Detects suspicious activity and provides alerts.	Detects and automatically prevents malicious activity.
Deployment mode	Out-of-band monitors passively.	In-line, placed directly in the traffic flow.
Response to threats	Manual mitigation action required.	Automatic mitigation action is taken in real-time.
Impact on the network	No impact on network throughput or latency.	May introduce latency if not configured properly or overburdened.
Complexity	Easier to deploy and manage.	Increased complexity due to in-line deployment and active blocking.

***Table 7.1**: IDS vs. IPS*

DDoS protection

DoS or DDoS attacks make a website, application, or server unavailable by overwhelming it with a flood of traffic. While a DoS attack uses a single source to target the victim, a DDoS attack employs multiple, distributed devices that may be part of a botnet to overwhelm the target's network bandwidth or server resources, rendering it inaccessible. The distributed nature of DDoS attacks makes them far more difficult to defend against.

Types of DDoS attacks

DDoS attacks can be orchestrated at different layers of the OSI model. Different types of DDoS attacks are as follows:

- **Volumetric attacks**: These are carried out at layer 3 and 4 and are the most common type of DDoS attack, designed to consume all available network bandwidth. This type of attack floods the target with a large volume of traffic from multiple sources, preventing legitimate traffic from reaching the destination. Common examples of volumetric attacks include UDP floods, which overwhelm a host's ports, and ICMP floods, which inundate a network with error messages and hog its bandwidth.

- **Protocol attacks**: These are computational attacks that are carried out at layer 3 and 4. This type of attack exploits vulnerabilities in network protocols to consume resources of servers and routing devices. Instead of relying purely on volume, they exploit vulnerabilities in the protocols to overwhelm the targets.

- **Application layer attacks:** These are layer 7 attacks that mimic legitimate user behaviour to target specific parts of an application, such as a search API or login page.

These attacks, though smaller in volume than volumetric attacks, are highly effective as they are difficult to filter out and can exhaust application resources, rendering the application unavailable.

The following table gives the details of various types of DDoS attacks. An actual attack may employ attack vectors from all these categories to achieve its objectives:

Attack category	Target OSI layer	Technical example	Operational goal
Volumetric	Layer 3 and 4 (network, transport).	UDP floods, ICMP floods, and DNS amplification/ reflection.	To saturate the target's network bandwidth with a massive flood of traffic.
Protocol	Layer 3 and 4 (network, transport).	SYN flood, ping of death.	To exploit weaknesses in protocols to exhaust a server's computational resources.
Application layer	Layer 7 (application).	HTTP floods, Slowloris attacks.	To mimic legitimate user behaviour to exhaust application-specific resources (e.g., login pages or APIs).

Table 7.2: *Types of DDoS attacks*

Attack vectors

DDoS attacks exploit technical vulnerabilities in protocols and applications. Some of the attack vectors are as follows:

- **SYN flood attack**: This attack targets the TCP three-way handshake. In a normal connection, a client sends a SYN packet, the server responds with a SYN-ACK, and the client sends a final ACK to establish the connection. In a SYN flood, the attacker sends a very large number of SYN requests but never responds with the final ACK. This results in a large number of half-open connections at the server, which are tracked in its TCP connection table. Eventually, the table fills up, and the server is no longer able to accept any new connections, even legitimate ones, resulting in DoS to legitimate users.

- **UDP flood attack**: This is a volumetric attack that leverages the stateless nature of the UDP protocol. The attacker sends a large volume of UDP packets on random ports to the target host. Since the victim's system cannot find an application associated with these packets, it responds by sending an ICMP Destination Unreachable message back to the spoofed source address. As the target gets overwhelmed by the attack traffic and the subsequent *Destination Unreachable* responses, it becomes unresponsive and unavailable to legitimate users.

- **HTTP flood attack**: This is an application layer attack that mimics legitimate web traffic. The attacker sends a flood of HTTP GET or POST requests to a web server. Since these requests appear normal, the firewalls or intrusion detection systems find it difficult to filter them. The objective is to overwhelm the server's processing capabilities or memory, causing it to slow down or crash.

DDoS mitigation process

A robust DDoS defense strategy must include a comprehensive response plan. Effective DDoS protection is a continuous, multi-stage process. It can be broken down into four stages:

- **Detection**: The first step is to identify an attack in its early stages. This is achieved by continuously monitoring the network traffic patterns for unusual activity. Modern systems leverage advanced analytics and ML to flag anomalous behaviour.
- **Response**: Once an attack is detected, the system responds rapidly to prevent service disruption. This involves activating preconfigured countermeasures or routing traffic through specialized protection services.
- **Mitigation**: This is the active process of neutralizing a DDoS attack. It involves employing a variety of techniques to filter out malicious traffic while allowing legitimate traffic to pass through.
- **Analysis**: After the attack is mitigated, a post-incident analysis is conducted to understand the attack vectors, improve existing controls, and strengthen security against future attacks.

DDoS mitigation techniques

DDoS protection leverages a combination of tools and techniques to absorb and neutralize attacks. Some of these are as follows:

- **Traffic scrubbing**: This is the core mitigation technique against large-scale volumetric attacks. This technique diverts suspicious traffic to a specialized scrubbing center where the packets are analyzed in real-time, the malicious traffic is filtered out, and the clean, legitimate requests are forwarded to the origin server. These centers are generally provided by cloud-based DDoS protection providers. This service can be configured as *always-on*, i.e., the traffic always passes through the scrubbing center, or it can be activated *on-demand* during an attack.
- **Rate limiting:** This is a simple yet highly effective technique that places a limit on the number of requests that can be made within a defined time frame from an IP address. This technique is especially useful against application layer attacks, as the malicious traffic can be throttled without completely blocking legitimate users.
- **Behavioural analytics:** Contemporary DDoS protection platforms use ML to establish a baseline of normal network behaviour. They continuously monitor traffic and flag

any significant deviations. This allows them to defend against sophisticated attacks that mimic legitimate traffic to evade signature-based detection.

- **Blackhole routing:** This is a severe technique that is employed as a last resort to survive the attack. When activated, all incoming traffic for the targeted IP address is dropped by diverting to a *black hole* or *sink hole*. While protecting the network infrastructure, it blocks all the legitimate traffic as well, effectively taking the service offline.

Secure remote access

The proliferation of remote and hybrid work models, coupled with the widespread adoption of cloud-native applications and services, requires secure access to systems, applications, and networks. The two primary technologies used for secure remote access are VPN and **Zero Trust Network Access** (**ZTNA**). While the VPN technology has been historically used for secure remote connectivity, its foundational principle of *trust-but-verify* is increasingly misaligned with the present-day security needs in view of the evolving threat landscape. In contrast, ZTNA is built on the principle of never-trust, always-verify. It offers a more agile, scalable, and secure network access solution. ZTNA is an essential component of the **secure access service edge** (**SASE**) framework, a cloud-delivered architecture proposed by *Gartner Inc.* that converges essential networking and security functions into a unified platform. SASE's purpose is to provide a cloud-based solution for secure and consistent access to applications and data for a distributed workforce, regardless of their location. It integrates capabilities such as ZTNA, **software-defined wide area network** (**SD-WAN**), **secure web gateway** (**SWG**), **cloud access security broker** (**CASB**), and **firewall as a service** (**FWaaS**) into a single, comprehensive solution. We will discuss the SASE framework and its components subsequently in *Chapter 11, Cloud Security*. Let us delve into the two primary technologies of VPN and ZTNA.

Virtual private network

A VPN establishes secure and encrypted connections over an untrusted network, such as the public internet. The underlying technical mechanism for this process is tunnelling. This is achieved by encapsulating network messages from a user's device and replaying them at the VPN server on the other side of the tunnel. This encapsulation makes the traversing of the public network transparent to the applications at either end. The integrity of this tunnel is maintained by encrypting the communication. Various protocols, such as **Internet Key Exchange version 2** (**IKEv2**), OpenVPN, and IPsec, are used to implement VPNs, each with its own combination of encryption and transmission standards. The IKEv2 protocol is often utilized for securing mobile devices and supports robust 256 bit **Advanced Encryption Standard** (**AES**) encryption. OpenVPN leverages the OpenSSL encryption library and TLS to provide a high-level of protection. The IPsec protocol, which uses the IKE protocol to set up tunnels, can be used on its own or in conjunction with other protocols like L2TP to provide secure network access.

VPNs come in two primary architectural variants to address different use cases. Remote access VPNs, also known as **client-to-site VPNs**, are designed for individual users who need to securely connect to a corporate network from a distant location. This is accomplished via client software installed on each user's device, which creates a secure tunnel to the corporate network. In contrast, site-to-site VPNs connect entire networks, such as a branch office to a corporate headquarters, allowing them to share resources as if they were part of the same extended network.

VPN trust model

The security philosophy of traditional VPNs is based on a perimeter-based trust model. This approach assumes that once a user has successfully authenticated and established a connection to the network via a VPN gateway, they can be implicitly trusted and granted broad access to the internal resources. The security posture of the network is thus defined by the network perimeter, and any individual or device inside the perimeter is considered safe. This is the trust-but-verify model, where the verification process is mainly confined to the initial authentication at the network's edge. This legacy trust model creates a large attack surface and has severe limitations in a security landscape where threats can originate from anywhere. Once an attacker gains access to a network by compromising a single user's credentials or device, they get unrestricted freedom to move laterally across the entire network and access sensitive resources. Additionally, traditional VPNs typically do not assess the security posture of end devices accessing the network. This effectively means that if a device is compromised, it can inadvertently become a conduit for malware to spread across the entire network, turning a single point of failure into a major security incident.

Limitations of VPN

Some limitations of VPNs that hinder their effectiveness and usability in modern, distributed network environments are as follows:

- **Performance and latency**: VPNs route all user traffic through a central server, which introduces additional steps of encryption and decryption. This process of traffic backhauling adds latency and can lead to slower speeds, especially when working with large files or resource-intensive applications.
- **Scalability and management**: As an organization grows and the number of remote users increases, scaling a VPN solution often requires the acquisition of additional hardware and extensive, time-consuming configuration changes. This creates significant administrative overhead and can be resource-intensive, particularly for larger enterprises.
- **User experience**: The process of connecting to a VPN can require manual logins and use of dedicated client software, which can be cumbersome for non-tech-savvy users and require ongoing support. This friction can hinder productivity and may even encourage users to circumvent the security policies to get their work done more efficiently.

- **Cloud access limitations**: The traditional VPN architecture was built for on-premises environments. Due to architectural and technology limitations, they often struggle to integrate seamlessly with modern cloud applications and services. This can introduce performance degradation for users and lead to inconsistent performance.

Zero Trust Network Access

ZTNA represents a fundamental shift in the approach to secure remote access, discarding the perimeter-based security model. Its foundational principle is *–never trust, always verify*. This means that no user, device, or system is implicitly trusted, regardless of their location or prior access history. Every single access request, whether originating from inside or outside the network, is treated as a potential threat and is rigorously verified before access is granted. This core principle is inextricably linked to the principle of least privilege. ZTNA is designed to ensure that users are only granted the bare minimum level of access that is necessary to perform their tasks. By assigning these permissions in a granular, role-based manner, ZTNA significantly reduces the potential damage that could be caused by a compromised account or a malicious insider.

ZTNA architecture

ZTNA is an identity-centric and application-centric access model. Unlike a VPN that grants access to the entire network, ZTNA only grants access to specific applications or services for which a user is authorized. This is achieved by establishing a secure and encrypted outbound connection between the end user's device and the specific application. The user is not granted access to any other part of the network.

At the heart of the ZTNA framework is a designated trust broker or secure gateway that evaluates every access request. The process of granting access is not a one-time event but a continuous verification cycle that checks the following factors, among others, before and during a session:

- **User identity**: The user's credentials are a primary factor, and ZTNA leverages authentication and authorization from existing **identity providers** (**IdPs**) to confirm the user's identity.
- **Device posture**: The security status of the device requesting access is assessed for compliance with organizational security policies. This includes checking for parameters such as up-to-date operating systems, running antivirus software, and proper patch management.
- **Contextual factors**: The access request is further evaluated based on dynamic contextual data points. These can include the user's location, time of day, and user behaviour patterns.

Advantages of ZTNA

ZTNA offers the following strategic advantages that are critical for protecting information systems:

- **Minimizes the attack surface**: An organization's private applications and services are hidden from unauthorized users by creating a virtual boundary around the organization's assets, drastically reducing the attack surface. This proactive measure makes it more difficult for attackers to even discover the resources, minimizing the probability of an attack.
- **Limits lateral movement**: Even if an attacker manages to compromise an account, their ability to navigate through the organization's ecosystem is restricted to the specific applications that the user is authorized to access. This confinement prevents the attacker from easily moving to other resources, thereby limiting the potential impact of a breach.
- **Enhanced threat detection**: The continuous verification and logging of every access request offer granular insights into user activity and application access. This detailed audit trail is extremely valuable for proactive threat hunting and can be leveraged for real-time threat analysis and response.
- **Inherently scalable**: ZTNA architecture is built to function seamlessly with cloud platforms and can scale automatically to accommodate an increasing number of users without requiring additional hardware, thus avoiding any performance bottlenecks.
- **Seamless user experience**: It offers a seamless, always-on user experience that works transparently in the background. Secure connections are established and security policies applied automatically. This provides a seamless experience to the user, making security an enabler of productivity rather than a hindrance.

The detailed analysis of VPN and ZTNA reveals a fundamental divergence in their architectural philosophies and suitability for modern enterprise systems. While both solutions provide secure remote access, their underlying principles, technical architectures, and strategic implications are fundamentally different. The following table gives a comparative summary of the key features provided by VPN and ZTNA:

Feature	VPN	ZTNA
Trust model	Trust but verify	Never trust, always verify
Access granularity	Broad, network-level access	Granular, application-level access
Authentication	User-based (often one-time)	Continuous user and device verification
Device posture	Not typically checked	Continuously validated
Performance	Latency and bottlenecks	Direct access, seamless performance
Scalability	Complex, resource-intensive	Cloud-native, elastically scalable

Table 7.3: *VPN vs. ZTNA*

Wireless security

Wireless networking has revolutionized connectivity by offering flexibility and mobility. However, this convenience introduces security challenges that are unique to the wireless environment and necessitate robust security measures to protect data transmitted over the airwaves.

Wi-Fi standards

The technical foundation of **wireless local area networks** (**WLANs**) is predominantly based on Wi-Fi standards defined in the IEEE 802.11 family of standards. These standards represent successive generations of Wi-Fi technology, each bringing improvements in terms of data transfer rates, operational range, and efficiency. The wireless standards have progressed significantly from early standards such as 802.11a/b/g to the more recent ones like 802.11n, 802.11ac, and 802.11ax (Wi-Fi 6). The collective development of these standards has enabled faster, more reliable, and more ubiquitous wireless connectivity.

Wireless security protocols

While the wireless networks provide flexible and seamless access to users, the ease of access also presents an easy target for hackers, who continuously attempt to exploit the vulnerabilities in their cryptographic and authentication mechanisms. As such, the wireless security protocols have evolved continuously over time to counter these threats. The progression from older and less secure standards to the recent and more robust ones underscores the dynamic nature of wireless threats and the ongoing challenge of securing wireless networks. The evolution, limitations, and enhancements offered by these protocols are as follows:

- **Wired Equivalent Privacy (WEP)**: WEP was one of the earliest security protocols for Wi-Fi. It is now considered outdated and highly insecure due to significant cryptographic weaknesses that make it easily crackable.

- **Wi-Fi Protected Access (WPA)**: WPA was an interim solution to address the severe vulnerabilities found in WEP. While it was an improvement over WEP, it also has known weaknesses and is now considered outdated and not secure for use.

- **WPA2**: WPA2 utilizes AES encryption in counter mode with **Cipher Block Chaining Message Authentication Code Protocol** (**CCMP**) for data encryption with a 128 bit key. It has personal and enterprise versions. For personal use (WPA2-Personal), it relies on the **pre-shared key** (**PSK**) method, where users enter a shared password for network access. The authentication process involves a 4-way handshake for key exchange. For enterprise environments (WPA2-Enterprise), it leverages the 802.1X framework with a RADIUS server for more robust authentication. WPA2 is vulnerable to offline dictionary attacks and the **key reinstallation attack** (**KRACK**) vulnerability.

- **WPA3**: WPA3 is the latest wireless security protocol designed to address the vulnerabilities in WPA2 and previous protocols. It provides the following enhancements:
    - **Encryption**: WPA3 utilizes AES in **Galois/Counter Mode** (**GCM**), which is considered a more robust and secure encryption algorithm than AES-CCMP. WPA3-Enterprise mandates 192 bit AES support for enhanced security.
    - **Authentication**: A key enhancement of WPA3 is the introduction of the **Simultaneous Authentication of Equals** (**SAE**) protocol. SAE provides stronger protection against offline dictionary and password-guessing attacks and is resistant to KRACK attacks.
    - **Individualized data encryption**: WPA3 offers individualized data encryption for each device connected to the network, even in open Wi-Fi networks. This implies that each device has its own unique encryption key, which significantly enhances privacy and security. This is a major improvement over WPA2, where all devices share the same key.
    - **Public network security**: WPA3 introduces Enhanced Open security mode that employs **Opportunistic Wireless Encryption** (**OWE**) to provide encryption between the device and the access point, even in open Wi-Fi networks where no password is needed.
    - **Forward secrecy**: WPA3 incorporates forward secrecy. This cryptographic property ensures that if a session key is compromised, it cannot be used to decrypt previously captured data from past sessions.
    - **Protected Management Frames (PMFs)**: WPA3 mandates the use of PMFs to protect management frames against spoofing and eavesdropping. The use of PMF was optional in WPA2.

The following table provides a comparison of security enhancements provided by WPA3 as compared to WPA2:

Feature	WPA2	WPA3
Encryption algorithm	AES-CCMP (128 bit AES).	AES-GCM (128 bit, Enterprise mandates 192 bit AES).
Authentication method	PSK for personal, 802.1X/ RADIUS for enterprise.	SAE.
Protection against offline dictionary attacks	Vulnerable, especially with weak passphrases.	Stronger protection, even with weak passphrases.
Protection against KRACK attacks	Vulnerable (4-way handshake).	Resistant (SAE key exchange).

Feature	WPA2	WPA3
Individualized data encryption	All devices share the same encryption key.	Individualized encryption for each device, even in open networks.
Security for public networks	No security for open networks.	Enhanced Open mode provides encryption without a password.
Forward secrecy	Not supported.	Provided.
Protected Management Frames (PMFs)	Optional.	Mandated.

Table 7.4: *WPA2 vs. WPA3*

Wireless security best practices

While the choice of a strong security protocol like WPA3 is critical for wireless network security, it can still be compromised if other vulnerabilities exist. The security of the protocol is closely intertwined with user practices and the security of the hardware.

The wireless router is the gateway to the network and is a frequent target of attack. Following best practices for router configuration can be adopted to provide a secure network foundation:

Action	Rationale
Change the default admin password	Default passwords are publicly known and provide a common entry point for attackers to gain full control over router settings.
Change default network name (SSID)	Default SSIDs can be used by attackers in conjunction with rainbow tables to launch pre-computed password attacks. A unique name provides an added layer of security.
Enable strong encryption (WPA3/ WPA2)	This is a critical step to encrypt data transmissions and prevent unauthorized access. The use of AES-based encryption is highly recommended.
Disable WPS, UPnP, and remote management	These features introduce significant security risks by allowing easy access to the network without a password or opening unnecessary ports.
Enable the router's firewall	The built-in firewall provides an additional layer of protection, filtering out malicious traffic and blocking unauthorized connection attempts.
Set up a guest network	This isolates untrusted devices from the primary network, preventing them from accessing and infecting other connected devices.

Action	Rationale
Regularly update router firmware	Firmware updates patch security vulnerabilities and fix bugs, ensuring the router is protected against the latest known threats.
Log out as administrator	Failing to log out of the admin panel after making changes leaves the router's configuration open to compromise if an attacker gains access to a connected device.

Table 7.5: Best practices for wireless router configuration

Conclusion

In this chapter, we explored the fundamental concepts and technologies that form the backbone of network security. We began with a discussion on the OSI and TCP/IP models. Understanding these models is critical for network security, as they provide a structured framework to analyze how data travels through a network and help in identifying the controls to be applied. We also examined the essential networking devices like routers, switches, bridges, and hubs, which facilitate the movement of data across networks. These devices, while enabling connectivity and communication, also represent potential points of vulnerability if not configured and secured properly.

The core of network security lies in specialized security protocols and devices that protect the network from unauthorized access, cyberattacks, and consequent data breaches. Firewalls serve as the first line of defense, filtering incoming and outgoing traffic based on defined security rules. While the basic firewalls provided protection at layers 3 and 4, the UTMs and NGFWs carry out deep packet filtering and provide additional protection at the upper layers of the protocol stack. WAFs provide targeted protection against web application attacks, such as SQL injection and XSS. IDS monitors the network traffic for any suspicious activity and detects potential attacks, and IPS proactively blocks them. DDoS protection mechanisms are employed to defend against DoS attacks and are crucial in protecting information systems against such attacks that aim to overwhelm network, application, or server resources.

We also discussed secure remote access technologies that have become indispensable in view of the remote and hybrid modes of working. We covered VPN technology, which provides an encrypted data tunnel for secure communication over public networks, and also the more advanced and granular ZTNA, which implements stringent and continuous identity verification and least-privilege access models, ensuring that trust is never implicit.

Finally, we addressed wireless network security, which presents unique challenges due to its broadcast nature. Following wireless security best practices and implementing strong encryption protocols like WPA3, along with a robust authentication mechanism, is essential to protect wireless networks against unauthorized access and eavesdropping.

As networks continue to evolve in scale, complexity, and architecture, network security must be approached as a continuously evolving discipline. Ongoing monitoring, regular risk assessment, and adaptation to emerging threats are essential to maintaining an effective network security posture.

In the next chapter, we will delve into the strategies to secure devices that connect to the network, i.e., the endpoints, which are an equally critical component of information security. In the next chapter on endpoint security, we will discuss strategies and technologies required to protect endpoint devices, such as servers, dockers, containers, and end user devices.

Exercises

1. Discuss the OSI model for computer networking and explain the functions of various layers of the model.
2. What are the different layers in the TCP/IP model? Discuss their correspondence with the layers of the OSI model.
3. Discuss encapsulation and decapsulation in the context of networking.
4. The networking protocols were designed primarily for data transfer across networks, not necessarily with security in view. Discuss.
5. Discuss how SSL/TLS facilitates the secure transfer of data across networks.
6. What is VLAN routing, and how do VLANs enhance network security? Discuss.
7. How do firewalls protect networks? Briefly discuss different types of firewalls.
8. Distinguish between IDS and IPS.
9. VPN and ZTNA both offer secure remote access. Discuss the foundational architecture of the two and bring out how ZTNA provides enhanced security over VPN.
10. Discuss the security enhancements provided by WPA3 over WPA2.

CHAPTER 8
Endpoint Security

Introduction

Endpoints are physical or virtual devices that connect to a network. They represent an increasingly heterogeneous attack surface encompassing devices such as laptops, desktops, servers, tablets, smartphones, **virtual machines** (**VMs**), and **Internet of Things** (**IoT**) devices, besides others. As endpoints are generally the first point of interaction with network services and applications, they are often the prime target of attackers to gain access to enterprise networks and data stores. Endpoint security is a methodology of safeguarding information systems, which includes strategies, technologies, and practices that protect the endpoint devices from compromise, unauthorized access, or data exfiltration.

The conventional paradigm for enterprise security focused on securing the network perimeter, where anything within the organization's perimeter could be implicitly trusted. With the advent of remote work, proliferation of personal mobile devices, and widespread adoption of cloud-based services, the traditional network perimeter has become increasingly porous or altogether disappeared. With this fundamental shift, the endpoint attack surface has grown exponentially, and the network-centric approach is no longer adequate to meet enterprise security requirements. Endpoint security addresses this challenge by shifting the security focus to the device itself. It ensures a consistent and compliant device security posture, whether the device connects to the office **local area network** (**LAN**), home network, or any public **Wireless Fidelity** (**Wi-Fi**) network.

Modern endpoint security extends beyond traditional signature-based antivirus tools and adopts a layered, defense-in-depth approach to protection. Contemporary solutions increasingly rely on technologies such as **endpoint detection and response** (**EDR**) and **extended detection and response** (**XDR**) to provide continuous visibility into endpoint behaviour and enable timely detection and response to any malicious activity. These solutions also align closely with Zero Trust principles, where devices are not implicitly trusted but are continuously assessed for security posture and compliance before being granted access to enterprise resources.

Besides detection and response capabilities, effective endpoint security also depends on proactive hardening and configuration controls. These include **operating system** (**OS**) and application hardening, secure configuration of remote access services, and continuous monitoring. This chapter examines the evolving endpoint threat landscape and presents practical strategies for securing endpoints, covering EDR, XDR, **endpoint protection platforms (EPP)**, OS hardening, virtualization security, and policy-driven controls. These measures provide a structured approach to reducing endpoint risk in decentralized environments.

Structure

In this chapter, we will discuss the following topics:

- Endpoint threats and security challenges
- Endpoint security solutions
- Zero Trust for endpoints
- OS hardening
- Securing remote access
- Securing virtualized environments
- Future trends in endpoint security

Objectives

By the end of this chapter, you should be able to understand the significance of endpoint security within an organizational security framework and describe the growing challenges posed by heterogeneous devices and emerging threat vectors. You will be able to explain the core components of endpoint security and evaluate advanced endpoint security solutions such as EDR, XDR, and EPP. You will be able to apply hardening techniques across OSs, remote access protocols, and virtualized environments, including VMs and containers. The chapter will also enable you to develop endpoint security policies aligned with Zero Trust principles and appreciate emerging trends in endpoint protection.

Endpoint threats and security challenges

Endpoints serve as the gateways into enterprise networks and, as such, remain among the most attractive targets for adversaries. They face a wide spectrum of threats, and the organizational environments in which they operate add further layers of complexity. In today's distributed digital landscape, where employees work remotely, data is accessed from diverse devices, and corporate resources extend far beyond the traditional perimeters, the endpoint has become both the most critical and the most vulnerable link in the security chain. Protecting it is therefore a central imperative of modern cybersecurity.

Endpoint threats

Endpoints are exposed to a diverse and continuously evolving set of threats that are designed to exploit not only system vulnerabilities but also human behaviour. While some attacks rely on familiar forms of malware, others take advantage of trust relationships, memory-resident techniques, and social engineering to compromise devices and gain unauthorized access to enterprise networks. Some of the commonly encountered endpoint threats are as follows:

- **Malware**: The traditional malware, such as viruses, worms, Trojans, and ransomware, remains a significant threat to endpoints. Ransomware attack, in particular, in which attackers encrypt critical data and demand ransom in exchange for decrypting it, has emerged as one of the most potent threats. These attacks not only cause financial loss to an enterprise but also result in downtime, reputational damage, and regulatory consequences.

- **Spyware**: These are malicious software that silently monitor user activity, keystrokes, and network traffic to harvest sensitive data such as login credentials or financial information.

- **Fileless malware**: Fileless techniques are increasingly observed in **advanced persistent threats** (**APTs**), where stealth and persistence are paramount. Fileless malware executes directly in system memory instead of relying on files stored on disk, making it difficult to detect them. Additionally, as they leverage trusted administrative tools such as PowerShell, **Windows Management Instrumentation** (**WMI**), and Office macros, the line between legitimate and malicious activity gets blurred, which makes the detection even more difficult.

- **Phishing**: Humans remain a critical weak link in securing endpoints. Sophisticated phishing campaigns can trick users into downloading malicious attachments, clicking on links, or revealing credentials to gain unauthorized access to endpoints and consequently to enterprise networks.

- **Supply chain attacks**: Supply chain attacks bypass even the most sophisticated defenses by compromising trusted third-party applications and services. Defense against such attacks requires organizations to extend security focus beyond their own infrastructure to monitor vendor relationships and audit their software supply chains.

The infamous outbreak of the WannaCry ransomware in May 2017 and the Kaseya ransomware attack of July 2021 demonstrate how attacks on endpoints can paralyze organizations. The WannaCry ransomware exploited a vulnerability in the **Server Message Block** (**SMB**) protocol on Windows systems to spread rapidly across global networks. Thousands of organizations, including banks, healthcare, and public services, were crippled as their endpoints were encrypted, and a ransom was demanded. In the Kaseya attack, hackers exploited vulnerabilities in Kaseya's remote management software to deploy ransomware across thousands of customer endpoints. Unlike WannaCry, which spread directly through vulnerable machines, the Kaseya incident exploited trusted tools that manage endpoints at scale. The attack paralyzed a large number of small and medium-sized enterprises worldwide, demonstrating how supply chain dependencies can be exploited to maximize impact.

Endpoint security challenges

Securing endpoints is one of the most challenging aspects of enterprise information security. Unlike centralized network infrastructure or data centers, endpoints are highly diverse and geographically distributed. They operate across multiple platforms, connect from varying network conditions, and are exposed to a variety of external and internal threats. This diversity introduces several challenges, each of which requires tailored strategies.

Expanding attack surface

As organizations embrace digital transformation, the number and variety of endpoints have increased dramatically. Earlier, the endpoints were largely limited to desktops and laptops within an office environment. These days, one commonly comes across laptops, smartphones, tablets, IoT devices, thin clients, virtual desktops, and even containerized applications running in the cloud. Each of these device types introduces unique vulnerabilities. This diversity in OS, firmware, and applications requires organizations to adopt specialized security measures for each environment. This challenge is magnified due to remote working and **bring your own device** (**BYOD**) policies. Employees often access enterprise resources using personal devices connected through home routers, unsecured public Wi-Fi, or shared networks. Unlike traditional office setups, these endpoints operate outside the organization's perimeter firewall and are not always covered by enterprise-grade security controls. Enforcing consistent security policies across such a heterogeneous environment is complex and often leaves gaps that attackers exploit.

Evasive malware

Traditional antiviruses rely heavily on signature-based detection, where known malicious file patterns trigger alerts. Sophisticated malware, however, increasingly adopts stealth techniques that bypass these defenses. Fileless malware, for instance, operates entirely in memory without writing files to disk. This allows them to evade file-based scans and persist only for the duration of system activity, making forensic detection extremely difficult. Attackers often leverage legitimate administrative tools such as PowerShell or WMI to execute malicious code. Since these tools are commonly used for legitimate administrative tasks, distinguishing between malicious activity and normal operations becomes challenging. Therefore, behavioural monitoring techniques and EDR capabilities need to be employed rather than relying solely on traditional antivirus.

Insider threats

While the majority of security measures are focused on external attackers, insider threats remain a persistent and dangerous challenge. Insider threats may arise from malicious insiders such as disgruntled employees or contractors who intentionally exfiltrate data, sabotage systems, or abuse privileged access. The *Edward Snowden* case (2013) remains a textbook example of insider threat, where a contractor with legitimate access to the U.S. **National Security Agency** (**NSA**) systems exfiltrated a huge amount of classified data without triggering security alerts. Even well-meaning staff may inadvertently introduce malware via phishing emails, the use of insecure USB devices, or weak credentials.

Insider threats are difficult to detect because their actions often resemble legitimate user activity. For instance, a system administrator copying data to external storage may be a routine activity, but it could be an attempt to exfiltrate data. Insider threat detection requires a combination of **user behaviour analytics** (**UBA**), access control measures, and continuous monitoring. Policies such as restricting USB usage, enforcing encryption, and logging privileged activities can help mitigate these risks to a great extent.

Software vulnerabilities

Unpatched systems, particularly those with zero-day vulnerabilities, pose a major challenge to securing endpoints. A zero-day vulnerability is a flaw in software or firmware that is unknown to the vendor and has not yet been patched. Attackers exploit such vulnerabilities before fixes are made available, leaving endpoints unprotected during the intervening period. Even after patches are released, many enterprises struggle with timely deployment due to operational constraints or compatibility issues, leaving a window of opportunity for attackers to exploit the endpoints.

Endpoints are particularly susceptible to zero-day attacks as they rely on complex OS and applications that may not be updated regularly. Attackers often bundle these exploits into phishing emails, drive-by downloads, or exploit kits to gain initial access to the endpoints.

Challenges of virtualized environments

VMs and containers introduce additional attack surface. Without proper security controls, attackers can breach these environments and move laterally across the enterprise infrastructure. The key challenges faced in virtual environments are as follows:

- **VM escape**: It is a vulnerability unique to virtualized environments that allows malicious code inside a VM to break out and interact with the hypervisor or other VMs on the host. It is critical to keep hypervisors patched and restrict unnecessary services to prevent such attacks.
- **Insecure container images**: Containers frequently use base images downloaded from public repositories. If these are not updated or scanned for vulnerabilities, organizations may inadvertently deploy insecure workloads.
- **Privileged containers**: Running containers with root privileges can allow attackers to escalate control to the host system.
- **Orchestration risks**: Tools like Kubernetes introduce complexity and administrative overhead. Misconfigured access control or open dashboards can provide attackers with unauthorized entry points to the containers.

Endpoint security solutions

Over the years, endpoint security has evolved significantly. In the early days, the focus was primarily on deploying preventive tools such as antivirus software and host-based firewalls to block known threats. While these basic controls remain indispensable, they have limitations in handling the sophistication of modern attacks that evade traditional detection methods. Contemporary endpoint security solutions have grown beyond the foundational technologies and evolved into advanced solutions that offer detection, response, and analytics capabilities against highly adaptive and sophisticated attacks.

Core components of endpoint security

Securing endpoints requires a combination of complementary technical controls rather than reliance on a single protective mechanism. The core components of endpoint security represent the minimum set of safeguards that should be present on every enterprise endpoint, irrespective of its location or operating environment. These controls focus on preventing common forms of compromise, limiting the impact of successful attacks, and reducing the overall attack surface of the device. Together, they provide protection against malware execution, unauthorized network communication, and misuse of applications, forming the basis upon which more advanced detection, response, and monitoring capabilities can be built. The following components represent the foundational building blocks of endpoint security, each addressing a specific aspect of the endpoint threat landscape and collectively contributing to a secure and resilient endpoint posture.

Antivirus and antimalware

The primary purpose of these tools is to protect endpoints from malicious software. While the core functionality of these tools remains the same, the methods of detection have evolved to combat new threats. The traditional software primarily relied on signature-based detection, which involves scanning files for known malware signatures. While this method is highly accurate and efficient at detecting known threats, it is fundamentally incapable of identifying previously unknown malware or polymorphic malware that constantly changes its code to evade detection. The limitations of signature-based detection are addressed by employing a heuristic analysis technique. Instead of relying on a signature database, the heuristic-based detection analyzes the behaviour, structure, and attributes of a program or human activity. A program or activity that displays suspicious behaviour, such as attempting to modify a critical system file, spawn an unusual process, or make unauthorized network connections, may be flagged as malicious even if there is no previously known pattern. This proactive approach is essential to detect zero-day and fileless malware.

Host-based firewalls

A host-based firewall runs directly on the endpoint. It filters inbound and outbound network traffic to and from the endpoint. Unlike network firewalls that protect an entire perimeter, the host-based firewalls protect individual devices, providing granular and device-specific controls. This is particularly critical for remote and mobile endpoints that operate outside the protected enterprise network. These firewalls restrict access to open ports and block unauthorized communication, significantly reducing the attack surface of the device. They can also control which applications and services can communicate over the network, monitor outgoing connections, and block unauthorized remote connections, thus reducing the risk of lateral movement and data exfiltration.

Application control

Application control is a security mechanism that prevents unauthorized software from running on an endpoint and restricts execution to a pre-approved list of programs. This is a highly effective control that can stop many types of attacks, as it prevents attackers from running their malicious executables on a compromised machine. Two primary methodologies are used for application control:

- **Whitelisting**: This is a restrictive approach that, by default, restricts execution to a pre-approved list of programs, and only software that is whitelisted is permitted to run. By preventing unknown or unauthorized applications from running, whitelisting drastically reduces the attack surface. This approach is particularly effective against zero-day exploits, since unknown malware cannot execute if it is not explicitly allowed. However, this approach requires careful management to avoid disrupting legitimate workflows.

- **Blacklisting**: This is a more permissive approach that allows all applications to run unless explicitly blacklisted. A list of known malicious or unwanted applications is maintained, and any application on that blacklist is blocked. This is easier to implement but is ineffective against new or unknown malware that are not on the blacklist.

Device control and data loss prevention

Controlling access to and from peripheral devices and implementing **data loss prevention (DLP)** solutions are essential controls to prevent data exfiltration and propagation of malware via endpoint devices. These controls are as follows:

- **Device control**: Removable media such as USB drives remain a popular vector for malware propagation and data theft. Endpoint security platforms allow administrators to enforce device usage policies, such as blocking all external drives, enabling read-only access, or restricting usage to encrypted devices. Implementing device control policies is crucial to prevent data exfiltration and to prevent the introduction of malware from an infected external device.

- **DLP**: These tools monitor endpoints for attempts to copy, email, or upload sensitive data such as **personally identifiable information (PII)** and intellectual property. Key features of DLP solutions include content inspection, endpoint enforcement, and implementing context-aware controls, i.e., identifying risky activities. DLP policies can enforce what users are allowed to do with data once they have access to it. For example, a policy can prevent users from copying confidential files to a USB drive, restrict copy-and-paste functionality in unapproved applications, or block the sending of sensitive data in an email.

Patch management

Patch management is the systematic process of identifying, acquiring, testing, and deploying updates and patches to software and systems. It is a foundational security control for protecting information systems. A significant number of cyberattacks exploit known vulnerabilities that remain unpatched on endpoints. A robust patch management program ensures that all endpoints are kept up-to-date with the latest security fixes, thereby closing a critical window of opportunity for attackers. The outbreak of WannaCry ransomware that we discussed in the section on endpoint threats clearly demonstrates the devastating consequences of delayed and poor patching.

Advanced endpoint protection solutions

The endpoint threats have increased in complexity and sophistication. Attackers increasingly use fileless and adaptive malware against which traditional antivirus-based protection is not adequate. Advanced endpoint protection solutions such as EDR, XDR, and EPP have been developed to counter the stealthier attack techniques used by threat actors. These solutions adopt an integrated multi-layer approach that moves beyond the traditional tools into continuous detection, behavioural monitoring, and automated response.

EDR

EDR refers to platforms that continuously monitor endpoints to identify suspicious or malicious behaviour. Unlike preventive tools, which focus primarily on known threats, EDR emphasizes detection, investigation, and response to unknown and evolving attacks.

The raw telemetry is transmitted to a central server, where it is normalized, correlated, and analyzed in real-time. EDR systems utilize sophisticated real-time analytics and deep learning algorithms to analyze this data to identify deviations from established baselines that signal potential compromise or malicious behaviour.

The core functions of an EDR solution include:

- **Continuous monitoring**: A lightweight agent is installed on the endpoints to continuously monitor and collect granular telemetry data. The agents collect complete system data that includes details on process execution, file system changes, network connections, user activities, and configuration changes. This telemetry data is transmitted to a central server for analysis.

- **Behavioural analysis**: The aggregated telemetry data is normalized, correlated, and analyzed in real-time. EDR systems utilize sophisticated real-time analytics and deep learning algorithms to analyze this data to identify deviations from established baselines that signal potential compromise or malicious behaviour.
- **Automated response**: EDRs enable quick containment. Upon detecting a threat, an EDR can take immediate and automated actions, such as isolating the infected endpoint from the network, terminating a malicious process, or quarantining a suspicious file to contain the threat and reduce its impact.
- **Threat hunting**: An EDR provides a detailed audit trail of events, providing forensic analysts a complete picture of an attack's timeline, scope, and impacted systems. This information is invaluable for post-incident investigations and proactive threat hunting. It aids security analysts in actively searching for **indicators of compromise (IOCs)**, **indicators of attack (IOAs)**, and other hidden threats that may have evaded the initial detection.

The following figure depicts the typical workflow of an EDR:

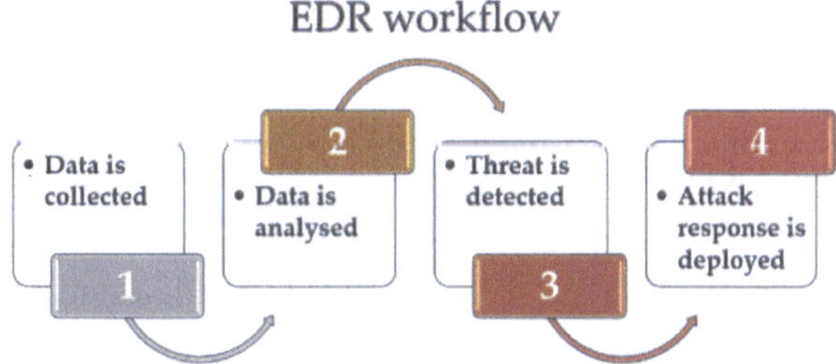

***Figure 8.1**: Typical EDR workflow*

XDR

Modern attacks are rarely confined to a single device or platform. APTs often span across multiple layers, including identity systems, email, networks, endpoints, and cloud workloads. This complexity led to the emergence of XDR solutions. While an EDR solution is focused on the single security layer of the endpoint, XDR extends that concept beyond the endpoint to deliver a unified cross-domain visibility, detection, and response capability.

Core capabilities of XDR are as follows:

- **Unified data collection**: XDR aggregates data and telemetry not just from endpoints but also from a wide array of security platforms such as EDR, firewalls, email gateways, cloud platforms, and identity providers.
- **Correlation and contextualization**: The data collected from diverse sources is normalized and correlated using **machine learning** (**ML**) and **artificial intelligence** (**AI**) into a single incident. This capability is critical for identifying complex attacks involving multiple attack vectors that might be missed by a single security tool. The

XDR correlation engines connect seemingly isolated alerts into a cohesive attack storyline. For instance, a phishing email alert from an email gateway may be correlated with a suspicious process on a user's laptop or unusual login attempts in the **Active Directory** (**AD**) server.

- **Improved detection accuracy**: Since alerts from multiple layers are combined in a single platform in the XDR, it reduces the false positives. An anomalous process on an endpoint becomes much more significant if it correlates with a compromised user account or a lateral movement attempt.
- **Automated response across domains**: XDR platforms enable cross-environment remediation. For instance, if a malicious process is detected on an endpoint, XDR can take simultaneous actions to quarantine the device, block the malicious IP address at the firewall, and disable the compromised user account in AD.
- **Threat intelligence integration**: XDR platforms can also integrate with threat intelligence feeds, which enables organizations to detect emerging attack infrastructure or campaigns. Additionally, as XDRs provide a centralized dashboard, they simplify investigation and automate threat hunting across the entire environment, improving detection and response efficiency.

The following table provides a comparison between the capabilities of EDR and XDR:

	EDR	XDR
Primary focus	Endpoint devices (desktops, laptops, servers, VMs).	Multiple domains (endpoints, networks, cloud, email, identity).
Visibility	Detailed visibility into endpoint activities (processes, files, registry, connections).	Cross-domain visibility with correlations across multiple security layers.
Detection approach	Behavioural analysis, anomaly detection.	Correlates events from different sources, uses analytics to identify multi-stage attacks.
Response capabilities	Endpoint specific	Orchestrated response across domains
Integration	SIEM/SOAR integration for extended use.	Vendor-driven ecosystem, built-in integrations across tools.
Strengths	Granular endpoint forensics	Unified incident view reduces alert fatigue and is stronger against multi-vector attacks.
Limitations	Narrow scope - endpoint only	Vendor lock-in risks are complex to deploy.
Suitable for	Organizations focusing on endpoint visibility and targeted attacks.	Enterprises need enterprise-wide, correlated detection and response in hybrid environments.

***Table 8.1**: EDR vs. XDR*

EPP

EPPs represent the convergence of multiple endpoint security controls that integrate and consolidate a wide range of endpoint security technologies into a single platform. An EPP is a multi-layered solution that typically includes **next-generation antivirus** (**NGAV**), EDR, device control, and DLP capabilities. Microsoft Defender for Endpoint is an example of an EPP that integrates antivirus, firewall, device control, and EDR in a single suite. The key advantage of an EPP is that it provides a single consolidated view for security operations, which simplifies management and enhances the overall security posture. Advanced EPPs are often cloud-native, leveraging global threat intelligence and behavioural analytics to deliver a more dynamic and effective defense.

Zero Trust for endpoints

The Zero Trust security model operates on the principle of never trust, always verify. Instead of assuming trust based on network location, Zero Trust enforces continuous verification of every device, user, and application request, irrespective of its geographical location. The concept of Zero Trust for endpoints integrates well with the cloud and hybrid environments. It helps in the dynamic enforcement of security policies across managed and unmanaged devices and provides strong protection against credential theft and lateral movement attempts.

Key principles of Zero Trust applied to endpoints are as follows:

- **Device posture assessment**: Each endpoint must prove its integrity before being granted access. This involves checking OS patch levels, security software status, disk encryption, and device compliance with corporate policies. For example, an unmanaged personal laptop without encryption may be denied access to corporate email, even if the user has valid credentials.
- **Identity-centric security**: Endpoint access is tied to strong user authentication methods such as **multi-factor authentication** (**MFA**) and device certificates.
- **Least privilege access**: Users and applications are granted only the minimum permissions required for their role. This is enforced by endpoint privilege management tools that restrict local admin rights.
- **Micro-segmentation**: Even if an endpoint connects successfully, it is only permitted to access the specific applications or resources it is authorized to access. This reduces the risk of lateral movement.
- **Continuous monitoring**: The endpoint posture and behaviour are continuously monitored for deviations. For instance, a device that suddenly connects at an unusual time or from an unusual geographic location may trigger re-authentication or be quarantined.

OS hardening

The default configurations of most OS are designed to facilitate ease of use and system compatibility and are not focused on maximum security. As a result, the default installations often include unnecessary services, open ports, and system settings that can be exploited by attackers. OS hardening is the practice of disabling the unwarranted components, implementing strong security policies, and applying configurations that make the systems more resilient. It is one of the fundamental controls for endpoint security that complements other endpoint security solutions. Proper OS hardening drastically reduces the attack surface, minimizes exposure to threats, lowers the risk of data breach, and helps in regulatory compliance.

The **Center for Internet Security** (**CIS**) provides authoritative benchmarks for secure OS configurations. These benchmarks are guidelines that offer prescriptive controls for most versions of Windows, Linux, and macOS, which can be scoped and adapted to specific environments based on the risk profile. CIS Benchmarks define two levels of security settings:

- **Level 1 profile**: This is the basic profile that recommends essential security requirements that should cause little or no interruption of service or reduced functionality.
- **Level 2 profile**: This profile recommends security settings for environments requiring greater security that could result in some reduced functionality.

The biggest operational challenge that system administrators face is ensuring the consistent deployment of these policies across the heterogeneous endpoints. CIS provides not only the documentation but also tools like CIS hardened images (pre-configured VMs) and CIS build kits (**Group Policy Objects (GPOs**) or bash scripts) to help automate the implementation of these baselines.

The following table summarizes CIS-aligned foundational controls essential for OS hardening:

Security control area	Description	Implementation mechanism
System hygiene	Remove unnecessary services, applications, and drivers. Enable only required services.	**Windows**: Disable superfluous optional features. **Linux**: Mask or disable unused systemd services.
Patching and updates	Ensure continuous and automatic application of patches, updates, and service packs.	Configuration Management tools, Windows Update for Business/Windows Server Update Services, and native package managers.
Application control	Utilize application whitelisting to allow only trusted and approved applications to run.	**Windows**: **Windows Defender Application Control** (**WDAC**), **Linux**: AppArmor/ SELinux **mandatory access control** (**MAC**), **macOS**: Gatekeeper.

Security control area	Description	Implementation mechanism
Access control	Implement **role-based access controls** (**RBAC**) and restrict administrative privileges.	Utilize least privilege accounts, enforce risk-based MFA.
Auditing and logging	Enable comprehensive logging of all system activities.	Integration of OS logs with SIEM.

Table 8.2: Summary of OS hardening foundational controls

Windows OS hardening

Windows is a widely deployed OS and hence a frequent target for attackers. For Windows deployments, the OS hardening strategy revolves around automation, and GPOs are the primary tool for deploying and enforcing secure configuration settings. The primary Windows native features used for OS hardening are as follows:

- **Group policies**: Group policy is a powerful feature in Windows that can be used to simultaneously enforce a wide range of security policies and configurations across a network of endpoints. Group policies can be used to enforce strong password policies, disable legacy protocols, and apply consistent firewall rules. Microsoft Security Compliance Toolkit can be leveraged to manage and compare GPOs against recommended security baselines to ensure configuration consistency and reduce drift.

- **User Account Control (UAC)**: It is a security feature that helps prevent unauthorized changes to a system. By setting UAC to *always notify*, users are prompted for permission before a program can make changes that require administrative privileges, which prevents stealthy privilege escalation attacks.

- **Secure boot**: This is a crucial security feature that ensures that the boot process of a device is secure. It prevents unsigned or unauthorized OS loaders from executing, thus protecting the system from low-level rootkits and other malicious software.

- **Disk encryption**: Mandatory full-disk encryption (BitLocker) can be implemented for all OS and fixed data drives. Implementing BitLocker on computers with a **Trusted Platform Module** (**TPM**) version 1.2 or higher and configuring 128 bit **Advanced Encryption Standard** (**AES**) encryption is the recommended best practice.

- **Virtualization-based security (VBS)**: Features like *Credential Guard* and *Device Guard* are leveraged to strengthen the security of Windows systems. VBS uses the Windows hypervisor to create an isolated virtual environment that serves as the root of trust. This isolates security assets like authenticated user credentials (Local Security Authority Secrets) from a potentially compromised OS kernel.

- **Application whitelisting**: Microsoft integrated security suite includes a host-based firewall and WDAC tool. WDAC can be used to implement application whitelisting to strictly control which executables, scripts, and DLLs are permitted to run. This prevents untrusted applications from executing and is a crucial defense against fileless malware-based attacks.
- **Identity protection**: Windows Hello for Business using biometrics or **personal identification number** (**PIN**), and Windows Defender Credential Guard can be configured to protect against unauthorized access and credential theft.

Linux OS hardening

Linux is the widely used OS in server environments and is often targeted by attackers to gain access and expand control in enterprise networks. Linux OS hardening relies heavily on command-line tools, configuration files, and configuration management platforms. CIS Build Kits often utilize Bash shell scripts for automating the process.

Some of the key technical controls for hardening enterprise Linux distributions are as follows:

- **Disabling unused services**: This is one of the core principles of any OS hardening. All unnecessary services and applications are removed or disabled to minimize the attack surface.
- **MAC**: Linux distros offer MAC frameworks such as:
    - **AppArmor**: This is the default MAC framework for Ubuntu and openSUSE. It controls applications using profiles that define the resources and files they are allowed to access. The *aa-genprof* utility can be used to automatically generate a profile for an application by monitoring its activity; thereafter, *aa-enforce* can be used to enforce the profile's rules, and *aa-complain* can be used to audit any violations.
    - **SELinux**: This is the default framework on **Red Hat Enterprise Linux** (**RHEL**). While a more powerful tool, it is also more complex and difficult to manage. It is used to define policies that restrict the capabilities of processes. Tools such *Udica* can be utilized to analyze container specifications and generate custom policies and define fine-grained security rules.

  These frameworks supplement the traditional **discretionary access controls** (**DACs**) by restricting applications and users to a specific set of permissions, even if they have elevated privileges. For instance, utilizing these kernel security modules, systems enforce the least privilege principle and ensure that even the root user inside a container or process is considered a regular user and is governed by the defined security profiles.
- **Kernel hardening**: Specific kernel configuration options and boot parameters must be set to reduce the attack surface. Enabling memory randomization makes repeat

exploits much more difficult to execute by randomizing memory locations. Disabling verbose debug helps ensure that sensitive backtrace information is not leaked upon a kernel panic. Enabling memory poisoning to overwrite freed memory reduces the risk of information leak from old data. Kernel security can be enhanced by the kernel integrity subsystem, **Integrity Measurement Architecture** (**IMA**), and **Extended Verification Module** (**EVM**).

- **Secure Shell (SSH) hardening**: Disable direct root login and enforce strong, key-based authentication.
- **Auditing**: All system activity must be logged by configuring and utilizing the Linux audit daemon (*auditd*) for forensic analysis and compliance purposes.

macOS hardening

macOS includes several robust built-in security features that can be configured to harden the OS. These are often managed via **unified endpoint management** (**UEM**) solutions for large-scale deployments.

The key macOS native security features and controls are as follows:

- **Gatekeeper**: It helps ensure that only trusted software runs on the Mac. It checks downloaded applications for security issues and signature validity before allowing them to run. This helps prevent users from inadvertently running malicious code.
- **System Integrity Protection (SIP)**: It is a security feature that provides kernel level protection and prevents even the root user from modifying certain core system files, folders, and processes. This significantly limits the OS attack surface and helps protect against root-level malware.
- **Hardware root of trust**: Latest macOS versions have an in-built security co-processor that handles critical security functions and enforces a cryptographic chain-of-trust during the secure boot process. It ensures that only legitimately signed code runs at each stage. It houses the **Secure Enclave Processor** (**SEP**) that protects the biometric data of Touch ID and handles the FileVault encryption keys. It also provides always-on, hardware-backed encryption for the **solid-state drive** (**SSD**) that is independent of FileVault.
- **FileVault**: It provides a mandatory full-disk encryption feature with keys managed by the SEP for hardware-backed security.
- **Startup security utility**: For maximum security, it should be configured to enforce secure boot and prevent the Mac from starting from external or removable media.

Securing remote access

Remote access protocols like SSH, **Secure File Transfer** (**SFTP**), and **Remote Desktop Protocol** (**RDP**) are essential for system administration and remote work. Proactive hardening of these services is critical for securing the endpoints, as they are frequently targeted by attackers to gain unauthorized access.

SSH hardening

SSH is a secure protocol used for remote system administration, particularly in Linux environments. Its default settings are quite liberal and can be a liability. The following best practices can be implemented for securing SSH connections:

- **Enforce key-based authentication**: Password-based authentication is vulnerable to brute-force attacks. Whenever feasible, password authentication should be disabled, and only key-based authentication should be used, as it is far more secure and resistant to brute-force attempts.
- **Limit authentication retries**: Configuring the server to disconnect a user after a specified number of failed login attempts can prevent brute-force attacks from succeeding.
- **Disable remote root login**: Direct root access via SSH is a major security risk. It is highly recommended to disable remote root login and use a standard user account with sudo privileges for performing administrative tasks.
- **Implement two-factor authentication (2FA)**: 2FA, such as a code from a mobile app, in addition to key-based or password authentication, provides an additional layer of defense. This ensures that even if an attacker obtains a private key or password, they cannot gain access without the second factor.
- **Restrict access by IP address**: Limiting SSH access to known and trusted IP addresses or subnets vastly reduces the attack surface and prevents malicious connections from unknown sources.

SFTP hardening

SFTP is a protocol that is commonly used by system administrators for secure transfer of files across systems and networks. It is built on the SSH protocol and mostly requires similar hardening configurations. Some of these are as follows:

- **Use key-based authentication**: As in the case of SSH, key-based authentication is more secure than password authentication for SFTP file transfers.
- **Restrict SFTP users to their home directory**: This is a critical security control. The SFTP users are restricted to their home directory by using *chroot*. This prevents them from navigating to other directories and accessing sensitive data in them.

- **Disable shell access**: SFTP users need to execute only limited commands for file transfer and do not require full shell access. It is recommended to disable shell access for such users who only require file transfer capabilities.
- **Limit SFTP access by IP address**: SFTP servers should not have unrestricted access. Restricting access to a limited set of IP addresses reduces the attack surface and ensures that only approved users and devices can initiate file transfer.
- **Enforce strong encryption and passwords**: Use the highest levels of encryption cipher strength. If password authentication is being used, strong password policies and MFA, if necessary, should be enforced.
- **Use logging to monitor file transfers**: SFTP logging should be enabled for detecting unusual or unauthorized file transfers.

RDP hardening

RDP is a very common protocol used for remote desktop access. Given its versatility, it is also a frequent target for cyberattacks. The following best practices are recommended for RDP hardening:

- **Do not expose RDP to the internet**: This is the single most important rule for RDP security. RDP should never be exposed to the internet publicly. It should normally be accessible through a **virtual private network** (**VPN**) or a dedicated RDP gateway.
- **Enforce strong passwords and MFA**: Long and complex passwords, along with MFA, can prevent brute-force attacks and credential theft.
- **Enable network-level authentication (NLA)**: This security feature requires a user to authenticate before an RDP session is fully established. This prevents attackers from launching **denial of service** (**DoS**) attacks or exploiting vulnerabilities that do not require authentication.
- **Disable unused features**: RDP includes a variety of features, like clipboard redirection and drive redirection, to ease administration. These features can be exploited by attackers to move files and data between the remote desktop and the local computer. Such features should be disabled by default and enabled explicitly for business needs only.
- **Limit number of concurrent sessions**: The default Windows configuration permits a single RDP session at a time; however, for server editions, this can be changed to allow two concurrent sessions. This feature should be enabled only on a need basis, as it increases the likelihood of misuse.
- **Monitor RDP logs**: RDP logs should be monitored for any suspicious activity.

Securing virtualized environments

Modern endpoints frequently exist in virtualized or containerized forms. Securing these environments requires specific attention to the underlying layers that host them. The following section discusses security issues unique to virtualized environments and best practices followed to secure the virtualized workloads.

VM security

VMs run in a virtualized environment and provide a high degree of isolation. A VM runs its own OS and applications that are distinct from the underlying physical host and other VMs on the same host. This isolation is managed by a hypervisor, which acts as a layer of abstraction between the VMs and the physical hardware. However, despite this isolation, there exists a risk of a VM escape attack. A VM escape occurs when a program running inside a VM breaks out of its isolated environment and is able to interact with the host OS or other VMs on the same host. If an attacker achieves a hypervisor compromise, it undermines the very foundation of virtualization security and can lead to unauthorized access to sensitive data and compromise of other VMs. To mitigate these risks, securing the hypervisor is critical.

Best practices for hypervisor security are as follows:

- **Isolation of the management plane**: Administrative interfaces used to manage the hypervisor should be separated from the guest networks and production traffic to prevent any lateral movement.
- **Patching and maintenance**: The hypervisor is the root of trust of the virtualized environment. It is therefore essential that the hypervisor kernel and host OS are continuously monitored and that immediate patches are applied to address new vulnerabilities and threats.
- **Access controls**: Strict RBAC and strong, risk-based authentication should be enforced for hypervisor administrative accounts. All unnecessary protocols and interfaces must be disabled.
- **System hardening**: The hypervisor and host OS should be hardened by disabling unnecessary features and services to reduce the attack surface.

Container security

Containers offer a more lightweight form of virtualization than VMs. While a VM provides hardware-level isolation, containers provide OS-level isolation by sharing the same kernel with the host and other containers. Since containers share the host OS kernel, any vulnerability in the host kernel can affect the containers. Therefore, security must be enforced across both image build-time and container runtime.

The recommended measures for container security are as follows:

- **Build-time security is focused on image scanning and least privilege**:
  - **Secure base images**: Official or verified Docker images from trusted sources should be used. It is always good to start with a minimal, small base image to reduce the attack surface.
  - **Image scanning**: Container image scanning should be integrated into the **continuous integration/continuous deployment** (**CI/CD**) pipeline. This ensures that the container images are scanned for known vulnerabilities and misconfigurations before deployment. It is also important to continuously scan to detect newly discovered vulnerabilities.
- **Runtime security ensures isolation and kernel restrictions**:
  - **Principle of least privilege**: Images must be configured to run containers using a dedicated non-root user ID. This drastically limits the damage in the event of a compromise.
  - **Restricting capabilities**: Containers often possess unnecessary root-level kernel capabilities. Docker and Kubernetes offer mechanisms to explicitly drop these unwarranted capabilities, which reduces the scope of potential kernel interaction if the container is exploited.
  - **MAC**: Secure computing profiles and AppArmor/SELinux profiles should be applied to limit the set of system calls a container can execute. This further helps in securing the boundary between the container and the host kernel.
  - **Resource limits**: Setting explicit memory and **central processing unit** (**CPU**) limits prevents a single compromised container from launching a DoS attack by consuming all shared resources, thus starving other applications.
  - **Storage and host interaction risk**: Use of Kubernetes hostPath volumes should be strictly avoided, particularly in production environments, as they directly mount directories from the host's file system into the container, posing a great risk.

Future trends in endpoint security

The future of endpoint security lies in leveraging AI and automation. As the volume of data and the velocity of modern sophisticated attacks continue to increase, the analysis and response capability of existing tools is getting outpaced. In such a scenario, AI becomes indispensable for providing actionable insights into huge datasets and correlated alerts. Automation, in turn, helps in security orchestration and automated response. It provides the necessary response capability to match the speed of modern-day attacks. Automation enables security solutions to respond swiftly and limit damage by automatically isolating impacted devices and blocking malicious processes without the need for any human intervention. This shift enhances real-time defense and response capability, making security proactive rather than reactive. Automation and AI-powered solutions are increasingly leveraging ML techniques, along with capabilities such as predictive analytics and automated threat hunting to deliver more effective and efficient endpoint protection.

Conclusion

Over the years, the information security landscape has undergone a fundamental transformation. With increased adoption of remote working, the proliferation of mobile devices, and a shift towards cloud computing, security efforts are increasingly focused on securing endpoints, in addition to protecting the core enterprise network. The endpoint threat landscape itself has been evolving. Contemporary malware has grown beyond static file-based code to sophisticated fileless malware that lives off the land and is specifically designed to evade legacy systems. This tactical shift has rendered signature-based antivirus solutions mostly ineffective and has necessitated a move towards a proactive, multi-layered defense.

To address the limitations of legacy systems, advanced endpoint security solutions such as EDR, XDR, and EPP have been developed to supplement the core endpoint security controls. In addition, this layered approach also encompasses hardening, detection, policy enforcement, monitoring, and integration with the overall enterprise security architecture. When aligned with Zero Trust principles, these technologies work together to provide continuous visibility into endpoint behaviour, enable rapid detection and response to threats, and enforce dynamic access decisions based on real-time device posture rather than implicit trust. This multi-pronged strategy provides the real-time visibility and automated response capabilities that are critical for swift detection, effective containment, and recovery from endpoint compromises.

Endpoint security challenges continue to grow due to the expanding attack surface, driven by the proliferation of IoT devices and the persistence of AI-driven attacks. Therefore, the key to proactive endpoint security is to develop tools and processes that adapt to emerging threats and provide constant vigil and protection.

Having discussed solutions and strategies for endpoint security, we now shift our focus to applications that run on servers and endpoints. In the next chapter, we will explore application security and secure software development practices.

Exercises

1. What are the common challenges encountered in securing endpoints in a remote or hybrid work environment?
2. Discuss the limitations of traditional antivirus software in protecting endpoints.
3. What is EDR, and how does it differ from legacy antivirus solutions?
4. Discuss how XDR enhances threat detection as compared to EDR.
5. Why is OS hardening critical for endpoint security? Discuss important configurations for securing Windows and Linux systems.
6. How does a security baseline (e.g., CIS Benchmarks) help in OS hardening?
7. What are the security risks associated with RDP, and how can they be mitigated?
8. Discuss the best practices for securing SSH on Linux systems.
9. What are the main security considerations for VM security? What is VM escape, and how can it be prevented?
10. Your organization uses Docker for deploying applications. You suspect that a container has been compromised. How will you investigate the incident, and what preventive measures can be taken to avoid such incidents?
11. You are tasked with deploying endpoint protection for a large remote workforce using company and personal laptops. What challenges do you anticipate? What endpoint security solution will you recommend and why?

Chapter 9
Application Security

Introduction

In the digital world, applications serve as the primary interface between organizations and their users. Businesses, governments, and individuals rely on web and mobile applications to deliver and consume services remotely. These applications form the backbone of a digital ecosystem that provides interactive platforms for e-commerce, banking, communication, and enterprise operations. Since these applications are publicly accessible over the internet, they also become potential targets for attackers seeking to exploit vulnerabilities, gain unauthorized access, and exfiltrate sensitive data. Ensuring application security is therefore critical for organizations.

Application security is the comprehensive practice of identifying, mitigating, and preventing security vulnerabilities throughout the lifecycle of an application. It focuses on protecting applications from unauthorized access, data breaches, and malicious activities that may compromise the confidentiality, integrity, or availability of data. It is not a one-time activity but a continuous, integrated process that spans the design, development, deployment, and operations phases.

As software development practices have evolved, so too has application security. In traditional development models, security was treated as a sequential phase or a centralized toll gate applied at the end of each development stage. While this approach aimed to establish a secure foundation by progressively adding security controls, it often resulted in delayed detection of vulnerabilities and higher remediation costs. The rise of agile software development and the need for rapid, continuous delivery have resulted in a paradigm shift towards **development, security, and operations** (**DevSecOps**). In this approach, security is embedded into every stage of the **continuous integration/continuous deployment** (**CI/CD**) pipeline, closely aligning with the *Shift Left* philosophy of integrating security controls early in the development process. By incorporating automated testing, continuous monitoring, and proactive risk management into the development workflow, organizations can build applications that are both agile and secure by design.

Structure

In this chapter, we will discuss the following topics:

- Secure software development lifecycle

- DevSecOps
- Common application vulnerabilities
- Securing web application
- API and microservices security
- Mobile application security
- Application security frameworks
- Emerging trends

Objectives

The objective of this chapter is to provide a comprehensive understanding of application security principles, methodologies, and practices essential for developing and deploying secure and resilient applications. By the end of this chapter, you will understand the methodology of secure software development and gain the knowledge to identify, analyze, and mitigate application-level risks during various stages of software development and application deployment. You will gain practical insights into secure software development principles, application security frameworks, and integration of security within DevSecOps pipelines to ensure continuous protection of web, mobile, and **application programming interface** (**API**) based applications.

Secure software development lifecycle

Historically, software security was treated as a separate function, often addressed only during the late testing or post-development phases. This reactive approach inherently introduced significant risk, as security concerns were either overlooked during early stages or confined to non-functional requirements. As a result, vulnerabilities that originated in design or coding often remained undetected until the later stages, when remediation became far more costly and complex. In today's dynamic and hostile threat landscape, such an approach is no longer tenable. Software security can no longer be treated as an afterthought or confined to isolated testing at the end of development. This demands a fundamental transformation in how software is conceptualized, designed, and delivered.

Secure software development lifecycle (**SSDLC**), which is an extension of the traditional SDLC, embodies this transformation. It embeds security considerations, controls, and assurance mechanisms into every phase of the development process. While SDLC defines how software is built, SSDLC ensures it is built securely. It bridges the gap between functionality and protection by integrating security practices directly into requirements, design, implementation, testing, deployment, and maintenance stages.

At the heart of SSDLC lies the *Shift Left* philosophy, the principle of moving critical security activities, such as threat modelling, compliance validation, and security testing, earlier in the development lifecycle. By positioning security closer to the source of change, SSDLC prevents vulnerabilities from emerging rather than merely detecting them later. For example, identifying design-level flaws before they propagate into the codebase drastically reduces both the effort and expense of remediation. Thus, SSDLC promotes a proactive and preventive mindset to ensure that software is secure by design and secure by default. By systematically integrating security into every phase, SSDLC ensures application resilience along with development agility and compliance assurance.

The key objectives of implementing SSDLC are as follows:

- **Early identification of vulnerabilities**: This is one of the primary objectives of SSDLC. The aim is to detect and address potential weaknesses during the design and coding phases before they become expensive to fix.
- **Integration of security controls**: Incorporate security requirements, secure coding standards, and testing mechanisms throughout the software lifecycle.
- **Continuous assurance**: Maintain visibility into the security posture of applications through regular testing, review, and monitoring.
- **Compliance and governance alignment**: Ensure that applications adhere to organizational policies, regulatory mandates, and industry standards.
- **Security as a shared responsibility**: Make security an integral part of the development culture by fostering collaboration among developers, security professionals, and operations teams.

Phases of SSDLC

SSDLC mirrors the traditional SDLC in structure, but with an explicit focus on integrating security into every stage. Each phase, from requirements gathering to maintenance, includes defined security objectives and activities to ensure that security concerns are addressed continuously, and it is not left as a final toll gate.

Planning and requirements gathering

This phase marks the secure initiation of the software project. Its objective is to identify both functional and non-functional requirements, including those related to security, privacy, and compliance. The goal is to define clear security objectives and determine necessary regulatory mandates right from the project's inception stage.

During the planning, requirements gathering, and analysis stage, security activities focus on translating business objectives into concrete security requirements. These requirements must be explicitly incorporated into the functional specifications and system architecture to ensure that security considerations drive design choices. All relevant compliance and regulatory obligations, such as data protection, access control, and auditability, should be addressed at this stage. The initial selection of technologies, platforms, and third-party components must also undergo a security review, supplemented by **software composition analysis** (**SCA**) to identify vulnerabilities in open-source or external dependencies.

Additionally, it is essential to establish the system's criticality and perform information classification. This is required to determine the sensitivity of data that the system will process and the potential impact in case of a security breach. A structured risk assessment and threat analysis should also be conducted to identify potential threats, assess their likelihood, and understand their possible business impact. This proactive assessment builds the foundation for designing appropriate security controls and setting the overall risk management strategy for the application.

Secure design and architecture

The design phase is critical for secure software development, as it provides the foundation for implementing the *Shift Left* strategy. During this stage, the security requirements are translated into architectural and design elements that minimize potential vulnerabilities. A secure design ensures that systemic weaknesses are identified and mitigated before coding begins, thereby reducing downstream risks, development rework, and remediation costs.

Threat modelling is one of the central security activities performed during this phase. Threat modelling is a structured process that helps identify potential attack vectors, clarify trust boundaries, and determine appropriate security controls. It is conducted early in the design stage and continuously refined as new features or architectural changes are introduced. Common methodologies such as **Spoofing, Tampering, Repudiation, Information Disclosure, Denial of Service, and Elevation of Privilege** (**STRIDE**) and **Process for Attack Simulation and Threat Analysis** (**PASTA**) are widely used to analyze threats and prioritize mitigation systematically.

The secure architecture review is also conducted during this phase. It ensures that the system is designed with layered defenses for defense-in-depth, along with principles of least privilege and isolation of critical assets. Core security design principles such as fail-safe defaults, open design, and separation of duties are applied to ensure robustness and transparency.

At this stage, it is also important to validate the technology stack, including third-party components, frameworks, and libraries, for security maturity and known vulnerabilities. This process helps prevent inherited risks from external dependencies. A detailed data flow analysis is also conducted to map how sensitive information traverses the system. Appropriate encryption, data integrity verification, and access control mechanisms must be applied wherever confidential or sensitive data is processed, stored, or transmitted.

By embedding these security considerations into the design phase, it is ensured that the applications are not only functional and efficient but also resilient by design and provide a strong security foundation before the first line of code is written.

Secure coding and implementation

This phase aims to prevent the introduction of new vulnerabilities while the source code is being created. The objective is to develop application code that adheres to secure coding practices to minimize the introduction of vulnerabilities during development. A foundational requirement for secure software development is to educate developers on secure coding practices.

Some of the key security activities during this phase include:

- **Adherence to secure coding standards**: Language-specific guidelines, such as the **Open Worldwide Application Security Project** (**OWASP**) secure coding practices, are followed.
- **Input validation and output encoding**: This prevents injection attacks, **cross-site scripting** (**XSS**), and similar flaws in the code.
- **Use of approved libraries and APIs**: Unverified or outdated components that may contain known vulnerabilities are avoided.
- **Static application security testing (SAST)**: Automated static code analysis is conducted to detect security flaws early in the development process. SAST is a white-box testing methodology that analyzes source code, byte code, or binary code without executing the application. It searches for insecure coding practices, weak algorithms, and suspicious patterns.
- **Code review and peer validation**: Manual review processes focusing on logic flaws, authentication, and data handling are incorporated to identify any weaknesses.
- **Secrets management**: Hardcoding credentials, API keys, or encryption keys within source code must be strictly avoided.

Testing and verification

The testing phase plays a crucial role in validating the overall security posture of the application before it is released into production. During this stage, runtime validation is performed to verify that the implemented controls effectively meet the defined security objectives and that the application is resilient against both known and emerging threats. The goal of verification is to ensure that the software satisfies its functional and security requirements while uncovering exploitable weaknesses within a running environment through systematic testing and analysis.

This phase employs a combination of automated and manual techniques to uncover application vulnerabilities. The key security activities performed are as follows:

- **Dynamic application security testing (DAST)**: DAST evaluates running applications and APIs for runtime vulnerabilities and misconfigurations. It is a black-box testing methodology that simulates external attacks to validate the application's behaviour under real-world conditions. Being language-agnostic, DAST focuses on how the application responds to malicious inputs and ensures that implemented controls function as intended during execution.

- **Interactive application security testing (IAST)**: IAST combines the strengths of static and dynamic testing to provide more accurate and contextual vulnerability detection. It uses lightweight agents that monitor the application's behaviour in real-time. By merging the internal code visibility of SAST with the runtime insights of DAST, the IAST can trace vulnerabilities back to their exact source code location and execution context. This hybrid approach enhances test accuracy and provides developer-friendly feedback that accelerates remediation.
- **Penetration testing**: Penetration testing involves conducting controlled, simulated attacks to assess the exploitability of the identified vulnerabilities. It helps in validating the effectiveness of security controls and reveals complex, multi-step attack paths that automated scanners may overlook.
- **Dependency scanning**: Dependency scanning focuses on identifying vulnerabilities in third-party components and open-source libraries used by the application. Continuous scanning against databases of known **Common Vulnerabilities and Exposures** (**CVEs**) ensures that outdated or insecure dependencies are promptly remediated.
- **Fuzz testing**: Fuzz testing evaluates how the application handles unexpected, malformed, or random input data. It helps uncover memory corruption issues, input validation flaws, and logic errors that may not be detected through traditional testing.
- **Security regression testing**: This is conducted after each code update or bug fix to ensure that previously resolved vulnerabilities remain fixed and verify that new changes have not introduced additional weaknesses.

Secure application deployment

During the deployment phase, the software is moved from a controlled development environment to the production stage. During this phase, it is critical to ensure configuration integrity, environment security, and operational readiness of the application. Secure deployment focuses on validating that the production environment enforces the same or higher level of security controls as those tested in pre-production. This phase involves securing the build and release pipelines, verifying the integrity of deployment packages, and ensuring that only authorized and verified code is promoted to production. Build artifacts should be cryptographically signed and validated prior to deployment to prevent any kind of tampering. Configuration management also plays an equally important role, as insecure and inconsistent configurations are among the most common causes of security breaches. Implementing hardened baseline configurations, disabling unnecessary services, and enforcing the principle of least privilege reduces the attack surface. Secrets such as API keys, certificates, and credentials must be securely managed through vaults or key management systems rather than embedded in code or configuration files. Pre-deployment security validation, including final vulnerability scans and configuration audits, should confirm that the system meets all security and compliance requirements before going live. Post-deployment verification ensures that logging, monitoring, and alerting mechanisms are functional.

Maintenance and monitoring

After the application is deployed, continuous security is ensured through a cycle of maintenance, monitoring, and improvement. The objective during this phase is to sustain the security posture of the application against evolving threats and environmental changes. Maintenance involves the timely application of security patches, regular updates to third-party components, and review of configurations to ensure continued compliance with security baselines. The vulnerability management processes must be well-defined to detect, prioritize, and remediate newly discovered vulnerabilities in a structured and timely manner.

It is also essential to ensure proactive security monitoring to promptly detect any policy deviations, anomalies, and potential security incidents. Security related logs from applications, servers, and network components should be aggregated into a centralized **security information and event management** (**SIEM**) system for correlation and alerting. Continuous monitoring helps in identifying intrusion attempts, unauthorized access, or suspicious activities before they escalate into significant security incidents. Security metrics and audit trails also provide valuable input for assessing ongoing control effectiveness. Over time, lessons learned from operational incidents and new threat intelligence are incorporated into earlier SSDLC phases. This helps in refining requirements, design, and coding standards to improve the subsequent development cycle. The maintenance and monitoring phase ensures that security is not static but adaptive. It helps in maintaining a secure operational environment and enables continuous improvement through feedback, vigilance, and timely response.

DevSecOps

In the traditional software development models, such as the Waterfall and Spiral models, security activities are performed in distinct, sequential phases, typically towards the end of development or just before release. While these models provide structured and formal control, they lack the flexibility to respond to rapidly evolving business needs and emerging threats. As software delivery cycles have become more iterative and dynamic, this static approach to security is no longer considered sufficient. The shift to agile software development and continuous delivery demands a new paradigm, one that integrates security as an intrinsic part of the development workflow rather than an external gate. This evolution has led to the emergence of DevSecOps, a model that brings together development, security, and operations as a unified, collaborative process.

DevSecOps represents the natural evolution of DevOps by embedding security into every stage of the software delivery pipeline. It extends the CI/CD philosophy by incorporating continuous security. The goal of DevSecOps is to make security a shared responsibility across all teams involved in the software lifecycle, rather than confining it to a specialized group at the end of development. The security checks are integrated into the software development process early and continuously. This ensures that vulnerabilities are identified and mitigated in near real-time, reducing the cost and complexity of remediation.

Principles of DevSecOps

The DevSecOps philosophy is anchored on the following core principles:

- **Security as code**: In this approach, security configurations, policies, and compliance checks are defined and managed as code, version-controlled, and deployed through the same automated pipelines that deliver the application.
- **Automation and integration**: Automated tools are employed to continuously perform code analysis, dependency scanning, configuration validation, and runtime monitoring as part of the CI/CD process.
- **Continuous feedback**: The findings from automated scans and runtime environments are fed back to the developers immediately, which helps in prompt remediation.
- **Collaboration and shared responsibility**: All stakeholders, including the development, security, and operations teams, work together seamlessly, supported by open communication and integrated workflows.
- **Immutable infrastructure**: The infrastructure is treated as disposable and reproducible through code [**infrastructure as code** (**IaC**)], while enforcing least privilege and continuous verification of all identities and connections.

Security integration in DevSecOps

Security in DevSecOps is embedded across each phase of the CI/CD pipeline to ensure that security controls evolve along with the codebase and deployment environments. The details of security related activities performed during various stages are as follows:

1. **Code stage**: In the coding stage, developers follow secure coding standards and employ SAST tools to identify insecure coding patterns before code is merged. Secrets management solutions such as HashiCorp Vault or Secret Manager are used to prevent hard-coded credentials. Source code repositories are used to enforce pre-commit checks and security policy validations.
2. **Build stage**: During the build process, automated SCA tools scan third-party libraries and dependencies for known vulnerabilities. The build systems also verify that packages are obtained from trusted sources and are digitally signed. This ensures that open-source components are used securely and remain updated.

3. **Testing**: At this stage, automated DAST and TAST tools analyze running applications to detect runtime vulnerabilities such as input validation flaws, injection risks, or misconfigurations. Fuzz testing and container image scanning are also carried out to strengthen assurance before further version release.

4. **Release and deployment**: As the applications are moved into production, IaC templates are validated through **policy as code** (**PaC**) tools such as Checkov or Terraform Validator to detect misconfigurations. The container orchestration environments, such as Kubernetes, are tested for compliance with the security baselines. Deployment gates are setup for secure deployment and to ensure that builds failing security criteria are not released.

5. **Operation and monitoring**: Once the application is in production, continuous monitoring solutions provide visibility into the application's security posture and operational health. **Runtime Application Self-Protection** (**RASP**), endpoint protection, and cloud workload protection platforms detect and respond to active threats. The telemetry from these systems is fed back into earlier pipeline stages to reinforce the cycle of continuous improvement.

Automation and tooling

Automation is central to the DevSecOps approach. It enables consistency, speed, and reliability in executing the security tasks. The CI/CD platforms, such as *Jenkins, GitLab CI, GitHub Actions*, and *Azure DevOps*, integrate with specialized tools for SAST, DAST, SCA, container scanning, and policy enforcement. For instance, *SonarQube* and *Checkmarx* perform static analysis, OWASP **Zed Attack Proxy** (**ZAP**) and Burp Suite execute dynamic testing, Snyk and Dependency-Check handle SCA. Automating these checks ensures that every code commit or deployment undergoes security validation automatically and consistently.

For security practitioners, the following table provides a representative DevSecOps toolchain, illustrating how common security tools are aligned with each stage of the CI/CD pipeline to enable continuous and automated security controls:

CI/CD stage	Security objective	Tool types	Tool examples
Code	Detect insecure code and dependencies early	• SAST • SCA • Secrets detection	• SonarQube, Checkmarx • Snyk, OWASP Dependency-Check • GitGuardian, TruffleHog
Build	Secure packaged applications	• Container scanning • Artifact integrity and signing	• Trivy, Aqua, Anchore • Cosign, Notary

CI/CD stage	Security objective	Tool types	Tool examples
Test	Detect runtime vulnerabilities	• DAST • IAST	• OWASP ZAP, Burp Suite • Contrast Security, BlackDuck
Deploy	Prevent insecure infrastructure and configurations	• IaC security • Configuration validation	• Terraform with Checkov • **Open Policy Agent** (**OPA**)
Run	Protect applications at runtime	• RASP • Perimeter protection	• Contrast Protect, Aikido • WAF
Monitor and respond	Detect and respond to attacks and anomalies	• Logging and monitoring • Incident response automation	• ELK Stack, Prometheus • Splunk SOAR, Cortex XSOAR

Table 9.1*: Modern DevSecOps toolchain across CI/CD pipeline*

While the specific tools used may vary across organizations, the underlying principle remains consistent: security controls are aligned with each stage of the CI/CD pipeline and executed automatically as part of the delivery workflow.

To understand this better, consider the following example. An e-commerce or banking and financial services company is developing a cloud-based web application that handles sensitive customer information such as personal details and payment data. To ensure both agility and a strong security posture, the organization adopts a DevSecOps approach by embedding automated security controls into every stage of its CI/CD pipeline. The process begins at the code commit stage, where developers use secure coding guidelines and local security checks integrated within their **Integrated Development Environments** (**IDEs**). Pre-commit hooks automatically scan for secrets, such as API keys or passwords, and for known vulnerabilities in third-party libraries through SCA. Once the code is pushed to the repository, the CI pipeline triggers automated testing through SAST to detect insecure coding constructs and logic flaws before the build is completed.

During the build phase, the system performs integrity checks on dependencies, applies digital signing, and carries out container image scanning to ensure that no vulnerable or unverified components are included in the deployment package. The CI pipeline also enforces policy gates that block builds failing to meet the defined security baselines. As the application progresses to the CD phase, DAST tools simulate real-world attacks on the running application to uncover runtime vulnerabilities such as injection flaws or XSS. In parallel, IaC templates are scanned to detect misconfigurations in cloud or container environments, ensuring that security baselines are met before deployment. Once deployed to production, the application environment is continuously monitored through SIEM and RASP to provide real-time detection for detecting and blocking anomalous activities or exploit attempts.

The insights from production monitoring are fed back into the development cycle, creating a continuous feedback loop that enables proactive remediation and iterative hardening of both code and infrastructure. This automated, integrated approach allows the organization to release updates frequently while maintaining consistent compliance and security assurance. By embedding testing, monitoring, and compliance into every step of the CI/CD process, the web application achieves security-by-design and security-by-default.

The following figure illustrates continuous embedding of security controls across a DevSecOps CI/CD pipeline, from code commit to runtime operations:

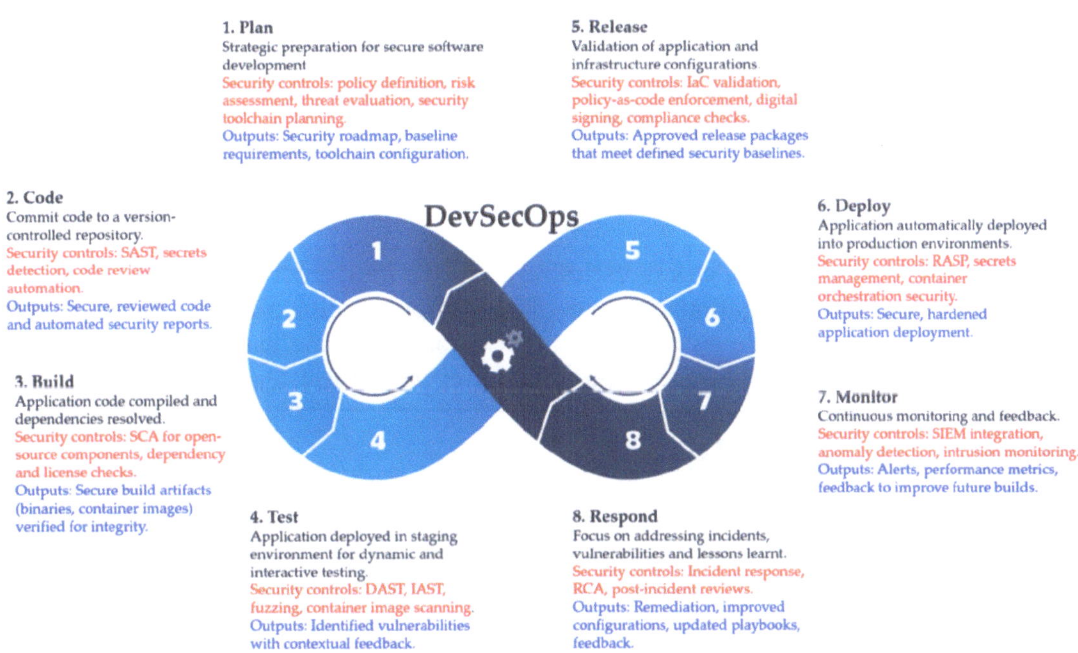

***Figure 9.1**: DevSecOps and continuous application security*

Common application vulnerabilities

Applications are complex systems that process user input, handle sensitive data, and interact with other components across networks and APIs. This inherent complexity, coupled with rapid development cycles and third-party dependencies, often leads to the introduction of vulnerabilities that attackers can exploit.

The OWASP periodically publishes a list of the most critical security risks for various types of applications. These serve as a baseline for identifying and mitigating common weaknesses in modern applications.

Broken access control

Access control enforces user privileges and ensures that users can only access resources and perform actions for which they are authorized. **Broken access control** (**BAC**) arises from flaws in implementing these mechanisms that allow users to act beyond intended permissions. Such failures typically result from violations of the principle of least privilege and the absence or improper enforcement of authorization checks.

Common manifestations of BAC include **Insecure Direct Object Reference** (**IDOR**) and privilege escalation. IDOR occurs when an application accepts and processes user-supplied object identifiers, such as account parameters in **Uniform Resource Locators** (**URLs**) or API requests, without verifying whether the authenticated user is authorized to access the referenced resource. This may allow attackers to view, modify, or delete another user's data. Privilege escalation can occur in two ways: horizontal escalation, where a user gains access to another user's resources, and vertical escalation, where a standard user acquires administrative or higher level privileges.

Preventing BAC requires architectural discipline and consistent enforcement of access control in trusted environments. Mitigation strategies include implementing **role-based access control** (**RBAC**), enforcing server-side authorization checks, applying the least privilege principle, and performing comprehensive access validation for every request.

Cryptographic failures

Cryptographic failures involve improper protection of sensitive information, either in storage, processing, or transmission. Weak or outdated cryptographic algorithms, improper key management, and transmitting data without **Transport Layer Security** (**TLS**) can expose confidential data such as passwords, financial details, or personal identifiers to unauthorized individuals. Cryptographic failures can be prevented by enforcing strong encryption standards such as **Advanced Encryption Standard-256** (**AES-256**), **Rivest–Shamir–Adleman-2048** (**RSA-2048**), secure key management, using TLS 1.3 or higher, and by avoiding hardcoded keys or secrets in code and configuration files.

Injection vulnerabilities

Injection vulnerabilities arise when an application allows untrusted input to be directly incorporated into commands or queries executed by an interpreter, such as database queries, **operating system** (**OS**) commands, or client-side scripts. These flaws enable attackers to alter program logic, manipulate execution flow, and potentially compromise the underlying system. Common forms of injection include **Structured Query Language** (**SQL**) injection, command injection, and **Lightweight Directory Access Protocol** (**LDAP**) injection. In injection attacks, malicious input is crafted to retrieve or modify data, execute arbitrary commands, or gain unauthorized control over application components.

The most effective defense against injection is the use of parameterized queries or prepared statements, which clearly separate command structure from user-supplied data to ensure that the input is processed strictly as data rather than executable code. Other measures include rigorous input validation to enforce expected data types and formats, and output encoding of untrusted data before rendering it to users, thus preventing injection through the user interface or dynamic content.

Insecure design

Insecure design refers to architectural or logical weaknesses that result from the absence of a structured, secure design process. Unlike coding defects, these vulnerabilities originate from flawed business logic, inadequate threat modelling, or failure to anticipate potential abuse cases. Typical examples include missing security controls, insecure workflows, and the absence of rate limiting mechanisms.

Mitigating design flaws requires incorporating threat modelling early in the development lifecycle, applying secure design principles such as least privilege, defense-in-depth, and fail-safe defaults, and validating design assumptions throughout the development lifecycle.

Security misconfiguration

Security misconfiguration is one of the most widespread and recurring application vulnerabilities. It arises from the use of insecure default settings, overly permissive configurations, exposed administrative interfaces, or verbose error messages that reveal sensitive system details. Such misconfigurations inadvertently expose critical information or create exploitable system states that attackers can leverage to compromise applications and infrastructure.

To mitigate these risks, organizations should establish secure configuration baselines, disable unnecessary features and services, and restrict access to administrative interfaces. The use of automated configuration management and IaC tools such as Ansible or Terraform with embedded security policies can ensure consistent, repeatable, and verifiable configuration across environments.

Vulnerable and outdated components

Most applications depend heavily on third-party frameworks, libraries, and open-source modules to accelerate development and reduce complexity. However, when these components are outdated, unpatched, or sourced from untrusted repositories, they may introduce vulnerabilities into otherwise secure applications. Attackers actively exploit these weaknesses to gain access, execute arbitrary code, and compromise critical systems.

Mitigating this risk requires maintaining a comprehensive inventory of all third-party and open-source dependencies and performing regular SCA to detect known vulnerabilities and licensing issues. It also requires establishing an effective vulnerability management function to ensure timely patching and upgrades, monitoring of vulnerability databases, and avoiding the use of unsupported components.

Identification and authentication failures

Identification and authentication mechanisms form the foundation of application trust. Failures in these controls, such as weak password policies, insecure session handling, or flawed authentication logic, can allow attackers to impersonate legitimate users or hijack accounts. Common examples of threats include credential stuffing, session fixation, and brute-force attacks against poorly protected login systems.

To mitigate these risks, applications must enforce strong authentication mechanisms such as **multi-factor authentication** (**MFA**), secure password hashing algorithms, and proper session management with timeouts and secure cookie attributes. Additionally, account lockout policies, *CAPTCHA* for automated login attempts, and strict TLS should be implemented to reduce the likelihood of compromise.

Software and data integrity failures

Software and data integrity failures occur when critical updates, configurations, or data flows are not protected against unauthorized modification. Insecure update mechanisms, compromised build pipelines, or unverified software dependencies can lead to the introduction of malicious code or altered configurations during deployment.

Software and data integrity can be ensured by enforcing digital signatures and code signing, securing build and deployment pipelines with strict access controls, and using cryptographic integrity verification for software artifacts and configuration files. Continuous validation of software lineage and the use of trusted repositories also help maintain the integrity of deployed applications.

Security logging and monitoring failures

Effective logging and monitoring are essential for detecting, analyzing, and responding to security incidents targeting the applications. When applications fail to log important events or generate incomplete or inconsistent logs, attacks can go undetected for extended periods. This lack of visibility hampers both incident response and forensic investigation.

To address these issues, applications should implement comprehensive, centralized logging that captures authentication attempts, authorization failures, input validation errors, and administrative actions. Integration with the SIEM system enables real-time correlation and alerting. For effective incident detection and response, it must be ensured that logs are correctly timestamped, protected from tampering, and regularly reviewed.

Server-side request forgery

Server-side request forgery (**SSRF**) vulnerabilities occur when an application fetches resources from user-supplied URLs or inputs without adequate validation. Attackers can exploit this weakness to make unauthorized requests from the vulnerable server to internal or external systems, bypassing network controls and potentially exposing sensitive data or administrative interfaces.

Mitigation of SSRF involves implementing strict input validation and URL allowlists, segregating internal and external request handling, and restricting outbound network access for application components. Additionally, deploying network-level controls, such as firewalls or API gateways, can prevent SSRF attacks from reaching sensitive internal systems and services.

While the OWASP Top 10 vulnerabilities highlight the most common and critical risks, the application threat landscape continues to evolve rapidly. The increased adoption of microservices, APIs, and cloud-native architectures has introduced new categories of vulnerabilities. Staying secure in the evolving threat environment requires a proactive and continuous approach to security. This entails integrating threat intelligence, automated testing, and incorporating adaptive controls into every stage of the software lifecycle.

Securing web applications

Web applications form the backbone of the digital ecosystem, enabling service providers to deliver services and interact with users over the internet. They are inherently vulnerable to a wide range of threats as they often process user-supplied data and interact with backend systems such as databases, authentication servers, and APIs.

At its core, web application security involves safeguarding both server-side and client-side components that together handle user interactions, data processing, and session management. Threats to web applications often exploit flaws in authentication, session handling, input validation, or business logic. As discussed earlier, attackers typically target weaknesses such as injection vulnerabilities, XSS, **Cross-site request forgery** (**CSRF**), IDOR, and improper session management to gain unauthorized access or exfiltrate sensitive information.

Core principles of web application security

The core principles of web application security include:

- **Defense-in-depth**: This involves implementing multiple, independent layers of security controls such that the failure of one does not compromise the entire system.
- **Secure defaults**: Configuring all components to the most secure state by default to reduce exposure due to human error.

- **Least privilege**: Granting only the permissions necessary for specific functions to minimize the impact of any potential breach.
- **Fail-safe design**: Ensuring that in the event of an error or failure, the system reverts to a secure state rather than an insecure one.

Layered defense

Securing a web application requires adopting a layered defense strategy that begins at the design stage and extends through the development, deployment, and maintenance stages. Secure coding practices must be complemented by proper configuration of web servers, databases, and APIs. The use of secure frameworks and libraries that provide built-in protection against common attack vectors significantly reduces the development burden while improving baseline security. Modern application development frameworks such as Spring Security, ASP.NET Core Identity, or Django provide standardized mechanisms for authentication, authorization, and input sanitization that help prevent common vulnerabilities.

Authentication and session management

Authentication and session management are critical controls for web application security. Weak password policies, unprotected session tokens, or improper handling of cookies can expose applications to credential theft and session hijacking. Secure session management involves using strong random session identifiers, transmitting them only over **Hypertext Transfer Protocol Secure** (**HTTPS**), and enforcing session expiration and re-authentication for sensitive transactions. Implementing MFA provides an additional layer of protection against credential-based threats.

Input validation and output encoding

Input validation and output encoding offer protection against injection and scripting attacks. Every input received from a user or external system is validated for type, length, format, and range before processing. The output encoding control is deployed immediately before rendering untrusted data back to the user's browser. All dynamic content rendered to users is properly encoded to prevent injected scripts from executing in the client's browser. Using parameterized queries and prepared statements is an essential safeguard against injection attacks.

Mitigating XSS and CSRF attacks

XSS and CSRF are two of the most pervasive web vulnerabilities. XSS arises when an attacker injects malicious scripts that execute in another user's browser, while CSRF tricks authenticated users into unintentionally taking unwanted actions on a trusted web application. These can be mitigated through output encoding, **Content Security Policy** (**CSP**), same-site cookies, anti-CSRF tokens, and strict input validation.

Securing the transport layer

TLS is a fundamental control for web application security that ensures the confidentiality and integrity of data in transit. All sensitive communications, including authentication and data exchange, should be performed exclusively over HTTPS. Strong encryption, proper certificate management, and periodic TLS configuration audits are essential to maintain secure communication channels.

Besides the technical controls, secure deployment practices and ongoing maintenance are vital for sustaining a robust web security posture. Configuration hardening, timely patching of frameworks and servers, and periodic review of access controls prevent drift from secure baselines.

Advanced security controls for web applications

Modern web applications operate in complex, distributed environments that integrate APIs, microservices, cloud infrastructure, and third-party components. Securing them requires adopting advanced and adaptive controls.

Key controls that strengthen application resilience and ensure protection across the application development and operational lifecycle are as follows:

- Enforce identity-centric security using the Zero Trust principle of *never trust, always verify*. Apply continuous authentication and authorization at every request rather than relying on implicit session trust.
- Use next-generation **web application firewalls** (**WAFs**) capable of behavioural analysis, anomaly detection, and integration with CI/CD pipelines to automatically block common attacks such as SQL injection, XSS, and brute-force attempts.
- Embed runtime protection mechanisms within the application to monitor and block malicious actions in real-time, even if an exploit bypasses external defenses.
- Implement strict CSP headers to control the execution of scripts and mitigate XSS and data injection attacks in browsers.
- Enforce secure, *HttpOnly*, and *SameSite* attributes for cookies. The secure setting ensures that the cookie is only transmitted over an HTTPS connection. *HttpOnly* blocks client-side JavaScript access to the cookie. This is essential for mitigating the impact of XSS attacks, as session hijacking often relies on JavaScript access to session identifiers. In addition, short-lived tokens and centralized session invalidation should be used to reduce the impact of session hijacking.
- Protect APIs with authentication tokens such as OAuth 2.0 and **JSON Web Token** (**JWT**), input validation, schema enforcement, and strict rate limiting to prevent abuse and mass assignment attacks.

- Apply security headers such as **HTTP Strict Transport Security** (**HSTS**), X-Content-Type-Options, X-Frame-Options, and X-XSS-Protection to strengthen browser-side defense mechanisms.
- Use SCA tools to detect vulnerabilities in open-source libraries and automate dependency patching during builds.
- Harden container images, enforce minimal privileges, and integrate vulnerability scanning into container registries. Apply cloud-native security controls such as identity-based access management and workload isolation.
- Integrate SAST, DAST, and IAST tools into CI/CD pipelines. Automate vulnerability detection, prioritization, and remediation feedback loops.
- Use centralized logging, SIEM, and threat intelligence feeds to correlate web application events with known attack indicators for faster incident response.

API and microservices security

As web and mobile applications increasingly rely on modular, service-oriented architectures, APIs have become the essential backbone of digital interaction. While APIs facilitate seamless communication between frontend clients, mobile apps, and backend services, they significantly expand the attack surface. As APIs often expose direct access to data and business logic, securing them demands specialized controls that go beyond conventional web application defenses. API security focuses on verifying every individual request for identity (authentication), permissible actions (authorization), and resource limits (rate limiting).

Unlike traditional web applications, APIs operate primarily through machine-to-machine communication using standardized protocols such as **representational state transfer** (**REST**) or GraphQL. This model introduces unique risks associated with how data is structured, transmitted, and authorized. Consequently, API security focuses on controlling how data is exposed and determining who can access it. It ensures that every request is authenticated, validated, and monitored throughout its lifecycle.

The OWASP API Security Top 10 highlights vulnerabilities that are unique to API design and implementation. Among these, **Broken Object Level Authorization** (**BOLA**) is ranked as the most critical risk. BOLA occurs when an API fails to verify whether an authenticated user is authorized to access a specific object, effectively representing an IDOR vulnerability at the API layer. Because BOLA exploits valid API calls and legitimate request structures that differ only in object identifiers, it often evades traditional WAFs, which are designed to detect anomalous or malformed traffic rather than authorization logic flaws. Other common weaknesses include unrestricted resource consumption, broken authentication, excessive data exposure, mass assignment, and insecure deserialization. Unsafe deserialization, in particular, allows attackers to manipulate serialized objects to execute arbitrary code or alter application logic.

API authentication and authorization

Strong identity enforcement forms the cornerstone of API security. APIs must authenticate every client and service consuming them. They typically use token-based mechanisms such as OAuth 2.0 and **OpenID Connect** (**OIDC**), which provide standardized and scalable ways to issue and validate access tokens. JWTs are frequently employed for stateless authentication; however, their implementation requires secure signing algorithms, short lifespans, and proper revocation mechanisms to avoid replay or misuse. Poorly secured APIs, lacking proper authentication, input validation, or rate limiting, are frequently targeted by attackers. Similarly, insecure JWT handling, such as using weak signing algorithms or exposing tokens in URLs, can result in impersonation or privilege escalation. Enforcing robust authentication, validating claims, and rotating keys periodically are key to mitigating API-related risks. It is equally important to ensure that the authenticated users access only authorized resources. Enforcing fine-grained authorization using RBAC or **attribute-based access control** (**ABAC**) can prevent privilege escalation and unauthorized data retrieval.

Input validation

APIs often process structured data such as JSON, XML, or form data, which makes input validation and data filtering critical. It is essential to enforce schema validation to reject malformed or unexpected input and restrict fields that can be updated or queried by clients. Excessive data exposure is a common issue in the API ecosystem, where APIs return entire objects or unnecessary fields instead of limiting responses to only the required data. Implementing response filtering and output whitelisting minimizes leakage of sensitive information. Similarly, APIs must sanitize incoming parameters to prevent injection attacks that could compromise backend databases or logic.

API abuse prevention

Since APIs are often public-facing and easily scriptable, they are highly susceptible to brute-force, enumeration, and DoS attacks. Enforcing rate limiting, quota management, and **Internet Protocol** (**IP**) reputation-based throttling helps maintain service availability and prevent automated abuse.

Properly configured API gateways can dynamically enforce request limits and trigger automated protective controls when abnormal traffic patterns are detected.

Inter-service communication

Services within a microservices architecture frequently communicate over internal networks. Implicit trust based on network segmentation is insufficient in such an environment. It should, therefore, be ensured that all API communication occurs exclusively over HTTPS using strong TLS configurations for the confidentiality and integrity of data in transit. For highly sensitive operations, **mutual TLS (mTLS)** must be used. mTLS is the technical realization of the Zero Trust principle applied to service-to-service communication. It requires both the client and the server to present valid digital certificates for verification. This guarantees not only encrypted communication but also mutual authentication. In dynamic environments like Kubernetes, a service mesh such as Istio is used to manage the complexity of certificate issuance and rotation and ensure that mTLS is automatically enforced. The service mesh establishes a robust security foundation by authenticating every new service instance before it can communicate with others.

API gateway

An API gateway is a fundamental control for securing microservices. It acts as a centralized enforcement point that receives all client calls and serves as a security enforcement point that manages traffic between clients and microservices. It performs authentication, authorization, logging, and payload inspection before requests reach the backend. The gateway is vital for application resilience as it can implement rate limiting and request throttling to manage traffic surges and prevent DoS or credential stuffing attacks. API gateways can also integrate with **identity providers (IdPs)**, support JWT validation, and include built-in anomaly detection capabilities. This is complemented by techniques, such as RASP and behavioural monitoring tools, to analyze live API traffic to detect anomalies, injection patterns, and potential exploitation attempts in real-time.

Continuous protection

For continuous protection, API security demands proper governance, automated testing, and visibility across the entire lifecycle. One of the most significant risks in modern API environments arises from shadow and zombie APIs. These are endpoints that are deployed or left exposed without the knowledge or oversight of security teams. Shadow APIs are typically created by development teams outside formal governance processes, while zombie APIs are deprecated or legacy endpoints that remain accessible in production. Since these APIs can bypass security controls, they have become a leading attack vector in large-scale enterprise environments.

Mitigating these risks requires maintaining a centralized and continuously updated API inventory with clear versioning, ownership, documentation, and deprecation tracking. Automated API discovery and governance tools integrated into the CI/CD pipeline help identify undocumented or unmanaged APIs and enforce compliance with defined security baselines. Similarly, incorporating API fuzz testing, dynamic analysis, and automated vulnerability scanning helps identify logic flaws and edge-case vulnerabilities that may be otherwise missed.

Mobile application security

Mobile application security requires a distinct set of controls due to the unique characteristics of the client-side execution environment and platform-specific constraints. Key differences exist between the mobile platforms, particularly concerning sandboxing, inter-app communication, and permission models. Additionally, the mobile applications face a broader attack surface compared to web applications due to device diversity, user behaviour, and third-party dependencies. Common threats to mobile applications include reverse engineering of application binaries, data leakage through insecure storage, untrusted device environments, malicious code injection, and **man-in-the-middle** (**MitM**) attacks. Reliance of the mobile ecosystem on app stores and third-party **software development kits** (**SDKs**) also creates risks of supply chain compromise and unauthorized data collection. Rooted or jailbroken devices further increase the exposure by bypassing OS controls.

Mobile Application Security Verification Standard

Mobile application security focuses on specific domains where mobile apps are uniquely vulnerable due to their deployment on diverse platforms, integration with device hardware, and operation in untrusted user environments. The OWASP **Mobile Application Security Verification Standard** (**MASVS**) is the industry-recognized standard for defining security and privacy requirements for mobile applications. MASVS provides a structured framework used by mobile architects, developers, and security professionals. MASVS, in conjunction with the **Mobile Application Security Weakness Enumeration** (**MASWE**) and the **Mobile Application Security Testing Guide** (**MASTG**), provides a comprehensive system for auditing and testing mobile applications.

Data storage

Local data storage on mobile devices poses a major security concern. Applications frequently cache or store data to enhance user experience. Insecure handling of this data can lead to exposure if the device is lost or compromised. Therefore, sensitive data should not be stored insecurely on the client device, i.e., in plaintext or easily accessible files. Mobile applications should use platform-provided secure storage mechanisms such as the Android Keystore system or iOS Keychain, which safeguard credentials and cryptographic keys using hardware-backed security modules. In addition, sensitive files should be encrypted using strong algorithms such as AES-256 and stored in app-specific directories with restricted access. Caching of confidential data should be minimized.

Secure communication

Mobile application security standards mandate secure network communication. All network communication must be protected using TLS 1.3 or higher to ensure confidentiality and integrity. Mobile apps should enforce certificate validation and implement certificate pinning to prevent MitM attacks. APIs used by mobile clients must require authentication and authorization tokens that expire within defined intervals. Further, applications should never transmit sensitive information via unencrypted channels such as HTTP, SMS, or unprotected Bluetooth.

Code protection

Mobile apps are often distributed publicly, making them vulnerable to reverse engineering. Attackers can decompile application binaries, such as `.apk` files for Android or `.ipa` files for iOS, to extract intellectual property, hardcoded secrets, or security logic. To mitigate this risk, anti-reversing and anti-tampering controls such as code obfuscation, minification, and resource encryption techniques should be employed to prevent malicious users from modifying or analyzing the compiled application code. Tools like ProGuard, R8, or DexGuard for Android, and Apple's bitcode-based optimization for iOS, make reverse engineering significantly harder. Integrity checks and tamper detection mechanisms can further prevent execution of modified or repackaged apps.

Runtime protection

The mobile application runtime environment introduces additional security concerns, especially on compromised or emulated devices. Implementing root/jailbreak detection, debugger detection, and emulator detection helps in identifying insecure execution contexts. Advanced safeguards, such as RASP, help in monitoring app behaviour in real-time to detect injection, code modification, and unauthorized API calls. These runtime checks reinforce resilience against sophisticated attacks that occur post-deployment.

SDK security

Most mobile apps integrate external SDKs for analytics, advertising, or social login. Unverified or outdated SDKs can introduce vulnerabilities and privacy risks. Every third-party library should be reviewed, version-controlled, and subjected to SCA. Overprivileged SDKs should be avoided, unused components disabled, and updates must be applied promptly. Using dependency management tools like *Gradle* or *CocoaPods* with integrity checks ensures consistency and reduces the likelihood of supply chain compromise.

Continuous security validation

Security testing for mobile applications must include both static and dynamic analysis to identify coding flaws and runtime vulnerabilities across platforms. In addition to SAST and DAST, MASTG frameworks provide a comprehensive assessment by combining code analysis, network traffic inspection, and behavioural testing. Tools such as the **Mobile Security Framework** (**MobSF**) support both Android and iOS applications by enabling automated static analysis of `.apk` and `.ipa` files, along with dynamic analysis using emulators or physical devices. For deeper runtime inspection, *Frida* is commonly used for dynamic instrumentation on Android and iOS, allowing testers to intercept function calls, modify application behaviour at runtime, and identify platform-specific weaknesses that may not be detectable through automated scans.

Application security frameworks

Application security frameworks provide necessary structured guidelines and tools to manage application risks and standardize application security practices. The OWASP **Application Security Verification Standard** (**ASVS**), **International Organization for Standardization/International Electrotechnical Commission** (**ISO/IEC**) 27034, and **National Institute of Standards and Technology** (**NIST**) **Special Publication** (**SP**) 8000-218 are some of the important standards and frameworks that deal with application security. These frameworks establish best practices across the SDLC, from requirements gathering and design to deployment and maintenance, which helps organizations align their efforts with regulatory obligations and industry benchmarks. They define *what* needs to be achieved and *how* security should be integrated into the application. These frameworks can be adapted and scoped to match organizational development methodologies, regulatory environments, and risk appetites.

OWASP ASVS

The OWASP ASVS provides a formal framework that defines detailed security requirements for designing, developing, and testing web applications and web services. It provides a comprehensive framework and checklist for secure development requirements and facilitates assessing the degree of trust that can be placed in the web applications. It guides developers on security controls and establishes a basis for specifying verification requirements in contracts.

ASVS is structured into escalating levels of assurance that correlate the rigor of security controls with the application's risk and data sensitivity. These assurance levels are as follows:

- **Level 1 (basic assurance)**: Suitable for low-risk applications, relying primarily on automated vulnerability assessments to address known weaknesses.
- **Level 2 (standard assurance)**: Recommended for most applications that handle sensitive business data or perform important transactions. Level 2 requires both automated testing and substantial manual verification, including elements of design and code review.
- **Level 3 (high assurance)**: Reserved for mission-critical applications, such as those handling highly sensitive financial, medical, or government data. This level mandates comprehensive security verification, requiring in-depth design review, rigorous code review, and extensive testing designed to withstand attacks from skilled, determined adversaries.

ASVS is intended to be integrated into the SSDLC from the initial stages. The requirements corresponding to the chosen ASVS level must guide the security design and planning phases to ensure that security controls are engineered into the application rather than being retrofitted. The structure of ASVS, particularly the mandates in levels 2 and 3 for mandatory design and code reviews, formally validates the necessity of the SSDLC and the *Shift Left* philosophy. It transforms security integration from an abstract goal into a specific, measurable set of requirements necessary for achieving high application security maturity.

ISO/IEC 27034

ISO/IEC 27034 is an international standard that provides a formalized framework for integrating security into the application development processes. It defines the **Application Security Management Process** (**ASMP**) that emphasizes roles, responsibilities, and documentation to ensure that security controls are consistently applied throughout the SDLC, ensuring security is integral to the design process. It aligns closely with the broader **information security management system** (**ISMS**), like the ISO/IEC 27001.

NIST SP 800-218

NIST SP 800-218, the **Secure Software Development Framework** (**SSDF**), published by the U.S. NIST, offers practical, implementation-oriented guidance for building security into the software lifecycle. It complements DevSecOps practices by recommending baseline activities such as defining security requirements, implementing secure coding standards, conducting threat modelling, and verifying software integrity before release. It also assists in analyzing findings and developing targeted mitigation strategies and serves as a key reference for establishing effective security assessment programs.

While each of these frameworks offers distinct advantages, practical adoption entails integration and alignment of these frameworks rather than adopting one in isolation. A typical enterprise may use OWASP ASVS for control verification, ISO/IEC 27034 for process governance, and NIST SSDF for operational alignment within the DevSecOps pipelines. Automation tools can further enforce compliance by embedding verification checks into the CI/CD workflows, thus converting abstract standards into actionable controls.

Emerging trends

As software ecosystems become increasingly complex and interconnected, the boundaries of application security are expanding rapidly. Increased adoption of cloud-native architectures, containerization, and CI/CD pipelines has introduced new attack surfaces that demand adaptive and intelligent defense. To counter these threats, application security has evolved towards a comprehensive practice that integrates visibility, automation, and resilience into every layer of the software lifecycle. Let us discuss some of these emerging trends that are reshaping how applications are secured.

Supply chain security

The widespread adoption of open-source software, third-party libraries, and automated build pipelines has made the software supply chain critical to application security. Threat actors increasingly exploit vulnerabilities in dependencies, compromised build systems, or poisoned packages to inject malicious code into trusted software. High-profile incidents such as the SolarWinds Orion breach and the compromise of Codecov's testing platform have demonstrated how the infiltration of a single software component can propagate across the supply chain, compromising thousands of dependent applications and organizations.

Supply chain security focuses on ensuring integrity, authenticity, and provenance across all software dependencies and build processes. Key practices include SCA to detect vulnerable or tampered packages, cryptographic signing of source code and build artifacts, and adopting **software bill of materials** (**SBOMs**) for traceability. Frameworks such as **Supply-chain Levels for Software Artifacts** (**SLSA**) and NIST SSDF provide structured approaches for securing build pipelines to ensure that every component from source to deployment remains trusted and verifiable.

RASP

Traditional perimeter defenses like WAF often lack visibility into an application's internal behaviour, making them reactive rather than adaptive. RASP bridges this gap by embedding security logic directly into the application runtime. It monitors application behaviour in real-time and can detect or block malicious activity such as injection, privilege abuse, or session manipulation as it occurs.

In the earlier sections, we discussed RASP as an implementation-layer defense, however, its strategic importance lies in facilitating context-aware, autonomous protection. By instrumenting applications with sensors that understand logic flow and data usage, RASP provides fine-grained visibility and automated mitigation without requiring infrastructure reconfiguration. This shift towards self-protecting applications is a significant advancement in proactive and adaptive security.

Zero Trust architecture for applications

The Zero Trust paradigm is being increasingly applied to application security. Instead of inherently trusting the internal components, every service, API call, and user request is authenticated, authorized, and continuously validated. At the application-level, this entails enforcing strong identity verification, micro-segmentation, continuous access evaluation, and dynamic policy enforcement based on contextual factors such as device posture, session risk, and behavioural patterns. As discussed in earlier sections, the principles of Zero Trust are increasingly embedded into API gateways, service meshes, and CI/CD pipelines. Emerging frameworks such as BeyondCorp and OPA can be leveraged to implement consistent Zero Trust policies programmatically to ensure application resilience even in distributed and multi-cloud environments.

Application security posture management

As organizations adopt multiple security tools, such as SAST, DAST, SCA, container scanning, and runtime monitoring across the application lifecycle, security findings often become fragmented, inconsistent, and difficult to prioritize. **Application security posture management (ASPM)** is an integrative discipline that provides centralized visibility and control over the entire application security ecosystem. ASPM solutions continuously aggregate, correlate, and contextualize security data from various sources within the CI/CD pipeline and production environments. By mapping vulnerabilities to specific applications, assets, and business risks, ASPM helps in transforming raw scan outputs into actionable risk intelligence, which enables teams to prioritize remediation efforts.

The key capabilities of ASPM include centralized visibility, contextual risk prioritization, continuous posture assessment, and integration with DevSecOps workflows. By establishing a continuous feedback loop across development, testing, and production, ASPM shifts application security from a reactive process to a data-driven, risk-oriented discipline. This approach helps organizations maintain measurable, consistent assurance across complex application portfolios.

Security of AI-integrated applications

Generative artificial intelligence (**GenAI**) and **large language models** (**LLMs**) are being increasingly integrated in modern applications. LLMs embedded within applications provide conversational interfaces, automate workflows, and support decision-making. While these capabilities enhance functionality, they also introduce security risks that are not adequately addressed by traditional application threat models.

The OWASP Top 10 for LLM applications identifies vulnerabilities that arise from the unique characteristics of LLM-driven systems, including probabilistic behaviour, prompt-based control, and reliance on external data sources. Among the most significant risks for LLM-based applications is prompt injection, which occurs when an attacker manipulates input prompts to override system instructions or safety controls. This can be achieved directly or indirectly. While direct prompt injection involves explicit malicious input from a user, indirect prompt injection exploits untrusted external content, such as documents or web data consumed by the model to influence its behaviour. Another critical risk is excessive agency, where LLM-enabled applications are granted the ability to autonomously invoke tools, APIs, or workflows beyond their intended authority. When insufficiently constrained, such capabilities can allow manipulated models to perform unauthorized actions, significantly amplifying the impact of prompt injection and logic flaws.

AI-integrated applications can be secured by extending established application security principles into this new domain. Key controls include strict separation of system prompts and user input, limiting model permissions in accordance with least privilege, validating external data sources, and ensuring that AI-generated outputs are never implicitly trusted.

AI components must be treated as untrusted actors within the application architecture and subjected to the same authorization, monitoring, and audit controls as any other component.

We will explore AI security in greater detail in *Chapter 12, Emerging Technologies and Information Security*.

Conclusion

Application security is a foundational element of information security, as the protection of digital systems ultimately depends on the security of the software that drives them. It is not just a technical necessity but a business imperative that sustains trust, compliance, and operational resilience.

Application security must begin at the design stage, mature through secure development, and continue through regular testing, monitoring, and adaptation. The evolution from traditional SDLC to SSDLC and DevSecOps marks a shift from reactive security to a proactive and embedded approach. Contemporary applications adopt an integrated approach to security that combines secure coding, configuration management, encryption, and real-time monitoring. While cloud-native deployments, microservices, and automation have widened the attack surface, they also provide opportunities to embed security at scale. Automated testing, continuous validation, and adaptive controls help ensure that applications are secure by design and secure by default.

Effective application security is a continuous process that evolves with technology, threats, and business needs. It relies on close collaboration between all the stakeholders, including developers, operations, and security teams, and on a culture of continuous learning and improvement. When embedded effectively, application security can become a strategic enabler for building digital trust and supporting innovation.

Having discussed the core components of information security, we transition to the operational domain in the next chapter and explore the functioning of the **security operations center** (**SOC**). We will explore the structure, functions, and processes of the SOC, and its role in maintaining organizational security through continuous monitoring, systematic threat detection, and coordinated incident response.

Exercises

1. Define application security. Explain why it is considered a critical component of an organization's overall information security strategy.
2. Differentiate between secure SDLC and DevSecOps. How does each model address security challenges at different stages of software development?
3. Discuss the OWASP Top 10 web application vulnerabilities. Choose any three and describe their causes, potential impacts, and common mitigation techniques.

4. Explain the concept of Shift Left security. Why is it considered an effective approach to minimizing vulnerabilities in the development pipelines?
5. Describe how API security differs from traditional web application security. What are the unique risks associated with APIs, and how can they be mitigated?
6. What role do frameworks and standards, such as NIST SP 800-218 and ISO/IEC 27034 play in establishing a structured approach to application security?
7. Analyze a real-world security incident, such as the SolarWinds, Log4Shell, or Equifax incident, and identify the application-level weaknesses that contributed to the breach. Suggest how they could have been prevented.
8. Consider a simple web login form with username and password fields. Identify at least five potential vulnerabilities that could exist in the underlying code or configuration. Suggest secure coding or architectural controls to address each of the weaknesses.
9. Using any secure coding checklist or OWASP resource, assess an open-source application or API you are familiar with. Identify one example each of a security misconfiguration, an insecure data handling practice, and a missing input validation control. Write a short note on how these issues could be remediated.
10. Discuss emerging trends in application security. How do modern technologies such as RASP, software supply chain security, and Zero Trust architecture influence the future of secure application design?

CHAPTER 10
Security Operations

Introduction

In the preceding chapters, we discussed the information security strategy and the core security domains that guide how an organization identifies its critical assets and selects the right security controls. While strategic security governance defines what must be protected and why, the understanding of core domains helps in identifying and deploying the right controls. Once security controls are deployed, the real test lies in how well they operate in a live, evolving environment. This is where security operations take over. Security operations focus on ensuring that the controls continue to work as intended, day in and day out. It ensures that vulnerabilities are addressed before they can be exploited, and threats are detected and contained in a timely manner. This is achieved through continuous security operations focused on monitoring, detecting, investigating, and responding to threats that target the information systems.

In the modern threat landscape, attacks unfold continuously without warning and demand constant vigil. This vigil is maintained in the **security operations center** (**SOC**), the organization's operational nerve center, where people, processes, and technology converge. Through proactive monitoring, structured analysis, and rapid response, the SOC ensures that any suspicious activity is detected quickly and acted upon before it can escalate into a security incident.

At its core, cyber security operation is about reducing risk through decisive action. This implies capturing **indicators of compromise** (**IoC**) early, containing malicious activity before it spreads, and handling incidents with consistency and precision. To accomplish these aims, SOC analysts perform a broad set of functions that include vulnerability management, **incident response** (**IR**), threat hunting, and threat intelligence analysis. They rely on a robust ecosystem of technologies to support and streamline these functions, including **security information and event management** (**SIEM**) platforms for centralized visibility, **security orchestration and automated response** (**SOAR**) tools for orchestrated response, deception technologies for adversary detection, vulnerability scanners for identifying software and system vulnerabilities, and threat intelligence platforms for enriched contextual insights.

In this chapter, we will explore how these components come together to form an effective security operations capability. We will discuss how a SOC functions, how incidents are detected and analyzed, how threat intelligence enriches the detection process, and how response teams contain and eradicate threats. We will examine operational functions, the teams that perform them, the processes that guide their work, and the technologies that power their decisions.

Structure

In this chapter, we will discuss the following topics:

- Purpose of security operations
- Organization of SOC
- Core functions of SOC
- SOC tools and technologies
- SOC efficacy and maturity

Objectives

The objective of this chapter is to provide a comprehensive understanding of how security operations function in a modern enterprise, and how SOCs are organized, staffed, and equipped to detect and respond to cyber threats. By the end of this chapter, you will understand the strategic and operational role of a SOC and how people, processes, and technology work together to provide continuous defense. You will be able to identify the major operational functions within a SOC and understand how they contribute to risk reduction. You will also appreciate the importance of foundational security activities such as vulnerability management, configuration baselining, and patching. The chapter will help you distinguish between key technologies used in security operations, such as SIEM, SOAR, honeynets, vulnerability scanners, and threat intelligence platforms, and understand their role in detection and response.

You will develop a holistic view of security operations that integrates monitoring, detection, analysis, response, and continuous improvement. You will also learn how SOC maturity progresses over time and the indicators associated with each maturity level. By the end of the chapter, you will have a clear understanding of how modern security operations keep an organization resilient in the face of relentless and evolving threats.

Purpose of security operations

A SOC plays a critical role in enabling an organization to identify and respond to cyber threats promptly, effectively, and consistently. Its purpose extends far beyond deploying tools or monitoring dashboards. Security operations encompass the ongoing activities that keep an organization's security posture intact day after day. This includes monitoring infrastructure, analyzing suspicious events, detecting anomalies, investigating alerts, handling incidents, and coordinating mitigation actions. Security operations are inherently proactive, blending threat hunting, continuous vulnerability assessment, and intelligence-driven analysis to stay ahead of the adversaries. In practice, these functions are carried out by a structured operational team within the SOC, where people, processes, and technology come together to maintain situational awareness, reduce risk exposure, and preserve business resilience in the face of evolving adversary tactics.

Security operations revolve around the following key objectives:

- **Maintaining real-time visibility across the environment**: A SOC must have clear visibility into networks, endpoints, cloud workloads, applications, and user behaviour. Without visibility, any meaningful detection is not feasible. Log collection, telemetry, baselines, and accurate asset inventories provide the foundation for this awareness.
- **Detecting anomalies, threats, and security events**: Detection is both an art and a science. Effective detection involves rule-based correlation, analytics-driven anomaly detection, and intelligence-informed alerting. The aim is to identify suspicious activity early, before it can cause any damage.
- **Reducing response time and containing incidents**: Speed is critical once a threat is detected. Security operations focus on narrowing the gap between compromise and containment. Well-defined IR procedures, playbooks, automated enrichment, and rapid decision-making workflows enable faster recovery and limit damage.
- **Proactively reducing the attack surface**: Security operations are not limited to reactive monitoring. They also work to minimize opportunities for attackers. Vulnerability management, configuration hardening, baseline assessments, and patch management all help reduce the attack surface and build a more resilient environment.
- **Supporting business continuity, governance, and compliance**: SOC activities also support governance and assurance functions. They generate evidence for audits, assist with compliance requirements, and help maintain the organization's overall security posture. Clear reporting and measurable metrics make SOC performance transparent and accountable.

Together, these objectives define the mission of a SOC, which is focused on protecting the organization's digital assets through continuous, coordinated operational oversight.

Organization of SOC

The effectiveness of a SOC depends heavily on its organizational design, i.e., how responsibilities are distributed, how communication flows, and how leadership guides both strategic and tactical decisions. The organization of SOC varies widely across industries and the SOC maturity levels. While some organizations operate an internally staffed SOC, others adopt hybrid or fully outsourced models to achieve 24×7 coverage. Regardless of the structure, a SOC's success depends upon clearly defining roles and responsibilities, seamless coordination among teams, and strong governance mechanisms. In the absence of these, even the most advanced SOCs with state-of-the-art tools and mature processes struggle to deliver consistent operational value. A well-organized SOC creates predictability, consistency, and accountability. It ensures that alerts are handled methodically, investigations progress systematically, incidents receive the right level of escalation, and improvements happen on an ongoing basis.

SOC operating models

The way a SOC is structured has a significant impact on its effectiveness, scalability, and ability to support the organization's broader security strategy. SOCs are not one-size-fits-all. Enterprises adopt operating models based on their risk profile, budget, regulatory obligations, skills availability, and operational maturity. Broadly, SOCs can be categorized into four models, which include in-house SOC, managed / outsourced SOC, hybrid SOC, and virtual or distributed SOC. Each model offers distinct benefits and trade-offs, and the choice often reflects an organization's long-term security vision as much as its present operational constraints.

In-house SOC

An in-house SOC is fully owned, staffed, and operated by the organization. All analysts, engineers, incident responders, threat hunters, and SOC leadership are part of the internal workforce. This model provides the highest level of control over security operations because the organization manages the entire lifecycle of detection and response. Teams have direct access to internal systems, logs, business context, and IT owners, which makes investigations smoother and containment decisions faster. In-house SOCs also benefit from deep institutional knowledge as analysts are familiar with the organization's architecture, normal behaviours, and historical threat patterns. In-house SOC is suitable for enterprises with strict regulatory controls, sensitive data, or complex environments that demand customized monitoring and response workflows. However, building and maintaining such a SOC requires significant investment. It demands a mature governance framework, 24×7 staffing, continuous skill development, specialized tools, and strong cross-functional collaboration. Smaller organizations often struggle with these commitments, and even large enterprises face challenges such as analyst burnout, retention, and the escalating cost of technology.

Managed SOC

A managed or outsourced SOC delegates most operational activities to a specialized external **managed security services (MSS)** provider. The service provider handles monitoring, alert triage, initial investigation, and in certain cases, even the IR.

The benefits of a managed SOC are as follows:

- It is suitable for organizations that lack the resources or expertise to operate a SOC internally.

- It offers predictable costs and access to skilled resources and advanced detection technologies without heavy upfront investment.
- Outsourced SOCs typically leverage established operating procedures, mature playbooks, and global intelligence feeds that allow them to detect emerging threats quickly across clients.

The following are the limitations:

- Managed SOC can introduce operational challenges around contextual insights, response speed, and service provider dependency. External analysts may not have full visibility into internal assets or a deep understanding of the organization's business processes, which can adversely affect the speed and accuracy of investigations.
- Communication delays and contractual boundaries can slow down containment actions.
- Organizations that adopt the outsourced model must trust their service provider to handle sensitive data responsibly and meet regulatory obligations. This underscores the need for strong vendor governance and rigorous **service level agreement** (**SLA**) enforcement.

Hybrid SOC

A hybrid SOC blends internal capabilities with external support, creating a shared responsibility model. This model is often the preferred choice for mid-sized and large enterprises aiming to balance control with operational efficiency. Organizations typically retain strategic functions, such as IR leadership, threat hunting, and final investigation, and outsource the foundational tasks like alert monitoring, routine triage, and infrastructure management. This model allows organizations to maintain control where it matters most while benefiting from the scale, staffing flexibility, and expertise of a managed SOC. Hybrid SOCs often work best when internal teams focus on high-context analysis and tailored detection, while external teams handle the operational workload that requires round-the-clock coverage. The main challenge is coordination and integration. Both sides must operate in a coordinated manner, using shared playbooks, unified ticketing systems, and consistent communication channels. Without strong governance, hybrid SOCs risk misalignment, duplicated effort, or gaps in responsibility during active security incidents.

Virtual or distributed SOC

A virtual or distributed SOC is built on a decentralized model where analysts, tools, and processes operate across locations, time zones, or organizational units. Rather than functioning as a single physical facility, the SOC exists as a coordinated set of capabilities delivered remotely. This model is common in global enterprises, cloud-native organizations, and companies with remote-first operational structures. It provides flexibility, scalability, and access to talent across geographies. Virtual or distributed SOCs leverage cloud-based SIEMs, collaboration platforms, encrypted communication channels, and automated workflows to maintain seamless operations regardless of analyst location. They often incorporate follow-the-sun monitoring to achieve continuous coverage without night shifts. However, this model requires strong leadership and collaboration frameworks, standardization of tools, clearly defined processes, and disciplined communication practices to prevent operational silos. Maintaining culture, ensuring time-sensitive handoffs, and protecting sensitive investigation data across jurisdictions are additional considerations for successful SOC operations.

SOC roles and responsibilities

A SOC is built on a set of specialized roles that work together to monitor the information environment, detect threats, investigate suspicious activity, and respond to incidents. Although every SOC is organized differently depending on its size, maturity, and operating model, the core responsibilities largely remain the same. In smaller teams, several of these roles may be combined, with analysts often wearing multiple hats, from monitoring and investigation to basic threat hunting and initial response. Larger SOCs, on the other hand, assign these responsibilities across dedicated specialists. Regardless of how the roles are organized, the goal remains consistent, which is to ensure reliable, round-the-clock security coverage and handle alerts with the right mix of expertise and discipline.

SOC analyst

SOC analysts are the backbone of day-to-day operations, with responsibilities expanding progressively. SOC teams typically utilize a tiered model, as discussed, to ensure efficient workflow management, clear escalation paths, and differentiated responsibilities across tiers. The details are as follows:

- **Tier-1 analyst (alert monitoring and triage)**: Tier-1 analysts serve as the first line of defense. Their primary responsibility is to monitor the SIEM console and other platforms, validate alerts, perform initial triage, and escalate the alerts that require deeper investigation. They differentiate between false positives and legitimate threats, enrich alerts with quick contextual checks, and ensure that no alert of interest is overlooked. This role demands attention to detail, familiarity with common attack patterns, and the ability to make quick judgments. Their efficiency directly affects response time and SOC workload balance.

- **Tier-2 analyst (investigation and incident analysis)**: Tier-2 analysts handle escalated alerts and conduct deeper investigations. They analyze network traffic, endpoint telemetry, authentication patterns, and logs from various systems to understand the scope and impact of an event. They correlate IoC, perform root cause analysis, and recommend containment actions. Their role requires advanced analytical skills, familiarity with threat actor tactics, and the ability to reconstruct attack paths.

- **Tier-3 analyst (advanced investigation and threat hunting)**: Tier-3 analysts deal with complex incidents, evasive threats, and advanced adversary behaviour that cannot be addressed through routine procedures. They conduct in-depth forensic analysis, reverse-engineer malicious artifacts when required, and identify detection gaps. They are also responsible for proactive threat hunting, looking for hidden or emerging threats that have bypassed existing controls. Tier-3 analysts are often involved in developing custom detection rules and analytics, and improving the overall SOC capability. Through proactive threat hunting, they help refine detection logic, reduce blind spots, and strengthen resilience against sophisticated threat actors.

Incident responder

An incident responder steps in when an event crosses the threshold of an incident. The role of an incident responder is to contain, eradicate, and recover from security breaches with minimal business impact. They coordinate response activities across teams, lead evidence collection, perform containment actions such as isolating hosts or revoking credentials, and work towards restoring normal operations. They maintain detailed documentation for post-incident review and ensure that lessons learned translate into improved playbooks, controls, and preventive measures. The incident responder role is often combined with the Tier-3 SOC analyst role.

Threat intelligence analyst

Threat intelligence analysts gather, validate, and operationalize intelligence from both internal data and external sources such as **information sharing and analysis centers** (**ISACs**), vendor feeds, **open-source intelligence** (**OSINT**), and dark-web monitoring. They distill raw intelligence into actionable insights that help the SOC anticipate and detect threats more effectively. Their task includes analyzing threat actor **tactics, techniques, and procedures** (**TTPs**), mapping IoCs to operational context, and advising on developing detection rules or defensive adjustments. They also contribute to strategic intelligence that supports risk assessment and long-term planning.

SOC engineer

SOC engineers maintain the technical backbone of SOC operations. They manage SIEM platforms, logingestion pipelines, **endpoint detection and response** (**EDR**) tools, SOAR solutions, and other monitoring tools and technologies. Their responsibilities include establishing data integrations, tuning correlation rules, maintaining tool performance, and ensuring that alerting logic aligns with the evolving threats. SOC engineers work very closely with analysts to reduce false positives, fix telemetry gaps, and introduce new data sources to improve visibility.

Automation specialist

Automation specialists design and maintain automated workflows that accelerate detection and response. They create SOAR playbooks, integrate **application programming interfaces (APIs)**, automate enrichment steps, and orchestrate repetitive tasks such as IoC lookups, containment actions, and ticket creation. Automation helps reduce analyst fatigue, improves consistency, and enables the SOC to respond quickly even during high-volume events.

Forensic expert

Forensic experts conduct detailed technical investigations when an incident requires deep evidence analysis or legal defensibility. They preserve digital evidence, analyze file systems, memory dumps, logs, and malware samples. They also document findings in a manner that supports legal or regulatory proceedings. Forensics expertise is essential during major breaches, insider incidents, and cases where attribution, compromise assessment, or data exfiltration analysis is required.

Vulnerability management analyst

Vulnerability management analysts review vulnerability scan results, validate risk ratings, identify remediation priorities, and track the closure of high-risk findings. They collaborate with system owners, patch management teams, and governance functions to ensure that exploitable weaknesses are addressed proactively, reducing the attack surface. Although vulnerability management is closely linked to SOC operations, in some enterprises it is run as a separate function.

SOC manager

The SOC manager oversees the overall functioning of the SOC. Their responsibilities include staffing, process governance, shift management, performance tracking, and continuous improvement. They ensure that analysts follow established playbooks, coordinate escalations with other teams, and maintain consistent operational quality. The SOC manager also provides reporting to senior leadership, highlights emerging risks, and ensures that the SOC maintains alignment with organizational security objectives.

Head of security operations

At the leadership level, the head of security operations sets the strategic direction for the SOC. They define the operating model, oversee technology upgrades, manage budgets, and ensure that the SOC aligns with the business goals. They track long-term trends, drive maturity improvements, engage with external partners, and ensure regulatory compliance. This role bridges technical operations and executive decision-making.

The SOC roles do not operate in isolation. The effectiveness of SOC operations ultimately depends on how well these teams work together as a coordinated unit. Analysts maintain continuous monitoring, threat hunters uncover hidden threats, and incident responders manage crises with precision. Engineers keep the underlying tools reliable and responsive, while intelligence analysts enrich detection with timely insights. The leadership, in turn, ensures that the SOC evolves continuously and adapts to the changing threat landscape. Each role in the SOC brings its own expertise, and together they form the continuous, coordinated defense that protects the enterprise on an ongoing basis.

Core functions of SOC

SOC carries out a set of core functions that, together, enable real-time detection, analysis, and response to cyber threats. These functions translate strategic intent into day-to-day operational defense. While tools and technologies play an important supporting role, it is the thorough and disciplined execution of these functions, including alert monitoring, IR, threat hunting, intelligence integration, and vulnerability management, that ultimately determines the SOC's effectiveness. Each function contributes a specific action, and together they create a detection and response capability that is continuous, coordinated, and resilient.

Continuous monitoring

Continuous monitoring is the frontline function of a SOC and the primary mechanism through which security teams maintain real-time awareness of what is happening across the organization's digital environment. Its purpose is to ensure that potential threats and suspicious activities are detected as soon as they occur. Without rigorous and continuous monitoring, threats may linger undetected, and the entire IR process becomes reactive and inefficient. Continuous monitoring ensures that relevant alerts are identified proactively and acted upon promptly. It forms the foundation upon which rapid detection, accurate analysis, and effective containment are built.

Security monitoring spans across networks, endpoints, cloud platforms, applications, identity systems, and any other component that generates security-relevant telemetry. For continuous monitoring, the SOC analysts rely on a diverse set of technologies, such as SIEM platforms, EDR solutions, network sensors, cloud-native security tools, and threat analytics engines. These systems generate alerts based on correlation rules, behavioural models, and anomaly detection techniques. SOC analysts review these alerts and perform initial triage to determine which events require deeper investigation. This involves checking contextual information, enriching alerts with threat intelligence, analyzing user and entity behaviour, reviewing historical patterns, and assessing the criticality of the affected assets.

Effective monitoring depends on well-tuned detection rules, a clear escalation matrix, and a solid understanding of what normal activity looks like in the organization. Analysts must balance speed with accuracy. They need to act quickly enough to catch early warning signs, yet be careful enough to avoid unnecessary escalations.

Incident response

IR is one of the most critical functions of a SOC, as it determines how quickly and effectively an organization can limit the impact of a security incident. While continuous monitoring identifies suspicious activity, IR delivers the structured and coordinated actions that follow. A well-executed IR process reduces disruption, shortens downtime, protects organizational assets, and prevents incidents from escalating into business-impacting crises.

Effective IR follows a repeatable, phased cycle that guides the SOC from the first indication of an issue through containment, recovery, and post-incident analysis. This lifecycle typically includes detection, triage, containment, eradication, recovery, and post-incident analysis. Throughout the process, incident responders collaborate closely with system owners, network and cloud teams, legal and compliance functions, and, when necessary, external partners or regulators to ensure a coordinated and timely response.

Detection

Detection is the point at which a potential security issue is first identified. Alerts may originate from any of the security platforms, including SIEM, honeynets, endpoint detection tools, threat intelligence feeds, or automated anomaly detection systems. At this stage, the SOC analysts must distinguish between ordinary activity and behaviour that warrants further investigation. Accurate detection is essential, as it sets the stage for the subsequent response actions.

The activities during the detection stage include:

- Identifying unusual or suspicious events.
- Validating that the alert corresponds to a real issue and not a false positive.
- Collecting initial contextual information such as affected user, system, activity type, timestamp, and IOCs.

Triage

Triaging implies determining the severity, scope, and urgency of the incident. The SOC analysts evaluate the incidents based on the following criteria:

- **Impact**: *What systems or data are affected?*
- **Criticality**: *Does the activity threaten business operations or sensitive assets?*
- **Urgency**: *How quickly must the SOC act to prevent further damage?*
- **Confidence**: *How certain are we that this is a genuine security incident?*

Based on these considerations, the incidents are categorized into predefined severity levels, such as critical, high, medium, or low. Triage also involves assigning the incident to the appropriate team or responder to ensure that the right expertise is applied early in the process.

Containment

Containment aims to limit the spread and impact of the incident. This phase can involve both short-term containment, which stops immediate harm, and long-term containment, which stabilizes the environment until permanent fixes are applied. The immediate objective is to limit the spread of the incident and prevent further damage while analysis continues.

Depending on the nature of the incident, containment may involve the following activities:

- Isolating affected endpoints from the network.
- Blocking malicious IPs, domains, or URLs.
- Disabling compromised user accounts.
- Applying temporary firewall rules or segmentation controls.
- Halting malicious processes or tasks.

Eradication

Once the threat is contained, the next step is to remove the root cause. Eradication ensures that the threat actor cannot regain access and that the environment is clean before restoring normal operations. This involves:

- Eliminating malware, backdoors, persistence mechanisms, or malicious configurations.
- Patching vulnerable systems or updating misconfigured security controls.
- Resetting passwords or updating access controls.
- Removing unauthorized tools, scripts, or users left by the attacker.

Recovery

Recovery focuses on restoring affected systems or services to normal operation in a secure and validated state. The recovery process must be coordinated to prevent further disruptions while ensuring business continuity. The activities during this stage include:

- Rebuilding systems from known-good baselines.
- Restoring data from backups.
- Reconnecting previously isolated machines to the network.
- Performing careful testing to ensure the threat is fully removed.
- Monitoring for signs of reinfection or lingering attacker activity.

Post-incident analysis

After the incident is resolved, the SOC conducts a detailed review to understand what happened, how it unfolded, and how future incidents can be prevented or detected earlier. This stage includes:

- Documenting the full incident timeline and attack chain.
- Assessing gaps in detection rules, monitoring coverage, or response procedures.
- Reviewing what went well and what challenges responders faced.
- Updating processes, playbooks, and SIEM rules.
- Sharing insights across security teams and relevant stakeholders.

Post-incident analysis transforms each incident into an opportunity for continuous evolution and improving the SOC efficacy and maturity. The following figure represents a typical cybersecurity IR cycle:

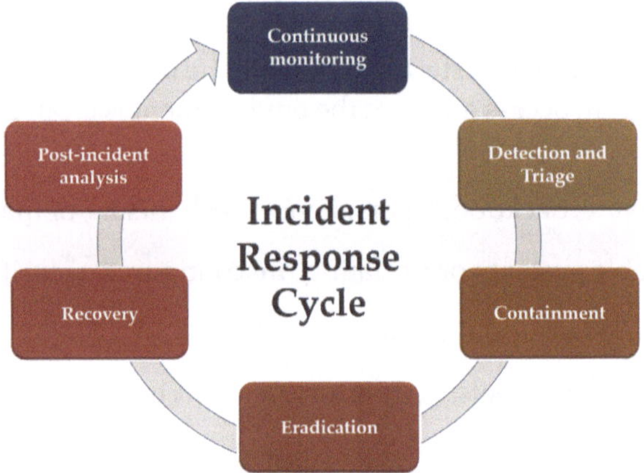

***Figure 10.1**: Cybersecurity IR cycle*

Digital forensic investigation

Digital forensic investigation focuses on uncovering how an incident occurred, what systems or data were affected, and whether an attacker maintains any level of persistence within the environment. While IR deals with containment and recovery, digital forensics digs deeper and attempts to reconstruct the adversary's actions to identify the exploited weaknesses and determine the full scope and impact of the compromise. This detailed examination enables understanding the incident in its entirety and eliminates any residual footholds an attacker may have left behind.

Evidence collection and preservation

A forensic investigation typically begins once the immediate containment measures are in place and the environment has stabilized. The first step often involves acquiring and preserving digital evidence from affected systems, logs, and network devices. Forensic experts must ensure that the evidence remains intact, unmodified, and defensible, especially if legal or regulatory proceedings are anticipated. To accomplish this, they rely on sound forensic acquisition methods such as creating bit-level images of disks, capturing volatile data from memory, and securely exporting log files. These artefacts must be collected in a manner that maintains their integrity and authenticity throughout the investigative process.

Evidence handling is governed by the principle of chain of custody, a formal, documented trail that records exactly how evidence was collected, who accessed it, where it was stored, and how it was transferred. A clear and unbroken chain of custody is essential for ensuring that the evidence can be trusted and accepted by legal authorities, if needed. Each handover or interaction with the evidence is recorded, typically using tamper-evident storage, digital signatures, or logs that demonstrate that the artefacts have remained unaltered since collection. Even in purely internal investigations, maintaining a clean chain of custody reinforces the credibility and accuracy of the forensic analysis.

Evidence examination and analysis

Once evidence is acquired, analysts proceed with examination and analysis of the evidence. This involves reconstructing the incident timeline and identifying the attacker's actions on the compromised systems. The artefacts collected from the host and network devices must be analyzed together for a holistic view of the malicious activities and a broader view of attacker behaviour across the environment.

Host-based forensic analysis focuses on endpoint artefacts such as file system metadata, registry entries, browser history, execution logs, scheduled tasks, system event logs, and traces of persistence mechanisms. Investigators look for malicious activities such as unusual processes, privilege escalations, unauthorized account creation, malicious binaries, lateral movement patterns, and indicators of data exfiltration. Memory forensics plays a vital role here, as volatile data can reveal injected code, decrypted payloads, in-memory implants, active network connections, and credentials exposed by running processes.

Network forensics is carried out to complement these findings by analyzing packet captures, firewall logs, proxy traffic, and DNS records to trace communication patterns. This helps identify command-and-control activity, lateral movement, reconnaissance actions, and suspicious data flows.

Root cause analysis and compromise assessment

A thorough forensic investigation helps in identifying the root cause of the security incident and carrying out a compromise assessment to assess its impact. Root cause analysis determines exactly how the compromise originated and identifies the conditions that enabled the attack. This may involve identifying an unpatched vulnerability, a misconfiguration, a successful phishing attempt, exposed credentials, insecure APIs, or weaknesses in third-party components. Understanding the root cause ensures that the underlying conditions that led to the attack are addressed so that similar incidents do not recur.

Compromise assessment extends beyond root cause to determine the full extent and impact of the security incident. It helps determine which systems were accessed, what data was viewed or exfiltrated, whether any backdoors or persistence mechanisms remain, and whether the threat actor moved laterally within the environment. The goal is to ensure that the compromise is completely eradicated and that the organization has a complete and accurate picture of the attacker's footprint.

Once the forensic investigation is over and the full scope of an incident is understood, the digital forensics experts may shift focus to threat hunting to proactively uncover stealthy or undetected attacker activity.

Threat hunting

Threat hunting focuses on proactively identifying threats that may have gone undetected through traditional detection mechanisms. While alert-driven monitoring depends on predefined rules, signatures, and models, threat hunting assumes that an adversary may already be present in the environment, operating quietly and evading automated detection. The goal is to uncover stealthy activity before it evolves into a security incident. Threat hunting combines human expertise, analytical reasoning, and contextual intelligence. Instead of depending on alerts, threat hunters actively explore telemetry, logs, behavioural patterns, and threat intelligence to find subtle indications of malicious activity. This shift from reactive detection to proactive discovery significantly strengthens the organization's security posture.

Threat hunters operate with the premise that no detection system is infallible. Attackers routinely use techniques designed to bypass detection rules, exploit blind spots in logging, abuse legitimate credentials, and hide within normal traffic patterns. Threat hunting helps uncover such hidden activity by identifying threats that do not trigger alerts, reducing attacker dwell time, validating and improving existing detection logic, and exposing gaps in logging, monitoring, and telemetry.

Threat hunting approaches

Threat hunting approaches can be broadly categorized as follows, based on the source of insight that drives the process:

- **Intelligence-led hunting**: This approach uses threat intelligence, such as IOCs, TTPs, malware indicators, or adversary campaign reports for threat hunting. For instance, the threat hunters may search for registry changes associated with a known ransomware family, hunt for process patterns resembling an **advanced persistent threat** (**APT**) group's lateral movement tactics, or look for command-line artefacts tied to zero-day exploitation campaigns. This approach helps ensure that the SOC remains aligned with global threat trends and emerging techniques.

- **Hypothesis-driven hunting**: In hypothesis-driven threat hunting, hunters begin by forming a reasoned assumption based on attacker behaviour, knowledge of the environment, or observed anomalies. For example, they may ask whether unusual Kerberos ticket activity indicates privilege escalation after a service account compromise, or whether suspicious PowerShell execution patterns suggest misuse of living-off-the-land tools. This approach mirrors a scientific investigation, which entails defining a hypothesis, gathering evidence, testing the hypothesis, and refining it based on the findings.
- **Analytics-driven hunting**: In analytics-driven threat hunting, statistical models, anomaly detection systems, and machine-learning tools discover unusual behaviour that warrants human investigation. This may include abnormal login patterns across geography or time, unusually large data transfers to an external domain, or rare parent-child process relationships that deviate from normal system behaviour. This approach blends automated detection with human expertise to uncover subtle or sophisticated threats that traditional monitoring systems might miss.

Threat hunting process

A well-structured threat hunting follows a systematic progression, ensuring that analysts move from a clear starting point to actionable outcomes. The process typically involves the following stages:

- **Planning and hypothesis formation**: The hunt begins by defining its scope, objectives, and working hypothesis. Analysts determine what they intend to uncover, such as a specific threat actor's behaviour, suspicious patterns, or deviations from established baselines. Clear scoping ensures that the process remains focused, measurable, and aligned with organizational priorities.
- **Data collection and preparation**: Threat hunters gather and prepare the required telemetry, which may include EDR logs, network captures, identity and access logs, process execution records, proxy/firewall logs, cloud activity logs, and application or authentication logs. Data quality, completeness, and coverage are critical for success. Gaps in logging not only hinder threat hunting but also reveal areas where monitoring must be strengthened.
- **Investigation and analysis**: Using advanced queries, visualization tools, statistical techniques, and correlation logic, analysts sift through the data to identify rare behaviours, tactics aligned patterns such as persistence or privilege escalation, unusual event sequences, or indicators linked to threat intelligence. This requires both technical depth and investigative skills.

- **Validation and escalation**: Once potentially suspicious activity is identified, analysts validate their findings by cross-referencing additional logs, checking against known-good behaviour, consulting asset owners, and comparing evidence with relevant threat intelligence. If the activity is confirmed to be malicious or high-risk, it is escalated to the IR team for containment and remediation.
- **Documentation and reporting**: Threat hunters document the hunt's objectives, scope, data sources used, analytical methods or queries, findings, and any detection gaps discovered. Comprehensive documentation ensures transparency, repeatability, and effective integration into the broader SOC workflows.
- **Improvement of SOC detection capability**: The insights from hunting often lead to new SIEM correlation rules, updated signatures, refined playbooks, enhanced logging configurations, updated threat models, and analyst training on new or emerging attack techniques. This feedback loop strengthens detection capabilities and drives continuous SOC maturity.

Threat intelligence integration

Modern cyber threats evolve rapidly, with adversaries constantly refining their TTPs. To stay ahead, SOCs cannot afford to rely solely on internal telemetry. They also need timely and contextualized information about emerging threats in the broader landscape. This is where threat intelligence becomes an essential component of security operations. Threat intelligence is far more than a mere feed of IoCs. Mature programs analyze adversary behaviour, campaign patterns, geopolitical drivers, and sector-specific risks. They convert raw data into actionable insights that SOC can utilize to make informed, timely decisions.

Threat intelligence can be categorized as follows:

- **Tactical**: This includes IoCs such as malicious IPs, domains, file hashes, and signatures that can be directly integrated into SIEM, EDR, and firewalls.
- **Operational**: This type of threat intelligence provides insight into current campaigns, malware families, TTPs, and threat actor infrastructure used for enhancing detection logic.
- **Strategic**: This provides high-level analysis of threat trends, industry risks, and anticipated shifts in adversary behaviour, used by leadership for planning and investment decisions.

Sources of threat intelligence

A mature SOC draws threat intelligence from a wide range of sources to ensure both breadth and depth of insight. Commercial intelligence providers supply curated reports, malware analyses, and sector-specific threat updates, while OSINT offers community-driven indicators, public advisories, and technical research. Industry ISACs contribute valuable, peer-shared information relevant to specific industries, and national **Computer Emergency Response Teams** (**CERTs**) provide authoritative alerts on active campaigns or emerging vulnerabilities. In addition to external sources, organizations also generate internal intelligence through incident investigations, threat hunting, telemetry analysis, and detection engineering. Some SOCs further enhance situational awareness through monitoring of surface, deep, and dark-web forums for leaked data, exposed credentials, or discussions of potential targeting. Together, these diverse sources provide a well-rounded picture of the threat landscape.

Threat intelligence platforms

Threat intelligence platforms (**TIPs**) help SOC organize, analyze, and operationalize the intelligence they collect. **Malware Information Sharing Platform** (**MISP**) is one such open-source threat intelligence sharing platform that can be used for this purpose. A TIP aggregates data from multiple feeds, removes duplicates, enriches indicators with contextual information, maps adversary behaviour to frameworks such as MITRE ATT&CK, and assigns risk scores based on relevance. It also automates the distribution of intelligence to downstream systems, including SIEM, SOAR, EDR, and firewalls. By acting as the intelligence hub, a TIP ensures that analysts get high-quality, prioritized, and contextualized intelligence rather than raw, unfiltered data, enabling faster and more informed decision-making.

When integrated into daily SOC workflows, threat intelligence significantly enhances the effectiveness of threat detection. It strengthens correlation rules, enriches behavioural detections, and ensures that monitoring aligns with current adversary techniques. During IR, it provides the context needed to understand attacker intent, campaign linkages, and appropriate containment strategies.

Vulnerability management

Information environments evolve continuously, so do the weaknesses within them. Vulnerabilities may emerge in custom-built applications, commercial software, shared libraries, container images, operating systems, firmware, or even in cloud control planes. As systems become more interconnected, a single unpatched weakness can provide attackers with an entry point to compromise an entire environment. A mature vulnerability management process ensures that organizations can identify, assess, prioritize, and remediate such weaknesses in a systematic and repeatable manner, thereby reducing overall exposure.

Effective vulnerability management requires more than running scanners or publishing reports. It brings together scanning, analysis, validation, remediation coordination, and ongoing measurement into a continuous cycle. The SOC often plays a central role by providing the visibility, data correlation, and operational oversight needed to ensure that vulnerabilities are discovered early and addressed proactively. A well-defined vulnerability management program includes a series of activities such as **vulnerability assessment** (**VA**), **baseline assessment** (**BA**), **penetration testing** (**PT**), and patch management.

Vulnerability assessment

VA involves the systematic discovery of weaknesses across endpoints, servers, network devices, **virtual machines** (**VMs**), container images, and cloud resources. Automated scanners perform network-based and agent-based assessments to identify outdated software versions, missing patches, insecure configurations, misconfigured services, exposed ports, weak cryptographic settings, and known **Common Vulnerabilities and Exposures** (**CVEs**). In modern environments, applications rely heavily on third-party libraries, APIs, container-based images, and open-source components. Weaknesses often emerge not in the application code itself but in these embedded components. Integrating **Software Composition Analysis** (**SCA**), dependency checks, and container image scanning into VA enhances visibility across the full technology stack.

However, scanning alone does not guarantee accuracy or insight. SOC analysts and vulnerability management teams must validate high-risk findings, eliminate false positives, map vulnerabilities to real assets, and evaluate exploitability in the organization's context. For instance, the presence of a critical CVE on an isolated system with no external exposure may pose less risk than a medium-severity flaw on a publicly accessible server.

Baseline assessment

BA ensures that systems adhere to secure configuration standards before vulnerabilities emerge. It focuses on verifying compliance with hardened baselines such as **Center for Internet Security** (**CIS**) Benchmarks, **Defense Information Systems Agency** (**DISA**) **Security Technical Implementation Guides** (**STIGs**), or internal security policies.

BA typically checks for the following:

- Authentication and access control settings.
- Logging and monitoring configurations.
- Network service exposure.
- File system and registry permissions.
- Installed software and unnecessary services.
- Kernel, OS, or cloud workload configuration parameters.
- IAM policies and cloud control plane settings.

Weak or inconsistent baselines often contribute to vulnerabilities that attackers exploit laterally. Aligning systems to a well-defined baseline significantly reduces the attack surface and reduces the attack surface and prevents configuration-driven vulnerabilities from appearing later. Configuration management tools such as *Ansible*, *Chef*, *Puppet*, along with cloud configuration policies, enable these baselines to be applied consistently at scale.

Penetration testing

PT complements VA and BA by simulating attacks and focuses on exploiting the vulnerabilities to understand their real-world impact. Penetration testers attempt to exploit weaknesses, chain multiple vulnerabilities, bypass security controls, and escalate privileges to demonstrate the practical impact of security gaps.

PT provides value by:

- Validating the effectiveness of preventive controls.
- Revealing exploitation paths not visible to scanners.
- Testing SOC detection and response readiness.
- Offering concrete evidence to prioritize remediation.

Penetration tests may be scheduled periodically or triggered by major application releases, architectural changes, or newly emerging threats. While automated tools assist, PT is ultimately human-driven and therefore provides richer insight.

Patch management

Patch management ensures that vulnerabilities identified across the environment are remediated in a timely, controlled, and auditable manner. This includes patches for operating systems, applications, firmware, container images, and third-party dependencies.

A mature patching process includes the following:

- Continuous monitoring of vendor advisories.
- Categorizing patches based on risk and exploitability.
- Testing updates in controlled environments.
- Coordinated rollout across production systems.
- Post-deployment verification.
- Exception handling for systems that cannot be patched immediately.

Patch management is closely tied to service availability and, therefore, must balance security requirements with operational constraints. Delayed patching remains one of the most common root causes of breaches, underscoring the need for structured, automated, and well-governed patching practices. It must be ensured that vulnerabilities are remediated in the right order and within acceptable timelines. A risk-based approach is essential, one that considers **Common Vulnerability Scoring System (CVSS)** severity, exploit availability, asset criticality, lateral movement potential, and real-world threat intelligence to prioritize what should be patched first.

SOC tools and technologies

A SOC relies on a diverse ecosystem of technologies that work together to detect, analyze, contain, and respond to threats. These tools provide visibility, automate workflows, enrich context, and support investigations, thus facilitating efficient SOC operations. While each tool serves a specific purpose, its true value emerges when it is integrated into a cohesive detection and response architecture.

Key SOC tools and technologies include the following:

- **SIEM**: A SIEM collects logs and events from across the environment, normalizes them, and correlates patterns to detect suspicious activity. It acts as the central hub for monitoring, alerting, and compliance reporting in the SOC.
- **SOAR**: A SOAR platform automates repetitive tasks, enriches alerts with contextual information, and executes predefined response actions through playbooks. It helps in reducing analyst workload and accelerates incident handling.
- **EDR:** It is an endpoint security solution that provides deep visibility into endpoint activities and helps in detecting malicious behaviour such as fileless attacks, privilege escalation, or lateral movement. EDR tools also support rapid investigation and containment at the device level.
- **Extended defense and response (XDR)**: An XDR expands the capabilities of EDR by correlating telemetry across endpoints, networks, cloud workloads, and identities. It offers unified threat detection and response.
- **User and entity behaviour analytics (UEBA)**: This technology uses behavioural baselines and **machine learning** (**ML**) models to identify abnormal or risky actions by users, devices, or applications. It is particularly effective for insider threats and compromised accounts.
- **Network detection and response (NDR)**: Monitors network traffic for anomalies, command-and-control activity, and lateral movement. It complements endpoint-level visibility with network-centric detection.
- **Identity threat detection and response (ITDR)**: Monitors identity systems such as **Active Directory** (**AD**), **identity and access management** (**IAM**) platforms, and authentication workflows for signs of credential compromise, privilege misuse, or lateral movement. ITDR strengthens the detection of identity-centric attacks that often bypass traditional security controls.
- **Deception technology**: Deploys decoy systems, fake credentials, honeynets, and simulated assets across the environment to attract attackers and reveal malicious activity early. These deceptive technologies generate precise alerts that help security teams observe attacker behaviour safely.

- **Attack Surface Management (ASM)**: Continuously discovers internet-facing assets, misconfigurations, and exposures to reveal what attackers can see and target. ASM helps reduce external attack surface risks.
- **Vulnerability scanners**: The vulnerability scanners identify missing patches, misconfigurations, and known weaknesses in servers, endpoints, and applications. These tools form the backbone of vulnerability management and help prioritize remediation.
- **Email security gateways**: These gateways analyze inbound and outbound email to detect phishing, malware, impersonation attacks, and malicious attachments or links. They are essential for defending against social engineering.
- **Data loss prevention (DLP)**: These solutions monitor and restrict the movement of sensitive data across endpoints, networks, email, and cloud services. DLP prevents accidental or malicious data leakage.
- **Digital forensics and IR (DFIR) tools**: DFIR tools support evidence collection, timeline reconstruction, compromise assessment, and root cause analysis. DFIR platforms enable deep analysis of incidents and support investigations.
- **Cloud security tools**:
  - **Cloud security posture management (CSPM)**: It detects misconfigurations and compliance gaps in cloud environments.
  - **Cloud workload protection platform (CWPP)**: It protects cloud workloads such as VMs, containers, and serverless functions from runtime threats.
  - **Cloud-native application protection platform (CNAPP)**: It integrates CSPM, CWPP, and other cloud security capabilities to secure cloud-native applications across their lifecycle.
  - **Data security posture management (DSPM):** It maps, classifies, and monitors sensitive data across cloud environments to prevent exposure or misuse.

This list covers most of the tools and technologies used in a SOC, but it is by no means exhaustive. The set of tools continues to grow as SOC capabilities evolve in response to the changing threat landscape. In real-world implementations, several of these functionalities are consolidated into integrated platforms to provide broader visibility, reduce tool sprawl, and streamline SOC operations.

We now focus on a detailed examination of the core SOC technologies, including SIEM, SOAR, honeynets, vulnerability scanners, and email security solutions. Endpoint-focused tools such as EDR and XDR were discussed in detail in *Chapter 8, Endpoint Security*, and network-focused technologies such as IDS/IPS were covered in *Chapter 7, Network Security*. Cloud-native security tools will be examined in depth in *Chapter 11, Cloud Security*.

SIEM

SIEM is one of the most essential technologies in a SOC. It provides centralized visibility and the analytical foundation upon which all other security operations depend. It collects logs, events, and telemetry from across the organization's IT landscape and brings them together into a unified platform where threats can be analyzed, correlated, and acted upon. Without a well-implemented SIEM, detecting multi-stage attacks, reconstructing incidents, or understanding the true security posture becomes extremely difficult.

Log collection and normalization

A SIEM begins by gathering logs from a wide range of systems, including endpoints, servers, firewalls, IAM platforms, cloud services, applications, databases, and network infrastructure. Each of these systems produces logs in different formats; this data must be parsed, standardized, and normalized. Normalization ensures that fields such as user IDs, source IPs, timestamps, event types, and process names follow a consistent structure to enable reliable search, analytics, and detection. This normalized data is stored in a searchable repository that allows analysts to perform investigations, reconstruct timelines, review historical activity, and support forensic needs.

Correlation and detection logic

The real intelligence of a SIEM comes from its ability to correlate events across systems. Instead of relying on a single alert, SIEM correlation rules look for meaningful patterns and sequences of actions that, when viewed together, indicate a potential threat. These rules may detect patterns such as:

- Multiple failed login attempts followed by a successful one.
- Privilege escalation events after an abnormal authentication.
- Suspicious command-line executions on sensitive servers.
- Data transfers that deviate from normal baselines.
- Simultaneous login attempts from geographically distant locations.

Correlation rules may be simple threshold-based logic or complex behavioural patterns aligned with MITRE ATT&CK techniques. As new threats emerge, the detection logics evolve through continuous tuning and threat intelligence integration.

Advanced analytics

The modern SIEM platforms go beyond static rules and incorporate advanced behavioural analytics. These capabilities use statistical profiling and ML models to detect anomalies that would otherwise go undetected. These include UEBA, for instance, an employee logging in at an unusual hour, a service account accessing systems it has never interacted with, or a rare parent-child process relationship suggesting malicious execution. This combination of rule-based and behavioural analytics significantly improves the detection of insider threats, account compromise, and living-off-the-land attacks.

Alert enrichment and contextualization

Alerts generated by a SIEM are enriched with additional context to help analysts prioritize effectively. Enrichment may include the following:

- Known malicious indicators from threat intelligence feeds.
- Business criticality of the affected asset.
- Existing vulnerabilities in the system.
- User risk scores.
- Historical activity of the account or device.

This context reduces false positives and allows analysts to make informed decisions quickly, particularly during triage and investigation.

Operational visibility

SIEM dashboards provide real-time visibility into the organization's threat landscape. They present summaries of high-risk events, authentication anomalies, malware activity, network anomalies, and cloud misconfiguration alerts. These dashboards enable SOC leadership to track trends and monitor operational health. SIEM platforms also serve as a central source of evidence for audits and regulatory requirements by generating reports that demonstrate effective monitoring and log retention. They also provide long-term log retention capability that is critical for conducting forensic investigations and root cause analysis. Stored logs help reconstruct the full sequence of attacker actions, identify lateral movement, and determine the impact of security incidents.

SIEM acts as the analytical backbone of the SOC by integrating with a wide range of security technologies. These integrations include SOAR tools for automated response, EDR/XDR for endpoint telemetry, NDR for network behavioural insights, TIPs for IoC enrichment, vulnerability scanners for prioritized remediation, and ITDR tools for identity-centric threat detection. Together, these integrations create a unified detection and response ecosystem in which the SIEM serves as the central hub, correlating alerts from across the organization and enabling coordinated security operations.

The following figure represents a high-level architecture of SIEM:

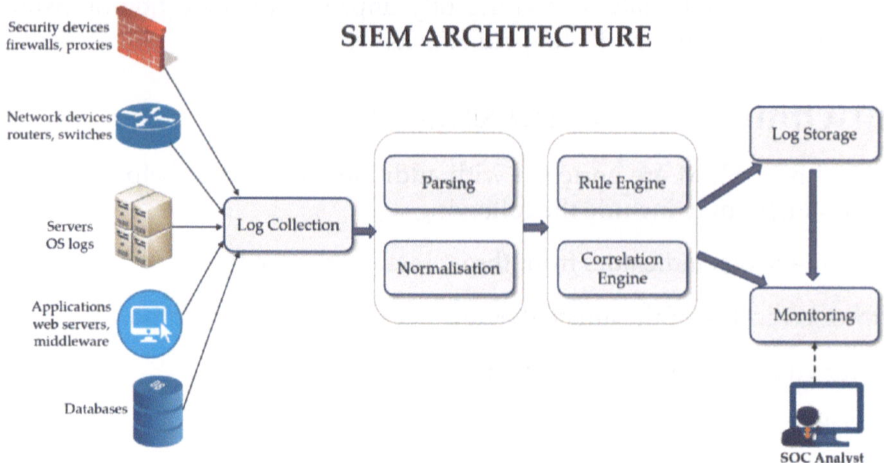

Figure 10.2: SIEM architecture

SOAR

SOAR platforms complement SIEM by operationalizing and accelerating the response workflow. While SIEM centralizes detection and correlation, SOAR translates those alerts into structured, repeatable actions. It does this by integrating with a wide ecosystem of tools such as EDR/XDR, firewalls, ticketing systems, TIPs, cloud security controls, and identity systems. Automated SOAR actions are orchestrated through playbooks that enrich alerts, validate indicators, contain threats, and trigger notifications without requiring continuous human intervention.

SOAR tools rely on API-driven integrations and modular actions that can be chained into conditional workflows. For instance, upon receiving a SIEM alert, a playbook may query threat intelligence sources, ascertain asset criticality, pull relevant endpoint telemetry, or run sandbox analysis. Based on predefined logic, SOAR can isolate an impacted host, block an IP on perimeter firewalls, disable compromised accounts, or create security incidents along with contextual evidence. This reduces **mean time to respond** (**MTTR**), improves consistency, and eliminates manual, error-prone steps in incident handling.

The SOAR platforms also help standardize the incident handling process by embedding organization-specific runbooks into automated workflows. They enable analysts to focus on advanced analytical investigation while routine tasks such as enrichment, containment, status updates, and reporting are handled by the platform. In effect, SOAR forms the execution layer of the detection–response process and ensures that security alerts are handled in a coordinated, consistent, and automated manner. In modern implementations, the SOAR functionality is often integrated into the SIEM platform itself.

Honeynets and deception technologies

A honeynet is a network of decoys designed to attract, detect, and study malicious activity. Modern deception platforms extend this concept far beyond the traditional honeypots by deploying distributed decoys, lures, and traps across endpoints, servers, identities, and cloud environments. Their primary objective is to detect lateral movement attempts by attackers who have bypassed the preventive controls and are now operating inside the environment, with stealth techniques that produce limited telemetry.

Deception technology is based on the idea of high-confidence detection with minimal false alarms. Since legitimate users have no operational reason to interact with decoys, any connection attempt, credential use, file access, or network scan targeting a deception asset is treated as a strong indicator of compromise. Deception systems replicate realistic identities and services and include artefacts, such as fake AD objects, enticing file shares, seemingly vulnerable services, exposed API keys, or misconfigured containers. The purpose is to draw threat actors away from production assets and reveal their TTPs. Telemetry collected from these interactions provides insights into attacker behaviour, including privilege escalation attempts, lateral movement techniques, command sequences, and exploited vulnerabilities.

Honeynets integrate into SOC processes by enriching detection, response, and threat intelligence workflows. Their alerts can be routed into SIEM and SOAR platforms to trigger automated containment actions, initiate investigation playbooks, or correlate adversary behaviour with known threat actor profiles. Because deception systems operate invisibly without affecting production performance, they add a proactive detection layer that complements EDR, NDR, and identity security solutions. Mature SOCs use deception not only for early breach discovery but also for validating defensive controls, conducting blue-team readiness assessments, and analyzing emerging attacker techniques in a controlled environment.

Vulnerability scanners

Vulnerability scanners such as *Tenable* and *OpenVAS* are specialized tools designed to identify security weaknesses in systems, applications, network devices, and cloud environments by comparing observed configurations and software versions against known vulnerability databases. These tools rely on continuously updated knowledge bases, such as CVE repositories, vendor advisories, exploit data, and misconfiguration benchmarks to detect outdated software, unsafe settings, exposed services, missing patches, and insecure policies. Scanners play a crucial role in providing objective visibility into an organization's technical risk surface. Their accuracy, coverage, and frequency of scans significantly influence downstream SOC operations.

Scanning techniques

Vulnerability scanners operate using a combination of active, passive, and agent-based techniques. These are as follows:

- **Active network probing**: This technique involves probing systems over the network, sending crafted requests, analyzing service banners, performing version identification, and validating misconfigurations through authenticated or unauthenticated checks.
- **Authenticated scanning**: Authenticated scans, which use temporary or delegated credentials, provide deeper insight into installed packages, registry values, kernel modules, startup services, permission structures, and local configuration settings.
- **Unauthenticated scanning**: Unauthenticated scans rely on banner grabbing and externally accessible information to assess perimeter exposure and identify internet-facing weaknesses. They offer comparatively limited visibility.
- **Agent-based telemetry collection**: Modern scanners provide agent-based scanning, where lightweight agents installed on endpoints collect detailed telemetry continuously and send it to a central platform. This approach helps minimize scan-related network load while enabling near-real-time detection of new vulnerabilities.

Email security solutions

Email is one of the most heavily targeted communication channels. It remains a leading vector for phishing, malware delivery, credential harvesting, and **business email compromise** (**BEC**). Email security solutions are a critical security layer for SOC as they help in preventing, detecting, and responding to threats hidden in messages, attachments, and URLs. Email security platforms combine signature-based detection, behavioural analytics, threat intelligence, machine learning, and policy enforcement to secure both inbound and outbound communication.

Email security solutions are typically deployed either as **secure email gateways** (**SEGs**) positioned between the internet and the organization's mail server or as cloud-native API-integrated platforms that sit inside **software as a service** (**SaaS**) email systems like *Microsoft 365* or *Google Workspace*. Regardless of the deployment mode, their core objective is to analyze every message and enforce policies that prevent malicious content, data leakage, or account compromise.

An email security solution generally includes the following functionalities:

- **Inbound filtering**: All inbound emails are analyzed to detect spam, phishing campaigns, malware-laden attachments, spoofed domains, and anomalous sender behaviour.
- **Outbound filtering**: This helps in preventing data leakage, unauthorized transmissions, and compromised accounts from distributing harmful content.

- **Internal message scanning**: This is carried out to identify lateral phishing attacks originating from compromised internal accounts.
- **Encryption and policy enforcement**: This involves applying DLP controls, **Transport Layer Security** (**TLS**) policies, digital signatures, and automated encryption to protect sensitive content.

Threat detection techniques

Email security platforms use a broad set of detection methods that operate at different stages of message processing. Common threat detection techniques include:

- **Signature and reputation checks**: Email attachments, hashes, URLs, and IPs are matched against known malicious indicators from the threat intelligence feeds.
- **Sandboxing**: Suspicious attachments or embedded URLs are executed in isolated environments to observe malicious behaviour such as macro abuse, command-and-control beacons, or privilege escalations.
- **Impersonation and spoofing detection**: Sender behaviour, header anomalies, domain alignment, and unusual communication patterns are analyzed to prevent impersonation attacks and BEC.
- **URL rewriting and detonation**: URLs embedded in received emails are rewritten to route them through security filters and detonated in sandboxes on click to detect credential harvesters or exploit kits.
- **ML classifiers**: This involves identifying subtle phishing indicators such as crafted language, urgent phrasing, anomalous tone, or deviations from typical communication patterns.
- **Attachment analysis**: Techniques include static analysis, file structure inspection, heuristics, and sandbox-based dynamic analysis to detect malware, exploits, and obfuscated payloads.

Data protection

Email security solutions also help in protecting sensitive data by enforcing organizational policies. These controls are essential for preventing accidental or intentional leakage of sensitive information. Email security solutions typically offer the following capabilities:

- **DLP**: All outbound messages are scanned for sensitive data or confidential business information, and the messages are blocked or encrypted based on the policy.
- **Content and attachment controls**: This entails restricting potentially dangerous file types (e.g., `.exe`, `.scr`, `.lnk`), enforcing size limits, and applying digital rights management where required.

- **Email encryption**: Applying automatic or user-triggered encryption (S/MIME, PGP, or gateway-based encryption) depending on message sensitivity and compliance rules.

Email security tools integrate closely with SOC workflows, helping analysts correlate email-related threats with broader attack campaigns. They play a central role in SOC operations by combining threat detection, content filtering, data protection, deception-aware analysis, and advanced behavioural analytics. As attackers increasingly use social engineering and multi-stage campaigns, these tools not only block malicious content but also provide rich telemetry for correlation and IR.

As organizations adopt SaaS-based email services, security approaches have evolved. API-integrated cloud-native solutions provide deeper visibility and more flexible controls than traditional gateways. Whether implemented as gateways or cloud-native API-integrations, email security solutions remain foundational to protecting an organization's communication channels.

SOC efficacy and maturity

A SOC delivers value only when it can reliably detect, analyze, and respond to threats in line with the organization's risk expectations. SOC efficacy is measured by how well it detects and responds to threats. This implies that the efficacy is not measured by the number of alerts handled or dashboards monitored, but by how well the SOC reduces real-world risks and supports business resilience. SOC maturity reflects how well-established, repeatable, and adaptive the SOC processes and capabilities are. It focuses on capacity and consistency for sustainable and repeatable performance. Assessing SOC maturity helps determine whether its operational capabilities are reactive, structured, proactive, or fully intelligence-driven. It provides a roadmap for continuous improvement.

Measuring SOC efficacy

SOC performance is assessed using a combination of quantitative and qualitative indicators. These metrics help evaluate whether SOC operations are delivering the expected levels of accuracy, speed, and consistency. While no single metric can fully capture overall SOC efficacy, taken together, they offer a balanced view of detection capability, response performance, and business alignment. Broadly, these indicators can be grouped into three categories based on what they measure: detection effectiveness, response efficiency, and business impact.

Detection effectiveness

These metrics measure how well the SOC identifies suspicious activity and avoids noise. Some of these metrics are as follows:

- **Mean time to detect (MTTD)**: It measures the average duration it takes the SOC to identify a security event from the moment it occurs. A lower MTTD indicates faster recognition and stronger monitoring coverage. This is a crucial metric as it limits the attacker's dwell time.

- **True positive rate**: It represents the proportion of genuine security incidents correctly detected by the SOC. A higher true positive rate shows that alerting logic is accurate and effective.
- **False positive rate**: Indicates how many alerts are incorrectly classified as threats. A lower false positive rate reduces analyst workload and prevents alert fatigue.
- **Coverage metrics**: Assesses how many relevant attack vectors, assets, and use cases the SOC is monitoring. Higher coverage suggests fewer blind spots across the environment.
- **Threat visibility**: It reflects the SOC's ability to observe relevant telemetry across endpoints, networks, cloud workloads, and identities. Strong visibility improves both detection depth and contextual understanding.

Response efficiency

These indicators assess how quickly and effectively the SOC moves from detection to containment and recovery. These are as follows:

- **MTTR**: Measures the time taken to confirm, contain, and remediate an incident after detection. A lower MTTR shows efficient workflows and strong coordination among responders.
- **Mean time to investigate (MTTI)**: Captures how long analysts spend analyzing and validating an alert. Efficient investigation reduces backlog and accelerates incident handling.
- **Containment time**: Indicates how quickly the SOC isolates affected systems or stops attack progression. Faster containment reduces the chance of lateral movement or escalation.
- **Escalation rate**: Shows how often Tier-1 analysts escalate alerts to higher tiers. A balanced rate suggests appropriate triaging rather than over-escalation or under-escalation.
- **Automation utilization**: Measures how much of the SOC's repetitive or low-level activity is handled by automation tools or SOAR. Higher utilization indicates streamlined operations and reduced manual workload.

Business impact metrics

These metrics connect SOC activity with organizational outcomes. Some of these are as follows:

- **Dwell time**: Represents how long an attacker remains undetected within the environment. Lower dwell time directly reduces business risk and limits potential data loss or damage.

- **Cost per incident**: Estimates the financial impact of responding to an incident, including personnel cost, tool usage, and recovery efforts. It helps assess operational efficiency and justify SOC budgeting.
- **Incident recurrence rate**: Shows how often similar incidents reappear, indicating whether long-term fixes and root cause actions are effective. A declining recurrence rate signals durable security improvements.
- **Compliance**: Measures whether the SOC meets predefined response and resolution timelines with business units. High compliance demonstrates reliability and consistent service delivery.
- **Business downtime attributable to security incidents**: Tracks the amount of operational disruption caused by security events. Less downtime signals more effective protection and quicker recovery.

SOC maturity model

SOC maturity reflects how consistently and effectively a SOC performs its detection and response responsibilities. It captures how well the people, processes, and technologies in the SOC operate as a unified system, and how reliably they can deliver repeatable outcomes under varying levels of threat conditions. Several maturity frameworks are commonly used for assessment, including the **Capability Maturity Model Integration** (**CMMI**) inspired five-level model, the **NIST Cybersecurity Framework** (**NIST CSF**) implementation tiers, and organization-specific variants. While these models differ in format, they broadly evaluate visibility, process standardization, automation, threat intelligence integration, analyst competency, and SOC's alignment with the wider organizational risk objectives.

The following table provides a conceptual SOC maturity model, representing how operational capabilities progress from foundational to advanced levels:

SOC maturity level	Characteristics
Level 1 **Initial/Reactive**	Limited visibility, heavy manual effort, and inconsistent processes. Detection and response largely depend on analyst judgment.
Level 2 **Repeatable**	Basic procedures and use cases established, improved logging, and investigations follow a more consistent pattern.
Level 3 **Defined**	Formal processes, runbooks, and escalation paths. Integrated visibility across key systems. Structured incident handling.
Level 4 **Managed and measured**	KPIs and reporting are adopted. Automation supports triage and containment. Threat intelligence is integrated for detections.

SOC maturity level	Characteristics
Level 5 **Optimized/** **Intelligence-driven**	Highly automated operations with advanced analytics, proactive hunting, strong business alignment, and continuous improvement embedded in operations.

***Table 10.1**: SOC maturity model*

As the SOC advances through maturity levels, its operating model shifts from reactive alert handling towards more analytical and intelligence-driven operations. Earlier stages typically focus on establishing log coverage, foundational use cases, and consistent documentation. Mid-level maturity brings stronger governance, well-developed workflows, and measurable performance indicators. At higher levels, automation, behaviour-based detections, and contextual threat intelligence shape a more resilient and predictable detection–response capability. Critical enablers across all stages include analyst skill development, rationalized tooling, integration across IT and cloud teams, and clear process ownership.

Maturity assessments are generally conducted at regular intervals to identify gaps in visibility, process consistency, automation, and staffing. Common obstacles to SOC maturity include fragmented tools, limited use case tuning, insufficient analyst training, and a lack of integrated telemetry. More mature SOCs address these challenges through structured improvement roadmaps, periodic threat-modelling exercises, red and purple-team engagements, and continuous refinement of runbooks and detections. SOC maturity should be viewed as an ongoing progression rather than a destination, ensuring that the SOC remains effective and resilient in the face of an evolving threat landscape.

Future SOC, unified and autonomous

As SOCs progress to higher maturity levels, the natural evolution is towards greater unification and intelligence in operations. Modern security environments generate telemetry from endpoints, networks, cloud platforms, identities, applications, and third-party services. This diversity often leads to fragmented tooling and siloed analysis. Mature SOCs aim to consolidate the capabilities of SIEM, SOAR, EDR/XDR, NDR, ITDR, TIP, vulnerability management, and cloud-native security controls into an integrated platform that provides complete visibility and unified correlation across all layers of the environment. This consolidation reduces tool sprawl, enhances analyst efficiency, and enables more accurate, context-rich detections.

This unification enables the SOC to leverage AI and ML to operate at scale. These technologies support faster triage, behavioural anomaly detection, automated investigation, and real-time decision-making. As models learn from historical incidents and environment-specific patterns, they improve predictive capabilities and reduce manual workload. This shift marks the gradual transition towards an autonomous SOC. The autonomous SOC is an operating model where routine detection, enrichment, containment, and reporting are largely automated, while analysts focus on threat hunting, complex investigations, governance, and strategic security improvements. This enables organizations to sustain high-levels of security effectiveness despite growing threats, expanding attack surfaces, and increasing operational complexity.

Conclusion

A SOC forms the nerve center of security operations. It lies at the heart of an organization's cyber defense capability, which brings together people, processes, and technology to deliver continuous protection in an increasingly hostile digital environment. In this chapter, we explored the operational foundations of a SOC, including its roles, core functions, investigative workflows, and the specialized tools that enable monitoring, detection, and response at scale. From IR and digital forensics to threat hunting, threat intelligence integration, and vulnerability management, each component contributes to a cohesive defense ecosystem that is both proactive and resilient.

Effective SOC performance depends not only on timely detection and swift response, but also on structured governance, repeatable workflows, and meaningful metrics that reflect business relevance. SOC maturity, therefore, is not defined by tool deployment alone but by the ability to integrate, automate, and refine operations in ways that steadily improve outcomes. A mature SOC is characterized by adaptability, intelligence, and operational discipline. It evolves continuously, learns from every incident, aligns closely with organizational priorities, and stays prepared for any emerging threats. This ability to anticipate, withstand, and recover defines the SOC's true value within the broader cybersecurity strategy. As the threat landscape becomes increasingly hostile, SOCs must also embrace unified platforms, data-driven decision-making, and AI-enabled automation to reduce noise, enhance visibility, and progress towards autonomous security operations.

In the next chapter, we shift our focus to securing cloud-native architectures, where distributed services, APIs, and dynamic workloads redefine how security is designed and implemented. We will build on the foundational concepts covered so far and extend them into the evolving world of cloud security.

Exercises

1. Explain the core objectives of a SOC. How does the role of a SOC differ from traditional IT security functions?
2. Differentiate between an in-house SOC, an outsourced SOC, and a hybrid SOC. Discuss the advantages and limitations of each model in the context of scalability, cost, and control.
3. Describe the key responsibilities of Tier-1, Tier-2, and Tier-3 SOC analysts. How does skill progression typically occur across these tiers?
4. Explain the stages of the IR lifecycle. For each stage, describe its purpose and how SOC teams collaborate with other stakeholders.
5. You are a SOC Manager. Your SIEM begins to generate a large number of failed login alerts from multiple geographies for a privileged account. Describe how a SOC should handle this from detection through triage, containment, and escalation. Clearly outline the decisions and actions at each step.
6. Discuss the role of threat intelligence in SOC operations. How does strategic, operational, and tactical intelligence enhance detection and response?
7. Explain the purpose of threat hunting in a SOC. Compare hypothesis-driven hunting with intelligence-driven hunting, and give an example of each.
8. A critical business application in your environment is found to be running an outdated library with a known remote-code execution vulnerability. Describe how the vulnerability management process, from assessment to patch management, should handle this situation. Include prioritization, communication, and verification steps.
9. List the key functions of SIEM and SOAR platforms. How do they complement each other in improving SOC efficiency and reducing analyst workload?
10. Define SOC maturity. Using any one maturity model, describe the characteristics that distinguish a reactive SOC from a proactive, intelligence-driven SOC.

Join our Discord space

Join our Discord workspace for latest updates, offers, tech happenings around the world, new releases, and sessions with the authors:

https://discord.bpbonline.com

Chapter 11
Cloud Security

Introduction

The rapid evolution of cloud computing has fundamentally transformed the way organizations design, deploy, and secure their digital environments. Instead of operating solely from on-premises data centers, organizations now rely on flexible architectures where computing resources and applications are distributed across public, private, hybrid, and multi-cloud environments. While this dynamic landscape offers unmatched scalability and agility, it also introduces a new and complex set of security challenges.

In a cloud-native setting, infrastructure is abstracted, workloads are ephemeral, and applications are primarily composed of microservices that communicate over **application programming interfaces** (**APIs**). As workloads, data, and identities are dispersed across multiple service layers and providers, the traditional security controls that rely on perimeter defense or static network segments no longer offer sufficient protection. Identity, context, and continuous validation have become the foundation of trust. Security must now be embedded into the architecture itself, supported by automation, policy-driven controls, and real-time monitoring to maintain assurance at scale.

Cloud security is not merely an adaptation of on-premises controls. It is a re-engineering of trust that is grounded in Zero Trust principles and is realized through automated, policy-centric frameworks that align with the elastic and distributed nature of the cloud. The shift towards cloud-native development built on containers, microservices, Kubernetes orchestration, and serverless computing demands continuous, integrated, and context-aware security. The convergence of these technologies with automation has led to the emergence of **cloud-native application protection platforms** (**CNAPP**), which provide unified visibility and protection across the modern application lifecycle.

In this chapter, we build on this perspective to examine how foundational security principles are interpreted and applied within cloud-native architectures. We explore how modern paradigms such as Zero Trust, **secure access service edge** (**SASE**), **infrastructure as code** (**IaC**), and automated posture management redefine security operations in the cloud. These concepts provide the structural and operational framework necessary to secure highly distributed, dynamic, and API-driven cloud environments.

Structure

In this chapter, we will discuss the following topics:

- Cloud-native architecture
- Shared security responsibility
- Organization management in cloud
- Identity and access management
- Cloud infrastructure security
- Cloud network security

Objectives

The objective of this chapter is to provide a comprehensive understanding of how security is architected, implemented, and managed in cloud environments. This chapter enables you to gain insight into emerging cloud security challenges and understand the shared responsibility model that forms the basis of cloud security. You will also understand how infrastructure, networks, identities, data, and workloads must be protected in a cloud environment, and how security posture must be continuously assessed and improved in alignment with organizational risk.

You will be able to identify the major components of cloud security, including **identity and access management** (**IAM**), infrastructure and network security, workload protection, data security, API security, and secure access architectures, and understand how they collectively provide layered, defense-in-depth protection. You will also appreciate the importance of cloud-native security techniques such as IaC, automated guardrails, continuous configuration monitoring, encryption, secure connectivity, and Zero Trust principles. The chapter will help you understand key cloud-focused security platforms and how they support visibility, compliance, workload protection, and identity governance. By the end of the chapter, you will have a clear understanding of how modern cloud security frameworks enable organizations to operate confidently in the cloud while managing risk effectively and maintaining strong security assurance across diverse cloud services.

Cloud-native architecture

Cloud-native architecture represents a fundamental shift in the way computing resources, applications, and services are designed and operated. Traditional enterprise networks are built around well-defined perimeters protected by firewalls, **intrusion prevention systems** (**IPSs**), and access gateways. These boundaries, once effective in containing risk, have steadily eroded with the rise of mobile workforces, remote access, and distributed application architectures. In a cloud-native environment, workloads, data, and users operate across multiple regions, service providers, and device types, creating a dynamic and borderless ecosystem. To support this scale and distribution, cloud-native systems emphasize elasticity, automation, and modularity, allowing organizations to build and evolve applications with far greater agility. This architectural model delivers unprecedented scalability, flexibility, resiliency, and cost efficiency.

Cloud computing forms the foundation of this architectural model. It refers to the delivery of computing resources, such as servers, storage, databases, networking, platforms, and applications over the internet on an on-demand basis. These resources are centrally pooled by cloud service providers and offered to consumers as scalable services that can be provisioned or released with minimal human intervention.

The **National Institute of Standards and Technology** (**NIST**) describes cloud computing as a model for enabling ubiquitous, convenient, on-demand network access to a shared pool of configurable computing resources that can be rapidly provisioned and released with minimal management effort or service provider interaction. This definition highlights the core advantage of the cloud, i.e., the ability to access shared resources quickly, efficiently, and at scale.

Abstraction and automation

Abstraction and automation are central to cloud-native architecture. They enable the core cloud features of elasticity, resilience, and rapid deployment, features that distinguish cloud environments from traditional, hardware-bound data centers.

Cloud computing achieves abstraction by decoupling applications from the physical infrastructure on which they run. Servers, storage systems, and networks are concealed behind virtualization layers, API-driven interfaces, and orchestration frameworks. Instead of dealing with physical devices, consumers work with logical constructs, such as **virtual machines** (**VMs**), containers, serverless functions, storage buckets, and managed services. This shift allows organizations to focus on applications and service delivery rather than provisioning or maintaining hardware.

Automation complements abstraction by enabling systems to respond dynamically to changing demand. Resource provisioning, scaling, failover, configuration, and monitoring are increasingly governed by automated policies rather than manual processes. This automation is essential for modern cloud environments, where workloads may fluctuate rapidly, and infrastructure components may be provisioned or deprovisioned within seconds. Together, abstraction and automation transform cloud infrastructure from a static set of resources into a responsive, programmable environment, enabling the speed and agility demanded by contemporary information systems.

Multi-tenancy

Multi-tenancy is another foundational element of cloud computing. It refers to the ability of a cloud platform to host multiple customers (tenants) on a shared physical infrastructure while keeping their data and resources logically isolated.

Multi-tenancy offers the following advantages:

- **Efficient resource utilization**: Physical resources are shared across multiple tenants, reducing costs.
- **Scalability**: The provider can allocate resources based on demand without dedicating hardware to any single customer.
- **Consistency**: Tenants operate on a standardized, centrally managed platform.

However, multi-tenancy also raises security concerns. Isolation controls, hypervisor security, storage separation, network segmentation, and strict identity management, therefore, become critical components of a secure cloud environment.

Characteristics of cloud environments

Cloud environments possess a distinct set of characteristics compared to traditional on-premises setups. NIST describes the following essential characteristics that not only enable the flexibility associated with cloud computing but also influence the way security controls are designed and implemented:

- **On-demand self-service**: Consumers can provision resources as-needed without requiring intervention from the provider.
- **Broad network access**: Services are accessible over the network from diverse devices, users, and locations.
- **Resource pooling**: Storage, processing, and networks are shared across multiple tenants using a multi-tenant model.
- **Rapid elasticity**: Resources can be scaled up or down automatically in response to workload changes.
- **Measured service**: Usage is monitored and billed based on consumption, creating transparency and cost accountability.

Cloud service models

Cloud services are commonly delivered through three primary service models. Each model distributes operational and security responsibilities differently between the cloud provider and the customer, ranging from customer-managed environments to fully provider-managed applications. The characteristics of these models are as follows:

- **Infrastructure as a service (IaaS)**: Provides virtualized compute, storage, and networking infrastructure. Customers manage the VMs, **operating systems (OSs)**, applications, and data, while the **cloud service provider (CSP)** manages the physical hardware. IaaS suits organizations that require granular control over workloads without owning physical infrastructure.

- **Platform as a service (PaaS)**: Offers a managed platform that includes the underlying infrastructure, runtime environment, middleware, and development frameworks. Customers focus on developing, deploying, and managing applications. PaaS accelerates development cycles by abstracting OS and middleware management.
- **Software as a service (SaaS)**: Delivers fully managed applications hosted and operated by the CSP. Customers access the software through web interfaces or APIs, with no responsibility for managing the underlying platform. SaaS is ideal for business applications where minimizing operational overhead is a priority.

Shared security responsibility

Security in the cloud operates on a shared responsibility model, where both the CSP and the customer play defined roles in securing the environment. Unlike traditional on-premises systems, where organizations managed every layer of the stack, cloud environments distribute responsibilities based on the service model in use. This division allows customers to benefit from provider-managed infrastructure while retaining control over the elements most closely tied to their data, applications, and business decisions. In essence, the provider secures the cloud, and the customer secures what they place in the cloud. However, these roles shift depending on whether the service being consumed is IaaS, PaaS, or SaaS. Understanding these distinctions is critical for preventing misconfigurations, ensuring compliance, and implementing effective security controls.

IaaS security

In an IaaS environment, the cloud provider is responsible for securing the physical data centers, server hardware, networking equipment, and the virtualization layer that supports the VMs. This includes maintaining the hypervisors, storage controllers, and the core infrastructure that ensures availability and resilience. The customer, however, assumes a broad set of responsibilities. They must install, patch, and harden OSs, configure VMs, and secure their own **virtual networks** (**VNets**), including firewalls, routing rules, and access control lists. They are also responsible for managing identities and access permissions, securing applications and middleware, protecting their data through encryption and classification, and enabling monitoring, logging, and incident response for the workloads they deploy. IaaS offers significant flexibility and control, but it requires strong governance and continuous management to maintain a secure posture.

PaaS security

PaaS further abstracts the underlying infrastructure, allowing organizations to develop and deploy applications without managing OSs or runtime environments. In this model, the cloud provider not only secures the physical infrastructure and virtualization layer but also manages the OSs, middleware, runtimes, and the orchestration mechanisms that support the platform. Customers continue to be responsible for securing the applications they build, enforcing access control and identity management, and protecting the data they store or process on the platform. They must configure application-level settings, secure exposed APIs, enforce encryption policies, and monitor application logs and user activity. PaaS reduces the operational burden seen in IaaS but still requires disciplined application-level and identity-centric security practices.

SaaS security

SaaS provides the highest level of abstraction, with the provider delivering fully managed applications over the internet. The CSP handles everything from physical infrastructure and platforms to application maintenance, security updates, feature upgrades, and service availability. The customer's security responsibilities are narrower but still crucial. They must manage user accounts and authentication policies, enforce appropriate access privileges, and configure the application's built-in security settings. Customers are also responsible for governing their data within the application, i.e., determining what is stored, how long it is retained, and how it is backed up or exported. Even in SaaS environments, weak access controls or misconfigured settings can lead to significant security incidents, making proper identity management and configuration hygiene essential.

The following figure depicts the shared security model in a cloud environment, highlighting the delineation of responsibilities between the providers and customers:

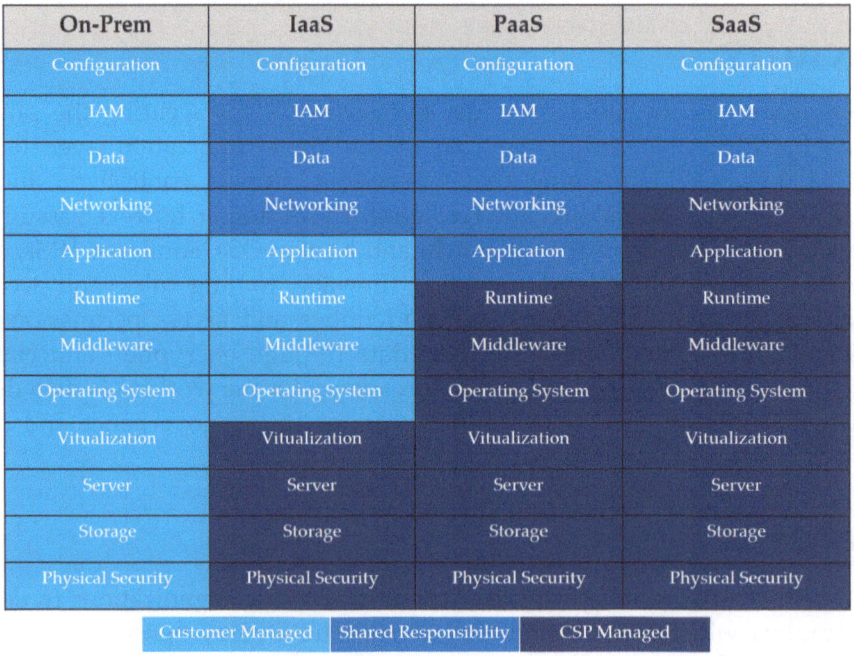

On-Prem	IaaS	PaaS	SaaS
Configuration	Configuration	Configuration	Configuration
IAM	IAM	IAM	IAM
Data	Data	Data	Data
Networking	Networking	Networking	Networking
Application	Application	Application	Application
Runtime	Runtime	Runtime	Runtime
Middleware	Middleware	Middleware	Middleware
Operating System	Operating System	Operating System	Operating System
Vitualization	Vitualization	Vitualization	Vitualization
Server	Server	Server	Server
Storage	Storage	Storage	Storage
Physical Security	Physical Security	Physical Security	Physical Security

Customer Managed | Shared Responsibility | CSP Managed

Figure 11.1: *Shared security responsibility in the cloud*

Organization management in cloud

Organization management refers to the overall management of a cloud environment. It is a foundational aspect of cloud security and governance. As enterprises adopt cloud environments at scale, they need to establish a structured hierarchy for managing accounts, resources, identities, and shared services across multiple teams and projects. Cloud platforms provide hierarchical management constructs that mirror traditional organizational boundaries, but with greater flexibility, centralized control, and automation. While these constructs help organizations apply consistent security baselines, enforce policies, standardize deployments, and consolidate billing, they still allow individual teams the autonomy needed for cloud-native development.

Organization hierarchy models

Cloud service providers implement different organizational hierarchy models, but the underlying objective is the same—to offer flexible, layered management that supports centralized governance while enabling decentralized deployment and operations. Although **Amazon Web Services** (**AWS**), Microsoft Azure, and **Google Cloud Platform** (**GCP**) use different terminology, their structures follow similar principles. Each platform defines a top-level organization node, introduces intermediate logical groupings for structure and policy inheritance, and uses individual accounts or projects as the leaf-level boundaries for deploying workloads.

In AWS, the root of the hierarchy is AWS Organizations. Under this, administrators can create **organizational units** (**OUs**), which group accounts based on business units, environments, compliance requirements, or functional separation. Each AWS Account operates as an isolated boundary for resources, billing, and access control. Governance is enforced through **service control policies** (**SCPs**), which can be applied at the organization, OU, or account level.

Microsoft Azure follows a similar layered design using tenants, management groups, and subscriptions. Tenants represent the overarching identity boundary, while management groups provide a hierarchical structure for organizing subscriptions according to organizational or regulatory needs. Azure subscriptions serve as the primary boundaries for resource deployment, access control, and cost management. Azure allows policies and **role-based access control** (**RBAC**) assignments to be applied at management group, subscription, and resource group levels to provide granular governance across the hierarchy.

In GCP, the highest level is the organization node, under which administrators can create folders to reflect business structures, departments, or compliance groupings. Projects are created under folders or directly beneath the organization node. GCP projects form the core deployment boundary and define the scope for IAM policies, quotas, billing, and resource ownership. They represent the fundamental unit for managing cloud workloads within GCP.

Organization-level security

At the organizational level, security begins with establishing a unified IAM strategy. Most enterprises integrate their corporate **identity provider** (**IdP**), such as **Active Directory** (**AD**), Azure AD (Entra ID), Okta, or Ping Identity, with the cloud platform. This integration allows for centralized authentication and role mapping, ensuring that cloud access follows the same identity lifecycle, **multi-factor authentication** (**MFA**) policies, and least privilege principles used across the enterprise.

Role mapping typically defines which groups or identity attributes correspond to cloud roles. For example, an engineering group may be assigned contributor-level permissions, while finance teams may receive read-only access for billing. Centralizing identity prevents the proliferation of cloud-native accounts and enforces uniform security controls across all business units.

Cloud providers additionally offer organization-wide policy frameworks that enable administrators to define baseline governance requirements. AWS uses SCPs to limit actions across accounts, Azure enforces governance through Azure policy and management locks, and GCP uses organization policies to control resource creation, regions, and service access. These policies form a preventive control layer that reduces misconfigurations before they occur.

Organization-level shared services

Shared services such as security telemetry and centralized logging operate at the organizational level and support workloads across the organizational units. These services are essential for threat detection, compliance, and unified visibility. By hosting them centrally, enterprises achieve consistency, reduce operational overhead, and ensure that all teams adhere to the same security standards.

These services may include:

- Central identity and authentication services.
- Logging and monitoring platforms, such as AWS CloudTrail, Azure Monitor, or GCP Cloud Logging, aggregated at the organization-level.
- Security operations tools, such as SIEM, **cloud security posture management** (**CSPM**), or CNAPP solutions.
- Network security and connectivity services, including central firewalls, **virtual private network** (**VPN**) gateways, **domain name system** (**DNS**), or hub-and-spoke network architectures.
- Key management and secrets handling, delivered through **key management system** (**KMS**), **hardware security module** (**HSM**), or enterprise vaulting tools.
- Backup and disaster recovery frameworks, centrally governed to ensure consistency.

Identity and access management

In cloud environments, the functions and services traditionally confined to data centers are delivered through unified, internet-accessible control planes. In this borderless model, identity becomes the new perimeter, making the cloud IAM layer the most critical control plane in the entire security architecture.

IAM functions in the cloud undergo a fundamental shift as compared to traditional on-premises settings. In on-premises architectures, IAM systems are typically confined to a single organization's internal network, rely on directory services, and operate within clearly defined perimeters. Cloud IAM, by contrast, is designed for distributed, multi-tenant, and internet-facing environments where identities interact with diverse services, APIs, and resources across geographic and organizational boundaries. As a result, the IAM layer becomes more expansive, more integrated, and more exposed, requiring stronger governance and continuous oversight.

The key features of cloud IAM are as follows:

- Cloud IAM spans multiple organizations and must support collaboration across suppliers, partners, contractors, and multiple internal business units, within the same cloud tenant or across federated environments.
- Cloud providers use their own proprietary IAM systems, which differ significantly from traditional directory services. For instance, AWS IAM, Azure Entra ID, and GCP IAM all implement their own roles, policies, and permission models.
- Cloud IAM provides central management for users, roles, service accounts, keys, and policies through unified control planes accessible over the internet, which increases both convenience and exposure.
- Managing identities in the cloud extends far beyond traditional directory services. Cloud IAM centralizes identity lifecycle operations, including provisioning, de-provisioning, role assignment, credential management, and federation across a globally accessible platform, with identities interacting with cloud resources through an API-driven, policy-based model.

Authentication

Implementing a robust authentication mechanism is critical for cloud security. Authentication in the cloud establishes a trust relationship between an identity and the cloud environment. It verifies who is attempting to access a resource and under what circumstances. Cloud authentication extends beyond traditional username-password checks and incorporates multiple contextual and adaptive mechanisms. The following elements capture the core aspects of authentication in public cloud environments:

- **Federated identity SSO**: Cloud environments commonly rely on federation with external IdPs such as *Azure AD/Microsoft Entra ID, Google Workspace*, or *Okta*. Instead of managing local credentials, cloud platforms validate tokens issued by the IdP, enabling seamless SSO, centralized lifecycle management, and unified credential governance across on-premises and cloud systems.

- **MFA**: It is mandatory for administrative identities and strongly recommended for all users. CSPs support a range of MFA methods, including authenticator apps, hardware tokens, SMS OTP, and certificate-based authentication. MFA adds a second layer of assurance, reducing the impact of credential theft or phishing attacks.
- **Workload and service authentication**: Cloud-native workloads such as serverless functions, containers, or VMs often authenticate using short-lived tokens, service accounts, managed identities, or workload identity federation. These eliminate embedded secrets and allow workloads to automatically rotate credentials, bind to specific resources, and operate with least privilege access.
- **Context-aware and adaptive authentication**: Authentication decisions incorporate contextual signals such as device posture, geolocation, IP reputation, session risk score, time-of-day patterns, and anomalous login indicators. Adaptive authentication can step up security, such as requiring MFA or blocking the request when risk exceeds predefined thresholds. This enables a more dynamic and resilient access boundary suited to the cloud's distributed nature.
- **Certificate and key-based authentication**: Many cloud services use certificates, API keys, or signed requests to authenticate service accounts. While often necessary for automation, these credentials must be rotated, monitored, and stored in secure vaults such as *AWS Secrets Manager*, *Azure Key Vault*, or *GCP Secret Manager*. Cloud IAM increasingly prefers short-lived, automatically issued tokens over long-lived static secrets.

Authorization

Authorization in cloud IAM is enforced through fine-grained, policy-driven mechanisms that specify what an identity can access, how it can interact with cloud resources, and under what contextual conditions. The following elements capture the core constructs of authorization in public cloud environments:

- **Policy-based access control (PBAC)**: Cloud platforms rely on declarative policy documents to define permissions. Examples include AWS IAM policies, Azure role definitions and GCP IAM bindings. These policies explicitly enumerate allowed or denied actions and the resources to which they apply, because policies are machine-interpretable, they can be version controlled, validated through automation pipelines and tested before deployment.
- **Resource-level granularity**: Authorization in the cloud goes far beyond traditional role assignments. Permissions can be scoped to extremely granular resource elements,

such as a specific **Simple Storage Service** (**S3**) object, a single API method, a VM's metadata server, a particular key version in KMS, or an individual function within a serverless application. This granularity allows precise access boundaries, reducing lateral movement risks and limiting blast radius during compromise.

- **Attribute-based access controls (ABACs)**: CSPs now support dynamic access decisions based on resource and identity attributes, such as tags, labels, project metadata, IP ranges, environment classification, or workload identity claims. ABAC enables policies that automatically adjust as attributes change, minimizing manual role assignments and simplifying governance in large, dynamic environments.

Managing permissions in cloud

Managing permissions in cloud environments requires a fundamentally different approach from traditional on-premises systems. The scale, dynamism, and distributed nature of cloud resources mean that permissions cannot be assigned, reviewed, or corrected manually. Cloud workloads, identities, and services are constantly created, modified, and deactivated, which makes static access configurations impractical and risky. As a result, organizations must rely on automation-driven least privilege strategies that continuously analyze usage patterns, score risk, right-size entitlements, and provide time-bound or **just-in-time** (**JIT**) elevation only when necessary. Automated assessment and enforcement are essential to prevent privilege creep, detect unused or excessive permissions, and maintain a defensible security posture. To support this, cloud platforms implement structured access controls through a range of policies that define how identities interact with resources.

Policy types

Cloud IAM relies on various policy structures that collectively define how identities interact with resources. Broadly, the IAM policy types can be categorized as follows:

- **Identity policies (user/group/service account policies)**: Define what an identity can do.
- **Resource policies**: Define who can access a resource and include policies such as S3 bucket policies and *Key Vault* access policies.
- **Permission boundaries**: This puts an upper limit on the maximum permissions an identity may obtain, even if assigned broader roles.
- **Organization-level policies**: These are guardrails such as AWS SCPs, Azure management group policies, or GCP organization policies that restrict actions across all accounts or projects.
- **Network-linked IAM policies**: Policies tied to identity-aware proxies, private endpoints, and API gateways, etc.

Privileged user management

Privileged access is highly concentrated in cloud platforms, where administrators can control global settings, encryption keys, and billing. Managing permissions for privileged accounts in cloud environments entails the following:

- **Separation of duties (SoDs)**: Breaking monolithic admin roles into narrowly scoped roles such as key admin, network admin, and billing admin.
- **Privileged identity federation**: Administrative identities authenticate through the enterprise IdP rather than local cloud accounts.
- **Approval-based elevation**: Users receive elevated privileges only after automated or workflow-based approval.
- **Privileged session monitoring**: Logging, recording, and analyzing admin actions via cloud-native services such as CloudTrail, activity logs, or audit logs.
- **Elimination of standing privileges**: Credentials of service accounts and break-glass accounts are tightly controlled, monitored, and frequently rotated.

Conditional access policies and perimeter management

In cloud environments, traditional network perimeters no longer define trust boundaries. Users, devices, workloads, and services operate across distributed networks and multiple cloud regions, making identity the primary control point for enforcing access. Modern perimeter management relies on conditional access policies that evaluate parameters such as device posture, geolocation, network conditions, risk scores, and session context before granting access. This adaptive approach ensures that access decisions are continuously validated rather than assumed based on network location. CSPs extend this model with features like identity-aware proxies, context-based session controls, device compliance checks, and trust zones that define permissible access pathways for users and workloads. Together, these controls create a dynamic, identity-centric perimeter that governs how internal and external entities interact with cloud resources.

As identity becomes the anchor of cloud access, the underlying infrastructure must enforce these decisions reliably and securely. This depends on how organizations design their cloud networks, segment workloads, manage traffic flows, and secure the underlying infrastructure that supports applications. The following section examines the foundational elements of cloud infrastructure and network security, and how they work in concert with IAM controls to maintain a robust security posture.

Cloud infrastructure security

Cloud infrastructure and networking form the foundation on which all cloud workloads operate, and securing these layers is essential for maintaining trust in any cloud environment.

Unlike traditional data centers, where organizations control the complete hardware, network, and virtualization stack, the cloud introduces a shared responsibility model. The responsibility for securing the underlying physical and virtualized infrastructure, including global data centers, hardware platforms, hypervisors, backbone networks, and the cloud management plane, always lies with the CSP. Providers such as AWS, Azure, and GCP secure these foundational components through hardened data center operations, hardware root-of-trust mechanisms, supply-chain integrity controls, strong hypervisor isolation, encrypted backbone networks, and continuous security monitoring at the platform level.

Responsibility for securing the virtualized infrastructure components that operate on this foundation shifts depending on the cloud service model. Understanding these boundaries is critical because cloud security is no longer enforced by a physical perimeter but by the secure configuration of virtual infrastructure, identity layers, and distributed network controls. This shared operational model defines how organizations implement guardrails, enforce configuration baselines, monitor risks, and maintain a resilient and well-governed cloud environment.

Infrastructure security techniques

Cloud infrastructure relies on layered, defense-in-depth security that protects the environment from the hardware layer up to the control plane. A secure cloud foundation begins with strong architectural design, where CSPs build multi-tenant platforms that enforce physical separation and robust isolation between customer workloads. Landing zones and baseline configurations provide a consistent security scaffold for all environments. CSPs also follow rigorous processes for secure development and configuration of their platforms, including systematic code reviews, continuous vulnerability testing, strict patch management, and deployment pipelines that validate every change before it reaches customer-facing environments.

Infrastructure as code

IaC transforms how cloud environments are deployed and secured. Instead of manual provisioning through consoles, IaC allows infrastructure to be defined through machine-readable templates and version controlled code. This offers the following security advantages:

- **Standardization**: IaC ensures that environments are deployed exactly the same way every time, ensuring consistency and removing human variability and configuration drift.
- **Version control**: The code templates become part of the organization's codebase, facilitating auditability, traceability, change history, and peer review.
- **Automated security testing**: Policies and scanners evaluate IaC templates before deployment, identifying insecure configurations, open ports, excessive permissions, or non-compliant architectures.

- **Rapid deployment**: Entire environments can be deployed or recreated securely within minutes, allowing quick recovery, scalable provisioning, and predictable behaviour.
- **Scalability and flexibility**: IaC supports complex architectures, including multi-region and multi-account deployments, while enforcing the same security baselines everywhere.

Cloud network security

Cloud network architectures are fundamentally built on **software-defined networking** (**SDN**), where networking functions such as routing, segmentation, filtering, and inspection are abstracted into programmable, virtualized components. This software-driven approach brings several security benefits. Policies can be centrally defined and enforced at scale, network paths can be dynamically reconfigured, segmentation becomes granular and identity-aware, and security controls can be embedded directly into the network fabric rather than relying on static, hardware-bound boundaries.

SDN enables a highly modular cloud network structure composed of virtualized components that collectively replace traditional switching and routing layers. These include components such as **virtual private clouds** (**VPCs**) / VNets, public and private subnets, route tables, **network security groups** (**NSGs**), **network access control lists** (**NACL**), network gateways, service endpoints, private service connectors, and load balancers. Each of these elements plays a role in determining traffic flow, enforcing segmentation, protecting workloads, and controlling exposure. The programmability of SDN allows the CSPs and consumers to implement network guardrails, automate segmentation, and continuously validate configuration against security baselines.

Network security controls

Cloud networks rely on a layered set of security controls that operate at different points within the VNet fabric to regulate traffic, enforce segmentation, and provide deep inspection where required. These controls complement the software-defined nature of cloud networking, allowing organizations to apply fine-grained filtering at the subnet, instance, application, and edge layers. From basic stateful filtering mechanisms to advanced threat-inspection technologies, these components work together to manage both east–west and north–south flows, contain lateral movement, and maintain visibility across distributed workloads.

Network security groups

NSGs serve as the primary distributed firewall within cloud networks and serve as the fundamental control for securing resources within a cloud environment. Unlike traditional perimeter firewalls that guard a physical boundary, NSGs operate as virtualized, stateful packet filters applied at the subnet or individual network interface level. They evaluate inbound and outbound traffic based on source, destination, protocol, and port, enforcing least privilege access between workloads.

A key security advantage of NSGs is that they scale horizontally with workloads. Every virtual machine or container host can have its own attached NSG, enabling micro-segmentation without the need to deploy additional components. When combined with automation frameworks and guardrails, NSGs ensure that network permissions remain consistent, auditable, and aligned to organizational security policies.

Cloud firewalls

Cloud-native firewalls offer scalable, centrally managed protection for both north–south (internet-facing) and east–west (internal) traffic. Unlike NSGs, which function primarily as packet-filtering controls, cloud firewalls provide layer 7 inspection, intrusion prevention, domain name filtering, **Transport Layer Security** (**TLS**) inspection, and threat intelligence enrichment. They integrate tightly with routing constructs like hub-and-spoke architectures or transit gateways to facilitate centralized filtering for multiple VNets. Their elasticity allows them to scale automatically with traffic volumes, removing the performance bottlenecks associated with physical firewalls.

Virtual network appliances

VNet appliances, also known as **virtual security appliances** or **virtual firewalls**, run as software-based instances within cloud networks and replicate the advanced security capabilities of traditional hardware appliances. These are typically provided by third-party vendors such as *Palo Alto*, *Check Point*, *Fortinet*, *Sophos*, *Juniper*, and others. These appliances provide sophisticated threat inspection using next-generation firewall capabilities, behaviour analysis, sandboxing, and threat intelligence correlation. They provide application-level controls, enabling traffic governance based on application signatures rather than simple IP and port rules. Many appliances also incorporate full **intrusion detection system** (**IDS**)/IPS capabilities, decryption and TLS inspection, and routing or segmentation functions that allow them to serve as virtual routers within a cloud network. They are commonly deployed in central inspection zones within hub networks, at internet egress points, or at cloud–on-premises interconnect boundaries to provide consistent and high-assurance inspection.

Web application firewalls

Web application firewalls (**WAFs**) add another layer of defense by protecting applications from HTTP-based attacks. Integrated with cloud load balancers and edge services, WAFs detect and block threats such as command injection, **cross-site scripting** (**XSS**), API abuse, bot-driven probing, and other web application vulnerabilities. They incorporate features like anomaly scoring, rate limiting, geo-based controls, and automated rule updates, enhancing the security of web applications and cloud-native API workloads.

Egress management

Controlling outbound traffic is a critical aspect of cloud network security, particularly for preventing data exfiltration and ensuring that workloads communicate only with approved external services. Egress controls such as NAT gateways, outbound proxies, firewall appliances, and policy-driven routing help regulate all outbound flows. In addition, controls such as private endpoints, private links, and private DNS restrict service access to internal, provider-managed networks rather than exposing workloads to the public internet. Most organizations adopt a default-deny egress posture, allowing outbound connections only when they are explicitly authorized. This approach greatly reduces the risk of unauthorized data transfer, accidental exposure, and **command and control** (**C2**) activity initiated through compromised workloads.

Container networking

Containerized environments introduce unique networking and security challenges because containers are ephemeral, lightweight, and highly dynamic. Unlike traditional workloads that operate in stable network segments, containers can be created, destroyed, or rescheduled within seconds. This fluidity makes manual network management impractical and increases reliance on automated, policy-driven controls. Container platforms also introduce a broader attack surface, including image vulnerabilities, insecure registries, misconfigured orchestration components, exposed APIs, and overly permissive network policies. The networking layer itself can be targeted if traffic between containers, pods, or services is not properly segmented or inspected. As container deployments scale across clusters, nodes, and cloud regions, securing east–west communication becomes as important as protecting north–south ingress and egress flows.

Container networking can be implemented in several ways, each carrying its own implications for performance, segmentation, observability, and security. The two most widely adopted technologies for container deployment and orchestration are Docker and Kubernetes.

Docker provides networking using virtual Ethernet interfaces, network namespaces, and bridge networks. From a security standpoint, isolating containers through dedicated namespaces is fundamental. Restricting container-to-container communication and using user-defined bridges helps enforce segmentation and reduce lateral movement. Network plugins offer advanced policy enforcement, but even in basic deployments, unnecessary port exposure should be avoided, and inter-container communication should follow strict least privilege principles.

Kubernetes builds on these concepts with a flat, cluster-wide networking model in which every pod receives its own unique IP address, enabling direct pod-to-pod communication without NAT. Security in this model is enforced through layered mechanisms. Network policies define rules using labels, namespaces, and traffic selectors, enabling declarative, fine-grained segmentation. **Container Network Interface** (**CNI**) plugins, such as *Calico, Cilium, Weave*, or *Azure CNI*, manage routing, enforce network policies, and often support encryption and advanced packet filtering. Many environments further strengthen security with service meshes like *Istio* or *Linkerd*, which add **mutual TLS** (**mTLS**), end-to-end encryption, identity-based service authentication, and Zero Trust service routing. At the cluster boundary, ingress and egress controllers manage external connections by enforcing TLS termination, applying WAF protections, rate limiting traffic, and restricting outbound flows, ensuring that both north–south and east–west traffic remain tightly controlled.

Zero Trust and secure access

Cloud environments operate without fixed perimeters, making traditional network boundary controls insufficient to determine trust. As workloads, users, and data move across public clouds, private clouds, and remote locations, secure access must be defined by identity, context, and continuous verification rather than static network positions. **Software-defined perimeter** (**SDP**) and **Zero Trust Network Access** (**ZTNA**) are two key technologies that play a central role in enabling this shift. Both embody the core Zero Trust principle of *never trust, always verify*, but they apply it at different layers of access and enforcement. Complementing these, *Gartner* SASE provides a broader architectural framework that converges networking and security functions into a unified, cloud-delivered platform. SASE integrates ZTNA with secure web gateways, **cloud access security brokers** (**CASB**), **firewall as a service** (**FWaaS**), and **software-defined wide area network** (**SD-WAN**) to deliver consistent, identity-driven access across distributed environments. Together, these technologies form the foundation of Zero Trust cloud access, replacing implicit trust with continuous, adaptive, context-aware security controls.

Software-defined perimeter

SDP is an architectural approach that removes implicit trust from network access by making applications and services completely invisible unless authentication and authorization have already been established. SDP operates on a *verify first, connect later* principle, inverting the legacy model where a user joins a network first and then accesses applications. It achieves this through a control plane–data plane separation, where authentication occurs at the control plane using identity attributes, device posture, geolocation, and risk assessments. Only after successful verification does the data plane establish a mutually authenticated, encrypted connection between the user and the specific application.

SDP relies on a combination of mTLS, **single-packet authorization** (**SPA**), micro-segmentation, and dynamic network overlays. SPA conceals application endpoints until a valid cryptographic request is received, significantly reducing attack visibility by preventing port scanning, banner grabbing, or service enumeration. The SDP gateway creates a one-to-one micro-tunnel between the user and the target resource, ensuring that users cannot access anything beyond the explicitly authorized application, because SDP abstracts applications from the underlying network and enforces identity-driven access, it provides strong protection for legacy systems, cloud workloads, and hybrid deployments.

Zero Trust Network Access

ZTNA extends Zero Trust principles into a scalable access framework for cloud environments. ZTNA replaces the traditional VPN-based perimeter with a context-aware, identity-centric access mechanism that authenticates and authorizes requests at the application-level rather than exposing entire networks. ZTNA operates through a broker or controller that evaluates identity, device health, MFA status, behavioural analytics, and environmental attributes.

A distinguishing feature of ZTNA is its continuous authorization model. Unlike static VPN sessions, ZTNA evaluates trust dynamically throughout the session. Any deviation in device posture, anomalous behaviour, or policy changes can trigger real-time revocation. ZTNA also enforces application segmentation, where each application becomes an isolated perimeter with dedicated policies. This significantly reduces lateral movement paths and prevents attackers from pivoting across environments.

ZTNA is particularly valuable in cloud-native environments where workloads shift frequently, employees work remotely, and applications may be distributed across SaaS, PaaS, IaaS, and on-premise environments. It supports both agent-based (device-controlled) and agentless (browser-based) modes, allowing flexible enforcement across managed and unmanaged devices. By abstracting applications from network exposure and applying granular access controls, ZTNA forms one of the core enforcement components of the Zero Trust architecture.

Secure access service edge

SASE is a framework introduced by Gartner that represents the convergence of networking and security into a unified, cloud-delivered architecture. Instead of relying on traditional network perimeters or centralized security stacks, SASE distributes security controls closer to users, devices, and applications—regardless of where they operate. It integrates identity-centric access, continuous trust verification, and cloud-native traffic inspection into a single service framework.

SASE combines several key technologies that operate cohesively to deliver secure, scalable, and policy-driven access. These include:

- **ZTNA**: VPN-style perimeter access is replaced with identity and context-based authentication for each session. It enforces least privilege, application-level access, ensuring that users never gain network-level visibility. Access decisions are continuously evaluated using factors such as device posture, user risk score, behaviour patterns, and geolocation.

- **CASB**: A CASB provides visibility and control over SaaS usage, enforcing policies such as DLP, anomaly detection, shadow IT monitoring, and OAuth app governance. It inspects user-to-cloud traffic, identifies risky behaviour, enforces encryption/tokenization, and integrates with identity systems to ensure safe consumption of enterprise cloud applications.

- **SWG**: They protect users from web-based threats by filtering outbound HTTP/HTTPS traffic. They perform URL categorization, malware inspection, SSL/TLS decryption, content filtering, and sandboxing. As part of SASE, SWGs extend these protections to remote and roaming users without forcing traffic through on-prem proxies.
- **FWaaS**: A FWaaS provides cloud-delivered, scalable firewall capabilities that replace hardware firewalls. It enforces layer 3–7 policies, intrusion prevention, application inspection, geo-blocking, and threat intelligence updates. FWaaS removes the need for appliance lifecycle management and ensures consistent perimeter controls across all network edges.
- **SD-WAN**: This forms the networking backbone of SASE, providing intelligent routing, link optimization, encryption, and application-aware traffic steering. It enables direct-to-cloud connectivity, bypassing legacy MPLS backhaul, and integrates with the SASE policy plane to dynamically route traffic through the correct security services.

A diagrammatic representation of the SASE framework is shown in the following figure:

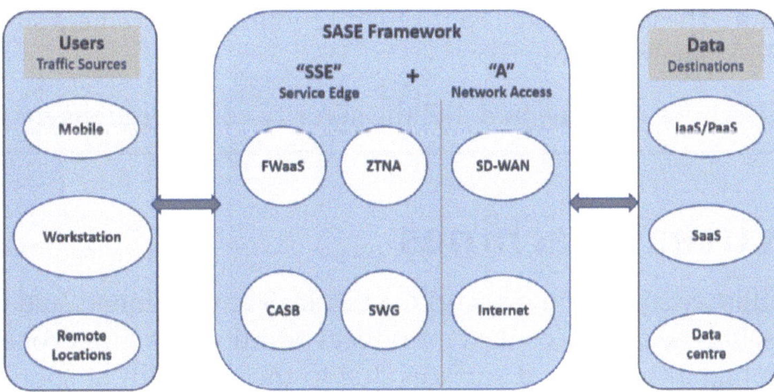

***Figure 11.2**: SASE unified framework*

Protecting cloud workloads

Cloud environments host a wide spectrum of workloads, including VMs, containerized applications, managed platform services, and serverless functions. Each of these workloads differs in architecture, lifecycle behaviour, deployment methods, and operational abstractions. As a result, securing cloud workloads requires a contextual approach that aligns security controls with the unique characteristics of each type of workload rather than relying on traditional, host-centric techniques.

Cloud workloads are ephemeral and immutable in nature. Unlike static on-premises servers that persist for years, cloud workloads can be frequently provisioned, scaled, or terminated. Most cloud-native architectures mandate immutable deployments, where workloads are not modified in place; patches, configuration updates, and changes are incorporated into new machine images, containers, or code packages. This reduces drift, enforces consistency, and shrinks the attack surface. However, it also requires security controls that operate automatically and continuously across highly dynamic environments.

Security must therefore adapt to workloads that may not exist long enough for manual hardening, traditional vulnerability scanning cycles, or ticket-based approvals. Automated, policy-driven guardrails, real-time visibility, identity-based permissions, runtime protection, behavioural analytics, and secure-by-design deployment pipelines become foundational to managing workload risks.

Consider a containerized microservices application that is deployed in a managed Kubernetes cluster. Suppose a newly introduced container image contains a vulnerable library with a known remote code execution flaw. An integrated cloud-native security platform that scans the container images during the CI/CD pipeline can block the deployment before it reaches production. Consider another scenario, where a compromised workload attempts to establish outbound communication with a known malicious C2 server. In such a scenario, runtime protection integrated with network policy enforcement can immediately isolate the pod and terminate the session. These automated controls and runtime enforcement significantly reduce risk in dynamic cloud environments.

The following subsections examine in detail the security considerations for each category of cloud workloads.

Securing virtual machines

VMs remain the most commonly used workload in IaaS environments and closely resemble traditional servers, but their cloud context introduces additional security considerations. They remain one of the highest-risk cloud surfaces due to their breadth of configuration options and runtime exposure. Strong security governance, hardening standards, and automated configuration checks are essential to maintain a secure posture.

Key principles for VM security include the following:

- **Secure images and golden templates**: Organizations should maintain hardened, **Center for Internet Security** (**CIS**) compliant images and use image pipelines that incorporate vulnerability scanning, configuration validation, and patch updates before deployment.
- **OS hardening and patch automation**: Cloud workloads must enforce secure configuration baselines, disable unnecessary services, rotate credentials, and apply patches automatically via tools such as *Azure Update Manager*, *AWS Systems Manager*, or *GCP OS Config*.
- **Endpoint and runtime protection**: VMs require **endpoint detection and response** (**EDR**), anti-malware, host intrusion prevention, and behavioural detection systems tailored for cloud environments.

- **Identity-based access**: VM access should rely on short-lived credentials, IAM roles, managed identities, and JIT access to eliminate static keys and reduce lateral movement risks.
- **Network and segmentation controls**: NSGs, host-based firewalls, and micro-segmentation should be used to ensure that VM communication is restricted to intended paths.
- **Disk, snapshot, and backup security**: Encrypting disks, snapshots, and images, along with strict access policies, prevents compromise of machine images.

Container security

Containers offer portability, low overhead, and rapid scaling, but they introduce unique risks due to their layered architecture and reliance on shared engines and orchestration platforms. Containers compress the traditional attack surface of application, OS, network, and runtime into a tightly integrated ecosystem that demands continuous scanning, strong isolation, and policy-based network enforcement.

Key container security areas are as follows:

- **Image security**: Enforce trusted registries, sign images, scan for vulnerabilities, and block deployments of unverified images.
- **Runtime isolation**: Use namespaces, control groups, and kernel security mechanisms such as seccomp, AppArmor, or SELinux to isolate containers and restrict capabilities.
- **Least privilege container design**: Run containers as non-root users, avoid privileged containers, minimize exposed ports, and restrict inter-container communications.
- **Network controls**: Apply Kubernetes network policies, CNI plugin enforcement, and service mesh-based encryption and identity management.
- **Secrets management**: Store API keys, tokens, and certificates in secure vaults rather than environment variables or image layers.
- **Orchestrator hardening**: Securing Kubernetes components such as the kube API server, etcd, kubelet, and admission controllers is critical due to their central role in orchestration.

Securing PaaS workloads

While CSPs secure the underlying platform, customers are responsible for the secure use of the service. PaaS security is primarily focused on configuration and governance. Customers need to ensure that the service is used securely, even though the infrastructure is managed by the cloud provider.

Key PaaS security considerations are as follows:

- **Configuration hardening**: Misconfigurations such as public exposure, weak firewall rules, or default access are the most common PaaS vulnerabilities.
- **Role enforcement**: Managed identities, service accounts, and granular IAM roles prevent misuse of platform services.
- **Network controls**: Use private endpoints, service endpoints, VNet integration, and firewall restrictions to eliminate public access paths.
- **Data security controls**: Enforce encryption at rest and in transit, rotate keys, use **customer-managed keys (CMKs)** where applicable, and restrict access using data classification.
- **Logging and monitoring**: PaaS services need continuous audit logging, diagnostic settings, and anomaly detection to detect misuse.
- **Secure API exposure**: API endpoints must use OAuth2, **JSON Web Token (JWT)** validation, certificate-based authentication, or gateway-level authorization.

Securing serverless workloads

Serverless or **function as a service (FaaS)** workloads, such as *AWS Lambda, Azure Functions,* and *Google Cloud Functions,* operate in a fully managed runtime where no servers are visible to customers. While offering significant security advantages, it also introduces unique risks.

Key security considerations for FaaS are:

- **Identity-centric access**: Functions must use granular IAM roles, least privilege permissions, and temporary credentials rather than environment keys.
- **Event and trigger security**: Misconfigured triggers for workloads such as S3 buckets, Event Grid, Pub/Sub, or API gateway can allow unintended invocation paths and privilege escalation.
- **Dependency risks**: Third-party libraries, outdated packages, and vulnerable dependencies are a major attack vector in FaaS deployments.
- **Runtime protection**: Functions should enforce timeouts, memory limits, and execution constraints to prevent any abuse.
- **Network restriction**: Where possible, functions should run inside private networks, access resources via private endpoints, and avoid public internet paths.
- **Observability and forensics**: Due to short-lived executions, logs, traces, and metrics must be captured in real-time.
- **Secure deployment**: Functions should be deployed via secure pipelines that validate code integrity, carry out regular testing, and enforce **policy as code (PaC)**.

Data security

Data is the most critical asset in any cloud environment, and its protection requires a combination of secure storage architectures, identity-driven access controls, encryption mechanisms, and strong key management. Unlike traditional data centers, where storage infrastructure is physically controlled and confined to fixed network boundaries, cloud storage is distributed, scalable, and exposed through APIs, creating both opportunities and risks. CSPs offer a variety of storage classes, such as object storage, volume storage, and databases, each with unique characteristics and security implications. Effective data security, therefore, depends on understanding the nature of each storage type and applying the right controls across its lifecycle.

Object storage

Object storage is the primary data storage model in cloud environments, designed for scalability, durability, and global accessibility. Securing object storage requires enforcing strict access controls through bucket-level and object-level policies that determine who can read, write, or manage stored data. CSPs support fine-grained controls using IAM roles, ACLs, and attribute-based policies that help limit exposure and enforce least privilege. Data must be protected using server-side encryption with customer managed or provider-managed keys. Where appropriate, client-side encryption can be used to ensure only trusted applications decrypt the data. Object storage systems can avoid exposure to the public internet and significantly reduce risk by using a private network or service endpoints.

Volume storage

Volume storage, typically attached to VMs as block devices, requires a security strategy that spans the underlying platform, the guest OS, and the application workloads using the disks. Data in volumes can be secured at several layers, including the application, database, file system, volume, or API layer. The correct layer of protection depends on data sensitivity, performance considerations, and regulatory requirements. Cloud providers support encryption at rest using disk-level encryption with managed keys, while applications may implement additional encryption for highly sensitive workloads. Access control must be tightly applied through instance profiles, mount permissions, OS-level privileges, and firewall rules that restrict who or what can access the volumes. Snapshots and backups must also be encrypted and access controlled, as they often contain full copies of sensitive datasets. To reduce the risk of data leakage, organizations should avoid re-attaching volumes across environments with different trust levels and should sanitize or securely wipe volumes before deletion or reuse.

Database storage

Securing cloud-based databases requires a combination of identity governance, encryption, network isolation, and continuous monitoring. Managed database services provide built-in security features that organizations must configure correctly to achieve a secure deployment. IAM-based authentication and role-based permissions ensure that users, applications, and services interact with the database using the principle of least privilege. Encryption in transit is enforced through TLS, while encryption at rest is applied using provider-managed or CMKs. Network-level protections, such as private endpoints, VPC peering, or service networks, prevent unauthorized public access and confine database communication to trusted segments. Additional controls, such as query auditing, configuration baselines, automatic patching, replication integrity checks, and backup encryption, strengthen the overall security posture. For highly sensitive workloads, **database activity monitoring** (**DAM**) and anomaly detection tools provide deeper visibility into misuse, data exfiltration attempts, or privilege escalation activities.

API security

APIs form the backbone of cloud architectures, powering interactions between microservices, serverless functions, container platforms, managed cloud services, and external consumers. Because cloud environments are inherently distributed and heavily automated, APIs often expose critical data and management functions over public or semi-public networks. This makes them a primary attack vector for threats such as credential misuse, injection attacks, **insecure direct object references** (**IDOR**), broken access controls, and compromised service-to-service communication. Securing cloud APIs, therefore, requires controls that operate at both the application layer and the cloud management plane.

Cloud providers embed several native mechanisms to protect APIs, especially those exposed through API gateways and managed services. API gateways in AWS, Azure, and GCP provide integrated authentication and authorization with IAM roles, OAuth tokens, and key-based access. They enforce rate limiting, throttling, schema validation, TLS termination, and request sanitization to reduce the risk of abuse or malformed traffic. Cloud WAFs and threat-protection engines additionally inspect API payloads for anomalies or attack signatures. For internal microservices, service mesh frameworks ensure API security by enforcing mTLS, identity-based routing, and fine-grained authorization at the service layer.

Integrated cloud security management platforms

As cloud adoption scales across multiple providers and architectural models, organizations require unified platforms that can continuously assess security posture, detect misconfigurations, manage identity risks, protect workloads, and secure sensitive data. Native tools from CSPs address individual layers of cloud security, but visibility often becomes fragmented across accounts, regions, and services. Integrated cloud security platforms bring these capabilities together, offering continuous monitoring, analytics, and automated remediation across complex environments. These solutions complement IAM, network, and workload controls by providing centralized governance and precise insights into cloud risks. Some of these solutions are as follows:

- **CSPM**: CSPM solutions focus on identifying and remediating misconfigurations across cloud services to maintain a secure and compliant posture. They provide the following capabilities:
  - o Continuously scan cloud configurations across services such as storage, networks, IAM, and compute.
  - o Identify misconfigurations, deviations from benchmarks (CIS, NIST, CSA), excessive permissions, and insecure defaults.
  - o Provide automated or guided remediation to enforce secure baselines across multi-cloud environments.
- **CWPP**: CWPP platforms secure workloads such as VMs, containers, and serverless functions through vulnerability management, runtime protection, and threat detection. They perform the following key security functions:
  - o Protect compute workloads across VMs, containers, Kubernetes, serverless functions, and PaaS services.
  - o Monitor runtime behaviour, detect anomalies, prevent malware, and enforce host and container hardening policies.
  - o Provide deep visibility into workload vulnerabilities, image risks, and lateral-movement paths.
- **Cloud infrastructure entitlement management (CIEM)**: CIEM tools manage and optimize cloud identities and permissions by detecting excessive privileges, anomalous access patterns, and policy drift. Their primary objective areas include:
  - o Addressing identity sprawl by analyzing permissions across cloud IAM systems.
  - o Detecting excessive, unused, or high-risk privileges and recommending least privilege reductions.
  - o Supporting automated entitlement right-sizing, privilege risk scoring, and continuous identity posture assessment.
- **Data security posture management (DSPM)**: DSPM solutions discover, classify, and monitor sensitive data across cloud storage systems to prevent exposure, leakage, and non-compliant handling. Their core data-centric capabilities include:
  - o Data discovery and classification across object stores, databases, data lakes, and backups.
  - o Identifying sensitive or regulated data exposures and evaluating encryption, access policies, and sharing settings.
  - o Mapping data flows and highlighting unauthorized access paths, public exposure risks, and shadow datasets.

- **Attack surface management (ASM):** ASM platforms provide external visibility into cloud-exposed assets and shadow resources to proactively identify weaknesses. Their major exposure-focused tasks include:
    - Providing external visibility into cloud-exposed services, APIs, domains, and ephemeral public endpoints.
    - Detecting shadow cloud assets, unmanaged resources, and externally visible misconfigurations.
    - Helping organizations reduce cloud attack surface by continuously scanning for internet-facing weaknesses.
- **CNAPP**: A CNAPP integrates posture management and workload protection into a single platform to secure cloud-native applications across the entire lifecycle. It provides the following comprehensive end-to-end security features:
    - Combines CSPM, CWPP, CIEM, and DSPM capabilities into a unified platform.
    - Secures the full application lifecycle, from IaC templates and deployment pipelines to runtime protection.
    - Integrates posture management, vulnerability scanning, entitlement analysis, and data security for end-to-end cloud protection.

Conclusion

With the rapid adoption of cloud technologies and services, cloud security has emerged as a foundational pillar of information security. This chapter examined the essential concepts and controls required to secure cloud environments, beginning with the fundamentals of cloud-native architecture across IaaS, PaaS, and SaaS models. Understanding these service models is crucial, not only because they influence how organizations deploy and operate workloads, but also because they determine how security responsibilities are distributed between the CSP and the customer.

The shared responsibility model remains central to effective cloud security. While CSPs secure the underlying physical infrastructure, global networks, and control planes, organizations must focus on securing identities, configurations, data, and access paths, along with workloads where applicable. This demands a structured approach to cloud organization design, hierarchical management, and standardized policy enforcement across all accounts, projects, and subscriptions.

IAM is one of the most critical components of cloud security. In an environment where traditional perimeters dissolve, identity becomes the primary control point. Managing cloud identities, defining granular authorization, implementing least privilege, and securing the IAM perimeter all directly shape the security of deployed workloads. Cloud infrastructure and network security extend these safeguards into the virtualized fabric that hosts applications, where software-defined networks, segmentation strategies, automated guardrails, and hardened platform services together form a resilient foundation for secure operations.

Zero Trust principles further redefine secure access in cloud environments, emphasizing continuous verification and context-driven controls. Technologies such as SDP, ZTNA, and SASE help operationalize these principles at scale. Further, ensuring the security of workloads and data, including VMs, containers, serverless functions, object storage, volume storage, and databases, is fundamental to a robust cloud security posture. Integrated cloud security management platforms such as CSPM, CWPP, CIEM, DSPM, ASM, and CNAPP provide the visibility, automation, and continuous assurance required to secure complex, dynamic, and distributed multi-cloud environments.

In the next chapter, we will explore emerging technologies such as artificial intelligence and quantum computing, and examine how they are reshaping the future of information security.

Exercises

1. Explain the difference between IaaS, PaaS, and SaaS from a security perspective. What specific security responsibilities remain with the customer in each model?
2. Describe the shared responsibility model in cloud security. Provide examples of controls that are always managed by the CSP.
3. Discuss how cloud organization management structures support governance and policy enforcement. Why is hierarchical design important for large deployments?
4. Identity is considered the new perimeter in cloud environments. Explain why this shift has occurred and list some IAM controls that help enforce least privilege in cloud ecosystems.
5. What are conditional access policies, and how do they form a key element of IAM perimeter defense? Provide an example of how such a policy can mitigate a real-world risk.
6. SDN introduces new ways to segment and secure traffic in the cloud. Compare traditional network segmentation with cloud-based segmentation using constructs such as VPCs/VNets and NSGs.
7. A large organization adopts a multi-cloud strategy and finds inconsistent security configurations across its environments. Which integrated cloud security management platforms would you recommend to identify and mitigate the risk, and why? Provide a brief justification for the recommendations.
8. Zero Trust access is increasingly adopted in cloud-native environments. Explain how SDP, ZTNA, and SASE each contribute to Zero Trust and describe a use case where SASE provides advantages over ZTNA alone.

9. A team is deploying a containerized microservices application on a managed Kubernetes cluster. Identify four key security controls that should be implemented across container images, orchestration, networking, and runtime. Briefly justify each control.
10. An organization needs to store regulated customer data in the cloud, including documents, database records, and application logs. For each storage type (object, volume, and database), recommend appropriate security controls related to access, encryption, and key management, ensuring compliance and minimal operational overhead.

Chapter 12
Emerging Technologies and Information Security

Introduction

The information security landscape is undergoing a period of rapid transformation. Technologies that were once experimental or niche are now shaping mainstream enterprise environments and influencing how trust is established, how data is protected, and how threats are detected and mitigated. In this chapter, we will take a holistic view, focusing on technologies whose impact spans multiple domains in the field of information security and reshapes both defensive strategies and adversarial capabilities.

One of the most significant influences in the evolving landscape is the increasing use of **artificial intelligence** (**AI**) in information security. **Machine learning** (**ML**) and **generative AI** (**GenAI**) are now deeply embedded in threat detection, behavioural analytics, and automated response, which enables security teams to operate at unprecedented scale and speed. You may have noticed that when you login to your bank's mobile application from a new device or unfamiliar location, the system triggers additional authentication. This response is often driven by ML models operating in the background that detect anomalies in real-time. What appears to the user as a simple security alert is, in reality, an AI-driven risk assessment process. While these technologies significantly enhance the security of information systems, they are also being weaponized by attackers to craft sophisticated phishing campaigns, evade detection, automate malware development, and conduct large-scale reconnaissance. This dual-use nature of AI has resulted in a more dynamic and adaptive threat environment in which both defenders and adversaries rely on data-driven decision-making and automation.

Besides AI, there are other emerging technologies that introduce new security challenges and opportunities. Quantum computing raises concerns about the long-term viability of widely used cryptographic algorithms, driving research in quantum-safe cryptography and key management. Blockchain-based systems offer alternative mechanisms for establishing trust to ensure data integrity and support decentralized identity models. Likewise, the growth of edge computing is shifting computation and data storage closer to users and devices, expanding the attack surface and weakening centralized security controls. These developments reflect a paradigm shift towards distributed, resilient, and adaptive security models. We will examine these emerging technologies and trends to gain an understanding of how information security is likely to evolve in the coming years.

Structure

In this chapter, we will discuss the following topics:

- AI in information security
- Quantum computing and quantum-safe cryptography
- Blockchain and information security
- Edge computing and distributed security

Objectives

The objective of this chapter is to provide a holistic understanding of emerging technologies and trends that are shaping the future of information security. By examining advances in technologies such as AI, quantum computing, blockchain, and edge computing, the chapter aims to highlight how these technologies influence the threat landscape, security architectures, and defense strategies across domains. It also seeks to develop an understanding of the dual-use nature of emerging technologies, where innovations strengthen security capabilities while simultaneously introducing new risks. By the end of this chapter, you should be able to understand the security implications of these technologies, assess their potential impact on existing security controls, and appreciate the need for adaptive, forward-looking security models in modern information systems.

AI in information security

The rapid adoption of AI by threat actors marks a fundamental shift in how cyberattacks are conceived and executed. Activities that once required significant technical skills, time-consuming reconnaissance, and manual effort are increasingly being replaced by automated, high-velocity, and highly personalized attack campaigns. Using GenAI, autonomous agents are being employed to conduct reconnaissance at scale, adapt attack paths, and facilitate lateral movement with minimal human intervention. This has lowered the entry barrier for cybercrimes while simultaneously increasing the speed and reach of cyberattacks.

The dark **large language models** (**LLMs**) such as *WormGPT* and *FraudGPT* provide attackers with ready-made capabilities for phishing, malware generation, and social engineering. By compressing the traditional dwell time of attacks, these tools allow adversaries to move rapidly from reconnaissance to exploitation and obfuscation. Automated malicious email campaigns, for example, now leverage AI-generated language that is context-aware, non-repetitive, and convincingly human, making it far more difficult for content-based security controls to identify and block such threats.

In addition, the widespread deployment of poorly secured AI-enabled applications exposes the AI systems to a different class of risk. Recent incidents have demonstrated that AI systems often inherit fundamental weaknesses from the environments in which they are deployed, including weak credential management, long-lived authentication tokens, and inadequate monitoring. Exploitation of AI integrations, such as token abuse in cloud-connected AI services or basic credential leakage in automated decision systems, highlights that many AI-related breaches are not the result of advanced model manipulation, but of familiar security failures amplified by automation. These incidents underscore a critical lesson that, as AI systems become more autonomous and interconnected, traditional security weaknesses can propagate faster, operate at greater scale, and cause more widespread impact than ever before.

AI-powered threats

The use of AI by threat actors has introduced a rapidly evolving class of threats that differ fundamentally from traditional cyberattacks. Rather than relying solely on technical exploitation or manual social engineering, attackers combine automation, generative models, and autonomous agents to conduct attacks at scale. In that context, AI is not merely another target within the attack surface; it has become an active enabler that reshapes how deception is carried out, how systems are probed, and how data is exfiltrated.

What makes AI-powered threats particularly challenging is their ability to camouflage technical exploitation with cognitive manipulation. Generative systems can produce content that closely resembles legitimate communication, behaviour, or system output, making it difficult to distinguish malicious activity from normal operations. When such capabilities are coupled with autonomous execution, attackers gain the ability to operate continuously and at scale. This places sustained pressure on detection, response, and trust mechanisms.

Some stack types in which AI is being actively weaponized by the threat actors are as follows:

- **AI-driven impersonation and social engineering**: Advanced text and voice generation tools enable highly convincing impersonation attacks targeting individuals and institutions. In some high-profile cases, AI-generated messages and voicemails have been used to impersonate senior government officials, creating a false sense of urgency and legitimacy. These attacks exploit trust rather than technical vulnerabilities, making them particularly effective against well-trained targets and difficult to detect using traditional security controls.

- **Automated reconnaissance and environment profiling**: AI-driven agents are increasingly used to automate reconnaissance activities, including system enumeration, vulnerability discovery, and credential harvesting. Through natural language interaction, attackers can instruct AI systems to analyze environments and assemble attack components with minimal manual intervention, accelerating early attack stages.

- **AI-assisted ransomware and extortion**: AI can support ransomware campaigns by generating adaptable payloads, refining encryption strategies, and tailoring extortion communications to specific victims. This personalization increases pressure on targets while lowering operational effort for attackers.

- **Synthetic identity creation and fraud enablement**: AI-generated identities, composed of fabricated personal attributes and plausible behavioural patterns, can evade traditional verification mechanisms. Such identities may be used for account creation, long-term fraud, or gradual infiltration of trust-based systems.

- **Compromise of biometric and media-based authentication**: The widespread use of facial images and voice samples for identity verification creates valuable datasets for attackers. AI models can exploit these data sources to generate deepfakes capable of bypassing biometric controls. What were once considered strong authentication mechanisms now risk becoming attack vectors when not combined with liveness detection and contextual verification.

- **Prompt injection and instruction manipulation**: Prompt injection has emerged as a major concern in AI-enabled applications. By crafting carefully designed inputs, attackers can manipulate models into ignoring safeguards, revealing sensitive information, or performing unintended actions. These attacks exploit the probabilistic and instruction-driven nature of LLMs, blurring the line between misuse and exploitation.

- **Abuse of AI-driven application interfaces**: AI components often act as intermediaries between users and backend services. When these interfaces lack proper isolation or validation, they may be manipulated to indirectly trigger traditional vulnerabilities such as unauthorized data access or script execution. Incidents involving compromised enterprise AI chatbots have demonstrated how a single malicious prompt can trigger cascading failures.

- **Model downgrade and safeguard bypass attacks**: Some attacks focus on influencing how AI systems balance safety, performance, and cost. By manipulating configuration paths or operational modes, adversaries may force systems into less restrictive states, weakening safeguards intended to limit harmful behaviour. Emerging techniques have shown how attackers can deliberately force AI systems to operate in less secure or lower-cost modes. Such downgrade attacks exploit design trade-offs between performance, cost, and safety, allowing attackers to bypass safeguards and access restricted behaviour.

Defense against AI-driven threats

As AI becomes integral to enterprise systems and security operations, defending against AI-driven threats requires a deliberate shift in how protection mechanisms are designed and applied. Traditional controls, which assume predictable inputs and bounded system behaviour, are insufficient for AI systems that learn, adapt, and interact dynamically with users and other systems. For instance, if an attacker subtly manipulates the training data used to build a fraud detection model, the system may learn incorrect patterns and begin approving fraudulent transactions. Such data poisoning attacks may go undetected until the compromised model is deployed, which highlights the criticality of safeguarding training data and model integrity. Effective defense, therefore, demands a holistic approach that spans governance, architecture, and operational security, while recognizing AI systems themselves as high-value and high-risk assets.

A key consideration in emerging defensive strategies is the need to secure the entire AI lifecycle. Vulnerabilities may arise not only during deployment, but also during data collection, model training, integration, and runtime operation. In response, governments, industry bodies, and security practitioners are developing structured frameworks and technical guidance to help organizations systematically identify risks, implement safeguards, and respond to incidents involving AI-enabled systems.

Key strategies and emerging mechanisms for strengthening defenses against AI-driven threats are as follows:

- **Policy-led and framework-based security initiatives**: Governments are beginning to articulate formal expectations for AI security in critical and high-impact environments. Initiatives such as the *U.S. Advanced AI Security Readiness Act* emphasize proactive identification of AI-related vulnerabilities, threat modelling across cyber and physical domains, and coordinated incident response planning. While such efforts do not prescribe specific technologies, they reinforce the principle that AI systems must undergo structured risk assessment and continuous oversight.
- **Adversarial testing and AI red teaming**: Red teaming has emerged as a cornerstone of AI security validation. By deliberately simulating misuse, manipulation, and adversarial prompting, organizations can uncover weaknesses that may not be visible through conventional testing. For example, attackers may inject carefully crafted malicious samples into training data to bias a model's decisions (data poisoning), or use deceptive prompts to trick a generative system into revealing restricted information or bypassing safeguards (prompt injection). AI red teaming, therefore, extends beyond model accuracy to examine data poisoning risks, prompt injection, unintended information disclosure, and unsafe autonomous behaviour across the entire AI pipeline.
- **Lifecycle-oriented security architectures for AI**: Defending AI systems increasingly involves applying controls at each stage of their lifecycle. This includes validating training data sources, enforcing secure model deployment practices, and implementing runtime monitoring for anomalous outputs or behaviour. Such lifecycle-based thinking aligns with emerging industry guidance that treats AI security as an ongoing process rather than a one-time configuration exercise.
- **Standardized control models and security baselines**: To bring consistency and rigor to AI security, industry organizations have begun defining comprehensive control frameworks. For instance, the *AI Control Matrix* by **Cloud Security Alliance** (**CSA**) maps AI-specific security objectives across multiple domains while aligning them

with established standards by organizations such as **International Organization for Standardization** (**ISO**) and **National Institute of Standards and Technology** (**NIST**). These models help organizations integrate AI security into existing governance and risk management structures rather than treating it as a standalone concern.

- **Secure design guidance for agentic and autonomous AI systems**: As AI systems increasingly act on behalf of users, clear guidance is emerging around secure agent design. Initiatives such as the *Securing Agentic Applications Guide* by the **Open Worldwide Application Security Project** (**OWASP**) emphasize principles such as least privilege, explicit trust boundaries, constrained tool access, and robust authentication between agents and backend services. Complementary guidance on AI-specific incident response highlights the importance of detecting, containing, and recovering from failures involving autonomous decision-making.

- **Convergence of AI security and cryptographic resilience**: Defensive strategies are also evolving to account for long-term cryptographic risks. Security platforms are beginning to integrate AI-driven analytics with cryptographic agility, ensuring that both automated decision-making and underlying trust mechanisms remain resilient as cryptographic standards evolve. This convergence is particularly relevant for security infrastructure expected to operate over extended time horizons.

- **AI-assisted defensive operations**: Defenders are increasingly using AI to augment security operations themselves. AI and ML are increasingly being embedded in security platforms such as **security information and event management** (**SIEM**) and **endpoint detection and response** (**EDR**) systems. AI-assisted tools can help identify misconfigurations, prioritize alerts, and recommend remediation actions across complex environments. When deployed with appropriate oversight and governance, these capabilities enhance human decision-making and help security teams manage scale without relinquishing control.

While specific regulations and standards continue to evolve, the underlying principles of lifecycle security, adversarial testing, standardized controls, and human oversight provide a durable foundation for securing AI-enabled systems. These foundations are explored further in the following section, which examines regulatory and governance frameworks for AI security in greater detail.

AI regulatory frameworks

As AI systems increasingly influence decision-making and security operations outcomes, proper governance is critical for managing risks. Unlike traditional software, AI systems often operate with probabilistic behaviour, opaque decision logic, and significant dependence on data quality. These characteristics challenge existing regulatory models and require new approaches that balance innovation with accountability, safety, and trust.

From an information security perspective, AI governance frameworks seek to address risks related to misuse, loss of control, systemic bias, and cascading failures across interconnected systems. Across jurisdictions and institutions, there is growing convergence around principles such as transparency, risk-based classification, secure-by-design development, and clearly defined responsibility for AI outcomes. While regulatory approaches differ in enforcement and scope, they collectively reflect recognition that AI systems must be governed with the same rigor as other critical digital infrastructure.

The following initiatives and frameworks illustrate how AI governance and regulations are evolving globally:

- **Risk-based legislative frameworks**: The **European Union** (**EU**) has taken a leading role through the EU AI Act, which classifies AI systems based on risk and imposes corresponding obligations related to transparency, security, and oversight. General-purpose AI systems are further guided by codes of practice addressing safety, copyright, and misuse. This layered approach reflects an effort to balance innovation with enforceable safeguards for high-impact use cases.
- **Transparency and accountability policies**: In the U.S., state policies such as California's SB 53 emphasize operational transparency, incident reporting, and protection for individuals who disclose unsafe AI practices. By requiring organizations to document safety measures and respond formally to incidents, such initiatives reinforce *trust, but verify* governance philosophy aligned with security assurance principles.
- **US national strategy–driven governance**: The U.S. AI Action Plan emphasizes maintaining technological leadership while addressing security risks associated with synthetic media, open-source AI, and large-scale automation. Rather than centralized regulation, the approach relies on secure-by-design principles, sector-specific guidance, and coordination across government and industry, reflecting the broader risk-based regulatory approach.
- **International principles and baseline governance norms**: At the international level, the **Organization for Economic Co-operation and Development** (**OECD**) AI Principles provide a widely adopted baseline for responsible AI, emphasizing robustness, security, accountability, and human-centric design. These principles influence national strategies and serve as a common reference point for aligning AI governance across borders.
- **Management system standards for operationalizing AI governance**: Recognizing the need for practical implementation, standards bodies have introduced management system-based approaches to AI governance. ISO 42001 defines requirements for establishing, implementing, and maintaining an AI management system, analogous to ISO 27001 for information security. Such standards help organizations integrate AI risk management into existing governance, audit, and assurance processes.

- **Multilateral and global coordination efforts**: International organizations, including the United Nations, have initiated expert panels and global dialogues focused on safe, secure, and trustworthy AI. These efforts aim to harmonize governance principles while addressing cross-cutting concerns such as workforce impact, energy consumption, and the misuse of advanced AI capabilities.

AI is not the only technology reshaping foundational assumptions in information security. Advances in quantum computing pose an equally significant challenge, threatening the mathematical basis of widely used cryptographic systems. Let us examine these implications and the emergence of quantum-safe cryptography as a necessary response to this approaching paradigm shift.

Quantum computing and quantum-safe cryptography

Quantum computing is one of the most revolutionary advancements in the field of computing. By leveraging principles of quantum mechanics, quantum computers can process and evaluate complex problems with a level of efficiency that is unattainable using traditional systems.

Although practical, large-scale quantum computers are still under development, progress in the field has accelerated steadily over the past two decades. Advances in qubit stability, error correction, and quantum architectures have transformed quantum computing from a largely theoretical pursuit into an emerging engineering discipline. Publications from major technology vendors and research institutions signal growing confidence in the long-term viability of fault-tolerant quantum systems. From an information security perspective, this is particularly significant, as quantum computing challenges the mathematical foundations on which many widely deployed cryptographic mechanisms rely.

Fundamentals of quantum computing

Quantum computing is based on the principles of quantum mechanics, the branch of physics that governs the behaviour of matter and energy at the atomic and subatomic levels. Unlike classical computing, in which information is represented using binary bits, quantum computing uses quantum bits or qubits. Qubits can exist in multiple states simultaneously, enabling new computational models that differ fundamentally from classical logic.

Quantum mechanics concepts

Three key quantum mechanics concepts that form the basis of quantum computing are as follows:

- **Superposition**: Superposition allows a qubit to represent a combination of multiple states at the same time, rather than a single deterministic value. While a classical bit must be either 0 or 1, a qubit can exist in a weighted combination of both states. This property enables quantum systems to process many possible inputs in parallel, which forms the basis for quantum computational advantage.

- **Entanglement**: Entanglement describes a phenomenon in which the states of two or more qubits become intrinsically linked, i.e., the state of one qubit cannot be fully described without reference to the others. Entangled qubits exhibit correlations that persist regardless of physical distance. This allows quantum computers to represent and manipulate complex relationships between variables more efficiently than classical systems.
- **Interference**: Quantum interference refers to the ability to amplify correct computational paths while suppressing incorrect ones through controlled interactions between quantum states. Interference is critical to extracting meaningful results from quantum computations, as it enables algorithms to converge towards desired outcomes despite operating over many possible states simultaneously.

These principles allow quantum computers to address certain categories of problems more effectively than classical systems. Some problems, such as integer factorization, are computationally time-consuming for classical computers but can be solved dramatically faster using quantum techniques. Other problems, such as optimization and simulation of physical systems, which are tractable classically, can be accelerated significantly using quantum computers as the problem size grows.

Quantum algorithms

Quantum algorithms are specifically designed to exploit superposition, entanglement, and interference to achieve performance advantages over classical approaches. While the number of known quantum algorithms remains limited compared to classical algorithms, a small set has profound implications for information security. These are as follows:

- **Shor's algorithm**: Introduced in the mid-1990s, it demonstrated that large integers could be factorized efficiently on a quantum computer. This result is especially important because the security of many public-key cryptographic systems depends on the practical difficulty of integer factorization. A sufficiently powerful quantum computer running Shor's algorithm would render these cryptosystems insecure.
- **Grover's algorithm**: This offers a different type of advantage by providing a quadratic speedup for searching unstructured datasets. Grover's algorithm has direct implications for symmetric cryptography and hashing, as it effectively reduces the security strength of symmetric-keys and hash functions. As a result, they need larger key sizes to maintain equivalent levels of protection.
- **Quantum fourier transform (QFT)**: It is a foundational subroutine used in several quantum algorithms, including Shor's algorithm. It provides an efficient method for transforming quantum states into frequency representations, enabling pattern extraction that would be computationally cumbersome using classical techniques.

Applications of quantum computing

Quantum computing has potential applications across diverse domains, including materials science, pharmaceuticals, finance, logistics, AI, and climate modelling. Many of these applications involve optimization, simulation, or pattern recognition problems that grow rapidly in complexity as variables increase.

From an information security standpoint, the most significant implication of quantum computing lies in its impact on cryptography. The ability to efficiently factor large numbers and solve related mathematical problems undermines the assumptions on which many classical cryptographic algorithms are built. Quantum technologies also introduce new possibilities for key management. **Quantum key distribution** (**QKD**), which leverages quantum properties, can be used to detect eavesdropping during cryptographic key exchange.

Impact of quantum computing on classical cryptography

The most far-reaching security implication of quantum computing lies in its potential to undermine the cryptographic foundations on which modern digital systems depend. Cryptography is deeply embedded in everyday digital activity, from securing communications and authenticating users to protecting financial transactions and critical infrastructure. A sufficiently powerful quantum computer that meets the threshold of cryptographic relevance would fundamentally alter the assumptions that these protections rely upon.

Classical cryptographic systems rely on mathematical problems that are computationally not feasible for today's computers to solve within a practical timeframe. Public-key or asymmetric cryptographic algorithms are based primarily on the difficulty of factoring large integers or solving discrete logarithm problems. While these problems are effectively unsolvable using classical supercomputers, quantum algorithms change this equation entirely. Shor's algorithm demonstrates that problems that would require an impractical amount of time on classical systems could be solved efficiently by a **cryptographically relevant quantum computer** (**CRQC**).

As a result, widely deployed asymmetric cryptographic mechanisms would become vulnerable. This includes public-key encryption, digital signatures, and key exchange schemes that form the backbone of secure communications. Protocols and algorithms such as **Rivest–Shamir–Adleman** (**RSA**), **Diffie–Hellman** (**DH**), **Digital Signature Algorithm** (**DSA**), **Elliptic Curve Cryptography** (ECC), and **Elliptic Curve DSA** (**ECDSA**) all derive their security from mathematical assumptions that do not hold in a quantum computing context. Once a CRQC becomes available, any system relying on these algorithms for long-term security would face immediate and systemic risk.

Symmetric cryptography and cryptographic hash functions are affected differently. Quantum computers do not render these algorithms obsolete, but they do weaken their effective security strength. Grover's algorithm provides a quadratic speed-up for brute-force search problems, implying that an attacker can search key or hash spaces more efficiently. While this improvement is significant, it does not eliminate security altogether. Instead, it necessitates stronger parameter choices. For symmetric encryption algorithms such as the **Advanced Encryption Standard** (**AES**), doubling the key size may be sufficient to restore the original security margin. In practical terms, AES with 256 bit keys is expected to provide security comparable to today's 128 bit strength in a quantum-enabled threat environment.

Cryptographic hash functions face a similar reduction in effective strength. A hash function such as **Secure Hash Algorithm 256** (**SHA-256**), while secure against classical attacks, offers a lower security margin against quantum-assisted brute-force or collision attacks. As with symmetric encryption, this risk can be mitigated by using longer hash outputs or quantum-resistant constructions, rather than abandoning hash-based mechanisms altogether.

The broader implications of these changes are very significant. Cryptography is often the final line of defense in digital systems, and the erosion of its foundational assumptions would have cascading effects across industries. Nearly all digital trust mechanisms rely on asymmetric cryptography in some form, whether for establishing secure channels, validating identities, signing software updates, or enabling secure financial and legal transactions. Importantly, the threat is not limited to future communications alone. Sensitive data encrypted today may be harvested and stored by threat actors, with the intention of decrypting it later once quantum capabilities mature.

Understanding the impact of quantum computing on cryptographic classes is therefore critical. While asymmetric algorithms face an existential threat and must ultimately be replaced with quantum-safe alternatives, symmetric encryption and hashing can remain viable with appropriate adaptations. This distinction forms the foundation of current efforts towards **post-quantum cryptography** (**PQC**) and highlights the urgency of preparing for a transition before quantum computing reaches operational maturity.

Quantum threat landscape

The quantum threat landscape is defined by the impact that future quantum computing capabilities may have on the cryptographic mechanisms that form the very basis of digital trust. The security risks posed by quantum computing are not limited to a distant or speculative future. They are increasingly being framed in terms of plausible timelines and concrete threat scenarios. Estimates from standards bodies, industry consortia, and academic research suggest that CRQC systems capable of breaking widely deployed public-key algorithms may emerge in the early 2030s. While precise timelines remain uncertain and depend on advances in error correction, qubit stability, and system scaling, the convergence of projections from multiple independent sources has elevated quantum risk from a theoretical concern to a strategic planning issue for information security professionals.

A defining characteristic of the quantum threat is its asymmetry in time. Threat actors do not need immediate quantum capability to benefit from future advances. Encrypted data can be collected and stored today, even if it cannot yet be decrypted. Once sufficiently powerful quantum systems become available, that same data may be retrospectively exposed. This *harvest now, decrypt later* scenario shifts the quantum threat from a distant future concern to a present-day risk. It is particularly concerning for information with long-term sensitivity, such as personal data, intellectual property, state secrets, health records, and cryptographic keys used in long-lived systems.

When CRQC emerges, the threat would extend beyond confidentiality breaches. It would affect not only encrypted data but also the mechanisms used to establish identity, authenticity, and trust across the digital ecosystem. Public-key cryptography, for instance, supports a range of mechanisms such as authentication, digital signatures, certificate validation, and secure software distribution. If these are compromised, attackers could impersonate trusted entities, forge digitally signed artifacts, and undermine the integrity of systems that rely on cryptographic proof. The resulting erosion of trust would affect financial systems, software supply chains, legal documentation, and critical infrastructure.

Need for cryptographic transition

Addressing the quantum threat requires action well before large-scale quantum computers become operational. Cryptographic transition is inherently slow, complex, and difficult to execute under pressure. Organizations that delay preparation risk being forced into reactive migrations with limited testing, incomplete coverage, and elevated operational risk.

One of the primary drivers for early transition is data longevity. Many categories of information, such as health records, financial histories, intellectual property, and classified communications, need to be secured for decades. Once such data gets exposed, it cannot be re-protected retrospectively. Preparing cryptographic protections today is therefore essential to preserving long-term confidentiality and trust.

The complexity of transition further reinforces the need for early planning. Cryptography is deeply embedded across enterprise systems, applications, protocols, hardware platforms, and third-party services. In many cases, organizations lack a complete inventory of where cryptographic algorithms are used, which keys protect which assets, and how dependencies propagate across systems. Transitioning to quantum-safe alternatives requires discovery, prioritization, redesign, testing, and staged deployment across this entire landscape.

Historical experience underscores the scale of the challenge. Previous cryptographic migrations, such as moving away from legacy hash functions or encryption standards, took many years to complete, despite affecting narrower portions of the technology stack. The quantum transition is broader in scope and touches nearly all public-key cryptography, making timelines longer and coordination more complex. Additionally, cryptographic transition is not confined only to systems that are under direct organizational control. Software vendors, cloud providers, device manufacturers, and integration partners also need to adopt quantum-safe mechanisms. This makes post-quantum readiness a supply-chain-wide effort rather than a purely internal initiative.

For these reasons, the cryptographic transition should be treated as a long-term transformation program rather than a one-time upgrade activity. Early preparations are needed to enable measured decision-making, reduce operational risk, and position organizations to adopt quantum-safe technologies in a controlled and resilient manner.

Quantum-safe cryptography

Quantum-safe cryptography, more commonly referred to as PQC, encompasses cryptographic algorithms designed to remain secure in the presence of both classical and quantum threats. Unlike traditional public-key algorithms, whose security is based on mathematical problems that are vulnerable to quantum attacks, post-quantum algorithms rely on problem classes for which no efficient quantum solutions are currently known. Their purpose is to preserve confidentiality, integrity, and authenticity as quantum computing capabilities mature.

A defining characteristic of PQC is its practicality. These algorithms are intended to operate on conventional computing platforms and integrate into existing communication protocols, operating systems, and applications. This makes them suitable for large-scale deployment across existing digital infrastructure. PQC algorithms are designed to protect against future CRQC while remaining robust against classical attacks.

PQC is not a single algorithmic approach, but a family of techniques based on diverse mathematical foundations. Prominent categories include lattice-based cryptography, hash-based cryptography, multivariate polynomial cryptography, and isogeny-based cryptography. This diversity reduces systemic risk by avoiding reliance on a single hard problem and provides flexibility when selecting algorithms suited to different performance, key size, and security requirements.

Recognizing the urgency of quantum preparedness, NIST has been leading a global effort to evaluate and standardize PQC algorithms. In August 2024, this process resulted in the standardization of three algorithms intended to replace widely used public-key mechanisms. These include a lattice-based algorithm for key establishment, the **Module-Lattice-Based Key-Encapsulation Mechanism** (**ML-KEM**), and two DSAs—the **Module-Lattice-Based DSA** (**ML-DSA**) and the **Stateless Hash-Based DSA** (**SLH-DSA**). These standards provide a concrete foundation for organizations to begin structured migration planning.

From an application perspective, PQC is critical to preserving trust across a wide range of online digital activities. Secure communications, certificate-based authentication, software signing, blockchain transactions, legal documentation, and long-term data protection all depend on cryptographic assurances that must remain valid over extended periods. In the absence of quantum-safe alternatives, these mechanisms would be vulnerable to compromise once quantum capabilities reach sufficient scale.

While PQC represents the most practical and widely applicable response to quantum threats, other quantum-safe technologies also play complementary roles. QKD is a method of securely exchanging cryptographic keys using the physical properties of quantum systems. Its security is rooted in the principle that observing a quantum state alters it, allowing eavesdropping attempts to be detected. **Quantum random number generators** (**QRNGs**) provide another supporting technology. These systems generate randomness based on inherently unpredictable quantum phenomena, rather than classical physical processes. As high-quality randomness is a cornerstone of secure cryptographic systems, QRNG can enhance the strength of both classical and post-quantum cryptographic implementations.

Regulatory standards and frameworks

The regulatory approach to quantum risk is evolving as governments and standards bodies acknowledge the long-term impact of quantum computing on cryptographic security. While binding mandates are still emerging, international standards bodies and regulatory institutions are playing a central role in shaping global readiness for quantum-era cryptographic risks by defining technical baselines, guidance, and transition pathways for quantum-safe security. Some of the initiatives are as follows:

- ISO is actively developing and updating cryptographic standards to incorporate PQC techniques, including extensions to existing standards for digital signatures and encryption, such as those within the ISO 14888 and ISO 18033 series.
- NIST initiated its PQC standardization program in 2016 and has since progressed to formal standard selection. Quantum-resistant algorithms for key establishment and digital signatures, including lattice-based schemes such as CRYSTALS-Kyber and Dilithium, are being adopted as reference standards for government and industry.
- The **European Telecommunications Standards Institute** (**ETSI**) has established dedicated working groups and task forces focused on quantum-safe cryptography, with particular emphasis on telecommunications networks, critical infrastructure, and long-lived systems.

Blockchain and information security

Blockchain technology is not a recent invention. Its foundational concepts have been in use for over a decade. However, recent advancements in scalability, smart contracts, interoperability, and enterprise adoption have elevated blockchain from a niche financial technology to a broader trust infrastructure. These developments are increasingly influencing information security architectures by introducing alternative models for establishing trust, ensuring data integrity, and enabling decentralized control in distributed systems.

From an information security perspective, blockchain's growing maturity is shaping how organizations think about integrity, non-repudiation, and cross-organizational trust. As enterprises explore blockchain-based solutions such as identity management, secure data sharing, and auditability, the security implications of blockchain design, cryptographic dependencies, and governance models become central to securing information systems.

Blockchain principles

The following core principles of blockchain contribute directly to its security properties:

- **Decentralization**: Control is distributed across multiple nodes rather than concentrated in a single trusted entity. This reduces single points of failure and makes systems more resilient to compromise.
- **Cryptographic integrity**: Each block contains a cryptographic hash of the previous block, forming an immutable chain. As a result, any unauthorized modification to historical data becomes immediately detectable.
- **Consensus mechanisms**: Algorithms such as proof of work, proof of stake, and byzantine fault tolerant protocols ensure that participants agree on the state of the ledger, even in the presence of faulty or malicious nodes.
- **Transparency and auditability**: Transactions recorded on a blockchain are verifiable by authorized participants, enabling strong audit trails and non-repudiation.

Security applications of blockchain

Blockchain has practical applications in several security-sensitive domains. Some use cases that demonstrate blockchain's value as a trust-enabling layer are as follows:

- **Data integrity and provenance**: Blockchain can be used to record hashes of critical data, ensuring tamper evidence and traceability without storing sensitive data directly on-chain. This is particularly useful in supply chain security, document verification, and digital evidence management.
- **Decentralized digital identity**: Blockchain-based identity frameworks enable self-sovereign identity models, where users control their credentials and selectively disclose attributes. Cryptographic proofs replace centralized identity providers, reducing identity fraud risks.
- **Access control and authorization**: Smart contracts, such as programmable logic deployed on blockchains, can enforce access control policies automatically, enabling transparent and auditable authorization decisions across organizational boundaries.

Blockchain security challenges

Despite the advantages, blockchain-based systems introduce the following notable challenges:

- **Privacy limitations**: Public blockchains expose transaction metadata that can lead to link and inference attacks. Techniques such as zero-knowledge proofs and privacy-preserving smart contracts are emerging, but they add complexity.
- **Scalability constraints**: Consensus mechanisms and data replication limit transaction throughput and latency, which makes many blockchains unsuitable for high-volume enterprise workloads without architectural trade-offs.

- **Smart contract vulnerabilities**: Programming errors in smart contracts can lead to irreversible financial and data loss, as code execution is often immutable once deployed.
- **Key management risks**: Blockchain security ultimately depends on cryptographic keys. Loss or compromise of private keys can result in permanent loss of assets or identity.

Edge computing and distributed security

Edge computing has existed for several years as a response to latency, bandwidth, and performance limitations of centralized cloud computing. However, recent growth in **Internet of Things** (**IoT**) deployments, real-time analytics, AI at the edge, and 5G connectivity has significantly accelerated its adoption. These developments are reshaping information security by extending computing and decision-making far beyond the traditional data centers.

This decentralization significantly expands the security perimeter and introduces new threats. As computing shifts towards the edge, security efforts need to focus on securing these highly distributed, resource-constrained, and often physically exposed environments. This evolution is influencing modern information security trends, including Zero Trust architectures, decentralized identity, and autonomous security controls.

Edge computing environments have the following characteristics that are distinct from centralized cloud environments. They are:

- Highly distributed across geographically dispersed locations.
- Heterogeneous, consisting of devices with varying hardware, operating systems, and capabilities.
- Often physically exposed, which increases the risk of tampering and device compromise.

These characteristics challenge the traditional perimeter-based security models. In such distributed, heterogeneous, and physically exposed environments, trust assumptions must be minimized, and security controls must operate autonomously at the edge, often with limited connectivity to central systems.

Edge computing risks

Edge computing introduces a broader and more complex threat model and attack surface, which exposes the edge environment to the following types of risks and attacks:

- Device-level attacks, such as firmware manipulation, hardware tampering, and malware injection.
- Network-based attacks, including man-in-the-middle attacks on edge-to-cloud or edge-to-edge communication.

- Data-centric threats, where sensitive data processed at the edge may be exposed, altered, or exfiltrated.
- Supply chain risks, as edge devices often rely on third-party hardware, firmware, and software components.

Securing the edge environment

Effective edge security requires a layered and adaptive approach. The following measures can be taken to protect edge environments:

- **Device security and hardening**: Ensure secure boot, trusted platform modules, firmware integrity checks, and minimal attack surfaces to protect edge devices.
- **Identity and authentication**: Implement strong device identity, certificate-based authentication, and Zero Trust principles to help ensure that only authorized entities participate in edge ecosystems.
- **Data protection**: Encrypt data at rest and in transit, combined with local data minimization and secure deletion to reduce exposure.
- **Monitoring and lifecycle management**: Implement continuous monitoring, remote attestation, and secure update mechanisms for maintaining security across large edge deployments.

As computing continues to move outwards, from centralized data centers to decentralized edge environments, the boundaries of traditional security architectures are being stretched. Securing edge ecosystems requires not only hardened devices and encrypted communications but also rethinking trust, visibility, and control in highly distributed settings. This shift mirrors a broader pattern wherein emerging and evolving technologies are fundamentally reshaping the foundations on which information security has long been built, demanding both technical adaptation and strategic foresight.

Conclusion

In this chapter, we examined how transformative technologies such as AI, quantum computing, blockchain, and edge computing are redefining the landscape of information security. While each technology introduces distinct capabilities and risks, a common theme that emerges is that security should not be treated as a static set of controls applied after systems are built. Instead, it must evolve alongside technological change, embedded deeply into design, governance, and operational decision-making.

AI has emerged as both a powerful security technology and a new attack surface. Its use in automation, detection, and decision support is enhancing the speed and scale of security operations, yet it also introduces challenges related to model integrity, data poisoning, misuse, and governance. Quantum computing, on the other hand, represents a different class of disruption that threatens the mathematical foundations of present-day cryptography. Although CRQC is not yet operational, the risks it poses are immediate due to the longevity of sensitive data and the feasibility of *harvest now, decrypt later* attacks. The emergence of PQC and related standards signals a necessary transition rather than a distant concern. Besides these disruptive technologies, blockchain and edge computing continue to influence security efforts as their adoption expands. Blockchain complements conventional trust models by enabling decentralized integrity and verification, while edge computing extends security responsibilities to environments that are highly distributed, resource-constrained, and often physically exposed.

Together, these emerging technologies illustrate a fundamental shift in information security, from reactive defense towards an adaptive, risk-aware approach. The key is to continually assess how emerging technologies alter threat models, assumptions, and security controls, and to respond proactively rather than retrospectively. As innovation accelerates, sustained vigilance and the ability to adapt security architectures proactively will become defining capabilities of resilient organizations. In an environment of constant technological change, trust will depend not only on robust controls but on the ability to evolve them continuously.

Exercises

1. Using examples from AI-powered threats and AI-enabled defenses, analyze how AI simultaneously strengthens and undermines security controls. How should security teams balance innovation with risk containment?
2. Explain the concept of harvest now, decrypt later. Why does this fundamentally change how organizations should approach cryptographic planning, even before CRQC becomes available?
3. Identify the key technical, operational, and governance challenges involved in transitioning to PQC. Why is cryptographic agility critical in this context?
4. Evaluate how blockchain technologies alter traditional trust and verification mechanisms in information systems. What security benefits do they introduce, and what risks or limitations must be carefully managed?
5. Compare the security challenges of centralized cloud environments with those of edge computing architectures. How do decentralization, physical exposure, and scale affect threat models and security strategies?
6. Assess the role of regulatory standards and frameworks in managing risks associated with AI and quantum technologies. How do global standards bodies and national regulators influence secure technology adoption?
7. As a **chief information security officer** (**CISO**), how would you prioritize investments across AI security, quantum-safe cryptography, blockchain, and edge security over the next five years? Justify your approach based on risk, maturity, and long-term impact.

Index

A

AAA Protocols 127
AAA Protocols, characteristics
- Diameter 128
- RADIUS 127
- TACACS+ 127

Access Control 107
Access Control, architecture 112, 113
Access Control, models
- Attribute-Based Access Control (ABAC) 134
- Discretionary Access Control (DAC) 132
- Mandatory Access Control (MAC) 133
- Role-Based Access Control (RBAC) 133
- Rule-Based Access Control (RuBAC) 135

Access Control, steps 113, 114
Adaptive Authentication 119
Advanced Endpoint Protection 184
Advanced Endpoint Protection, solutions
- EDR 184
- EPP 187
- XDR 185

Advanced Persistent Threats (APTs) Attack 32
AI 109
AI-Driven Threats 292
AI-Driven Threats, mechanisms 293, 294
AI-Integrated Applications 222
AI-Integrated Applications, practices 224
AI-Integrated Applications, trends
- ASPM 224
- RASP 223
- Supply Chain Security 223
- Zero Trust Paradigm 223

AI/ML 139
AI-Powered Threats 291
AI-Powered Threats, configuring 291, 292
AI Regulatory Frameworks 294
AI Regulatory Frameworks, illustrating 295, 296
AI, threats 34
Algorithm 86
Antivirus/Antimalware 182
API Security 284
Application Control 183
Application Control, methodologies
- Blacklisting 183
- Whitelisting 183

Application Layer Protocols 151
Application Layer Protocols, configuring 151, 152
Application Security Frameworks 221
Application Security Frameworks, types
- ISO/IEC 27034 222
- NIST SP 800-218 222
- OWASP ASVS 221

APTs Attack, configuring 33
APTs Attack, stages
- Exfiltration 33
- Expansion 33
- Infiltration 33

Architectural Security Models 128
Architectural Security Models, types
- Bell-LaPadula 129
- Biba 129
- Brewer/Nash 131
- Clark-Wilson 130
- Graham-Denning/Harrison-Ruzzo-Ullman 131
- Information Flow 130
- Non-Interference 131
- State-Machine 129

Artificial Intelligence (AI) 33

Asymmetric Encryption 91
Asymmetric Encryption, advantages 93
Asymmetric Encryption, applications 93
Asymmetric Encryption, characteristics
Deffie-Hellman (DH) 92
Elliptic Curve Cryptography (ECC) 92
Rivest-Shamir-Adleman (RSA) 91
Attribute-Based Access Control (ABAC) 134
Auditing/Monitoring 108
Audit Planning 75
Audit Planning, configuring 75, 76
Audit Planning, pitfalls 76
Audit Process 79
Audit Process, configuring 79, 80
Audit Program 76
Audit Program, configuring 76, 77
Audit Program, ensuring 77
Audit Project Management 74
Audits/Assessments 71, 72
Authentication 115
Authentication, factors 116-118
Authentication, types
Adaptive 119
Multi-Factor 119
Authenticity 9
Automation 207
Automation, configuring 207, 208
Availability 8

B

Bell-LaPadula Model 129
Biba Model 129
Blockchain 302
Blockchain, applications 303
Blockchain, challenges 303
Blockchain, principles
Consensus Mechanisms 303
Cryptographic Integrity 303
Decentralization 303
Transparency/Auditability 303
Brewer/Nash Model 131
Bridges 155

C

CIA Triad 5
Cipher Data Security 105
Cipher Data Security, strategies
Access Control 106
Auditing/Monitoring 107
Data Loss Prevention (DLP) 107
Data Masking/Tokenization 105
Ciphertext 85
CIS Controls Framework 18
CISO 49
Clark-Wilson Model 130
Cloud Adoption 284
Cloud Adoption, solutions
ASM 286
CIEM 285
CNAPP 286
CSPM 285
CWPP 285
DSPM 285
Cloud IAM 269
Cloud IAM, features 269
Cloud IAM, fundamentals
Authentication 269
Authorization 270
Managing Permissions 271
Cloud Infrastructure Security 272, 273
Cloud-Native Architecture 262, 263
Cloud-Native Architecture, characteristics 264
Cloud-Native Architecture, fundamentals
Abstraction/Automation 263
Multi-Tenancy 263
Cloud-Native Architecture, models
Infrastructure as a Service (IaaS) 264

Platform as a Service (PaaS) 265
Software as a Service (SaaS) 265
Cloud Network Architecture 274
Cloud Network Architecture, concepts
Container Networking 276
Network Security Controls 274
Zero Trust Network Access (ZTNA) 277
Cloud Workloads 279
Cloud Workloads, configuring 279
Cloud Workloads, terms
Container Security 281
FaaS Security 282
PaaS Security 281
Virtual Machines (VMs) 280
Code Injection Attack 26
Code Injection Attack, vulnerabilities
Cross-Site Scripting (XSS) 27
SQL Injection 27
Compliance 61, 62
Compliance Audits 68
Confidentiality 5
Container Networking 276
Container Security 194, 195
Continuous Authorization 278
Continuous Monitoring 235
Continuous Monitoring/Regular Evaluation 61
Cryptanalysis 87, 88
Cryptography 84
Cryptography, attacks
Brute-Force 103
Chosen-Plaintext 104
Frequency 104
Known-Plaintext 104
Side-Channel 104
Cryptography, techniques
Asymmetric 91
Digital Certificates 96
Digital Signatures 95
Hash Functions 93
Public Key Infrastructure (PKI) 97
Symmetric 88
Cryptography, terminology
Algorithm 86
Ciphertext 85
Cryptanalysis 87
Decryption 86
Encryption 85
Key Generation 87
Plaintext 85

D

Data Confidentiality 6
Data Confidentiality, impact 6
Data Confidentiality, measuring 6, 7
Data Lifecycle 97
Data Lifecycle, stages
Data Archival 100
Data at Rest 99
Data Creation 98
Data Disposal 100
Data in Transit 99
Data in Use 98
Data Loss Prevention (DLP) 107, 183
Data Masking/Tokenization 105
Data Masking/Tokenization, configuring 105
Data Security 108
Data Security, storage
Database 283
Object 283
Volume 283
Data Security, trends
AI 109
Homomorphic Encryption (HE) 108
PQC 108
DDoS Attacks 164
DDoS Attacks Mitigation, techniques
Behavioural Analytics 166
Blackhole Routing 167
Rate Limiting 166
Traffic Scrubbing 166
DDoS Attacks, stages
Analysis 166

Detection 166
Mitigation 166
Response 166
DDoS Attacks, types
Application Layer 164
Protocol 164
Volumetric 164
DDoS Attacks, vulnerabilities
HTTP Flood 166
SYN Flood 165
UDP Flood 165
Decentralized Identity (DID) 140
Decryption 86
Defense-in-Depth 13
Defense-in-Depth, principles
Continuous Monitoring 14
Layered Security 13
Redundancy 14
Variety Defenses 14
DevSecOps 205
DevSecOps, principles 206
DevSecOps, stages
Build 206
Code 206
Operation/ Monitoring 207
Release/ Deployment 207
Testing 207
Diameter 128
Digital Certificates 96
Digital Forensic Investigation 238
Digital Forensic Investigation, concepts
Evidence Collection/ Preservation 239
Evidence Examination 239
Root Cause Analysis 239
Digital Signatures 95
Digtal Threat Landscape 2
Digtal Threat Landscape, enhancing 2-4
Discretionary Access Control (DAC) 132
Distributed Denial of Service (DDoS) Attack 25
DNS Attack, techniques
Hijacking 31
Spooting 30
System Amplification 31
Tunnelling 31
Domain Name System (DNS) Attack 30
DREAD 39
Dynamic Routing 153

E

Edge Computing 304
Edge Computing, approaches 305
Edge Computing, risks 304
EDR 184
EDR, functions 184
Email Security Solutions 252
Email Security Solutions, functionalities 252
Email Security Solutions, terms
Data Protection 253
Threat Detection 253
Encryption 85, 86
Endpoint Security 180
Endpoint Security, architecture 182
Endpoint Security, challenges
Evasive Malware 180
Expand Attack Surface 180
Insider Threats 180
Virtualized Environments (VMs) 181
Zero-Day Vulnerability 181
Endpoint Security, components
Antivirus/ Antimalware 182
Application Control 183
Data Loss Prevention (DLP) 183
Host-Based Firewalls 182
Patch Management 184
Endpoint Threats 178
Endpoint Threats, techniques
Fileless Malware 179
Malware 179
Phishing 179

Spyware 179
Supply Chain Attacks 179
EPP 187

F

Federated Identity Management (FIM) 123
FIM, configuring 123
FIM, process
Open Authorization (OAuth) 125
Open Identity (OpenID) 126
Security Assertion Markup Language (SAML) 124
Financial Audits 68
Firewall 156
Firewall, architecture 159
Firewall, configuring 160
Firewall, terms
Next-Generation Firewalls (NGFWs) 158
Unified Threat Management (UTM) 157
Firewall, types
Application-Level Gateway 157
Circuit-Level Gateway 157
Packet Filtering 156
Stateful Inspection 157
Forensic Audits 69

G

Graham-Denning/Harrison-Ruzzo-Ullman Model 131

H

Hash Functions 93
Hash Functions, properties
Collision Resistance 94
Deterministic 94
Pre-Image Resistance 94
Uniformity 94
Homomorphic Encryption (HE) 109
Honeynets 251
Host-Based Firewalls 182
Hubs 154

I

IAAA 10
IAAA, elements
Accountability 12
Auditing 12
Authentication 11
Authorization 11
Identification 11
IaC, advantages
Automated Security Testing 273
Rapid Deployment 274
Scalability/Flexibility 274
Standardization 273
Version Control 273
IAM 135
IAM, configuring 138
IAM, solutions
Identity as a Service (IaaS) 137
Identity Governance Administration (IGA) 136
Privileged Access Management (PAM) 135
IAM, trends
AI/ML 139
Decentralized Identity (DID) 140
Identity Fabric 140
Password-Less Authentication 139
Identification 114
Identity as a Service (IaaS) 137
Identity Fabric 140
Identity Governance Administration (IGA) 136
Identity Management 120
Identity Management, protocols
Kerberos 121
LDAP 120
Single Sign-On (SSO) 120
Identity Registration/Proofing 115
Identity Registration/Proofing, configuring 115
IDS/IPS 163
IDS/IPS, configuring 163
IGA, capabilities 136
Incident Response (IR) 236
Information Flow Model 130

Information Security 4
Information Security, architecture 290, 291
Information Security, components
AI-Driven Threats 292
AI-Powered Threats 291
AI Regulatory Frameworks 294
Information Security, frameworks
CIS Controls Framework 18
ISO 27001 18
NIST Cybersecurity Framework (CSF) 17
SOC2 18
Information Security, pillars
Defense-in-Depth 13
IAAA 10
Least Privilege 12
Segregation of Duties (SoD) 13
Zero Trust 15
Information Security, principles
Authenticity 9
Availability 8
CIA Traid 5
Confidentaility 5
Integrity 7
Non-Repudiation 9
Information Security, strategies
Balanced Scorecard (BSC) 47
CMMI 47
SWOT Analysis 47
Information Systems Audit Frameworks (ISAF) 66
Infrastructure as Code (IaC) 273
Insider Threats 27
Integrity 7
Internet Layer Protocols 150
Internet Layer Protocols, configuring 150, 151
Internet of Things (IoT) Attack 32
IR, lifecycle
Containment 237
Detection 236
Eradication 237
Post-Incident Analysis 238
Recovery 237
Triage 236
ISAF, configuring 66, 67
ISAF, purpose
Operational Efficiency 73
Regulatory Compliance 73
Security Posture 73
ISAF, types
Compliance 68
Financial 68
Forensic 69
Operational 68
ISO 27001 18
ISO/IEC 27034 222

K

Kerberos 121
Kerberos, steps 122
Key Generation 87

L

LDAP 121
Least Privilege 12

M

Malware Attack 23
Malware Attack, vulnerabilities
Adware 25
Botnet 25
Cryptojacker 24
Fileless Malware 25
Ransomware 24
Rootkit 24
Trojan 24
Virus 23
Worm 23
Managing Permissions 271
Managing Permissions, resources
Conditional Access Policies 272
Policy Types 271
Privileged User Management 272
Mandatory Access Control (MAC) 133
Man-in-the-Middle (MitM) Attack 26
Microservices Security 216

Microservices Security, concepts
API Abuse Prevention 217
API Authentication/ Authorization 217
API Gateway 218
Continuous Protection 218
Input Validation 217
Inter-Service Communication 217
Mobile Application Security 219
Mobile Application Security, architecture 219
Mobile Application Security, fundamentals
Code Protection 220
Continuous Security Validation 220
Data Storage 219
Runtime Protection 220
SDK Security 220
Secure Communication 219
Multi-Factor Authentication (MFA) 119

N

NAT, ways
Dynamic 154
Port Address Translation (PAT) 154
Static 154
Network Address Translation (NAT) 154
Network Devices 154
Network Devices, functionalities
Bridges 155
Hubs 154
Routers 155
Switch 155
Network Security 144
Network Security, architecture 155
Network Security, components
DDoS Attacks 164
Firewall 156
IDS/IPS 163
Proxy 162
Web Application Firewall (WAF) 160
Network Security, concepts
OSI Model 144
TCP/IP Model 148
Network Security Controls 274
Network Security Controls, components
Cloud Firewalls 275
Egress Management 276
Network Security Groups (NSGs) 274
VNet 275
Web Application Firewalls (WAFs) 275
Network Security, protocols
Application Layer 151
Internet Layer 150
Transport Layer 149
Next-Generation Firewalls (NGFWs) 158
NGFWs, capabilities 158
NIST Cybersecurity Framework (CSF) 17
NIST SP 800-218 222
Non-Interference Model 131
Non-Repudiation 9

O

OAuth, configuring 125
OCTAVE 39
Open Authorization (OAuth) 125
OpenID, configuring 126
Open Identity (OpenID) 126
Operational Audits 68
Organization Management 267
Organization Management, platforms
Organization Hierarchy Models 267
Organization-Level Security 268
Organization-Level Shared Services 268
OS Hardening 188
OS Hardening, foundation
Linux 190
macOS 191

Window 189
OSI Model 144
OSI Model, layers
Application 145
Data Link 147
Network 146
Physical 147
Presentation 146
Session 146
Transport 146
OWASP 209
OWASP ASVS 221
OWASP ASVS, levels 221
OWASP, vulnerabilities
Accelerate Development 211
Broken Access Control 210
Cryptographic Failures 210
Identification/ Authentication 212
Injection Vulnerabilities 210
Insecure Design 211
Security Logging 212
Security Misconfiguration 211
Server-Side Request Forgery (SSRF) 213
Software/Data Integrity 212

P

PAM, functionalities 136
Password Attack 29
Password Attack, resources
Brute-Force 29
Credential Stuffing 29
Dictionary Attack 29
Key Logging 30
Password Spraying 29
Password-Less Authentication 139
PASTA 38
Patch Management 184
PKI, configuring 97
Plaintext 85
Post-Quantum Cryptography (PQC) 108
Privileged Access Management (PAM) 135
Proactive Hardening 192
Proactive Hardening, types
RDP 193
SFTP 192
SSH 192
Proxy 162
Proxy, role
Performance Enhancement 162
Policy Enforcement 162
Security 162
Proxy, types
Forward 162
Reverse 162
Public Key Infrastructure (PKI) 97

Q

Quantum Computing 296
Quantum Computing, algorithms
Grover 297
Quantum Fourier Transform (QFT) 297
Shor 297
Quantum Computing, applications 298
Quantum Computing, concepts
Entanglement 297
Interference 297
Superposition 296
Quantum Computing, terms
Classical Cryptography 298, 299
Cryptographic Transition 300
Quantum-Safe Cryptography 301
Quantum Threat Landscape 299
Regulatory Frameworks 302

R

RADIUS 127
RDP Hardening 193
Risk Assessment 56
Risk Assessment, steps
Control Analysis 57
Control Recommendations 59

Impact Analysis 58
Likelihood Determination 57
Results Documentation 59
Risk Determination 58
System Categorization 56
Threat Identification 56
Vulnerability Identification 57
Risk Management 55
Risk Management, concepts
Continuous Monitoring/ Regular Evaluation 61
Risk Assessment 56
Risk Mitigation 59
Risk Mitigation 59
Risk Mitigation Control, types
Administrative 61
Physical 60
Technical 60
Risk Mitigation, options
Risk Acceptance 60
Risk Avoidance 60
Risk Reduction 60
Risk Transference 60
Role-Based Access Control (RBAC) 133
Routers 155
Routing 152
Routing, types
Dynamic 153
Static 153
VLAN 153
Rule-Based Access Control (RuBAC) 135

S

SAML, fundamentals
Assertions 124
Bindings 124
Flows 124
Profiles 124
SASE, technologies
CASB 278
FWaaS 279
SD-WAN 279
SWG 279
ZTNA 278
Secure Access Service Edge (SASE) 278
Secure Data Across 101
Secure Data Across, stages
Encrypting 101
Long-Term Retention 103
Protecting 102
Safeguarding 101
Secure Disposal 103
Securing 102
Secure Remote Access 167
Secure Remote Access, technologies
Virtual Private Network (VPN) 167
Zero Trust Network Access (ZTNA) 169
Security Assertion Markup Language (SAML) 124
Security Governance 44, 45
Security Governance, activities 46
Security Governance, architecture 45
Security Governance, benefits 45, 46
Security Governance, factors
Asset Value 47
Audit Report 47
External Environment 46
Organizational Culture 46
Security Governance, metrics
Performance Management 54
Resource Management 54
Strategic Alignment 54
Value Delivery 54
Security Governance, policy
Baselines/Guidelines 53
Information Security 52
Security Governance, purpose
CISO 49
Information Security 47
Strategic Planning 49
Security Governance, roles
Auditors 51
Business Owners 51
CISO 51
Senior Management 50

System Administrators 51
Users 51
Security Operations (SOC) 228, 229
Segregation of Duties (SoD) 13
Sensitive Data 5
SFTP Hardening 192
Shared Responsibility 265
Shared Responsibility, model
IaaS Security 265
PaaS Security 265
SaaS Security 266
SIEM 248
SIEM, foundations
Advanced Analytics 248
Alert Enrichment/ Contextualization 249
Correlation/Detection Logic 248
Log Collection/ Normalization 248
Operational Visibility 249
Single Sign-On (SSO) 120
SOAR 250
SOC 2 18
SOC, architecture 229
SOC Efficacy 254
SOC Efficacy, terms
Business Impact Metrics 255
Detection Effectiveness 254
Response Efficiency 255
Social Engineering Attack 27
Social Engineering Attack, techniques
Baiting 28
Phishing 27
Pretexting 28
SOC Maturity Model 256
SOC, objectives 229
SOC Operating, models
Hybrid 231
In-House 230
Managed 230
Virtual/Distributed 231
SOC, roles
Automation Specialist 234
Forensic Expert 234
Head Security Operations 234
Incident Responder 233
SOC Analyst 232
SOC Engineer 233
SOC Manager 234
Theart Intelligence Analyst 233
Vulnerability Management Analysis 234
SOC, strategies
Continuous Monitoring 235
Digital Forensic Investigation 238
Incident Response (IR) 236
Threat Hunting 240
Threat Intelligence 242
Vulnerability Management 243
SOC, technologies
Email Security Solutions 252
Honeynets 251
SIEM 248
SOAR 250
Vulnerability Scanners 251
SOC, tools 246, 247
Software-Defined Perimeter (SDP) 277
Spoofing Attack 30
SSDLC 200
SSDLC, configuring 200, 201
SSDLC, phases
Maintenance/ Monitoring 205
Requirement Gather/ Planning 201
Secure Application Deployment 204
Secure Coding 203
Secure Design 202
Verification/Testing 203
SSH Hardening 192
State-Machine Model 129
Static Routing 153
Strategic Planning 49

Strategic Planning, plans
- Operational 49
- Strategic 49
- Tactical 49

STRIDE 37
Supply Chain Attack 31
Switch 155
Symmetric Encryption 88
Symmetric Encryption, applications 90
Symmetric Encryption, challenges 90
Symmetric Encryption, characteristics
- Advanced Encryption Standard (AES) 89
- Data Encryption Standard (DES) 89
- Notable Symmetric Algorithms 89

T

TACACS+ 127
TCP/IP Model 148
TCP/IP Model, layers
- Application 148
- Internet 148
- Link 148
- Transport 148

Threat Actors 22
Threat Actors, attacks
- Advanced Persistent Threats (APTs) 32
- Artificial Intelligence (AI) 33
- Code Injection 26
- Distributed Denial of Service (DDoS) 25
- Domain Name System (DNS) 30
- Insider Threats 27
- Internet of Things (IoT) 32
- Malware 23
- Man-in-the-Middle (MitM) 26
- Password 29
- Social Engineering 27
- Spoofing 30
- Supply Chain 31

Threat Actors, categories
- Cybercriminals 22
- Hacktivists 22
- Malicious Insiders 23
- Script Kiddies 22
- State Actors 22

Threat Actors, vulnerabilities
- Configuration 35
- Hardware 35
- Human 35
- Network 35
- Process 35
- Software 35

Threat Hunting 240
Threat Hunting, approaches
- Analytics-Driven 241
- Hypothesis-Driven 241
- Intelligence-Led 240

Threat Hunting, stages 241
Threat Intelligence 242
Threat Intelligence, architecture 242
Threat Intelligence, configuring 243
Threat Modelling 35
Threat Modelling, approaches
- Application-Centric 37
- Asset-Centric 36
- Attacker-Centric 37

Threat Modelling, methodologies
- DREAD 39
- OCTAVE 39
- PASTA 38
- STRIDE 37
- Trike 38
- VAST 39

Threat Modelling, steps
- Asset Identification 36
- Mitigation 36
- Review/Monitoring 36
- Risk Analysis/Prioritization 36
- Scope Definition 36
- Threat Identification 36

Transport Layer Protocols 149
Trike 38

U

Unified Threat Management (UTM) 158

V

VAST 39
Virtualized Environments 194
Virtualized Environments, layers
  Container Security 194
  VM Security 194
Virtual Private Network (VPN) 167
VLAN Routing 153
VM Security 194
VPN, configuring 168
VPN, limitations
  Cloud Access Limitations 169
  Performance/Latency 168
  Scalability/Management 168
  User Experience 168
Vulnerability Management 243
Vulnerability Management, activities
  Baseline Assessment 244
  Patch Management 245
  Penetration Testing 245
  Vulnerability Assessment 244
Vulnerability Scanners 251
Vulnerability Scanners, configuring 252

W

WAF Detection, methodologies
  Anomaly-Based 161
  Signature-Based 161
WAF Detection, modes
  Hybrid 161
  Negative Security 161
  Positive Security 161
Web Application Firewall (WAF) 160
Web Application Security 213
Web Application Security, ensuring 215
Web Application Security, principles
  Defense-in-Depth 213
  Fail-Safe Design 214
  Least Privilege 214
  Secure Defaults 213
Web Application Security, terms
  Authentication/Session Management 214
  Input Validation/Output Encoding 214
  Layered Defense 214
  TLS 215
  XSS/CSRF 214
Wireless Security 171
Wireless Security, architecture 171
Wireless Security, practices 173
Wireless Security, protocols 171, 172

X

XDR 185
XDR, capabilities 185, 186

Z

Zero Trust 15
Zero Trust Endpoints 187
Zero Trust Endpoints, principles 187
Zero Trust Network Access (ZTNA) 169, 277
Zero Trust, principles
  Assume Breach 16
  Least Privilege Access 16
  Verify Explicitly 15
Zero Trust, tenets 16
ZTNA, advantages 170
ZTNA, architecture 169
ZTNA, foundations
  Continuous Authorization 278
  Secure Access Service Edge (SASE) 278
  Software-Defined Perimeter (SDP) 277